THE SHADOW OF THE CRESCENT

THE SHADOW OF THE CRESCENT:
THE RENAISSANCE
IMAGE OF THE TURK

(1453—1517)

BY

ROBERT SCHWOEBEL

ST. MARTIN'S PRESS
NEW YORK
1967

Copyright © B. de Graaf, Nieuwkoop, 1967
First published in the Netherlands by
B. de Graaf, Publishers 1967

First published in the United States of America by
St. Martin's Press, Inc., 1967

Library of Congress Catalog Card Number: 67-27189

Printed in the Netherlands by
Drukkerij N. Miedema & Co., Leeuwarden

To Edward and Anna Schwoebel

CONTENTS

PREFACE.

It is not surprising to find writers sometimes comparing the confrontation of our so-called communist and free worlds with the clash of East and West in the Renaissance period. Indeed there are some remarkable parallels. In both cases one finds not only a struggle between competing powers but a conflict of ideologies, and contrasting social, economic and political systems. In the Renaissance, as today, the rivals—Latin Christendom and the Ottoman Turks—believed they were engaged in a struggle for survival. Each was determined to supplant the other's way of life. Both sides claimed they were charged with a divine mission and that their respective regimes offered the best hope for humanity. Then, as now, the ruling powers thought primarily in terms of a military solution. The fourteenth, fifteenth, and sixteenth centuries were filled with battles between the Turks and Christian powers. Full scale wars alternated with limited operations and with periods of uneasy peace comparable to our cold wars. But hostilities were also interrupted by diplomacy and peaceful relations. The protagonists negotiated, traded, and even engaged in cultural exchange. And whether at peace or war they were sensitive to matters touching prestige and public opinion; hence all parties promoted their policies with propaganda at home and abroad.

Such striking similarities must not obscure the essential differences between the two conflicts. Though a military state, the Ottoman empire, for example, was not totalitarian. Nor did the dynastic monarchies of Latin Christendom bear much resemblance to our modern western democracies. The contrasts, however, extend beyond the political structures peculiar to the two ages. In sorting out those characteristics by which we distinguish one historical epoch from another we have learned to look behind events and institutions and investigate aims and aspirations, basic assumptions, ideals, and values, and the variety of ways in which these were expressed. As Denys Hay put it, it is "the style of living" which really changes in history; and the style of living pertains not only to such things as "clothes and buildings and decoration; it involves the justification of the kind of life we lead, the adjustment between duty and pleasure, the way we learn and what we learn, the way we pray and what we pray for".

The eastern question was, of course, not new in the Renaissance; and during the fourteenth, fifteenth, and sixteenth centuries the Turkish peril was often viewed as the latest phase in the centuries-old assault of Islam upon Christendom. For their evaluation and understanding of the problem, Europeans of the time drew heavily upon the medieval corpus dealing with Islam and the Levant. Even under the pressure of momentous change they clung tenaciously to established categories and adapted a large body of new information to the forms of thought and expression developed in the anti-Moslem and crusading literature of the Middle Ages. At the same time they were unable to ignore the drastic alterations which had occurred and were still taking place both within and outside Latin Christendom. Major events such as the ill-fated crusades of Nicopolis (1396), and Varna (1444), and especially the fall of Constantinople (1453), the battle of Belgrade (1456), the seizure of Negropont (1470), and the assaults upon Rhodes and Otronto (1480), dramatized the fact that the Turks were established in Europe and were at the gates of the West. Moreover the advance of the Turks coincided with a concatenation of no less spectacular, though well-known events, which signaled the reorientation of Europe. Marked at one end by the close of the Hundred Years War and the invention of printing, and at the other by the voyages of Columbus, the French invasion of Italy (1494), and the revolt of Luther, the half century under consideration here was perhaps less a period of transition than one of crystallization. Changes long in the making now issued in new structures and patterns which were to be characteristic of European life until the Renaissance gave way to the modern age. Under such conditions even the most cherished traditions were called into question if only to be reaffirmed, if not modified.

The purpose of this book is to examine the western attitude toward the Ottoman Turks in the critical years 1453-1517. It is primarily concerned with the forms and content of European thought on that subject. Attention is given to the sources of information and ideas, to the media by which the latter were transmitted and disseminated, and to those forces and circumstances which chiefly conditioned the making of the Turkish image in the West. The function of these conceptions in the main stream of Renaissance intellectual history is touched upon but the systematic investigation of this problem must be the subject of another book. Inevitably the treatment of so large a topic requires a sampling of various opinions and attitudes. Further examples in each of the categories dealt with in the text may be readily discovered in the sources and in many instances additional references are provided in the notes. But the emphasis herein is given to the role and significance of prominent individuals and important groups representing particular points of view rather than to determining the extent to which the latter were held. It should be noted that much of the material on which the study is based was originally composed for propaganda purposes. Obviously it cannot be treated as accurately representing the true state of the Ottoman empire. It constitutes, however, an essential source for what westerners thought and felt about the Turks, and when used critically, reveals many of the subjective elements involved in their reaction. In order to catch something of the feeling and flavor of their response I have quoted liberally from the sources and frequently paraphrased texts without detailed criticism of their factual content. In short our main objective is not to determine whether the accounts of our authors are right or wrong but rather to discover what and why they thought and felt as they did.

It remains only to acknowledge the assistance and counsel which I have received. I am indebted to the American Philosophical Society, the Folger Shakespeare Library in Washington D.C., and to Temple University for grants which enabled me to pursue the research for this book. Among the many people who have taken an interest in my work and rendered advice and criticism I am particularly indebted to Professor Kenneth M. Setton, Professor Felix Gilbert, and Professor Norman Zacour. For their criticism, countless suggestions, and encouragement I owe a special debt of gratitude to Dr. Rudolf Hirsch, and to my wife, Barbara Schwoebel. I alone, of course, am responsible for errors in judgment and fact. Finally I wish to thank the editors of *History Today* and *Studies in the Renaissance* for permission to incorporate material from my articles which they first published.

St. Ottilien
June 25, 1967

LIST OF PLATES

ABBREVIATIONS

AHR	*American Historical Review*
Babinger, *Mahomet II*	Franz Babinger, *Mahomet II, le conquerant et son temps* (1432-1481), Paris, 1954.
Chastellain, *Chronique*	George Chastellain, *Oeuvres*, ed. Kervyn de Lettenhove. 8 vols. Brussels, 1863-1866.
CPR	*Calendar of Entries in the Papal Registers Relating to Great Britain and Ireland: Papal Letters.*
CPSMilan	*Calendar of State Papers and Manuscripts Existing in the Archives and Collections of Milan.*
CPSVen	*Calendar of State Papers and Manuscripts Relating to English Affairs Existing in the Archives and Collections of Venice.*
Daniel, *Islam and the West*	N. Daniel, *Islam and the West. The Making of an Image.* Edinburgh, 1960.
De Clercq, *Mémoires*	Jacques de Clercq, *Mémoires*, ed. J. A. Buchon in *Chroniques d'Enguerrand de Monstrelet*. Vol. XIII. Paris, 1826.
D'Escouchy, *Chronique*	Mathieu d'Escouchy, *Chronique*, ed. G. du Fresne de Beaucourt. 3 vols. Paris, 1863-64.
GW	*Gesamtkatalog der Wiegendrucke.* 7 vols. Leipzig, 1925-38.
Iorga, *GOR*	N. Iorga, *Geschichte des osmanischen Reiches.* 5. vols. Gotha, 1908-13.
Iorga, *Notes et extraits*	N. Iorga, *Notes et extraits pour servir à l'histoire des croisades au xve siècle.* Vols. 4-6. Bucharest, 1915, 1916.
Iorga, "Notes", *ROL*	N. Iorga, "Notes et extraits pour servir à l'histoire des croisades au xve siècle", *Revue de l'orient latin*, VIII (1900-1901).
Martène, *Thesaurus*	E. Martène and U. Durand, *Thesaurus novus anecdotorum.* Vol. I. Paris, 1717.

MHH	*Monumenta Hungariae Historica.*
NCMH	*New Cambridge Modern History, I: The Renaissance*, ed. G. R. Potter. Cambridge, 1961.
Pastor, *Acta inedita*	L. Pastor, *Acta inedita historiam pontificum romanorum.* Vol. I, Freiburg, 1904.
Pastor, *HP*	L. Pastor, *History of the Popes*, ed. and tr. F. Antrobus.
Pius II, *Commentaries*	*The Commentaries of Pius II*, tr. and ed. L. C. Gabel and F. A. Gragg. *Smith College Studies in History.* Vols. XXII, XXV, XXX, XXXV, XLIII. Northampton, Mass., 1936-1957.
Raynaldus, *Annales*	O. Raynaldus, *Annales ecclesiastici post Baronium ab anno 1198 usque ad annum 1565.*
RISS	L. Muratori, *Rerum Italicarum scriptores.*
Vaughan, *Europe and the Turk*	D. M. Vaughan, *Europe and the Turk, A Pattern of Alliances*, 1350-1700. Liverpool, 1954.
Wadding, *Annales*	L. Wadding, *Annales Minorum seu trium Ordinum a S. Francisco institutorum.* 3rd. ed. 25 vols. Quaracchi, 1931-1935.
Wolkan, *Der Briefwechsel*	R. Wolkan, *Der Briefwechsel des Eneas Silvius Piccolomine. Fontes rerum Austricarum.* Vols. 61, 62, 67, 68. Vienna, 1909-18.

CHAPTER I

The scourge of God

News of the fall of Constantinople spread throughout the Christian world during the summer of 1453. Three ships bearing refugees from the stricken city reached Crete early in June. A monk of the monastery of Agarathos recording the event observed that "nothing worse than this has happened, nor will happen", and he prayed God to deliver his island from the clutches of the Turks.[1] The chronicler Leontios Makharis wrote that "many good men came to Cyprus from Constantinople and many monks", and that the island's queen, Charlotte de Lusignan, deeply grieved and moved to pity by the plight of the refugees, "took St. George called Mangana and built them a monastery there, and gave them villages and many revenues. . .".[2] At the end of June, Jean de Lastic, grandmaster of the ancient crusading order of the Knights of St. John the Hospitallers, wrote from his headquarters on the island of Rhodes to Frederick II, margrave of Brandenburg, then a pilgrim in Jerusalem, informing the German prince of what had happened. De Lastic described the horrors of the siege and the bloody sack which followed. He implored Frederick and the rulers of Christendom to unite and resist this tyrant who had vowed to destroy them. For the Grand Turk fancied himself to be another Alexander, or, indeed even greater than the Macedon, since he planned to subjugate Italy and the whole of Europe, and at that very moment was raising a huge fleet to pounce upon the helpless islands of the Aegean.[3]

The tragic news was not long in reaching the West. A pilgrim from Basel, one Peter Rot, reported that on June 12, his vessel, which was bound for the Holy Land, intercepted three Venetian merchant ships off Modon. The merchantmen had unwittingly approached Constantinople to find it besieged and were bearing home the first reports of the Turkish victory.[4] On June 29, letters from the castellan of Modon and the bailo of Negropont announcing the catastrophe were read by the secretary of the Council of Ten to a mute Senate.[5] Obviously caught off-guard the Venetians revealed the panic which momentarily gripped the Republic in a letter dispatched the next day to Pope Nicholas V. The Turkish victory, they warned, was as perilous as it was grievous. The Venetians erroneously reported that Pera had fallen on May 28, and that all its inhabitants six years of age and above had been slain. Constantinople had succumbed the following day and a similar carnage had been perpetrated by the iniquitous sultan, the assassin and enslaver of Christians. Surely, the letter continued, the pope was best qualified to judge the significance of these events and knew what had to be done. Having watched the steady growth of Turkish might, however, Venice was no longer able to remain silent. Now that the Grand Turk had made Constantinople the capital it was going to be difficult to stop him. Unless God, the pope, and the Christian princes gave aid, the Senate predicted the submission of the Republic to the Turks and grave consequences for Christendom. The Venetians begged the pope to use all his power to raise help before it was too late.[6] On the same day the Senate sent instructions to Giovanni Moro, Venetian envoy to the court of Naples. Moro was directed to inform Alfonso V of the disaster and to remind him that "... the sultan was still young and that he passionately hated Christianity". The Senate noted that Mehmed II was stronger than any of his predecessors and possessed in Constantinople a strategic base of great importance for future operations. Moro was to emphasize the urgent need for unity and accord among the Christian rulers.[7]

On July 4, the messenger carrying the Venetian letter to Rome passed through Bologna and related the news to its citizens. Cardinal Bessarion, the eminent Greek humanist and apostle of church union who had long labored to save Byzantium, was then papal governor in the city and here first learned of the unhappy event.[8] The messenger finally reached Rome on July 8. A Franciscan popular preacher, Roberto Caracciolo, informed the Roman populace which mourned openly in the streets;[9] but the shock was such that when after a time confirmation did not arrive, many people refused to give credence to the report. Disbelief, however, was shortlived and was followed by panic when a rumor passed through the city that the Turks had captured the papal galleys. It was widely reported that the sultan was gathering a huge army and a fleet and planned to invade Sicily and Italy within two months. Francesco Sforza's envoy in Rome wrote that the pope and cardinals were "molto smariti e vergognosi del caso de Constantinopoli," that they planned to send ambassadors to all the rulers of Italy, and prayed God for a miracle.[10]

Meanwhile word had reached Genoa from Venice by July 6. As in Rome many at first refused to believe the news. But here too skepticism gave way to dispair. The signoria briefly discussed the possibilities of action against the Turks, but fear and frustration combined to paralyze the Republic. Defeatism prevailed and finally on November 25, the government wrote off its Black Sea colonies making them over to the *Banco di San Giorgio*. Genoa had reaped the full measure of a policy which a century earlier had led her to become the first Latin power to aid the Turks at the outset of their westward advance.[11]

The signoria of Florence, on the other hand, in a letter of July 17, to its ambassador in Genoa, Nicola Soderini, and in another of July 20 to Siena, wrote that it was not possible to describe the shock which the news caused in Florence. Cosimo de Medici was alleged to have observed that the fall of Constantinople was the most tragic event the world had seen for many centuries.[12]. Similarly King Alfonso of Naples enjoined his fellow Italians to consult and he promised to take immediate steps to halt the advance of the Turks. By autumn he was urging the pope to greater action. He recommended to Nicholas an envoy named Junius de Gratibus, from the despot of Serbia. Alfonso pressed the pope to find some means to aid immediately both the Serbians and the Hungarians, otherwise the despot would be forced to submit to the Turks and Christendom suffer still further losses.[13]

Refugees who had escaped the hands of the conqueror spread the news in the neighboring countries of the Balkans. A Greek bishop named Samuel accompanied by other Orthodox clergy travelled through Wallachia and into Transylvania. Reaching Hermanstadt in August the Greeks warned of an impending attack upon that area. [14] George Brankovich, despot of Serbia, was so disturbed by the news that for three days he withdrew to a solitary retreat. The emperor of Germany, Frederick III, learned of the tragedy early in July. The imperial court was at Graz when reports from Serbia arrived relating the details of the siege and plundering of the Byzantine capital.[15] Frederick was genuinely distressed and wrote by the pen of Aeneas Sylvius to Pope Nicholas the same day on which he heard the news. Forty thousand men, he bewailed, were blinded by the Turks. Many others were led into captivity. All the churches of the city had been destroyed or defiled. Numerous ships were seized. The former seat of the eastern empire was now under a Turkish lord. Frederick urged the pope to bring peace among the Christian princes while the evil deeds were still fresh in everyone's mind. He promised to neglect nothing in his own efforts to work for peace in Europe and prepare for a crusade.[16] From Graz the story spread to other parts of Germany and eastern Europe. Heinrich Reuss, commander of Elbing, writing to the grandmaster of the Teutonic knights, initially expressed his doubts concerning the truth of the reports. However, in a later letter to the grandmaster, Reuss sorrowfully acknowledged the Turkish triumph and gave evidence of his distress over the horrible atrocities committed by the Turks.[17] The news reached Cracow while the devout Franciscan, St. John Capistran was there on a mission. He at once declared his intention to preach the crusade, and on February 10, 1454, at the wedding feast of the king of Poland he called upon Casimir and his guests to take the cross.[18]

Letters from Venice, Rome, and the imperial court announced the event to the rest of Europe. Philip the Good of Burgundy heard from both Nicholas V and Frederick III. For many years a staunch advocate of the crusade, Philip now doubled his efforts.[19] The king of Portugal, when informed of the imminent danger, promised his support to the papacy.[20] A canon from the cathedral of Seville bore the news to the learned Koranic scholar and historian of the council of Basel, Juan de Segovia, in his monastery at Aiton in Savoy.[21] Thomas Gascoigne, chancellor of Oxford University, noted that a papal letter brought the news to Oxford; and a chronicler of London faithfully recorded: "Also in this yere, which was the yer of Ower Lord god MCCCCLiij was the Cite of Constantyn the noble lost by Cristen men, and wonne by the Prynce of Turkes named Mahumet".[22] To the farthest ends of the Christian world, couriers carried the tale of the great catastrophe. Christian I, king of Denmark and Norway, when informed of the event declared that the Grand Turk was the beast rising out of the sea described in the Apocalypse.[23] A Georgian chronicler wrote: "On the day when the Turks took Constantinople the sun was darkened".[24]

Following shortly the first notices, detailed reports became available as refugees from the captured capital began arriving in the West during the following months. One of the first eyewitnesses to reach Venice, whose account is extant, was a Florentine merchant named Jacopo Tedaldi.[25] He had fought throughout the siege and escaped at the last moment and was picked up in the harbor by one of several galleys which rescued some four hundred survivors. Arriving in Venice on July 5, he was granted a safe-conduct by the Republic in order to travel to Florence. The account of an eyewitness and participant in the defense of the city, the work was composed shortly after the event and soon reached a widespread audience.

Tedaldi reported that on April 5, the Grand Turk besieged the city with an army of 200,000, and began hammering its walls and fortifications with massed artillery. Particularly terrifying to the defenders was one huge cannon which the Turks fired more than a hundred times every day. Under intensive bombardment the old walls crumbled as dry clay. Initially denied entrance into the harbor by a bridge of ships and a massive chain, the sultan's fleet of nearly a hundred vessels took up stations in the Bosporus. About two weeks later, however, the Christians were dumbfounded when they awoke in the morning to find some 60 Turkish vessels in the upper end of the Golden Horn. Under cover of darkness the Turks had moved their ships across the short stretch of land from the Bosporus to the harbor. The city was now besieged by sea and land. The defenders, numbering no more than 7000,

4

insufficient even to man adequately the extensive walls, were worn down countering mining operations and probing attacks, and continuously repairing the damage wrought by the fierce and relentless bombardment. Tedaldi described the Turks' conduct of the siege, the composition of their forces, and their preparations for the final assault. Having determined to make an all-out effort to carry the city, Mehmed proclaimed a three day solemn feast in honor of Allah. For three nights preceding the day of the assault the Turks built huge fires which illuminated their whole camp, and they filled the air with shrieks and cries and beating their tambourines. Finally on May 28, the sultan gave the command which sent his vast army against the walls. The main effort was concentrated in the area of St. Roman's gate where the Turkish artillery had been most effective. The defenders at the gate were under the command of a Genoese, Giovanni Giustiniani, the only western captain to have responded voluntarily to the pleas of the emperor and who had brought a small force to fight in the city's defense. A courageous and able warrior he had stiffened the resistance of the Greeks and raised their hopes; but as the Turks moved forward Giustiniani fell mortally wounded and was removed to a ship in the harbor. When the sultan's troops mounted the walls the rest of the Christians believing Giustiniani to have fled, abandoned the struggle. "And thus the Turks entered Constantinople, in the morning of the 29th day of May, and put to the sword all whom they found and who resisted them."[26]

The Florentine merchant or a contemporary editor concluded the work with some remarks on the significance of Mehmed II's victory, a prediction concerning his future plans, and recommendations for a crusade. More infamous than Nero when it came to spilling Christian blood, he wrote, "the Grand Turk was bold and ambitious, and desired more than Alexander or Caesar to conquer the whole world". Mehmed, he continued, had histories read to him and enquired about the locations and conditions of Venice, Rome, and Milan. He planned to build a bridge from Megara to Venice to facilitate his invasion of the West. Now that he held Constantinople, he intended to make it his capital, the center of his empire, and the base for a great fleet. Mehmed boasted that every prince would become his tributary since he had captured the strongest city in the world. In addition his troops were bold and fearless; they were highly disciplined and he held them in constant readiness.[27]

In the years immediately after the fall of Constantinople dozens of crusading schemes were devised by statesmen, soldiers, churchmen and others. Too often these plans fell into a similar pattern displaying an ignorance of contemporary military developments. But the recommendations appended to Tedaldi's report, written shortly after the Turkish victory when fear of an attack ran high, are timely and somewhat original. The sultan, our author claimed, did not plan another campaign for that summer, for he needed time to consolidate his new conquests. The time was ripe then for a successful counter-offensive. The plan called for a combined land and sea operation. There were to be two armies. An Italian force was to pass by way of Albania and proceed East recruiting Christians as they marched through the Balkans. A second army of Hungarians, Bohemians, Poles, Wallachians, and others, under the command of the Hungarian hero, John Hunyadi, was to make its way south toward Adrianople. A naval force, comprising units from Aragon, Venice, Genoa, Florence, and other maritime powers, had the mission of blocking the Dardenelles, and preventing Turkish reinforcements from passing to Europe from Asia. The author of the plan counted on additional aid from Russia and the Turkish prince of Karamania, who "with some inducements may probably become a Christian". The armies were to receive logistical support from the Greeks who were expected to take part in the recovery of their own lands. The commanders of the three forces were to be instructed to maintain communications and to coordinate in the prosecution of the campaign.

Regarding the Turks, our authority writes that they are unable to put more than 200,000 men, including irregulars, into the field. Many of these are Christians, who, serving against their wills, could be encouraged to desert to the Christian cause. Indeed, since the Grand Turk would keep to the field, as always, desertions would be facilitated. Furthermore, cut off from the sea and harassed by the Greeks, the Turks would be at a disadvantage without supplies. By the time the two armies converged on Turkey, the sultan's troops would be almost starved and victory would be assured. The author of this plan, it is true, fell into some of the errors common to western architects of crusading projects in this period. The success of his scheme depended in part upon supplies and help received from the Greeks, who, it is well known, found it difficult to cooperate with the Latins. Despite his praise of the Turkish soldier's bravery and discipline, he played down the effectiveness of the huge Ottoman armies and perhaps erred by underestimating his enemy. On the other hand his attention to matters of logistics, coordination, and intelligence, evidence a realistic approach to the problem. The recommendation that the eastern force be commanded by the experienced Hunyadi was militarily and politically sound. Hunyadi was conversant with the Turks' methods of warfare and enjoyed a great reputation in the West. One revealing aspect of the plan was its complete disregard of any possible aid from England, and especially France and Germany, the former champions of the struggle against the Moslems.[28]

Toward the end of November, 1453, a vessel arrived in Venice bringing envoys from Rhodes and Cyprus and more refugees from Constantinople. Among the latter was the Greek prelate Isidore, metropolitan of the See of Kiev and All Russia and since 1439 a Latin cardinal. The cardinal's hat was a reward for his efforts in behalf of the union between the Greek and Latin churches. Isidore had first journeyed to the West for this purpose in 1434. A member of the Greek mission to the council of Basel he had warned that body of the need for peace in the church in face of the Turkish menace. He returned to the West in the entourage of Emperor John VIII Paleologus and played a prominent role in the negotiations which resulted in the act of union announced in Florence July 6, 1439. In the fall of 1452, he had gone back to Constantinople as papal legate accompanied by Leonard of Chios, archbishop of Mitylene and a token force of two hundred archers which he had raised on Chios at his own expense. He had taken part in the solemn service held in the great church of Hagia Sophia on December 12, 1452, when the decree of union was proclaimed. Isidore remained in the Byzantine capital throughout the siege, participated in its defense, was wounded by a Turkish arrow, and fell with the city into the hands of the victors. In disguise he escaped to one of the vessels which carried survivors to Crete. Now on his way to Rome he paused long enough in Venice to give an account of his harrowing experiences and to report on the sultan's designs concerning the West. He predicted that unless the Italians joined forces there was no hope for Italy. Commanding the largest army known to history (30,000 cavalry and a numberless infantry), and a fleet already 230 vessels strong, Mehmed planned to attack by way of Calabria or Venice and to occupy the peninsula within the next two years.[29]

Isidore's tale of the agony suffered in the last moments of the dying city was confirmed by a group of Franciscans who arrived with him at Venice and shortly afterward went on to Bologna. They too had witnessed the events of the siege and the final assault. They reported that 3000 men, including the emperor, perished when the Grand Turk carried the city; but only then did the blood bath begin. Thousands of innocent folk were murdered. The rest —young girls and boys, old men, monks, nuns, and priests—were led into captivity. From among 400 children sold into slavery the sultan sent some as gifts to the sultan of Egypt and to the Moslem rulers of Tunis and Granada. All the churches were destroyed or violated, and defiled. Also many Venetian noblemen and merchants, residents of the city, were robbed and slaughtered.[30]

Along with the refugees came envoys from the rulers of the Christian outposts now gravely imperiled by the Turkish victory. Their desperate appeals and tales of Ottoman atrocities further played upon the fears of western Christians. In writing to obtain much needed assistance, the grandmaster of Rhodes, Jean de Lastic, vividly portrayed his perilous position and the ultimate threat to Christian civilization. The Grand Turk, he wrote, was a wild beast who practiced every manner of cruelty and impiety upon Christians; and daily his savagery waxed greater. His thirst for human blood was insatiable and so uncontrollable that he had personally joined in the carnage. He allowed human bodies, naked and decapitated, to be left in the streets to be eaten by dogs. The danger to Rhodes mounted with each passing moment. Pera, Chios, and Mitylene had submitted to him. Serbia, Trebizond, and Kaffa paid him tribute. Even Cyprus had sent him envoys. "And now", de Lastic exclaimed, "that raging viper, having broken his oath and agreement with us, has demanded an annual tribute of 2000 ducats...." But the knights, he added, refused to pay and expected to be attacked at any moment. Situated perilously close to the Turkish mainland, the grandmaster described his island as a meek lamb in the midst of wolves and ferocious animals, and he concluded with an urgent appeal for aid.[31]

The tale of woe unfolded by the refugees and the desperate pleas for assistance from Levantine rulers stirred to action leading Christian spokesmen. Veteran proponents of the crusade proclaimed to an uneasy and apprehensive Europe the imminent peril which loomed over the whole Christian world. Too long, they declared, the West had ignored or watched indifferently the steady growth of the infidel power. Now there was little time before the sultan would unlease his monstrous forces against the West. Among the influential voices which spread the alarm and demanded unity at home and a crusade against the Turks, none was stronger, more eloquent, or more persistent than that of Cardinal Bessarion. For many years before the fall of Constantinople he had sought with little success to alert Europe to the impending danger. Along with his compatriot Isidore, he had labored in vain to heal the schism between the Greek and Latin churches so that they might face the Turk with a united front.[32] Now, he wrote to the doge of Venice, Francesco Foscari, he was no longer beseeching aid for his own country or its capital but for the safety and honor of all Christians. That which everyone had feared has happened! The barbarians have seized Constantinople, the home of so many celebrated and illustrious men. The chief city of all Greece, the splendor and glory of the East, the school of all the highest arts, has been captured, ravaged, and sacked by the savage enemies of the Christian faith, the fiercest of wild beasts. They have plundered the public treasure and the wealth of private citizens. They have stolen the treasure from the churches, the precious metals and stones, the rich ornaments, and the relics of the saints. The sanctuaries they have defiled with blasphemings, bloodshed, and outrages of every kind. They butchered the defenders as so many cattle—carrying off

8

I: Turkish raiders
(Joerg von Nuremberg, *Anzeygung*. Nuremberg, 1500).

the women, ravishing virgins, tearing children from the arms of their parents. The wretched survivors they sold into slavery, subjecting them to hideous tortures and reducing them to the lowest forms of servitude. For those who did not know the truth it was hard to believe the fate of the city.

The Venetians, however, Bessarion continued, were well acquainted with the details of the tragedy since many of their own people had perished there. He also realized that it was unnecessary to point out to them the extent of the danger which now threatened Italy. But he implored the Venetians to lend the weight of their authority in summoning the princes to common action. He begged them to use their influence in bringing to an end the wars among Christians which had encouraged the Turks to be bold and aggressive. Unless the Latin princes united and soon launched a counter-attack, the armies of Mehmed would complete their subjugation of Greece and the Aegean islands, and overrun Hungary and Albania. Italy too would then face the hour of reckoning.[33]

From courts and councils, pulpits and studies, those whose words chiefly influenced public opinion—statesmen, publicists, preachers, and scholars—proclaimed the tale of tragedy and dire warnings. In Germany the humanist-diplomat and future pope, Aeneas Sylvius Piccolomini, summoned the full power of his rhetorical skill to communicate his shock and distress. In his celebrated letter to Nicholas V, addressed from Graz on July 12, 1453, he wrote, "but what is this execrable news which is borne to us concerning Constantinople? My hand trembles, even as I write; my soul is horrified, yet neither is it able to restrain its indignation, nor express its misery. Alas, wretched Christianity!" Aeneas condemned an indifferent Latin world which had stood by while the Turks had seized the most renowned city. He lamented the unspeakable cruelties to which its inhabitants had been subjected. More than 40,000 people had died. He grieved the sack and pollution of the exalted Hagia Sophia and the defilement of a host of fine churches by the spurious creed of Mohammed. Words failed him, he cried, when he considered how many books, still unknown in the West, had been destroyed. "Alas, how many names of great authors have now perished? It is a second death for Homer and Plato." Of the two lights of Christendom, one has been extinguished. Indeed, all the glory of Greece has been destroyed. Christianity had suffered losses to the infidels in times past, but never was the danger so great. The Turks were now established in the very heart of Christendom. They controlled the Black Sea and the river Don. They had subjected the Wallachians and planned to conquer the Hungarians, and after them Germany. He pitied Pope Nicholas in whose reign the tragedy had occurred. Despite the pope's efforts Byzantium had fallen, and posterity would remember him for that above all else. He prayed Nicholas to do everything in his power to bring peace to Europe and assemble representatives from all the nations to prepare for the Holy War.[34]

The Turkish victory of May 29, 1453, marked the end of one empire and the beginning of another. Mehmed II had set the seal upon the accomplishments of his predecessors. The Turks now occupied the capital as well as the better part of the territories of Byzantium. It was, in the words of Paul Wittek, "an imperial deed; by it the conqueror defied the whole western world, thus showing that he was lord over the lands stretching from the Black Sea to the Mediterranean, and that he alone decided their fate".[35] For the West it meant relinquishing the time-honored practice of fending off the forces of Islam by piece-meal support of a buffer power. It meant that the commerce which passed through the former Byzantine lands, which the Italians especially had in large measure controlled, was now at the disposal of the sultan. For Latin Christendom it brought to an inglorious end the seemingly interminable negotiations to bring Greek Orthodoxy under the obedience of Rome. And, as Toynbee descriptively put it, "1453 signified that western Christendom had now become the trustee of the ancient Greek culture, which, at this date, the Franks equated with 'Culture' with a capital' C' ".[36] So much for the views of modern scholars. Although contemporaries of the event possessed a definite scheme of universal history (in general that adumbrated by St. Augustine in response to the fall of old Rome), they can hardly be expected to have shared the detachment and perspective of modern historians. What place then did the fall of Byzantium occupy in the thought and traditions of the period? How did it color the West's view of the Turks? How did contemporaries understand and explain it? And how did their reactions contribute to the significance of the event?

To begin with, the siege, capture, and sack of Constantinople together with the threat which the Turks seemed to pose to the religion and culture of Latin Christendom sharpened the instinct for tragic drama in contemporary writers. In their accounts prognostications, fortune, and capricious fate play a prominent role in the determination of events. Heroes of epic proportions are introduced and upon their individual decisions or actions the outcome of the struggle is made to depend. The ancient historiographical device of the speech, placed in the mouth of a participant to achieve dramatic effect, is also employed. Mehmed II and Constantine XI are both represented as delivering stirring orations before their assembled hosts prior to the final assault. Upon his triumphal entrance into the devastated capital one source has the conqueror respond to the cheers of his soldiers: "I thank Mohammed who has given us this splendid victory; but I pray that he will permit me to live long enough to capture and subjugate Old Rome as I have New Rome".[37] A still later writer pictures him standing amidst the ruins of the imperial palace meditating upon the fate of empires and recalling the words of the Persian poet:

> L'araignée a filé sa toile dans le Palais imperial
> La chouette a entonné son chant nocturne
> sur les tours d'Efrasiyab. [38]

The dramatic form in which the accounts are cast reveals something of the profound sense of the tragedy of life felt by that generation which experienced the last stages of the Hundred Years War, recurrent plague, widespread social and economic dissension, the emergence of the Renaissance prince, the spread of the mercenary system, the vestiges of papal schism and conciliarism, rampant heresy and superstition, technological progress, especially the invention of printing, the spread of humanistic learning and the proliferation of vernacular literature, as well as the threatening advance of the Turks, and which stood on the threshold to the Protestant reformation, the discovery of the New World, and a new critical skepticism which made possible the revolution of modern science. In its less noble form the sense of tragedy was expressed in a widespread and pronounced pessimism. One finds an attitude of despair and disillusionment emanating from the highest places. On his death bed Nicholas V confessed to two Carthusian monks that no one ever spoke the truth to him. "I am so perplexed with the deceptions of all those who surround me", he said, "that were it not for fear of failing in my duty I should long ago have renounced the papal dignity."[39] In a letter made famous by Gibbon, Aeneas Sylvius showed a similar reaction. Christendom, he wrote, was a body without a head, without laws, without magistrates. The pope and the emperor were mere titles, everyone was a law unto himself; nothing could bring order and unity out of the confusion and strife. Lacking leadership, discipline, and a common interest, any force which might be raised to oppose the Turks must fail.[40] In the same vein George Nevill, bishop of Exeter, writing after the battle of St. Albans (1461) to Francesco Coppino, apostolic legate in Flanders, deplored the bloodshed and anarchy in England. "O miserable and luckless race... would you have no spark of pity for our own blood of which we have lost so much of fine quality.... If it [St. Albans] had been fought under some capable and experienced captain against the Turks, the enemies of the Christian name, it would have been a great stroke and blow. But to tell the truth, owing to these civil discords, our riches are beginning to give out, and we are shedding our own blood copiously among ourselves, while we are unwilling to give help in men and money to the army of his Holiness against the infidel Turks...."[41] A contemporary in Germany echoed the same sentiment: "God help us, the whole empire is so shattered and torn on all sides that it nowhere holds together. Cities against princes, princes against cities, wage endless wars and no one is of too low estate to challenge his neighbor. There is no quiet corner in the whole of Germany; turn where you will, you have to guard against ambush, robbery, and murder; the clergy enjoy no peace, the nobility no honor."[42]

Inspired by such an outlook writers of the day gave considerable space to the description of catastrophic and bizarre happenings. They were often preoccupied with the more violent and cruel aspects of human behavior. As Huizinga put it, "it was, so to say, bad form to praise the world and life openly. It was fashionable to see only its suffering and misery...".[43] Western chroniclers repeated the tales of Turkish atrocities with meticulous pains, and seem never to have tired of describing the inhuman cruelties practiced by the Turks. They attributed every conceivable crime to the enemies of the faith. They accused Mehmed II of beheading the Greek emperor, and personally violating members of the royal family. Chastellain called him, "... the cruel enemy of God, a new Mohammed, violator of the cross and the church, despiser of God's law, and prince of the army of Satan...".[44] The details of the rape of Hagia Sophia were related with especial interest. Many Greeks had sought refuge behind its closed doors. They had placed their hopes in a popular prophecy which had predicted that the enemy would be turned back by divine intervention before reaching the sacred cathedral. When the Turks, therefore, entered the church, in addition to the riches they had anticipated, they found a host of captives waiting to be led away. Jacques de Clerq described the scene: the Turks found many women inside the church of Holy Wisdom. Among them were ladies of high authority, and their young daughters; "... ils [the Turks] eurent leur compagnie charnelle, de forche et outre leur gré et volonté, et en contempt de Dieu nostre createur et de la foy...". Mathieu d'Escouchy recorded that the Turks stabled their horses inside the sanctuary. They reserved the most handsome youths to be led into slavery, and it was their intention to convert them to the religion of Islam. All the wooden statues of the saints, he lamented, they burned, except one, a statue of Our Lady. They used it as an executioner's block, on which they beheaded many Christians. "On the night of the city's capture", d'Escouchy continued, "Mehmed II slept with the daughter of the emperor, who was the most beautiful damsel in all the empire." Throughout the night the Grand Turk tried to persuade her to renounce Christianity in favor of Islam, but with no success. The following morning he took her to the church of

Holy Wisdom, and showed her the beheading of the Christians. Again the sultan implored her to accept his religion; but, d'Escouchy proudly explained, she preferred death to apostasy. Dismayed, Mehmed II stripped her naked, and had her beheaded on the statue of the Virgin, and sent her head to the brother of Constantine.[45]

There is little to be gained by multiplying these examples of Turkish cruelty. "If I shoulde write", exclaims an English chronicler, "the detestable murder of men, the abhominable and cruell slaughter of children, the shamefull rauishment of women and Virgins, which were perpetrate and done by the vnmerciful Pagans and cruell Turkes, I assure you that your eares would abhorre the hering, and your eyes would not abyde the readyng, and therefore I passe them ouer." The details of the story differ from one chronicler to another but in general they cover the same ground emphasizing the brutality of the Turks, the wanton shedding of blood, the pollution of holy places, the wealth seized, and the unhappy lot of Christians carried into slavery.[46] While imagination encouraged writers to invent specific details, it would have been difficult for them to exaggerate the extent of the suffering inflicted upon the unhappy inhabitants of the fallen city. Indeed, no amount of explanation or rationalization can whiten the record of the Turkish soldiers' savagary during this period of conquest. The Ottomans, however, were far from unique in this respect. It is important to remember that the Turks were at war throughout the whole of our period, and lived constantly under conditions which brought out the worst side of human nature. Hence, most of the accounts which circulated in Europe about the Turks, dealt with their military exploits and the accompanying terrible deeds. The reports fanned the fear of the Turks which gripped Europe after the fall of Constantinople; while the fear itself magnified in the eyes of the Latins the inhuman qualities of the Ottomans. It is not common, of course, to imbue one's mortal enemy with praiseworthy attributes. These considerations together with that of the compelling attraction which the violent side of life held for contemporaries and which led them to dwell upon such morbid topics as the sack of Constantinople, go far to explain the reputation which the Turks enjoyed for excessive cruelty. As a result, the inhumanity of the Turks was emphasized above all else, and the stereotyped Turk—savage and bloodthirsty, swooping down upon innocent Christians, and massacring them indiscriminately—was firmly established in the traditions of the West.[47]

The prevailing pessimism further lent support to a deterministic view of history. Chroniclers of the period generally did not examine their sources with an eye to historical causation. Behind the course of human history moved the hand of God. Happy occasions were the blessings bestowed by a charitable Father; adversity the deserved punishment from a just Lord. Inevitably many Christians saw the fall of Constantinople and the rise of the Ottoman Turks in this light. God's judgment had been visited upon this wicked generation because of the sins of Christians everywhere.[48] Stories of miracles and prophecies describing both the triumph and the undoing of the Turks were popular throughout the fifteenth century. An English correspondent writing to King Henry V from the Council of Constance told of a miraculous victory over the Ottoman enemies of Sigismund the king of the Romans: "A wonderful circumstance, as is related, occurred. For the survivors of the infidels themselves are convinced, by a very ancient writing found amongst themselves, in which it is declared that, within the next five years, they will be wholly conquered by the Christians, or converted to the faith of the Christian religion". Such imagination, or wishful thinking, was not easily disturbed by the record. What Timur had done at the beginning of the century, Prester John, or an unknown champion, or a supernatural occurence was capable of repeating. The chronicler Jean Molinet wrote of a miraculous cross which arose in the sky in the year 1501 to repel a threatened Turkish invasion. One of the most popular prophecies was the work of a Dominican, Giovanni Nanni, *De futuris christianorum triumphis in Saracenos*, printed first at Genoa in 1480 and frequently thereafter. On the basis of astrological calculations Nanni successfully predicted the approaching death of Mehmed II, but erred by some four hundred and fifty years on the date of the ultimate collapse of the Ottoman empire.[49]

In examining the nature of man's sins, however, contemporaries probed the underlying causes of the catastrophe. The results of these examinations shed some light on the tangle of intellectual and spiritual conflicts of an agitated age in which neurotic and psychotic tendencies at once expressed themselves. The Latin West exhibited a sense of guilt on the one hand and blamed the Greeks for the misfortune on the other. Certainly the Christian princes at home came in for their share of condemnation. At that moment when the cherished structures and ideals of the past were visibly fading and the new order of society had not yet recognizably crystallized, criticism was bound to take a conservative turn. The so-called "new monarchs" had appeared on the stage, and were comporting themselves in a manner which was to become characteristic of political behavior for centuries to come. But their selfish foreign and domestic policies offended the susceptibilities of an age enamoured by the concept of the *Respublica Christiana*. The princes were accused of avarice and cupidity for having failed to rally to the cause of Byzantium and Christendom. Their political behavior caused them to be compared with the Turks; and, when expediency forced them into accomodations with the Moslems, they were ranked among the enemies of Christ.[50] The Spanish traveler, Pero Tafur, who wrote the account of his journey to the Levant sometime after 1453, rebuked the Christian princes along these lines. The glories of Byzantium are dead! "Today", he wrote, "for the sins of Christians, both nobles and villeins are afflicted with a grievous servitude, since their lords are the Turks, the enemies of the Faith." Although he admired some characteristics of the Turks, they remained for Tafur the sworn enemies of Christ. He had refused preferment at the hands of the emperor of Trebizond for, among other reasons, ". . . he was married to a daughter of a Turk, and . . . some harm would surely come to him from that". Tafur observed that when he was in the East (1436-1438), even before the fall of Constantinople, the Greeks were largely at the mercy of the Turks. The latter, he felt, had been reluctant to take the capital, for fear of arousing the Christian princes. The failure of the West to come to the aid of Byzantium, however, demonstrated how ill-founded such fears were. Alas, he concluded, ". . . if God had allowed it, and the Turks had dared more, they would have succeeded in all that they attempted, seeing that Christendom had made no effort to avenge the wrong".[51]

Genoa and Venice were singled out as particularly culpable. In view of their economic interests in the Levant, it was difficult for many to understand their failure to oppose the Turks. With great fleets at their disposal they might have saved Constantinople for Christianity! The possible conclusion of this line of reasoning was too tempting to resist. Selfish and materialistic, the Italian maritime powers had played the role of Judas Iscariot. Constantinople had been betrayed into the hands of the Turks for the preservation of economic privileges![52] In the chronicle of Viterbo, Niccolò da Toccia introduced a variation on the tradition of Constantinople's betrayal. In his fictional account Florence, represented by a merchant named Neri, was held responsible for the treachery. According to da Toccia, Neri had lived in Constantinople with his wife and four sons for thirty-six years. Having carried on business in all parts of Greece, he had become acquainted with the Grand Turk. At the same time he was in such favor with the Greek emperor that the latter had entrusted Neri with the keys to one of the city's gates to facilitate his commerce. When Constantinople was laid under siege by the Turks, and it became apparent that it could not hold out very long, Neri petitioned Mehmed II for a safe conduct from the city, for himself, his family, and his goods. Mehmed II declared his willingness to grant the Florentine his wish, providing Neri would admit the Turks through the gate to which he had ready access. Otherwise, Neri was told, he would be treated as an enemy of the Turks. On the morning of May 29, da Toccia continued, Neri opened the gate for the Turks; but, discovered by the Christians, he and one of his sons were killed on the spot. However, the damage was done; owing to this treachery, da Toccia lamented, the Turks entered the capital, completely destroyed it and killed more than 200,000 Christians![53]

While reproaching themselves, or one another, western Christians did not allow the Greeks to escape responsibility for the debacle. Latins and Greeks had nurtured a mutual hatred for centuries. They had obscured essential differences in a maze of jealousies, suspicions, and distrust. Reconciliation was impossible. On the eve of the Turkish triumph, with almost certain disaster facing the Greeks in Constantinople, voices were raised in Rome itself in opposition to sending aid. [54] On the other side, the Greek opponents of church union refused to compromise with the Latins even to gain the military assistance which might have saved the city. The often repeated statement attributed to the Grand Duke Notaras is indicative of the intensity with which the Greek opponents of church union spurned the West. For many Greeks the Turkish turban was less hated than the Roman tiara.[55] In this charged atmosphere of mutual recriminations we cannot expect to find much but bitterness and spiteful accusations. Barbaro denounced the Greeks for not having given their whole-hearted support to the defence of their own city. He claimed that on the very eve of the Turkish assault, the Greeks refused to join in the work of final preparations unless they were paid. In fact, he wrote, they refused to support the defense thourghout the entire siege except when they were paid.[56] The accusation of Greek avarice was often repeated in the West. Constantinople, the chronicler of Bologna recorded, "si perdè per l'avarizia de' Greci, perchè non vollero mai assoldare genti alcune". The same source asserted that the Turks found much wealth in Constantinople, and those who first entered the city became rich men. In the home of one Greek lady alone, the chronicler continued, the Turks found precious stones and metals, and money worth 150,000 ducats; in another house, they found treasure valued at 80,000 ducats.[57]

As a bizarre, catastrophic event revealing the foibles of Latins and Greeks while demonstrating the prowess of a barbarian people, the fall of Constantinople did not readily commend itself to treatment by the new humanistic historiography. Such matters were the meat of the traditional chroniclers.[58] In the mid-fifteenth century humanist historians, adhering more or less rigidly to their antique models and eschewing the Biblical cosmology of their medieval predecessors, lacked the conceptual framework for dealing objectively with such events. Moreover, one may suppose that the triumph of yet another tyrant was discouraging to those who had hailed the revival of true poetry and ancient wisdom as ushering in a new age of creative and rational human achievement. Indeed, it seems reasonable to conclude that the success of the Turks contributed to undermining the confidence and optimism of the humanists who a little more than two generations after Petrarch were on the point of reverting to the values and outlook of the fourteenth-century poet.[59]

It is perhaps, then, not surprising to find the Florentine humanist historian Poggio Bracciolini maligning the Greeks for their failure in a satirical work entitled *De miseria conditionis humanae*. Poggio presents his views in the form of a dialogue purporting to be a conversation between himself, Cosimo de'Medici, and the humanist Matteo Palmieri. The latter is made to declare that while the loss to learning was a grievous thing, the Greeks owing to their deceitfulness, their indolence, and greed got what they deserved. Palmieri recalls how they had exploited and duped the crusaders who had failed to take the Holy Land because of Byzantine intrigues. The Greeks, he continues, were so overcome by avarice and cowardice that they never lifted a finger to help themselves but begged for aid from the pope and others when in fact they were sufficiently wealthy to provide for their own defense. The discussion of the Turkish victory, however, serves mainly as a point of departure for Poggio who passes on to a lengthy discussion of the evils and misfortunes which plague his generation.[60] Such conversations, actually, did take place in Florence. In the protocols of the Pratica, a Florentine advisory council, it is recorded that at a session on November 10, 1496 one of the elders related the details of the fall of Constantinople as he had heard them from the Greek humanist John Argyropulos. The speaker was particularly concerned to point out that his informant had admitted that the city was captured because the Greeks were not willing to spend the money necessary for defense—a lesson, however, which the Florentines themselves failed to heed.[61]

A scathing recitation of Byzantine transgressions is to be found in the *Constantinopolis* of the Brescian humanist Ubertino Puscolo. The author, a pupil of Guarino da Verona, had gone to Constantinople for further study and was there when the Turks took over. His vehement and unrelenting denunciation of his former hosts is matched only by the more famous diatribe composed in the tenth century by Liutprand of Cremona. For Puscolo the Greeks had lost all sense of Christian virtue and humanistic values. Everything had its price in the capital. Honest labor was disdained. All men of rank drew their income from the public treasury and squandered it on the gaming tables. True worship was eschewed and holy feasts were completely commercialized. Puscolo found ultimate proof of the debased condition of the Greeks in the record of duplicity which passed for negotiations with the Latins on the question of church union:

O perfidious race
Of Greeks! What cruel fury drove you straight
On toward the abyss, possessed you to fall,
O men of Greece, that you should dig the gulf
In which you sank your land, your cherished homes,
Your wives, your children?

Having refused the union they were abandoned at last even by their heavenly protector, the founder Constantine; and so God's justice was done.[62]

The Greeks, however, were not universally despised in the West. Besides the loss to the Christian faith, which everyone mourned, and the loss to Greek learning, lamented especially by the humanists, there was some genuine grief expressed over the fall of the empire and the sufferings of the Greeks. "Et certes les nouvelles furent piteuse à ouyr", wrote the Burgundian courtier, Olivier de la Marche, "car, comme disoyent les voyagiers, c'estoit une moult noble cité. . .". He mourned the losses to the faith, but also the destruction of the Greek people, and the death of the emperor. His praise of Constantine XI was boundless: ". . . je juge l'Empereur de Constantinople, vivant, la plus noble personne du monde. . .". The German emperor, he reasoned, was emperor only by election, but the emperors of Constantinople had held their crown by inheritance for more than five hundred years.[63]

Few, if any, chroniclers of the event attributed the Turkish victory directly to the well-organized, highly disciplined, and amply supported army of Mehmed II; and yet, such a conclusion was implicit in all the more accurate accounts of the battle, as well as from the great alarm which spread throughout the West with the news of the tragedy. It was consistent with the character of the times to emphasize the negative aspects of any great happening. It was assuredly contrary to ingrained tradition to praise the merits of any infidel. Nevertheless, even the most one-sided accounts of the siege and capture of Constantinople did not fail to give recognition to the obvious prowess of the Turks. Thus indirectly Latin writers paid tribute to the following significant strengths of the Ottoman army: the great size of the Grand Turk's host which, to be used at all successfully, demanded well-planned and highly coordinated tactical maneuvering; extensive and effective employment of artillery; strict discipline which converted even the amorphrous mass of irregulars into a formidable opponent; and, sustained logistical support. Barbaro, Tedaldi, and others testified to the bravery, loyalty, and obedience of the Turkish soldier. All authorities were highly impressed with the Turks' artillery and the huge forces which the conqueror commanded.[64] Despite recognition of these facts, and the self-confessed alarm and fear that the Turks would soon march west, our authorities were generally unable to reach an objective assessment of the role of the Turkish army in the defeat of the Greeks. There is an obvious contradiction between the facts they present and the conclusions they draw. Their preconceived notions of the Turks as infidels and enemies of the faith, and therefore cruel and inhuman savages, were only confirmed by the sack which followed the Turks' victorious entrance into Constantinople. If the Turks were barbarians, it followed that they must be inferior to civilized Europeans on all counts; and, in the face of overwhelming evidence to the contrary, even the military abilities of the Turks were disparaged. The appraisal of the Turks which Aeneas Sylvius gave in an oration delivered before the Roman curia in 1452 was frequently repeated. "They are", he declared, "unwarlike, weak, effeminate, neither martial in spirit, nor in counsel; their spoils were taken without sweat or blood."[65] The Turks were a pernicious force sent, or permitted, by God to scourge Christendom for its sins; all that was needed was for Christians to repent and take up the defense of the faith.

The prosecution of this program and the responses to it in so far as they shed light on the West's conception of the Turks will be dealt with in the following chapters. It remains here to consider to what extent the views and reactions evoked by the capture of Byzantium were shared by the man in the street or the tiller of the soil. Our reconstruction of the spread of the news, immediate reactions, and contemporary interpretations is based largely upon accounts written by members of the ruling and educated classes—princes, diplomats, prelates, scholars, court and town chroniclers, a physician, a merchant, and one or two professional soldiers. Was it true, then, as one historian has recently asserted, that "only the papacy and a few scholars and romanticists scattered about the West had been genuinely shocked at the thought of the great historic Christian city passing into the hands of the infidel"?[66] Or as another has claimed: "The number of people who had any reliable account of Mohammed's conquest and any real conception of the Turkish peril was . . . small, and a still smaller minority was capable of attaching any significance to the event"?[67] Certainly the sources available to the historian of ideas and attitudes in the Renaissance are still largely from the pens of an intellectual elite. But this is not to say that there was not a considerable traffic in ideas and information from the higher to the lower levels of society and vice versa.[68]

Fortunately we are not left wholly dependent upon speculation. There exists a significant collection of popular ballads, *lamenti*, and apocryphal accounts inspired by the Turkish victory.[69] Traveling minstrels, peddlars and tinkers, pilgrims and mendicants no doubt recited comparable versions, now lost or never committed to writing, in the market squares and inns, church-yards and convents of even more remote places. The extant popular works, I am convinced, bring us as close as written records allow to the thought and feelings of the "people" whose reactions to such an event were inevitably conditioned by medieval conceptions of the meaning and purpose of universal history. The interaction between the accepted notions and commonly shared opinions regarding Christendom and, the new knowledge of external matters such as the Turkish empire, the Far East, and the discovery of the New World is a fertile field of investigation for the historian of cultural processes. These popular works are in general not distinguished by a wealth of accurate detail and so have been little used by historians who have found them un-reliable or containing "nothing new". In some cases, it must be admitted, the Turkish question is quite peripheral; but they show, when considered together with the works of more learned authors, that the fall of Constan-tinople had a greater impact upon the West than is recognized by those scholars who are satisfied to cite the failure of the princes to take the cross as proof of a general apathy.[70]

The general tenor of the popular pieces may be illustrated by a brief sum-mary of one of the longer laments. The ninty-nine stanzas which comprise the *Lamento di Constantinopoli* were written shortly after the Turkish victory by either Bernardino Cinglano or Matteo Pisano. [71] The author was not present at the siege but claims that his account is based on what he had heard and read. In his invocation he specifically rejects the inspiration of the muse of Parnassus and calls upon Jesus Christ and the Virgin Mary; there are few classical references but the work is informed by a deeply religious spirit.[72] He begins by berating the pope, the emperor, and the prelates whom he holds responsible for the continuous retreat of Christians before the advance of the infidels. First they abandoned the land of Christ's birth and the holy places, and now Constantinople. He praises the latter's glories, its strength and riches, and its holy relics. For long it stood as the protector and defender of all Christendom and was feared by Turks and other infidels. He repeats the thesis that the city was betrayed by the Genoese and he minces no words in denouncing them as traitors to the faith.[73] He was ignorant of or chose to ignore the heroic role played by the Genoese captain Giustiniani. He reviews the background to the final act in the history of Byzantium: the military buildup of Mehmed II; the appeals of Constantine XI to the West; the responses of Venice, the pope, and the king of Aragon; and the Turkish siege of the city.[74] There follows a long and plantive account of the sufferings of the defenders, both Greeks and Latins. In the massacre of the citizens more than 200,000 perished! And, not wishing one body to remain intact, the Turks cut them all into pieces. He laments the fate of the infants who were spared in order that they may be raised as Saracens. A thousand historians would not be sufficient to record the tragedy. Over 60,000 books of great value were burned or cast into the harbor.

> Piangete omai, filosofi e doctori,
> Piangete, greci, piangete, latini,
> Piangete voi, o grandi studiatori,
> Piangete sempre, poi ch'e saracini,
> Piangete, chè v'àn tolti e vostri onori;
> Piangete tucti, grandi e piccolini,
> Pianga ciascun omai col lamentarsi,
> Pianga per que' libri che son[o] stat' arsi.[75]

The second part of the lament consists of a prolonged petition to the powers of Christendom to avenge the honor of Christ. In contrast to many of the appeals of this period the author does call for the recovery of Constantinople; indeed, he looks forward to a restoration of Christian control in the Holy Land. He invokes the power of Christ to bring about a perpetual peace among Christians, and especially the Italians:

> E co' lor forze e l'animo veracie
> Che piglien l'arme contra alli pagani:
> Fallo, Signore Iddio, se a te piace,
> Acciò che quel[lo] paese si raquisti
> Dove nascesti e dove tu moristi.[76]

He implores Nicholas V as vicar of God to all Christians, to call the Italians, and all prelates and people:

> A fare impressa per mare e per terra
> Per fare agli pagani un' aspra guerra.[77]

He warns Frederick III that unless he arms and comes to the aid of the pope the infidels would soon be upon him. He pleads with the king of Aragon, the kings of France and England, the duke of Burgundy, and fifty-seven other powers whom he addresses by name to respond to the command of the pope, the shepherd of the church, for the defense of the faith and the recovery of Byzantium.

> La fede a tutti sia raccomandata;
> La fede tutti abbiate nella mente;
> La fede sempre sia da voi amata;

La fede di Cristo omnipotente;
La fede sempre sia da voi chiamata;
La fede vi ricordi, umana gente;
La fede mel combatter tutti quanti;
La fede vi farà fermi e costanti.[78]

The capture of the city, as we have seen, came as a shock to the Latins. Clearly they were not prepared for it and their surprise is some indication of how little many understood the affairs of the Levant. In accounting for the increase in popular writings on the Turkish problem after 1453, Nicolai Iorga suggested that "during the first half of the century one did not believe the danger so close or so great. . .". Despite the long record of Turkish victories in the Balkans and Greece, the debacles at Nicopolis and Varna, the warnings of eastern Christians and informed Latin observers, the threat, while often viewed as a serious matter demanding the attention of all Christians, was yet regarded as removed and for the most part not of the utmost urgency. The fall of Constantinople awakened the West to the fact that the Turks were the masters of southeastern Europe, a fact which historians well know was a *fait accompli* of more than fifty years standing.[79]

But the works of this genre reveal more than a feeling of alarm and a need for military action. They confirm the sense of guilt and insecurity betrayed in the accounts of the chroniclers. The scourge of God had chastened the Greeks and there were no indications that the rod had been withdrawn. The fall of Constantinople thus gave an added stimulus to the movement for reform. What greater proof was needed to show God's dissatisfaction with the administration of prince or pope, town council or local lord? The one hope for salvation was repentance—the purging of sins, usually described in detail in the ballads and laments, and a return to the virtues of an idealized past.[80]

Religious reform sentiment in the fifteenth century exhibited two dominant but conflicting tendencies. The pursuit of primarily regional or particular interests produced intense resentment toward the autocratic and highly centralized authority of Rome. On the other hand, preoccupation with the ideal of a unified Christian commonwealth tended to stress the divine ordination of the pope as the one true source of Christian unity. During the Great Schism and its immediate aftermath, the popularity of conciliar ideas, the emphasis on the responsibility of the individual, the series of concordats which curtailed the power of the pope over the churches of many regions, all seemed to point toward a victory for the proponents of a decentralized ecclesiastical structure. Indeed, the lessening of the administrative power of

Rome and the concomittant diminution of its prestige and international standing at that time greatly contributed to the ultimate destruction of church unity. But in the mid-fifteenth century both the process of decentralization and the flagging prestige were temporarily abated. Beginning with the victory of Eugenius IV over the council of Basel the papacy began successfully to reassert its claims to final and universal authority in matters of legislation and administration over the whole church. The new stimulus to reform engendered by the conquests of the Turks strengthened the claims of those who believed that the only hope for Christendom was to embrace the conservative program of the restoration papacy. Since the Ottoman menace was regarded popularly and by ecclesiastical publicists as the latest phase in the prolonged contest between the true faith and the infidel, its resolution required a new crusade. As the successor of St. Peter, charged with the leadership of Christendom, the pope alone had the authority to command the obedience of all Christians; and, like Urban II, charged with the defense of the faith, he was the sole legitimate author of the Holy War. The Turkish threat worked toward reviving a waning loyalty to the *Respublica Christiana* and gave new life to the old cry for peace and unity in a Christendom subject to the pope. Considered in this light, that is in its effect upon the public posture of the Renaissance papacy, it may be said that the fall of Constantinople contributed to postponing the Protestant revolt.

NOTES TO CHAPTER I

1. The text has been edited and translated from the British Museum Additional MS, 34060, by R. Browning, "A Note of the Capture of Constantinople in 1453", *Byzantion*, XXII (1952), 379-387.

2. *Recital Concerning the Sweet Land of Cyprus Entitled "Chronicle"*, ed. R. W. Dawkins, (Oxford, 1932), I, 683.

3. R. Röhricht, *Deutsche Pilgerreisen nach dem Heiligen Lande* (new ed., Innsbruck, 1900), pp. 122, 123.

4. A. Bernoulli (ed.), *Pilgerreisen der Basler Hans und Peter Rot, 1440 und 1453* (Basel, 1882), p. 90.

5. Marino Sanuto, *Vite de' duchi Venezia (RISS*, XXII, 1151); cf. Pastor, *HP*, II, 272; and F. Thiriet, *La Romanie vénitienne au moyen âge* (Paris, 1959), pp. 382, 383. The news also reached Vicenza on the 29th. See N. Iorga, *Notes et extraits*, IV, 53, 54.

6. Venetian letter to Nicholas V, June 30, 1453, in Martène, *Thesaurus*, I, cols. 1825-1826.

7. N. Iorga, "Notes", *ROL*, VIII (1900-1901), 100. Painfully aware of their exposed position and the losses already suffered, and skeptical about assistance from riva l

Latin powers, Venice took immediate action to protect her own interests, armed her galleys, strengthened the fortifications of her Levantine possessions, and began negotiations with the conqueror which issued in the peace of April 18, 1454. See the documents summarized in F. Thiriet, *Régestes des délibérations du sénat de Venise concernant la Romanie* (Paris, 1961), III, 187-190.

8. N. B. Tomadakis, "Répercussion immédiate de la prise de Constantinople", *L'Hellenisme contemporain, Supplement (1953): Le Cinq-centième anniversaire de la prise de Constantinople*, p. 57.

9. F. Torraca, "Frà Roberto da Lecce", *Archivio storico per le province napoletane*, VII (1882), 141-165; Pastor, *HP*, II, 272.

10. *Ibid.*, p. 273, 274; Stefan Infessura, *Diario della città di Roma (RISS*, III, ii, 1136); letter of Cardinal Estouteville to Francesco Sforza, Rome, July 19, 1453, in Pastor, *Acta inedita*, I, 35, 36; letter of Johann Hake to the archbishop of Trier, July 20, 1453, in J. Koch, "Nikolaus von Cues und seine Umwelt", *Sitzungsberichte der Heidelberger Akademie der Wissenschaft. Philosophisch-historische klasse*, XXXIV, Abt. 2 (1944-48), 97.

11. Letter of N. Soderini to Florence, July 8, 1453, in Iorga, *Notes et extraits*, II, 489. But see J. Heers, *Gênes au xvᵉ siècle. Activités économiques et problèmes sociaux* (Paris, 1961), pp. 363-406, who shows that the commercial activities of the Genoese in the Levant continued to be important long after the event. The plight of the Genoese at Pera is vividly set forth in a letter of Angelus Johannes Zaccharia, podestà of Pera, June 23, 1453, in *Notices et extraits des mss. de la Bibliothèque du Roi*, XI (Paris, 1827), 74-79. Cf. letter of Francesco Giustiniano written at Chios, September 27, 1453, in Iorga, "Notes", *ROL*, VIII, 105-108. Giustiniano concluded with a strong warning that the Turks were preparing to continue their attack upon Christendom: "Contremiscunt etiam omnia christianorum loca ipsis Teucris finitima, et eo maxime quia noviter preparare fecit, ut fertur, in Galipoli classem ducentum fustarum, triremium, biremium et uniremium, et dicitur infra mensem erit ordinata et parata; que quo itura sit ignoramus. Dominus sit nostrum custos et defensor!"

12. Florentine letters to Soderini and Siena in Iorga, *Notes et extraits*, II, 499-500. See also the letter from the signoria to Nicholas V in G. Müller, *Documenti sulle relazioni delle città Toscane coll' Oriente Cristiano e coi Turchi* (Florence, 1879), no. CXXV, pp. 178, 179.

13. Letter of Alfonso to Nicholas V, October 8, 1453, in Lajos Thallóczy and Antal Áldásy (eds.), *A Magyarország és Szerbia Közti Összeköttetések Oklevéltára, 1198-1526 (MHH*, XXXIII, Budapest, 1907), no. 244, 171, 172.

14. Iorga, *Notes et extraits*, IV, 65-68.

15. Letter from Aeneas Sylvius to Nicholas V, Graz, July 12, 1453, in Wolkan, *Der Briefwechsel*, Abt. III, Bd. I, no. 109, 199.

16. "Imperator summo pontifici spondet auxilio esse contra Turcos", in Aeneas Sylvius, *Opera*, epist. clxiii, 716, 717; cf. Frederick's letter to King Charles of France, January 9, 1454, in Luc d'Achery (ed.), *Spicilegium sive collectio veterum aliquot scriptorum* (new ed., Paris, 1723), III, 795, 796.

17. Iorga, "Notes", *ROL*, VIII, 115.

18. J. Hofer, *Giovanni da Capestrano. Una vita spesa nella lotta per la riforma della chiesa*, tr. G. di Fabio (Aquila, 1955), p. 593.

19. Chastellain, *Chronique*, III, 73; Jacques du Clercq, *Mémoires*, p. 85.

20. Pastor, *HP*, II, 285. On Alfonso V's enthusiasm for the crusade in support of which he had the "crusado" struck see Duarte Pacheco Pereira, *Esmeraldo. De situ orbis*, ed. and tr. G. H. T. Kimble *(The Hakluyt Society*, series 2, vol. lxxix, London, 1937), 103, 104; and on Prince Henry's search for Christian allies against the Moslems of North Africa as a main reason for his prosecuting the exploratory voyages, Gomes Eannes de Azurara, *The Chronicle of the Discovery and Conquest* of Guinea, trs. and eds. C. R. Beazley and E. Prestage *(The Hakluyt Society*, series 1, vol. xcv, London, 1896), I, p. 28.

21. D. Cabanelas Rodríguez, *Juan de Segovia y el problema islámico*)Madrid, 1952), p. 93.

22. *Loci e libro veritatum*, ed. J. E. T. Rogers (Oxford, 1881), p. 158; *Chronicles of London*, ed. C. L. Kingsford (Oxford, 1905), 164.

23. Pastor, *HP*, II, 285, 286. On the Turks referred to as Antichrist see J. Deny, "Les Pseudo-propheties concernant les Turcs au XVIe siècle", *Revue des études islamiques*, X (1936), 201-220; and H. Preuss, *Die Vorstellungen vom Antichrist* (Leipzig, 1906).

24. Quoted in A. A. Vasiliev, *History of the Byzantine Empire* (Madison, 1952), p. 655.

25. "Informations envoyées, tant par Francisco de France, à tres-reverend père en Dieu monseigneur le cardinal d'Avignon, que par Jehan Blanchin et Jacques Edaldy [sic] marchant Florentin, de la prinse de Constantinople par l'empereur Turc le xxix. jour de May MCCCCLIII. à la quelle ledit Jacques estoit personnellement", in Martène, *Thesaurus*, I, cols. 1819-1825. In 1862 C. Lefèbvre published the "Informations" from a manuscript of Cambrai, no. 1114, which he thought to have been previously unpublished. See *Revue des sociétés savantes des départements*, VIII (1862), 500-504. The work was very popular in the fifteenth century. It is found in a manuscript (B.N., fr. 2691) of Jean Chartier, *Histoire de Charles VII, roy de France*, ed. Denys Godefroy (Paris, 1661), 271-279; and a manuscript (Bibliothèque Royale, Brussels, 19684) of a Burgundian chronicle *(Chronique des Pays-Bas, de France, d'Angleterre et de Tournai*, ed. J. J. de Smet in *Corpus chronicorum Flandriae*, III, Brussels, 1856, 511-516; cf. V. Fris, "La Chronique des Pays-Bas, de France, d'Angleterre et de Tournai", *Compte-Rendu des séances de la Commission royal d'histoire*, 5th ser., X [1900], 65-82). Marie-Louise Concasty, in her article "Les 'Informations' de Jacques Tedaldi sur le siège et la prise de Constantinople", *Byzantion*, XXIV (1954), 95-110, gives four other French manuscripts of the work, and one Latin (published by Martène and Durand, *Veterum scriptorum et monumentorum historicorum, dogmaticorum, moralium, amplissima collectio*, V, Paris, 1729, cols. 785-800). The "Informations" is also found in a modified form in Nicole le Huen, *Le Grant voyage de Hierusalem* (Paris, 1522), fols. clxix-clxxii. Concasty believes that Tedaldi and Blanchin are responsible for the part of the text treating the details of the siege. The assessment of Mehmed II and the crusade plan, she writes, were added to the work at the time of its translation into French (1454), for the purpose of gaining adherents to the crusade. The edition used here is that of Martène, *Thesaurus*, based on the Ms. B.N., fr., 5036.

26. Martène, *Thesaurus*, I, 1819-1823.

27. *Ibid.*, 1823, 1824.

28. *Ibid.*, 1824, 1825.

29. For Isidore's career see J. Gill, *Personalities at the Council of Florence* (Oxford, 1964), pp. 65-78; G. Mercati, "Scritti d'Isidoro il cardinale Ruteno", *Studi e Testi*, XL (Rome, 1926); Pastor, *HP*, II, 287. "Isidorus, Cardinalis Ruthenus, Episcopus Sabinensis, Legatus Pontificis, universis Christi fidelibus", ed. P. A. Dethier *(MHH, XXI*, pt. i, no. 4), 687-695; cf. Raynaldus, *Annales*, ad an. 1453, nos. 5, 6; and Isidore's letter from Crete to Nicholas V, August 15, 1453 in Iorga, *Notes et extraits*, II, 522-524.

30. *Corpus chronicorum Bononiensium*, ed. A. Sorbelli *(RISS*, new ed., XVIII: Cronaca A, 186, 187); cf. "Rapporto del Superiore dei Franciscani, presente all' assedio ed alla presa di Costantinopoli", ed. Dethier *(MHH*, XXII, pt. i), 939, 940.

31. "Citazione del G. M. de Lastic a' Cavalieri del Priorato d'Alvernia, imponendo loro l'accorrere alla difesa di Rodi, minacciata dall' Ottomanno", in S. Pauli (ed.), *Codice diplomatico del sacro militare ordine Gerosolimitano*, II (Lucca, 1737), no. cvi, 131, 132. Cf. "Bulla Magni Magistri Johannis de Lastic, fratris ordinis equestris Sancti Johannis in Rhodo, ad fratrem Robertum de Lotil, priorem prioratus eiusdem ordinis in Anglia, Hibernia et Scotia, de excidio Constantinopolitano et de necessitate armandi contra Turcum eiusdem que classem magnam insulas archipelagi invasuram", ed., Dethier *(MHH*, XXII, pt. i), 878-886; and the address of ambassadors of the grandmaster to Nicholas V in *Cronaca di Viterbo*, ed. I. Ciampi (Florence, 1872), I, 229, 230; and letter from Jean de Lastic to Johann Losel, prior in Germany, July 6, 1453 in Iorga, *Notes et extraits*, II, pp. 520, 521.

32. For the career of Bessarion see L. Mohler, *Kardinal Bessarion als Theologe, Humanist und Staatsman*, 3 vols. (Paderborn, 1923-1927, 1942); and R. J. Loenertz, "Pour la biographie du cardinal Bessarion", *Orientalia christiana periodica*, X (1944), 116-149,

33. "Epistola Bissarion [sic] cardinalis Tusculani, legati Bononiensis natione Graeca. ad ducem Venetorum pro auxilio Constantinopoli exhibendo exhortatoria", in A. Vast, *Le Cardinal Bessarion (1402-1472). Étude sur la chrétienté et la renaissance vers le milieu du xve siècle* (Paris, 1878), appendix III, pp. 454, 455. This letter dated July 13, 1453, is not to be confused with Bessarion's well known *Orations Against the Turks*, as does D. Geanakoplos, *Greek Scholars in Venice*, p. 97, n. 93.

34. Wolkan, *Der Briefwechsel*, Bd. I, Abt. III, no. cix, 199-202.

35. Paul Wittek, *The Rise of the Ottoman Empire* (Royal Asiatic Society Monographs, XXIII, London, 1938), p. 51. The event, of course, has attracted the attention of historians from the fifteenth century to the present. Convenient summaries may be found in the numerous articles published in 1953; e.g. *L'Hellenisme contemporain. Supplement (1953): Le Cinq-centième anniversaire de la prise de Constantinople; Byzantinoslavica*, XIV (1953); S. Runciman et al., *The Fall of Constantinople. A Symposium Held at the School of Oriental and African Studies 29 May 1953* (London, 1955).

36. A. J. Toynbee, "The Ottoman Empire in World History", *Proceedings of the American Philosophical Society*, XCIV (1955), 120.

37. Lauro Quirini, "De urbis Constantinopolis jactura et captivitate", in Giovanni degli Agostini, *Notizie istorico-critiche intorno la vita, e le opere degli scrittori Viniziani* (Venice, 1752), I, 219.

38. D. Cantemir, *Histoire de l'empire othoman* (Paris, 1743), II, 45.

39. Quoted by Pastor, *HP*, II, 310.

40. Aeneas Sylvius, *Opera*, ep. 127, p. 656; Gibbon, *The History of the Decline and Fall of the Roman Empire*, ed. J. B. Bury (3rd ed., London, 1909), VII, 207.

41. *CSP Milan*, p. 62.

42. Pastor, *HP*, III, 157.

43. J. Huizinga, *The Waning of the Middle Ages*, tr. F. Hopinan (New York, 1954), p. 31.

44. Chastellain, *Oeuvres*, I, 11. Following a ten page summary of the events of world history until his time he concluded: "Et dernièrement, qui, pis vaut, s'est eslevé en mes jours l'ennemy cruel de Dieu, le grand Turc, un nouveau Mahomet, violeur du crucifix et de son Eglise, dispiteur de sa loy, prince de l'armée de Satan, lequel levant sa corne d'orgueil, par présomption de sa terrienne puissance en quoy se confie, a osté aux chrestiens leur bastille de Constantinople et soumise à sa dition en confuse et douloureuse attente cy-après".

45. Jacques de Clerq, *Mémoires*, p. 147; Jean Chartier, *Histoire de Charles VII*, p. 271; Leonard of Chios, "Epistola ad Papam Nicolaum V", ed. Dethier *(MHH*, XXI, pt. i, no. 3, 610-12*)*; G. Moravcsik, "Bericht des Leonardus Chiensis über den Fall von Konstantinopel in einer vulgärgriechischen Quelle", *Festschrift F. Dölger. Byzantinische Zeitschrift*, XLIV (1951), 428-436; Mathieu d'Escouchy, *Chronique*, II, 35, 36. There is a marked similarity between the fabrication concerning the emperor's daughter and the actual treatment of Anne Erizzo by Mehmed II after the fall of Negropont in 1470. See W. Miller, *The Latins in the Levant. A History of Frankish Greece (*1204-1566*),* (London, 1908), pp. 476, 477.

46. The quotation is from *Grafton's Chronicle* (London, 1809), I, 651. Among the eyewitness accounts the most sanguinary are Leonard of Chios, *op. cit.*, pp. 610-615; Cardinal Isidore's "Universis Christi fidelibus", ed. Dethier *(MHH*, XXI, pt. i, no. 4, 687-695); Niccolò Barbaro, *Giornale dell' assedio di Costantinopoli*, 1453, ed. Enrico Cornet *(MHH*, XXII, pt. i, no. 16); e.g. Barbaro recorded (p. 820), "el sangue se coreva per la tera come el fosse stà piovesto, o che l'aqua si fosse andada per rigatoli cusi feva el sangue; i corpi morti cusi de Christiani, come de Turchi, queli si fo butadi in nel Dardanelo, i quali andava a segonda per mar, come fa i meloni per i canali." Cf. in the secondary accounts, Johannes Trithemius, *Opera historica* (Frankfurt, 1601), p. 368; Antonio Bonfini, *Rerum Ungaricarum decades*, ed. I. Fógel, B. Iványi, and L. Joház *(Bibliotheca scriptorum medii recentisque aevorum*, Leipzig, 1936), III, 181, 182; an anonymous Slavic source discussed by Iorga in *Bulletin de la section historique. Académie Roumaine*, XIII (1927), 126; Niccolò da Toccia, *Cronaca di Viterbo*, pp. 227-230.

47. Cf. M. Gilmore, *The World of Humanism*, 1453-1517 (New York, 1952), pp. 20, 21, who believes that such a view of the Turk was the product of the literature of the sixteenth century.

48. The assertion was made time and again in the literature of the fifteenth and the sixteenth centuries. E.g. Chastellain, *op. cit.*, III, 109, who wrote that Mehmed II conquered "la forte ville de Constantinople et fit en icelle pluseurs dérisions abhominables que Dieu permist peut-être pour les péchies de son peuple...." Cf. comments in *Ein Wappenbuch Kaiser Maximilians I*, ed. Anna Coreth in *Festschrift zur Feier des Zweithundertjährigen Bestandes des Haus-Hof-und Staatsarchivs* (Vienna, 1949), I, 297. For its continuation in Elizabethan literature see C. A. Patrides, " 'The Bloody and Cruell Turke': the Background of a Renaissance Commonplace", *Studies in the Renaissance*, X (1963), 126-135.

49. "A Letter to King Henry the Fifth Written from the Council of Constance" in C. Munro (ed.), *Letters of Queen Margaret (Camden Society*, no. 86, London, 1863), p. 10; Jean Molinet, *Chroniques*, ed. G. Doutrepont and O. Jodogne (Brussels, 1935), II, 483-485; Giovanni Nanni, *De futuris Christianorum triumphis in Saracenos* (Genoa, 1480). This work also appeared at Leipzig, 1481; Gouda, 1482; Cologne, 1482; Lowen, ca. 1485; Nuremberg, 1485; Paris, 1495; and again at Cologne, 1497. See *GW*, II, cols. 332-337; nos. 2017-2024. Cf. Barbaro, *Giornale*, ed. Dethier *(MHH*, XXII, pt. ii, no. 16, 777, 793, 794, 804-809; Kritovoulos, *History of Mehmed the Conqueror*, tr. C. T. Riggs (Princeton, 1954), pp. 58, 59. For other prophecies and miracles associated with the eastern threat see Iorga, "Notes", *ROL*, VIII, 293-298.

50. Cf. *CSP* Ven., II, 5, 348, 349; Luca Landucci, *A Florentine Diary from 1450 to 1516*, tr. Alice de Rosen Jervis (London, 1927), pp. 182, 183.

51. *Travels and Adventures*, 1435-1439, tr. and ed. M. Letts (London, 1926), pp. 131, 137.

52. Gascoigne, *Loci e libro veritatum*, p. 158; Barbaro, *op. cit.*, pp. 757, 758, 763.

53. Niccolò da Toccia, *Cronaca*, p. 228.

54. Iorga, *Notes et extraits*, IV, 46-49; Pastor, *HP*, II, 254, 255. Cf. R. Guilland, "Les Appels de Constantin XI Paléologue à Rome et à Venise pour sauver Constantinople", *Byzantinoslavica*, XIV (1953), 226-244.

55. See H. Evert-Kappesowa, "La Tiare ou le turban", *Byzantinoslavica*, XIV (1953), 245-257. Cf. Setton, "Byzantine Background to the Italian Renaissance", pp. 42, 43.

56. Barbaro, *op. cit.*, p. 801; Leonard of Chios, *op. cit.*, 563, 564, 571, 572.

57. *Corpus chronicorum Bononiensium*, p. 186.

58. For a penetrating analysis of humanistic historiography see Felix Gilbert, *Machiavelli and Guicciardini. Politics and History in Sixteenth-Century Florence* (Princeton, 1965), pp. 203-235.

59. Cf. H. Baron, "Fifteenth Century Civilization and the Renaissance", *NCMH*, I, 73-75 on the changes in humanistic outlook in the second half of the *Quattrocento*.

60. Poggio, *De miseria conditionis humanae* in his *Opera* (Basel, 1538), pp. 88-131.

61. Cited by Felix Gilbert, "Florentine Political Assumptions in the Period of Savonarola and Soderini", *Journal of the Warburg and Courtauld Institutes*, XX (1957), 194, 204, n. 80.

62. The English translation is that of L. R. Loomis who claims that the ambivalent attitude of Italian humanists toward the Greeks prevented the fall of Constantinople from being imbued with symbolic significance comparable to that of Babylon, Jerusalem, or Rome. "The Fall of Constantinople Symbolically Considered", in *Essays in Intellectual History Dedicated to James Harvey Robinson* (New York, 1929), pp. 243-258. The complete text of Puscolo is found in *MHH*, XX, pt. i, no. 8, 101-261; see especially pp. 104-109, 119-128, 144-149.

63. Olivier de la Marche, *Mémoires*, ed. H. Beaune and J. d'Arbaumont Paris, (1884), II, 336, 337.

64. Cf. Barbaro, *op. cit.*, pp. 18, 22; Tedaldi, *op. cit.*, passim.

65. *Oratio*, ed. Dethier *(MHH*, XXII, pt. i, no. 13, 639).

66. S. Runciman, *The Fall of Constantinople 1453* (Cambridge, 1965), p. 179.

67. Gilmore, *The World of Humanism*, p. 15.

68. See e.g., Denys Hay, *The Italian Renaissance in its Historical Background* (Cambridge, 1962), p. 4.

69. E.g. *Lamenti storici dei secoli XIV, XV, e XVI*, ed. A. Medin and L. Frati, 4 vols. (Bologna, 1887-1894); Iorga, "Notes", *ROL*, VIII, 302-304; one lament commemorating the event, "La lamentatio Sanctae Matris Ecclesiae Constantinopolitanae", was put to music by Guillaume Dufay and sung in the churches in France. See B. Becherini, "Due canzoni di Dufay del codice fiorentino 2794", *La Bibliofilia*, XLIII (1941), 124-135; A. Grunzweig, "Notes sur la musique des Pays-Bas au xve siècle; I; Une lettre inedite de Guillaume Dufay", *Bulletin de l'institut historique belge de Rome*, XVIII (1937), 73-85; C. van den Borren, "Guillaume Dufay, centre de rayonnement de la polyphonie europeénne à la fin du moyen âge", *Bulletin de l'institut historique belge de Rome*, XX (1939), 181, 182.

70. As for example most recently in Runciman, *The Fall of Constantinople*, pp. 160, 180. For a discussion of the structure and function of *Volkslieder and Sprüche* in Germany see G. L. Waas, *The Legendary Character of Kaiser Maximilian* (New York, 1941), pp. 73ff.

71. In Medin and Frati, *op. cit.* II, 157-190.

72. *Ibid.*, p. 157.

73. *Ibid.*, pp. 158, 160.

74. *Ibid.*, pp. 160-162.

75. *Ibid.*, pp. 162-176.

76. *Ibid.*, p. 177.

77. *Ibid.*, p. 178.

78. *Ibid.*, pp. 178, 190.

79. Iorga, *ROL*, VIII, 267: "La plupart des nombreux écrits, plus ou moins populaires par le style et par la langue, qui concernent la croisade au xve siècle, sont postérieurs à l'année 1453, et il est facile d'en donner l'explication. Ce n'est que par la prise de Constantinople, par les pirateries des Turcs dans l'Archipel et la Méditerranée, par leur longue guerre contre Venise, par la conquête des colonies latines de l'Orient et par l'invasion de l'Italie et de l'Allemagne que la chrétienté fut complètement tirée de sa torpeur ou distraite des guerres qui la déchiraient. Pendant la première moitié du siècle, on ne croyait pas le danger si proche ni si grand, et on laissait la tâche de combattre au pape et à ceux qui avaient des intérêts immédiats en Orient."

80. For additional examples see below Chapter VIII, pp. 216-218.

CHAPTER II

The enemy of the cross

Nicholas V "attained success and fame in many great undertakings", wrote Aeneas Sylvius, "but was unhappy in the fall of Constantinople, which occurred during his pontificate and was a black stain on his reputation".[1] Though not wholly unconcerned with the problems of the Levant, before 1453 Nicholas was no great champion of the crusade. He did provide some assistance for the Hungarians, Albanians, and Bosnians in their struggles with the Turks, and some financial aid for the knights of Rhodes and the kingdom of Cyprus.[2] As for the Greeks he demanded consummation of the union as a precondition for substantial material support. With the accession of Constantine XI (January 6, 1449), Byzantium had stepped up its efforts to secure help from the West. A report from Genoa prompted by a Greek embassy to that city informed the pope that the new emperor was favorably disposed toward the union. The Genoese urged Nicholas to speed negotiations.[3] Early in 1451 Constantine sent Andronicus Bryennius Leontaris to the courts of Venice, Ferrara, Rome, and Naples. Bryennius was charged with the usual mission of seeking military aid but also carried a letter from the anti-unionist Orthodox clergy which showed that they were as implacable as ever in their opposition to the agreement reached at Florence. Indeed, their hostility was such that about the same time the pro-unionist patriarch, Gregory III, fled from the capital and eventually made his way to Rome by way of the Morea.[4] The pope's response to the Greeks dated September 27, 1451, ironically at the very moment when Mehmed II was at Adrianople busy with the final preparations for the siege', was in effect an ultimatum. Having failed to act in good faith in accordance with the agreement of Florence, Byzantium was under the judgment of God; in other words, no union, no aid. Unwittingly the pope had passed the sentence which the Turks were to carry out.[5] By the time Nicholas' letter reached the capital the intentions of the sultan were clear. New embassies were hastily dispatched to the West, but, as we have seen, the results were negligible.[6]

Of the Latin powers the Italians were certainly the best informed on the affairs of the Levant. Genoa, Venice, and Rome must have realized that sooner or later the city would succumb to the Turks. Yet psychologically they were unprepared for the decisive victory of May 29. The pope's biographer, the humanist Platina revealed the quandary in which Nicholas found himself when he wrote that nothing so unsettled the pope as when he heard that the Turks had taken Constantinople, "for he had intended to help the Greeks with troops and a fleet. . . but the city was taken so suddenly that he had hardly any time to think about sending aid".[7]

Once the damage was done, however, Nicholas did all that he could to meet new challenge. He dispatched three galleys to the Levant under the command of the Genoese Angelo Ambrogini and ordered five more to be outfitted at his expense at Venice. Toward the end of September 1453, he sent envoys to the rulers of Italy calling them to a congress in Rome the following month.[8] On September 30, 1453 he addressed a crusade bull to all Christendom. In it he denounced Mehmed as the cruelest persecutor of the church of Christ, the son of Satan, the son of perdition, the son of death who thirsted for the blood of Christians. He pronounced the sultan to be the great red dragon with seven heads crowned by seven diadems and with ten horns described by St. John. He called upon the princes of Europe to defend the faith with their goods and lives. He guaranteed a plenary indulgence to all who by February 1, 1454, would take part personally or furnish a combatant to fight against the Turks for six consecutive months. The pope announced what financial contributions he and the cardinals intended to make and imposed a general tenth on all Christendom. He threatened with the direst penalties anyone who shirked his responsibilities, and especially anyone who aided the infidels or supplied them with arms or goods.[9]

The pope's appeal was seconded by members of the Roman curia and a chorus of prelates throughout Christendom. Giovanni da Castiglione, bishop of Pavia, in an exhortation to King Ladislas of Hungary, warned that God would punish those who refused. The people themselves would not long suffer this shame! Moreover it was not only a question of avenging the Christian faith. Was it not the duty of a king to oppose an invasion? If Ladislas felt himself too young and overly burdened with his newly acquired responsibilities then it was up to his nobles to prosecute the war. He was warned not to count on truces granted by the sultan but admonished to follow the example of the pope.[10]

The cry of alarm and the exhortation of princes and people was raised also by the lesser clergy. From this period dates the *Ad excitandum omnes principes contra Theucram* of a canon regular, one Timothy of Verona. The author complained that he had labored his entire life for the cause of peace in Italy, but had despaired of achieving success. When, however, he heard of the capture of Constantinople, and how the barbarians had slaughtered the Christians like cattle, his hopes for peace in Italy were renewed. He reported that the sultan had concluded peace with his neighbors to the north and had prepared a fleet and manufactured cannon. He claimed that Mehmed was attracted to Italy by its riches and the graves of his Trojan ancestors. "Italy", he declared, "must prevent the attack and avenge the deaths of Christians." Timothy appealed first to Aragon and Venice to avenge their losses and prevent the Turks from seizing their commercial empires. They must refuse a criminal alliance with the Turks, and employ their ample forces in fighting them. He appealed to the condottieri Jacopo Piccinino, Sigismondo Malatesta, and Francesco Sforza, the last of whom he described as greater than all the generals of antiquity. It seemed to Timothy that Sforza especially had been destined for this task; after a long and successful career and being then advanced in age it was time for him to undertake a work of piety.[11]

The congress in Rome failed to establish peace in Italy. But on April 9, 1454, Venice and Milan signed the Peace of Lodi which ended the war of the Milanese succession. Then on August 30, Florence, Venice, and Milan concluded the treaty of Venice, the basic instrument of the Most Holy League, the first general peace in Italy. In January of the following year, Alfonso of Naples was the last to adhere to the covenant which bound all signatories to consult before concluding treaties and in case of a threatened attack. This grand alliance and pacification of Italy was the result of complex developments commencing long before the events of 1453-1454. In the negotiations, however, Pope Nicholas had played a principal role. There is no doubt that the fall of Constantinople and the Turkish threat together with the fear of impending French intervention in Italy strengthened his hand in bringing about the settlement.[12]

Meanwhile there were some signs that the pope's efforts might bear fruit north of the Alps in Germany. During 1454 and 1455, Frederick III called together on three occasions the princes of the empire. Although the emperor did not attend personally the first of these diets which was held at Ratisbon in April 1454, graced by the presence of Philip the Good, it possessed an air of universality and importance. Aeneas Sylvius, who represented Frederick at the gathering, recorded the brief response made by the duke of Burgundy to his own lengthy exhortation. "What is the use of long discussion? Aeneas has shown us our duty. Let others give their opinions; I will speak for myself", the duke declared. "I realize the crisis in which Christianity finds itself. If we wish to keep our faith, our liberty, our lives, we must take the field against the Turks and crush their power before it becomes any stronger." The duke of Burgundy declared his willingness to devote himself and his resources to the holy work if any other prince of appropriate stature would join him.[13]

At Ratisbon the princes agreed to support the war against the Turks and made promises of troops and money.[14] They met again toward the end of September at Frankfort. This time both the emperor and the duke of Burgundy were absent. The Germans were in less of a mood to discuss the crusade, but expressed their dissatisfaction with the pope and the emperor and clamored for reform. Aeneas Sylvius, once more representing Frederick, recorded that the Germans "could not bear to hear the name of the emperor or the pope, who, they said, were false and greedy and wanted to rake in gold, not make war. This was a fine sort of trick," he reported them as saying, "to proclaim a crusade against the Turks that money might be extorted from the Germans by artful wiles as from barbarians". Nonetheless at the urgent pleas of Aeneas Sylvius, St. John Capistran, and the Hungarian delegates, the princes promised to raise a force of 42,000 men, and to conclude the final arrangements in consultation with the emperor.[15] At the diet of Wiener-Neustadt which began in February 1455, the Turkish problem was subordinated to questions of German affairs. The emperor was confronted by the disgruntled princes who made their support of the crusade contingent upon his fulfilling their demands. The diet of Wiener-Neustadt ended having achieved no more conclusive results than its predecessors. The Germans, the chronicler of Speier observed, "had too many quarrels among themselves on their hands to want another with the Turks".[16]

Complaints that the self-seeking and divisive policies of Renaissance princes undermined the unity of Christendom, and denunciations of particular rulers for failing to render unqualified support to the papal crusade have been voiced with equal fervor by fifteenth-century writers and modern historians. These judgments reveal, in the case of the former, the conflict of values which plagued the conscience of the *Quattrocento*, and, on the part of many of the latter, an imperfect understanding of the complex springs of political action in the Renaissance.[17] A detailed analysis of the policies and diplomacy of the western powers *vis-à-vis* the Turks far exceeds the aims of this study. But when we analyze western attitudes toward the Turks we must understand the interplay between prevailing moral assumptions and the exigencies of practical politics. Failure to render unqualified support for the crusade, or even outright cooperation with the Turks need not mean that a prince was unconcerned with the Turkish threat, or opposed to the papacy's proposed solution. That the powers of Italy or southcentral Europe were more sensitive to the problem than, say, the kings of England or France is obvious. Geographical proximity and the extent of their economic or political interests in the Levant clearly influenced the policies of the rulers. Venice, for example, could ill-afford to antagonize the Turks by openly promoting a crusade which, even if it materialized, might adversely affect her interests in both Italy and the Levant. As for the princes farther west, they did not need a Machiavelli to tell them that to stay in business they must give priority to the most immediate or pressing problems, among which they counted the defense against supranational aspirations of pope and emperor. On the other hand there is no reason to expect that the princes were or ought to have been endowed with greater foresight than the rulers of our modern world; and indeed they were not as their reactions to the plights of Byzantium and Hungary show.[18]

Despite their dedication to national or regional aggrandizement most princes were not without some feeling for the mystical commonwealth of Christendom. Again it is important to remember that in an emergent society, such as Europe was at this period of the Renaissance, the sharp contrasts between theory and practical policy are an inevitable part of that painful quest for a new universally applicable moral authority.[19] The non-Christian justification of political behavior appropriated from classical stoicism by the Florentine humanists from Salutati to Bruni as yet meant little outside north-central Italy. And even there one sees in the second half of the fifteenth century a marked retreat to the ethical norms of orthodox Christianity albeit enshrined in the academy of Plato.[20] Machiavelli, of course was yet to write, but even well beyond him into the sixteenth century acceptance of his new morality was not widespread. A new emphasis on the exercise of human powers for the improvement of life in this world cannot be denied, but few were ready to discard the notion that both were divine in origin and purpose. Politics in the Renaissance rapidly assumed new forms, methods, and modes of expression which ultimately merged in a wholly new pattern of political life; but its reconciliation with, or separation from, the ideals of medieval Christianity was to be a long gradual process in which significant stages were accented by Machiavelli, Luther and Calvin, and the religious wars.[21] Thus the crusade talk and promises of princes and diplomats must not be dismissed as so much self-supporting publicity, though the value of the latter was not lost upon the more astute politicians among them. As long as the Turks were regarded as infidels and princes the defenders of the faith, the crusade was the obvious solution proposed to meet the Ottoman menace. Conscience-wise many a prince demonstrated that he felt a personal obligation to take the cross and a public responsibility to marshal his resources to oppose the Turks.[22] Moreover, these moral compunctions were translated into action. The Turkish question was too important not to be discussed at most every European congress. Many kept themselves informed of the Turks' activities. If closer interests and personal bias distorted their view, they had, at least, a general idea of the extent of the danger.[23] And if they sometimes appropriated the proceeds, they permitted a surprising number of papal agents to collect crusade funds through indulgences and other means. There are cases on record where they gave direct financial aid to those powers engaged in fighting the Turks.[24] They allowed and perhaps encouraged, again not without selfish reasons, private soldiers and men-at-arms to seek their fortunes in the Levant.[25] While the grand crusade did not materialize, small contingents of troops and ships were on various occasions dispatched to the East.[26] Although they were not prepared to drop everything else to fight the battles of a remote or rival power, like the Roman emperors of the fifth century, the princes of the West seem to have had a definite idea of just how far the new barbarians were to be allowed to go. And judging from the extent of his intelligence activities in the West and his reactions to the news of impending crusades we may conclude that the sultan was party to this thought.[27]

Meanwhile, as Tedaldi had predicted, the Grand Turk prosecuted no new campaign during the summer of 1453. Indeed, Mehmed II did not undertake an expedition against a major Christian power for nearly three years. After his triumphant entrance into Constantinople, the conqueror, as he was called from that time, remained in the city for twenty-four days, and then retired to Adrianople where he arrived on June 21, 1453. From Adrianople the news of his victory was dispatched to the rest of the Moslem world. The Christian rulers of the Levant hastened to pay recognition to the·new master of Byzantium. Chios, Mitylene, Trebizond, and Serbia sent envoys who discovered that Mehmed's success meant for them greater subservience and an increase in the tribute which they had to pay to the Turks.[28] Returning to Constantinople in the autumn of 1453 Mehmed II occupied himself with the problem of providing his conquests with a new administration. Constantinople had to be repopulated, and to some extent rebuilt. He remained in his capital through the autumn and into the winter supervising administrative reforms. During the winter he also visited Anatolia where he organized the government. Returning to Constantinople in the winter he went on to Adrianople where he planned a new campaign in the Balkans. In the spring of 1454 he marched at the head of his army into Serbia. The principal military gain was the capture of Omol and Ostrowitsa which submitted to the Turks under Ishak Pasha. His troops devastated the Serbian countryside, taking 50,000 Christians who were sent to Constantinople as slaves. The conqueror remained in Serbia during the summer of 1454 consolidating his new conquests.[29]

The West was kept informed of the Turks' progress by letters and ambassadors from Serbia and her neighbors. In a letter sent from Ragusa to the doge of Venice, dated August 8, 1454, we read of the terrors of the campaign as reported by Ragusan merchants who had been forced to flee Serbia and return home. The Grand Turk, having invaded the territory of George Brankovich, the despot of Serbia, with a huge army, devastated the entire province between the Danube and the Save rivers. The Turks burned, plundered, and slaughtered with such ferocity and cruelty that it appeared as if nothing could satisfy their thirst except Christian blood. They killed all the males over forty and led the women and young men into captivity. They also carried off various instruments of war and siege machinery. It was reported that the sultan had ordered supplies to be brought from every part of his empire, and it seemed to the Ragusans that he planned to subject to his will not only the territory of the despot, but the whole world.[30]

Before departing on his Serbian campaign in 1454, Mehmed II had concluded a treaty of peace with Venice on April 18, 1454, which granted the Republic trading rights in the Turkish empire, and the privilege of having a bailo in permanent residence at Constantinople. The sultan continued through this period to devote much of his attention to the reorganization of his state, and he made a number of new administrative appointments. He also occupied himself with the supervision of several major building projects in Adrianople and Constantinople. Early in 1454 he had provided for the government oe the Greek community which he had reestablished in Constantinople. Hd elevated Gennadios (George Scholarius) to the position of patriarch, anh granted the Greeks a charter outlining their rights and obligations as Turkish subjects. Sometime thereafter he made a similar arrangement with the Jewisg inhabitants of the city, appointing Moche Kapsali as grand rabbi, and holdinf him responsible for the behavior of his people. Finally at the very end of 1454, he granted a charter of rights and privileges to the noble families of the Peloponneseus.[31]

With the arrival of the spring of 1455, Mehmed II assembled his army in the plains before Adrianople, and led it to Kratovo. At Kratovo he was joined by a force under Isa-Beg, son of Ishak-Beg and governor of the northwest province. The combined army marched at once upon Novo Brdo, then one of the most important commercial cities in the Balkans, and rich in gold and silver mines. The Turks besieged it for forty days after which on June 1, it fell into their hands, and its inhabitants, except for the miners, were slaughtered or forced into captivity. The Turkish generals Karadja-Beg and Isa-Beg spent the rest of the summer of 1455 sugjugating the entire southwest portion of Serbia. Mehmed II, however, turned toward home, stopped at Salonika, and reached Constantinople sometime in October.[32]

During the spring of 1455 as Mehmed II was marshaling his forces for the siege of Novo Brdo, the leader of Christian opposition against the Turks lay dying in Rome. After a long illness and much suffering Nicholas V died on March 24, 1455.[33] The College of Cardinals elected, on April 8, Alfonso Borgia who took the name of Calixtus III. The new pope was crowned on April 20. Calixtus made it quite clear from the moment of his accession that he intended to prosecute the war against the infidels with every ounce of his energy; it was, wrote Pastor, ". . . the main object of his life".[34] Indeed, so that Christendom might fully understand the sincerity of his intentions the pope swore a solemn oath, copies of which he circulated about Europe. He vowed to the Holy Trinity, Father, Son, and Holy Spirit, to the Ever-Virgin Mother of God, and to the apostles Peter and Paul that he would do everything in his power, even sacrifice his life, if necessary, to reconquer Constantinople, ". . . which in punishment for the sin of man has been taken and ruined by Mehmed II, the son of the devil and the enemy of our Crucified Redeemer". He promised "to deliver the Christians languishing in slavery, to exalt the True Faith, and to extirpate the diabolical sect of the reprobate and faithless Mahomet in the East".[35]

In place of the general congresses which had proved to be futile in the past, Calixtus determined to work for the crusade by dealing with the princes individually. He began by taking advantage of the arrival in Rome of embassies to congratulate him upon his accession to open negotiations and to acquaint the powers with his plans and expectations. When the ambassadors from Florence led by their venerable Archbishop Antoninus appeared at the papal court on May 24, Calixtus spoke of his desire to take the offensive against the Turks, and expressed the hope that Florence would be among the first to come to the aid of the holy religion. Two days later Archbishop Antoninus replied in open consistory with a resounding approval of the pope's program. After a long eulogy on Calixtus' virtues and fitness for his high office, Antoninus elaborated on the Turkish problem. He commended the new pontiff for his eagerness to take up the holy work. He denounced the Turks as cruel beasts, blasphemers, and enemies of Christ. Mehmed he described as the son of Satan, the perverted enemy of the human race, and the personification of all evil.[36]

While his letters, legates, preachers, and money collectors hastened throughout Europe, Calixtus III implemented promptly his policy with what resources he had at hand. The papacy set an example by preparing its own fleet to oppose the Turks in Levantine waters. Even a small squadron might provide some relief for the beleaguered islanders of the eastern Mediterranean and Aegean Seas. Moreover a naval expedition in the vicinity of Constantinople might divert Mehmed II's attention from the troubled Balkans, and perhaps delay a major Turkish attack upon Hungary until a crusading host could be gathered. Calixtus looked to his old friend Alfonso V of Aragon and Naples for assistance in this project. Alfonso had given some help to Scanderbeg of Albania in his fight against the Turks and as recently as 1454 had promised to send a fleet against the infidels.[37] Now upon the accession of Calixtus he demonstrated new enthusiasm. On All Saints' Day, 1455, in a grand ceremony Alfonso and many of his nobles took the cross. [38] Throughout the months which followed he talked frequently about going personally against the Turks. In the spring of 1456 he informed his council that he had decided to dedicate the rest of his life to the cause of Christianity. He declared that he could not erase from his mind such tragedies as the submission of the king of Cyprus to a Moslem power, the failure of Christian arms at Varna, and the loss of Constantinople and the Greek empire. He pledged fifteen galleys to join the papal fleet and was awarded by the pope the tenth collected on ecclesiastical revenues to be applied to the cost of the galleys.[39]

Whatever his intentions may have been, Alfonso's interest in Italian affairs prevented his giving immediate succor to the pope. In fact his alliance with the condottiere Piccinino, who was at that moment disturbing the peace of Italy by attacking Siena, seriously hampered the pope's crusade plans and resulted in strained relations between Rome and Naples. In the following spring (1456), Alfonso became in the eyes of the pope an enemy instead of a defender of the church when he employed not only his own, but the galleys of the papacy in an attack upon the Genoese.[40] Calixtus, nonetheless, persisted in his efforts to raise a fleet, and despite many disappointments and setbacks his cherished project matured. Although it sailed too late to help the Hungarians in their moment of crisis, the papal squadron under the command of Cardinal Lodovico Trevisan, and including some Aragonese vessels, finally reached the waters of the Levant. There it provided protection for the harassed Christians, and in August, 1457, inflicted a defeat upon the fleet of Mehmed II at Mitylene. The news of this victory cheered the aging pontiff and raised his hopes for the ultimate overthrow of the Turks. He had a medal struck to commemorate the engagement. On it were inscribed the words: "I have been chosen for the destruction of the enemies of the Faith".[41]

Calixtus' dedication to the project of the fleet did not drive from his mind the realization that the Turkish threat to Hungary was the most critical problem facing Christendom. Alarming letters continued to arrive in the West predicting the direst consequences if Europe did not rise to the defense of Hungary. On May 15, 1455, Calixtus published a bull calling on all Christian princes and people to join and support the crusade. He designated March 1, 1456 as the time when the expedition should depart. He confirmed all graces and indulgences previously granted by Nicholas to those who joined in the holy war.[42] We cannot follow here the detailed negotiations which Calixtus and his legates carried on with the Christian princes.[43] We should note, however, that his envoys were sent not only to the great lords of Europe, but also to a host of minor rulers.[44] Preachers traveled through the countrysides of Italy, Germany, Hungary, Poland, and other places. Franciscan friars were especially active in preaching the crusade among the people.[45] We read in the chronicle of Viterbo how a Franciscan sought to arouse the people in that city on September 8, 1455. Stationing himself in the piazza near the fountain he drew the attention of the people by having drums and fifes played. Then he raised a silver cross with the figure of Christ on it, and proceeded to explain the crusade bull of Calixtus III.[46] For the most part the sermons of these preachers were not committed to writing but were delivered *ex tempore* and consisted mainly of a running commentary on the text of a crusade bull, as in the case at Viterbo, or that of a crusade indulgence. In any case we can be sure that they represented the Turkish threat as above all God's punishment of Christians for their sins, and stressed the need for repentance and the opportunity of expiation by war of a contribution to the holy cause or the assumption of the cross itself.[47]

This is precisely the vein in which the subject is presented in an English sermon dating from the early part of the century. Following a lengthy recital of the virtues of the Virgin Mary and the apostles and other saints the author deplores the lack of these qualities in Christians of his own day. Quoting Bernard of Clairvaux, he writes: "Serpit hodie putrida tabes *per omne corpus* ecclesie—fowle stynkynge *mater* of synne groweþ now thorowe-owte all Cristendom". The church is now more afflicted by sin than it was formerly by the persecutions and doctrinal heresies; and most lamentible of all is the absence of peace. Again from St. Bernard: "*Et* pax *est et* non est pax—þer is pece . . . in a man*er*, and ʒitt itt is no pes". By this the author explains there is peace for heathens and peace for heretics but "no pes aʒens synnefull lyvyng in all degrees temp*er*all and sp*i*ritu*a*ll of Cristes churche. For sic*ur*ly vertew is cast avey and man is fallyn in-to þe filthe of stynkyng synne". He bewails the schisms which rent the church, the internecine strife and loss of noble lords, Christians shedding the blood of Christians, "continually, gret *and* huge". The result of these calamities is that "welnyʒ in eu*er*y coost of þe marches Cristen mens lordeshippes decresses *and* goys downeward, *and* þe lordeshippes of hethen men groweþ vpward and in-creseþ; for seuerly our*e* Cristen prynces wi*th*-in þis xl ʒere *and* lasse haþ lost more þan þe þirde parte of Cristendom. Lo, þer peyn answeres to þer synnes. For lik as our*e* princes *and* lordes spoyleth *and* robbeþ þer suggett*us* *and* doþ daily, euen so

God suffreþ þe ethen princes to robb *and* spoile our*e* lord*e*s *and* princes, eu*e*n as þei do to oþ*ur*: 'In qua me*n*sura q*ua* mensi fueritis, remici*etur* vob*is*.' *Mathei* 7 capit*ul*o".[48]

In order to attract and hold the attention of their congregations and to be certain their message had the desired effect, popular preachers resorted to crude stage tactics and bizarre stunts. In a caricature of the crusade preacher Roberto Caracciolo, Erasmus depicts the Franciscan ascending the pulpit, sword in hand, and wearing the armor of a *condottiere* under his habit. Then after harranging his hearers on the subject of the war against the Turks and lamenting the apathy of Christians and especially the failure of their rulers to take the cross, Caracciolo is made to declare that if there were no other means he would strip off his habit and serve himself as a plain soldier or captain. With these words he cast off his mendicants robe and exposed the suit of armor in which he continued to exhort the crowd for another half hour.[49]

Owing to his unorthodox habits and vindictive quarrels with former superiors after passing from the observants to the conventuals, Caracciolo may have well deserved to be chosen by Erasmus as an example of the bigoted and cantankerous religious who was in part responsible for the rising tide of anti-clericalism.[50] Caracciolo was nonetheless a prominent member of his order serving as provincial vicar for Bosnia and vicar-general for the kingdom of Naples, and a loyal servant of the papacy which appointed him collector of the crusade tenth in Milan and apostolic preacher in Ferrara. He held at different times the Sees of Lecce and Aquino and was the author of an impressive number of sermons and devotional works, no longer read but immensely popular in his own time.[51] His renown as a preacher was due in part to the skill with which he stirred the consciences of his hearers. A sample of his technique, as it touches our subject, may be gleaned from a sermon of the hellfire and damnation genre in which Caracciolo alluded to the case of Constantinople as a foretaste of the final judgment before which all would quake—both good and wicked, pope, cardinals, bishops and prelates, friars and priests, monks, emperors, kings and princes, merchants, and workers, poor and rich—and the tortures of which he described in careful detail.[52] The effectiveness of such admonitions was no doubt heightened by his use of anecdotes and illustrations drawn not only from Scripture but from historical tradition and contemporary happenings. An extensive application of the latter may be seen in the first sermon of his *Spechio del la fede* where, in examining the various reasons why some lack faith, he cited the Moslems as an example under the title, "La terza principale rasone perche molti non hanno fede: si chiama de contrariatione". To show how this was the "speciale

II: Robert Caracciolo
(his *Prediche*. Milan, 1515).

peccato de infedelita" he divided his discussion concerning them into three parts: (1) La prima e la originatione; (2) La seconda la acceptatione; and (3) La terza la duratione. There is no need to review here Caracciolo's account of the rise and spread of Islam which he justified describing at length ". . . doue alchuni domando como e questa secto bestiale ed eronca ce concorsa tanta multitudine de gente e di populi". But it is important to note that he took pains to bring the account down to his own time sketching the main events of the career of Mehmed II from the fall of Constantinople to the capture of Otranto (1480).[53]

Of the many faithful preachers who obeyed the commands of Calixtus and announced to Christianity the imminence of the Turkish peril none was more devoted to the cause of the faith or enjoyed a higher reputation than John Capistran.[54] The holy Minorite friar of the Observance who had dedicated most of his years to the reform of the church, now gave life itself to its defense. During the months which followed the fall of Constantinople a stream of correspondence flowed between Capistran and the princes and prelates of Christendom. He sent the crusade bull of Nicholas V to Ladislas of Hungary and Bohemia, and urged him to turn to the defense of the faith. Nicholas of Cusa wrote Capistran from the diet of Ratisbon on May 28, 1454, urging him to work for a reconciliation between Poland and Prussia that their arms may be turned aginst the Turks.[55] On August 16, 1454, Cardinal Sbignev wrote him concerning the same problem. If the quarrel between Prussia and Poland were resolved, Poland could raise an army of 200,000 men to fight the Turks. The Cardinal of Cracow suggested, however, that the Tartars might be aroused by diplomacy and money to attack the Turks. Once the infidel dogs had destroyed one another it would be an easy task for the Christians to annihilate them completely.[56] Aeneas Sylvius wrote the holy Minorite from Wiener-Neustadt on July 26, and again on August 26, 1454. He informed Capistran of the forthcoming diet to be held at Frankfort. Then all Germany would gather to consult on the best means to defend the faith and avenge the injuries already sustained by the Savior. Aeneas urged Capistran to come to the diet, insisting that his presence was necessary for its success.[57]

Capistran obeyed the summons. On his way to Frankfort, he stopped at Munich where he again wrote to King Ladislas. He denounced the king's plans to attack Saxony, and pleaded with him to keep the peace and send delegates to Frankfort. The success of the diet depended upon the Hungarians. It was they who were most menaced by the Turks. He urged Ladislas to act before everything was lost.[58] Arriving at Frankfort toward the end of September, Capistran was greatly alarmed by the reports he received of the

Turks' activities. Cardinal Sbignev had written that a Turkish army of 40,000 men had invaded Serbia and was preparing to attack Belgrade and other cities along the Danube.[59] Capistran wrote from Frankfort, on October 28 to Nicholas V informing the pope that the Hungarian ambassadors at the diet had told him that the 42,000 troops promised by the Germans would not be sufficient. They insisted that the empire must raise a force of 70,000 and that unless they received help at once the Hungarians would have to make peace with the Turks. "Woe to you, o Italy! Woe to you, o Rome", he cried, "if, because aid is delayed, peace is concluded between the Hungarians and the Turks!" The Minorite bewailed the fact that the diet had postponed all major decisions for a new meeting to be held at Wiener-Neustadt in February, 1455. He urged the pope to see that the German forces join the Hungarians no later than May 1455.[60]

Following the close of the diet at Frankfort, Capistran traveled to Aschaffenburg, Würzburg, and Nuremberg preaching the crusade to the people in those places. At the end of December, 1454, he reached Vienna where he remained for three months. In Vienna he preached among the students many of whom responded to his call. In March he attended the diet of Wiener-Neustadt where he continued to urge one and all to awaken to the peril and defend the true religion.[61] On May 1, 1455, he wrote to the new pope Calixtus III. He called the pope's attention to the wrongs inflicted upon the church, the sufferings of Christian people, and the pressing need to resist the Turks. Yet the Germans planned to do nothing for another year! "Alas, most Holy Father," he cried, "how many Christian souls meanwhile will suffer rejection, and the danger of eternal damnation." He advised that it was better to attack the matter ahead of time than to seek a remedy after the damage was done. He begged the pope and the king of Aragon to take immediate action. Calixtus was urged to renew the bulls of his predecessors, and send zealous preachers, men of sound doctrine, who hated avarice and all evil, men who served the honor and glory of God alone and who were prepared to die for the defense of the holy catholic faith and the *Respublica Christiana*.[62]

In June 1455, Capistran attended the Hungarian diet held in Györ (Raab). The Hungarian nobles, we are told, were distressed by the news of Mehmed's victories in Serbia, and inspired by John Hunyadi made elaborate plans to take the offensive. Capistran related these plans to Calixtus III in a letter sent from Györ, June 21, 1455. A force of 40,000 men was to be raised by Hunyadi, King Ladislas, and George Brankovich, despot of Serbia. In the West the pope, the king of Aragon, and other Italian princes, and the duke of Burgundy had to recruit 60,000 men. Hunyadi believed, Capistran reported, that with an army of 100,000 it was possible to drive the Turks out of Europe; indeed, with such a large force he hoped to recover Jerusalem! Capistran assured the pope that if Hunyadi took the field with the proposed army, and the king of Aragon attacked the Turks by sea, there was great hope for recovering all that had been lost.[63]

Early in July the Franciscan saint left Györ. He spent some time with Cardinal Dionysius Széchy in Gran and preached in western Hungary. He also visited John Hunyadi in his home at Hunyad, and spent the last three months of 1455 preaching in Transylvania.[64] At the command of Cardinal Carvajal, he journeyed in January 1456 to Budapest. Carvajal had been appointed legate to Germany, Hungary, and Poland by Calixtus III in September, 1455. He had left Rome September 25, stopped at Florence and Venice, and reached Vienna late in November.[65] From Vienna he wrote to Capistran expressing considerable optimism for the success of the crusade. King Ladislas had promised to support the project, and of course the legate expected much aid from Hunyadi.[66]

The cardinal legate and King Ladislas arrived in Budapest February 6, 1456. There on the first Sunday of Lent (February 14), Carvajal delivered the pope's commission to Capistran granting him all faculties to preach the crusade. He also pinned on the Minorite a cross which the pope had blessed and sent to him. During the following weeks Capistran exercised his commission in Budapest, preaching daily and receiving the vows of those who took the cross.[67] Meanwhile the Hungarian nobility and prelates gathered in Budapest to attend the diet called by Ladislas. They agreed to raise money for an expedition against the Turks and made plans for recruiting an army. Nothing was to be done, however, before August 1. On April 6, 1456, the diet, having finished its work, informed the papal legate of its decisions, and adjourned.[68]

On the very next day news reached Budapest that Mehmed II was marching at the head of a huge army toward the southern border of Hungary. Since his capture of Constantinople the Grand Turk had viewed Hungary as the principal threat to the Turkish empire in Europe. The Serbian campaigns of 1454 and 1455 were calculated to prepare the way for a major expedition against Hungary. During the winter of 1455, the conqueror determined that the time had arrived to make the decisive move. He selected Belgrade, the gateway to Hungary from the south as his primary objective. He believed that once Belgrade was in his hands it would take him only two months to conquer the rest of Hungary. During the winter months (1455-56), Mehmed concentrated all his efforts on preparing for the campaign. He assembled troops from all over the empire. He stationed a large fleet at Vidin on the Danube. At Krushevac in Serbia, he had a foundry built where a large number of cannon were manufactured. He left no stone unturned in his search for supplies. It was alleged that he even organized legions of dogs to eat the bodies of the Christians slain in battle.[69]

Meanwhile Ladislas ordered his nobles to occupy the strongpoints and river crossings along the Danube, and appointed Hunyadi commander and chief of the Hungarian forces.[70] Cardinal Carvajal wrote to the pope on the same day (April 7), that the reports of the Turks' advance had reached Budapest. He informed Calixtus of the resolutions made by the Hungarian diet, and of the alarming news he had just received. Although King Ladislas had sent men to defend the Danube, Carvajal urged the pope to order the papal fleet to attack Constantinople and thus force the Turks to divide their power. The pope was also to arouse the other Christian princes to immediate action. The danger was such that a delay of one day, or even of a few hours, would lead to a catastrophe over which Christianity would weep forever.[71] Ten days later the cardinal legate wrote to Francesco Sforza. He declared that the danger no longer pertained to Hungary alone. If Hungary were to fall, the empire, the true faith, Milan, all would be imperiled. Peace with such an enemy as the Turks was impossible. They sought not only the subjection of Christians but the destruction of their religion. They had no greater pleasure than that of spilling Christian blood. The Christian princes had responded with words and promises. They believed God would not permit the Turks to succeed, and they thought human aid to be unnecessary. It was God's will, however, that the faithful gird on the sword and smite the enemy. Carvajal appealed to the duke of Milan to employ his great power to crush the Turks.[72]

During the next two months the Spanish cardinal, the Hungarian hero, and the Italian saint labored tirelessly to ready Hungary for the Turkish attack. Carvajal remained most of the time in Budapest endeavoring to reconcile the jealous princes and raise an army of Hungarian and German nobles.[73] Hunyadi hastened to Belgrade where he appointed Michael Szilagyi commander of the garrison, and went then to Szegedin and also urged the nobility to take up arms.[74] Capistran left Budapest and journeyed to the southern regions of Hungary to preach the crusade. He was ably assisted in Hungary, Germany, Poland, and elsewhere by a small band of devoted preachers.[75] On June 5 Cardinal Carvajal ordered Capistran to gather his crusaders and lead them to the threatened border. While King Ladislas and his court fled to the safety of Vienna, and the Hungarian nobles sought refuge in their castles, John Hunyadi departed Szegedin on June 12 and marched south with a small force. He informed Carvajal that he would station himself at Keve, forty miles south of Belgrade on the Danube at the mouth of the

Morava. He expected to be there by June 24, and hoped to prevent the Turkish fleet from passing up the Danube. He begged the cardinal to send him reinforcements. On June 22, Hunyadi summoned the German inhabitants of Transylvania to join him, warning them that the Turks were only four days' march south of the Danube. At the same time he appealed to Capistran who was preaching at Backa to proceed to Belgrade with the crusaders he had raised.[76]

In Rome Calixtus III watched apprehensively the developments in the Balkans. On June 29, 1456, he appealed to the prelates of Christendom to eschew the ways of the world, and by prayers, fasting, and penance "return to the Lord, that He may return to us". He commanded that on the first Sunday of every month processions were to be made and prayers were to be said in every diocese. The priests were to say the *Missa contra paganos*, and to preach to their congregations on the Turkish menace. He ordered all priests to repeat at every Mass the following prayer: "Almighty, everlasting God, to whom all power belongs, and in whose hand are the rights of all nations, protect thy Christian people, and crush by thy power the pagans who trust in their fortunes". Finally that all might be reminded of the imminent danger, the pope decreed that the bells in every church were to be rung daily between noon and vespers, and three "Our Fathers" and "Hail Marys" repeated.[77]

With a few thousand men Capistran hastened to Belgrade where he arrived July 2. Hunyadi had left orders for the Minorite to bring part of his followers to Keve. By this time, however, the Turks had entered the Danube, and the crusaders, unable to join Hunyadi, returned to the city.[78] During the following days crusaders continued to flock to Belgrade. In Hungary alone 40,000 had taken the vow. Capistran had personally pinned the cross on 27,000. Many more in Bohemia, Poland, Germany, and western Europe had pledged themselves. But the Turks had advanced a month before they were expected, and many crusaders would not reach Belgrade until the battle was over. By mid-July the crusading host was estimated to number 60,000. It was made up primarily of beggars, peasants, students, monks, and priests, commoners by and large untrained in the art of war or in the basic discipline necessary for survival in the field. Furthermore they came without armor and poorly armed with clubs, slings, staves, or swords. Only a few carried adequate personal weapons. Only here and there one might spot a well-equipped knight accustomed to bearing arms.[79]

On July 3, advanced units of Mehmed II's army took positions within sight of Belgrade. Four days later the main body of the Turkish force, estimated to number above 100,000, spread its camp from the Danube to the right bank of the river Save before the walls of the city. The Turks deployed their frightening siege artillery in three long lines in front of their camp. Well dug-in and protected, 200 cannon opened fire on Belgrade, battering its walls and buildings until the day of the final assault. The conqueror's fleet of 200 vessels, including 64 galleys, completed the encirclement of the city. While patrol vessels prowling the Danube kept a Christian squadron of 40 sail bottled up in the harbor of Belgrade, the bulk of the Turkish fleet stationed itself above Belgrade near the island of Semlin.[80] On Sunday, July 4, Capistran celebrated Mass inside the fortress, and exhorted the defenders (12,000 crusaders and the city's small garrison under Michael Szilagyi), to resist the Turks until relief forces should arrive. Leaving four friars including Giovanni da Tagliacozzo behind, he went to Slankamen where the crusaders had made their camp. Hunyadi, having fought his way back up the Danube from Keve, established his headquarters near the junction of the Danube and Theiss rivers, and met Capistran at Slankamen.[81]

Capistran pronounced a general absolution over the crusaders and rehearsed them in their war cry of "Jesus, Jesus, Jesus". Then under cover of a moonless sky, on the evening of July 14, the Christian host slipped down the Danube aboard several hundred small river craft. Before they reached the island of Semlin, they halted and most of the crusaders debarked to either shore. Hunyadi and 3000 men remained in some of the boats, while the other craft were filled with sand and rocks to be loosed in the river's current and dashed against the Turkish vessels. Capistran marched at the head of the crusaders on the right bank fifty to seventy feet above the water, where he and his banner of the cross were visible to all. At 8:00 on the morning of July 15, a Latin antiphon was intoned as the signal to attack. At once the crusaders streamed down both shores of the Danube while the weighted ships followed by those carrying Hunyadi's men crashed into the line of Turkish galleys. The Christian ships sailed out of the harbor of Belgrade and assailed the Turks from behind. The combination of surprise and the shock effect of Christian elements descending in force upon them from all sides resulted in confusion and disorder among the Turks. Three Turkish galleys were sent to the bottom of the river. Three more were captured and many more severely damaged. The Turkish fleet was finally forced to retire from its station at Semlin, and took up new positions below Belgrade. The blockade was broken.[82] The holy friar of the Observance now envisioned a great Christian victory. He saw the battle for Belgrade as a turning point in the struggle against the infidels which would not be complete until Europe and the Holy Land were in the hands of the faithful of God. During the week before the final assault he worked day and night in the camp of the crusaders which was located on

III: Siege of Belgrade, 1456
(Johannes de Turocz, *Chronica Hungarorum*. Augsburg, 1488).

the west bank of the river Save near Semlin. Capistran looked after their daily needs both material and spiritual. He preached regularly to the army, and he and the other priests celebrated Mass every day. Over and over the cry of "Jesus, Jesus, Jesus" was raised by the whole camp in unison.[83]

The Turkish final assault began on the evening of July 21. The defenders resisted valiantly and repulsed several charges. The Turkish advance units paid a heavy price in casualties as they passed over the trenches and stormed the walls. Some of the Turks penetrated the Christian defenses through the breaches made by their artillery. In the narrow streets of Belgrade they were met by the courageous crusaders who engaged them in bitter hand to hand fighting. The battle raged throughout the night, and more than once it appeared that the Christian cause was lost, and that the city had fallen to the Turks. The crusaders on the walls and in the streets, however, continued the struggle. At the height of the battle as thousands of Turks swarmed beneath the walls, the defenders, at a prearranged signal, simultaneously hurled bundles of ignited fagots and brushwood upon the attackers. The shock of this long wall of fire crashing down into their massed ranks stunned the Turks. The momentum of their attack was dissipated; the crusaders seized the initiative and fell upon the enemy with renewed vigor. They slew or drove back the Turks who had entered the city. The Turkish captains were unable to restore order; their troops fell back in confusion and fled from under the walls to the protection of their own lines of defense.[84]

As the light of day spread over the walls and trenches covered with the charred and torn bodies of thousands of Turks, Mehmed II decided to lift the siege of Belgrade. He gave orders to fire his fleet and began preparations for the withdrawal of his army. About mid-day (July 22), a handful of Christians clashed with some Turkish security elements near the latter's lines. A throng of crusaders, joined by St. John Capistran, rushed to the aid of their comrades, and pressed against the sultan's first line of defense. The surprised Turks fled from their positions abandoning their artillery. The inspired Christians pursued them and rushed on towards the final defenses before the Turkish camp. Mehmed II was forced to commit a part of his main force to contain the surprise attack. The sultan, enraged by his failure to take Belgrade and this unexpected and insolent interference with his preparations to withdraw, joined the counter-attack only to receive a serious wound. The crusaders were driven back from the Turkish camp, but held the enemy's advance positions and the artillery which they had captured. The encounter did not develop into a general engagement. As St. Magdalene's day closed the Turks withdrew from the field. The crusaders of St. John Capistran had saved Belgrade and halted the Turkish drive into Hungary.[85]

News of the battle traveled swiftly to the West. It reached Rome on August 6, where the aged pope, convinced that God had answered the prayers of the faithful, declared that it was the happiest moment of his life. He ordered feasts and celebrations, and all the bells of Rome were rung and processions held in all the churches. Throughout Europe preachers proclaimed the news. The crusaders at Belgrade had saved not only Hungary but Christendom! In processions and prayers the people thanked God for His mercy and praised Him for His goodness. As in Rome, so too in Siena, Viterbo, Bologna, and Venice, and elsewhere the people joined in rejoicing.[86] Thomas Gascoigne recorded that the good tidings were carried to England by a Hungarian priest named Erasmus Fullar who had fought in the battle and whose brother Oswald had died at the hands of the Turks. Fullar brought with him a letter from John Hunyadi which Gascoigne said he saw with his own eyes and which he claimed bore Hunyadi's seal. The victory was commemorated at Oxford. A procession was held, and in the church of the Blessed Virgin of Frideswida the "Te Deum" was sung, and Gascoigne preached a sermon. In his *Loci e libro veritatum* Gascoigne cited the battle of Belgrade as his example under the entry *bellum*. He recorded that Mehmed II, "who planned to obliterate the name of Jesus Christ from the face of the earth", invaded Hungary with a great evil force, but on the feast of St. Mary Magdalene 40,000 Christians issued from the city of Belgrade and assaulted the Turks. Led by the Franciscan John Capistran carrying a huge cross and shouting "Jesus, Jesus, Jesus", the Christians struck fear and terror among the perfidious pagan Turks who turned and fled from the face of God.[87]

George Chastellain, the Burgundian court historian and knight of the Golden Fleece, devoted an entire chapter in his chronicle to the event in which "Dieu fit et demonstra ses miracles a son peuple. . .". He wrote that he witnessed "les processions solempnelles et les sermons qui s'en firent en rendant graces a Dieu de sa bonte et misericorde", for the memorable victory. All were agreed that the infidels were overwhelmingly defeated and that the Grand Turk had been repulsed by the powerful arm of God. Chastellain declared that ever since his conquest of Greece the sultan had aspired to subjugate Hungary. Relying upon the vast numbers at his command he intended to conquer the whole world and convert all to the law of Islam. Mehmed had every reason to believe that he would succeed for Alexander the Great had conquered much of the world with far less. Furthermore the sultan was young and strong, rich in gold and his subjects were as numerous as the stars in the heavens. But God had not failed to heed the prayers of the faithful who under the leadership of the holy friar John Capistran had obtained "la victoire miraculeuse".[88]

Since the accession of Mehmed II, the Turks had enjoyed a series of successes which had carried them to the very doors of the West. At Belgrade an untrained army of crusaders had halted and driven back the grand army of the sultan. The Turks were not invincible; indeed, even a small army of professional fighting men would be sufficient to drive them completely out of Europe. Such was the opinion of King Ladislas, Hunyadi, Carvajal, and John Capistran whose letters circulated through the West spreading the news of the victory. Capistran in writing to the pope shortly after the battle declared that the time was now ripe: "The day of the salvation of Christendom has dawned! Now is the moment when the long cherished desire of your Holiness will be fulfilled, not only by the recovery of the Greek empire and Europe, but also by the conquest of the Holy Land and Jerusalem. Almighty God will surely help us if only your Holiness perseveres in your pious purposes". Capistran begged the pope to send 10,000 or 12,000 well-armed Italian horsemen to remain with him for at least six months. Together with the crusaders and the Hungarian nobles they would be able to capture enough of the enemy's wealth and supplies to pay the expenses of a campaign for three years. In the same vein Hunyadi wrote that "at the present time the emperor of the Turks is so completely crushed that if the Christians, as is proposed, would only rise against him they might easily, with the help of God, become masters of the whole Turkish kingdom".[89]

Calixtus persevered in his pious efforts; stirred on by the victory of Belgrade and the belief that the tide was turning against the Turks he raised with new enthusiasm his appeals to the Christian princes. His legates and preachers continued to marshal crusaders who gathered at Belgrade in large numbers during the last months of 1456. Meanwhile the pope negotiated with the Christian and Moslem neighbors of the Turks who also feared the sultan's growing power.[90] He gave direct support to Scanderbeg, the valiant leader of the Albanians who during 1456 and 1457 successfully resisted Turkish aggression and in several engagements gave the Turks a sound beating.[91] Finally in August 1457 the pope's own fleet defeated the Turks off Mitylene. Well might Calixtus declare: "I have been chosen for the destruction of the enemies of the faith." But his optimism was to be short-lived. Less than a month after the victory of Belgrade, the great captain of the Hungarian resistance, John Hunyadi, died (August 11, 1456), a victim of the terrible plague which took the lives of many Christians who had helped to save the city. On October 23, after a long period of suffering, St. John Capistran died from the same cause. The crusaders lost the one man in whom they had complete trust and to whom they would render obedience.[92] Calixtus did everything possible, but the favorable moment had passed. On August 6,

1458 the pope died without realizing his cherished aim. August 16, the cardinals entered conclave and three days later elected the humanist Aeneas Sylvius as the successor of Calixtus III.

NOTES TO CHAPTER II

1. Pius II, *Commentaries*, I, 74; cf. his letter to Nicholas V from Graz, July 12, 1453, in Wolkan, *Der Briefwechsel*, III, 200, 201. For contemporary sketches of Nicholas V see Manetti, *Vita Nicolai V summi pontificis (RISS*, III), 908-960 and Vespasiano da Bisticci, *Lives of Illustrious Men of the XVth Century*, tr. W. George and E. Waters (London, 1926), pp. 31-58.

2. Pastor, *HP*, II, 243ff. See also Massimo Petrocchi, *La politica della santa sede di fronti all' invasione ottomana*, 1444-1718 (Naples, 1955), pp. 24-27, and the old but still useful study by Frederick Kayser, "Papst Nicolaus V (1447-1455) und das Vordringen der Türken", *Historisches Jahrbuch der Görresgesellschaft*, VI (1885), 208-231.

3. Iorga, "Notes", *ROL*, VIII, 54; Gill, *The Council of Florence*, pp. 374, 375.

4. *Ibid.*, pp. 376, 377; R. Guilland, "Les Appels de Constantine XI Paléologue à Rome et à Venise pour sauver Constantinople (1451-1453)", *Byzantinoslavica*, XIV (1953), pp. 230, 231.

5. *Ibid.*, pp. 231, 232; Gill, *op. cit.*, pp. 378, 379.

6. C. Marinescu, "Notes sur quelques ambassadeurs byzantins en occident à la veille de la chute de Constantinople sous les Turcs", *Annuaire de l'institut de philologie et d'histoire orientales et slaves*, X (1950): *Mélanges Henri Gregoire*, II, 424-427; Guilland, *op. cit.*, pp. 238-242.

7. *Platynae historici liber de vita Christi ac omnium pontificum*, ed. G. Gaida *(RISS*, III, pt. i), 336.

8. Pastor, *HP*, II, 274, 289.

9. *Ibid.*, 276; Raynaldus, *Annales*, ad. an. 1453, nos. 9-11. Cf. M. Petrocchi, *La politica della santa sede*, p. 30.

10. Iorga, *Notes et extraits*, IV, 64.

11. Iorga, *Notes et extraits*, IV, 74, 75.

12. G. Mattingly, *Renaissance Diplomacy (Penguin Books*, Baltimore, 1964), pp. 74-76; Pastor, *HP*, II, 289-295; R. Aubenas and R. Ricard, *L'Église et la Renaissance (1449-1517) (Histoire de l'église depuis les origines jusqu'à nos jours*, ed. A. Fliche and V. Martin, vol. XV, Paris, 1951), pp. 33, 34.

13. Pius II, *Commentaries*, I, 70.

14. Cf. Iorga, *Notes et extraits*, IV, 90, 91; Wolkan, *Der Briefwechsel*, Abt. III, Bd. i, 481-484.

15. Pius II, *Commentaries*, I, 72; cf. the letters from Capistran at Frankfort to Nicholas V and Philip of Burgundy, Wadding, *Annales*, XII, 203-207.

16. Pastor, *HP*, III, 168; see the eloquent oration of Joannes Vitéz Zredna, "Oratio habita

in Nova Civitate coram Friderico III Imperatore" in *Orationes in causa expeditionis contra Turcas habitae*, ed. V. Fraknoi (Budapest, 1878), pp. 13-30.

17. For conflicting assessments of the policies of princes and popes, cf. Pastor *HP*, II, 286, 345, whose condemnation of the princes is unqualified: ". . .the leading Princes and States of Europe, with scarcely an exception, displayed the most deplorable indifference to the welfare of Christendom. So grievous were their dissensions, and such was the decay of zeal and heroism, that not one could rise above individual interests and animosities to gather round the banner of the Cross"; and H. Pfeffer-mann, *Die Zusammenarbeit der Renaissancepapste mit den Türken* (Winterthur, 1946), who finds the papacy guilty of duplicity in its dealings with the Turks.

18. Cf. D. Vaughan, *Europe and the Turk* and Franz Babinger, *Mahomet II*, and the latter's detailed studies of the relations of particular western powers with the Turks in the publications of the Bayerische Akademie der Wissenschaften and elsewhere, especially his "Lorenzo de' Medici e la corte ottomano", *Archivio storico italiano*, CXX (1963), 305-361.

19. See *e.g.* D. Hay, *The Italian Renaissance, passim;* and Lewis Spitz, *The Religious Renaissance of the German Humanists* (Cambridge, Mass., 1963), especially the introduction.

20. Cf. Hay, *op. cit.*, pp. 176, 177; Hans Baron, "Fifteenth-Century Civilization and the Renaissance", *NCMH*, I, 73-75.

21. The interplay of traditional Christian values and those derived from antiquity and contemporary experience in the discussions and writings on politics in Renaissance Florence is admirably presented by Felix Gilbert, *Machiavelli and Guicciardini*, pp. 28ff. A like confusion of ideals is to be found in the international diplomacy not only of our period but right through the sixteenth century. See e.g. Franklin Van Baumer, "England and the Turk and the Common Corps of Christendom", *American Historical Review*, L (1944-45), 26-48; "The Church of England and the Common Corps of Christendom", *Journal of Modern History*, XVI (1944), 1-21; and "The Corruption of Christendom in Renaissance England", *Jounral of the History of Ideas*, VI (1945), 131-156.

22. Most prominently the dukes of Burgundy and the royal family of Portugal. Charles VIII of France thought himself sincere in his intentions and so did Alfonso the Magnanimous of Aragon and Naples. Frederick III and Maximilian together with Mathias Corvinus were quite serious in their concern. Charles V actually prosecuted a crusade. Even the kings of England from Henry IV to Henry VII kept themselves informed and several vowed to take the cross.

23. See my article "Western Spies in the Levant", *History Today*, XIII (1963), 747-756.

24. See W. E. Lunt, *Papal Revenues in the Middle Ages* (New York, 1934), I, 43, 71, 76, 77, 102, 115-121, 125; R. Aubenas and R. Ricard, *L'Église et la Renaissance*, pp. 39, 40.

25. See below Chapter V, *passim*.

26. Cf. D. Vaughan, *Europe and the Turk, passim*.

27. On the sultan's espionage activities in the West see Franz Babinger, "Mehmed II, der Eroberer, und Italien", *Byzantion*, XXI (1951), 154. Latin visitors at the Grand Porte were closely interrogated by the Grand Turk, e.g. Pero Tafur, *Travels and*

Adventures, pp. 127, 128 and Arnold von Harff, *Pilgrimage*, ed. M. Letts (London, 1946), pp. 239, 240.

28. Babinger, *Mahomet II*, pp. 127-129. See the letter of the grandmaster at Rhodes to the prior of Alvernia, January 20, 1454, in Pauli (ed.), *Codice diplomatico del sacro militare ordine Gerosolimitano*, II, no. III, 131.

29. Babinger, *Mahomet II*, pp. 130-134. For some corrections of Babinger's chronology see Halil Inalcik, "Mehmed the Conqueror (1432-1481) and His Time", *Speculum* XXXV (1960), 412-418.

30. Thallóczy and Áldásy, *A Magyarország és Szerbia közti Összeköttetések Oklevéltára (MHH*, XXXIII), no. 249, pp. 185, 186. See also nos. 253, 254, pp. 189, 190.

31. Babinger, *Mahomet II*, pp. 129-131, 135-140, 143, 152, 170. For more details on the conqueror's treatment of the Greek church see T. H. Papadopoullos, *Studies and Documents Relating to the History of the Greek Church and Peoples under Turkish Domination* (Brussels, 1952), pp. 1-26; and G. Arnakis, "The Greek Church of Constantinople and the Ottoman Empire", *Journal of Modern History*, XXIV (1952), 235-250.

32. Babinger, *Mahomet II*, pp. 153-155. See reports on Turkish activities in Serbia in Wadding, *Annales*, XII, 253-255. A report on the discussions in Rome concerning what was necessary to oppose the sultan at this time is found in Thallóczy and Áldásy, *op. cit.*, no. 260, pp. 193-195.

33. Pastor, *HP*, II, 312, 313.

34. *Ibid.*, II, 345. Calixtus spent long hours discussing the subject, especially with the Minorites; Gabriel da Verona wrote that "the pope speaks and thinks of nothing but the crusade." See Wadding, *Annales*, XII, 290. See also the testimony of Aeneas Sylvius in J. Cugnoni (ed.), *Aeneae Silvii Piccolomini Senensis qui postea fuit Pius II Pont. Max. opera inedita (Atti della R. Academia dei Lincei*, 3rd series, VIII, Rome, 1883), ep. 58, p. 438.

35. Pastor, *HP*, II, 346. Latin text in Raynaldus, *Annales*, ad. an. 1455, no. 18.

36. Raynaldus, *Annales*, ad an. 1455, nos. 21-23. Cf. the eulogy of Calixtus by another eminent Florentine who praised the pope for his plans to fight the Turks. "Oratio exercitationis gratia edita ab Alamanno Rinuccino in creatione Calisti Pontificis Maximi de anno MCCCCLV", in Alamanno Rinuccini, *Lettere ed orazioni*, edited by Vito R. Giustiniani (Florence, 1953), pp. 3-10. Among the other envoys who came to congratulate Calixtus, those from Germany, led by Aeneas Sylvius and Johann Hinderbach, were particularly enthusiastic in their support of Calixtus' Turkish policy. Cf. Raynaldus, *Annales*, ad an. 1455, no. 23, and J. Cugnoni, *Opera inedita*, ep. 58, pp. 437-442. The embassy from Venice took a realistic stand on the matter and explained, "...quod quando videbimus alias potentias Christianas contra Teucros potenter se movere, nos quoque imitantes vestigia maiorum nostrorum reperiemur illius bone dispositionis, cuius per elapsum fuimus". Quoted by Pastor, *HP*, II, 342, n. Cf. letter from Venice to Calixtus III in Thiriet, *Régestes*, III, 205, where it is claimed that if it were not for Venetian efforts of 1453-54, the Turks would have perhaps invaded Italy and thus showing that the Venetians were indeed good Christians! See below Chapter III, pp. 75-77.

37. Vaughan, *Europe and the Turk*, p. 62; (Marinescu, "Le Pape Calixtus III (1455-1458), Alfonso V d'Aragon, roi de Naples, et l'offensive contre les turcs", *Bulletin de la*

section historique. Académie Roumaine, XIX (1935), 81; and on Alfonso's relations with Scanderbeg, A. Gegaj, *L'Albanie et l'invasion turque au xve siècle* (Paris, 1937), pp. 83ff., and A. Serra, *L'Albania e la Santa Sede ai tempi di G. C. Scanderbeg* (Cosenza, 1960).

38. Pastor, *HP*, II, 359, 360.

39. C. Marinescu, "Le Pape Calixte", pp. 86-89.

40. Pastor, *HP*, II, 362, 363.

41. P. Paschini, "La flotta di Callisto III", *Archivio della società romana di storia patria*, LIII-LV (1930-32), 177-253; Pastor, *HP*, II, 372-375, 438; Raynaldus, *Annales*, ad an. 1457, nos. 31, 32.

42. *Ibid.*, ad an. 1455, no. 19.

43. Alain de Coëtivy, called the Cardinal of Avignon, was appointed legate to France and its adjacent territories up to the Rhine river. On September 8, 1455, Calixtus personally conferred the cross on him along with Cardinal Carvajal, legate to Germany and Hungary, and Archbishop Urrea of Tarragona, captain of the papal fleet. Pastor, *HP*, II, 349, 350; Raynaldus, *Annales*, ad an. 1455, no. 27. On September 12, sixty-five bulls, including his commission, were delivered to Coëtivy, who left Rome on September 17, 1455. M. Concasty, "Les Informations", *Byzantion*, XXIV (1954), 106. Although the Cardinal of Avignon did not return to Rome until the spring of 1458, his mission was a complete failure as far as the crusade was concerned. Carvajal, along with Cardinal Dionysius Széchy, labored in Hungary on behalf of the crusade. His mission was much more of a success than that of Coëtivy. See the excellent work of Lino Gómez Canedo, *Un Espanol ad servicio de la santa sede, Don Juan de Carvajal* (Madrid, 1947), pp. 153-199. Nicholas of Cusa was appointed legate to England and Germany. Raynaldus, *Annales*, ad an. 1455, no. 27; cf. J. A. Twemlow (ed.), *Calendar of Papal Registers Relating to Great Britain and Ireland*, XI: *Papal Letters, 1455-1464* (London, 1931), pp. 19-21. Cusa, however, was deeply involved in a struggle in his diocese of Brixen and apparently never reached England.

44. Pastor, *HP*, II, 351, 352.

45. *Ibid.*, II, 352. A brief sketch of the activities and interest of the Franciscans in the crusade is given by Atanasio Matanich in his "San Giovanni da Capestrano oratore pontificio apostolo e difensore della 'Respublica Cristiana'", *Studi francescani*, LII-LIII (1955-1956), 225-228. On the preaching activities of the Franciscan, Roberto Caracciolo, "il principe de' predicatori del tempo suo", see Francesco Torraca, "Frà Roberto da Lecce", *Archivio storico per le province napoletane*, VII (1882), 141-165. Preachers of other orders were also active in raising money and troops for the crusade. Cf. Calixtus' order to the general and provincials of the Augustinians to have their preachers concentrate their efforts on this work (extract in Pastor, *HP*, II, appendix 39). The chronicler of Bologna described the preaching of the crusade in that city on August 31, by an Augustinian named Paulo da Roma, and added that the pope, ". . .eliesse alquanti predicaturi che andasseno per Ytalia, predicando et confortando li popoli che li dovesseno dare subsidio alla dicta armata". *Corpus chronicorum Bononiensium*, p. 238. Cf. Adrien de But, *Chronique*, p. 356.

46. Niccolò da Toccia, *Cronaca di Viterbo*, p. 243.

47. H. G. Pfander, *The Popular Sermon of the Medieval Friar in England* (New York, 1937), p. 45.

48. W. O. Ross, ed., *Middle English Sermons (Early English Text Society*. O.S. 209, London, 1940), no. 41, pp. 254, 255.

49. Erasmus, *Ecclesiastae sive de ratione concionandi lib. quatuor in Opera omnia* (Leyden, 1704), V, cols. 985, 986.

50. See e.g. the tale repeated by Vespasiano in his portrait of Cosimo de' Medici, *Lives of Illustrious Men*, p. 227.

51. See the article by L. Jadin, "Roberto Carraciolo", *Dictionnaire d'histoire et de geographique ecclesiastique* (Paris, 1949), XI, cols. 984, 985.

52. F. Torraca, "Frà Roberto da Lecce", 157, 158.

53. Roberto Caracciolo, *Spechio del la fede* (Venice, 1517), fols. vii^r-ix^r.

54. The best study of Capistran and his career is that of J. Hofer, *Giovanni da Capestrano. Una vita spesa nella lotta per la riforma dell chiesa*, tr. (from the German), G. di Fabio (Aquila, 1955).

55. Wadding, *Annales*, XII, 198, 210; Hofer, *op. cit.*, pp. 595, 596.

56. Wadding, *Annales*, XII, 199-202; Hofer, *op. cit.*, p. 596.

57. Wadding, *Annales*, XII, 202-203.

58. Hofer, *op. cit.*, pp. 597, 598.

59. *Ibid.*, p. 602; Wadding, *Annales*, XII, 201.

60. Wadding, *Annales*, XII, 207. From Frankfort Capistran wrote to Philip of Burgundy warning of the imminent danger and pleading with him to prepare to take the field: "Surge igitur, christianissime princeps", he urged, "et da non solum verbis, sed facto de te magni animi exemplum, ut nostrae salutis signifer videaris. Ecce venenosissimum serpens Turcarum imperator cum quadringentis millibus Rasciae terram invasit erecta cervice, putans christianae religionis nomen prorsus extinguere.... Totius christianae religionis salus post Deum a te dependet: in te oculi omnium sperant; qui Teucrorum ictibus modo percutiuntur, abs te solo certum expectant auxilium: ut solus Christianissimum in praesentiarum tibi vendicas nomen". *Ibid.*, XII, 205-207; cf. his exhortation to the king of England, *ibid.*, XII, 211-212.

61. Hofer, *op. cit.*, pp. 611-614, 621.

62. Wadding, *Annales*, XII, 246-248.

63. *Ibid.*, XII, 252-254.

64. Hofer, *op. cit.*, pp. 640-642.

65. Gómez Canedo, *Carvajal*, pp. 153-156.

66. *Ibid.*, p. 158; and cf. Carvajal's letter to Calixtus III from Vienna, January 16, 1456 in Wadding, *Annales*, XII, 320.

67. Although we do not possess the texts of these sermons, Christoforo a Varisio in his *Vita S. Joannis a Capistrano (Acta Sanctorum, Octobris*, X, Brussels, 1861, 531), gives us some idea of their general tone. Christoforo wrote: "Et quia inimicus crucis Christi, imperator Turcarum, cum magna potentia, juxta illud tempus, inclytum regnum Ungariae navali bello et terrestri violenter invadebat, zelantissimus Pater fidei christianae, licet jam esset decrepitus et incompos viribus, discurrebat tamen hinc inde praedicando Crucem contra Turcas cum fervore maximo, reducendo ad memoriam christianorum, quantum Salvator noster pro nobis passus est, quam gravia tormenta Martyres pro defensione christianae fidei pertulerunt, quam multis

miraculis vividissima et una fides Jesu Christi, extra quam non est salus, per omnes Sanctos roborata sit; insuper informabat, ut cogitarent quomodo canes illi, jugiter nomen Domini blasphemantes, fidem Christi derident, ecclesias destruunt, altaria sacra profanant, non abhorrentes, virgines super altaribus, Deo dicatis, deflorare, sanguinem christianorum truculenta rabie effundunt, eos in servitutem redigunt, fidem suam autem, a diabolico viro Mahometo eis traditam, spurcitiis et ignominiis plenam, extollunt, magnificant et exaltant. His et aliis sermonibus multitudinem hominum tam nobilium, quam ignobiblium, tam divitum, quam pauperum, ad defensionem catholicae fidei animavit, eosque signaculo crucis Christi contra Turcas insignivit."

68. Hofer, *op. cit.*, pp. 645, 646; Gómez Canedo, *Carvajal*, p. 156.

69. Babinger, *Mahomet II*, pp. 169, 170.

70. Hofer, *op. cit.*, p. 646.

71. Carvajal to Calixtus III, Budapest. April 7, 1456, in D'Achery, *Spicilegium*, III, 800.

72. Carvajal to Francesco Sforza, Budapest, April 17, 1456 in L. Thallóczy and A. Áldásy (eds.), *A Magyarország és Szerbia Közti Összeköttetések Oklevéltára (MHH*, XXXIII), no. 529, pp. 462-464. On Sforza's attitude toward the crusade see L. Fumi, "Il desinteresse di Francesco Sforza alla crociata di Callisto III contro i Turchi", *Archivio storico lombardo*, XVII (1912), 101-113.

73. Gómez Canedo, *Carvajal*, pp. 160-164.

74. R. Nisbet Bain, "The Siege of Belgrade by Muhammed II, 1456", *English Historical Review*, VII (1892), 242, 243.

75. Hofer, *op. cit.*, pp. 647-649.

76. *Ibid.*, pp. 652, 653.

77. Pastor, *HP*, II, 400, where the prayer is quoted. Raynaldus, *Annales*, ad an. 1456, 19-24. Adrien de But, *Chronique*, 356. Cf. the letters of Calixtus III to Francesco Sforza (Rome, April 27, 1456), and Charles VII of France (May, 1456), in Pastor, *Acta inedita*, I, 54-56.

78. Hofer, *op. cit.*, p. 655. The sources for the siege of Belgrade in 1456 have been carefully examined and evaluated by F. Babinger, "Der Quellenwert der Berichte über den Entsatz von Belgrade am 21-22. Juli 1456", *Sitzungsberichte der Bayerischen Akademie der Wissenschaften*, Heft 6 (1957), 1-69. See also Lechat, "Lettres de Jean de Tagliacozzo sur le siège de Belgrade et la mort de saint Jean de Capistran", *Analecta Bollandiana* (Brussels, 1921).

79. *Ibid.*, pp. 654, 669-672; cf. R. Nisbet Bain, "The Siege of Belgrade", pp., 242, 243.

80. Hofer, *op. cit.*, pp. 657-661. Babinger, *Mahomet II*, pp. 171, 172. Cf. Bonfini, *Rerum ungaricarum decades*, III, 184.

81. Hofer, *op. cit.*, pp. 658, 663-665.

82. *Ibid.*, pp. 666-668; Babinger, *Mahomet II*, p. 172.

83. Hofer, *op. cit.*, pp. 668-676.

84. *Ibid.*, pp. 676-678; Babinger *Mahomet II*, p. 173.

85. Hofer, *op. cit.*, pp. 679-682; Babinger, *Mahomet II*, p. 174. Cf. the "Relatio de victoria Belgradensi", of Giovanni da Tagliacozzo (Wadding, *Annales*, XII, addenda 795), who described the victory as a miracle. God, working through his blessed servant, John Capistran, had saved the city.

86. Report of Jacopo Calcaterra from Rome to Francesco Sforza, August 24, 1456, Pastor, *HP*, II, appendix no. 43; Raynaldus, *Annales*, ad an. 1456, no. 24; Wadding, Annales, XII, 380; Sanuto, *Vite de duchi di Venezia*, col. 1163; Niccolò da Toccia, *Cronaca di Viterbo*, p. 248; *Corpus chronicorum Bononiensium*, p. 243. On August 24 and August 28, Nicholas of Cusa preached at Neustift two sermons entitled "Laudans invocabo Dominum", and "Suadeo tibi emere a me" in commemoration of the victory; see E. Vansteenberge, *Le Cardinal Nicolas de Cues*, 1401-1464 (Paris, 1920), pp. 480, 481.

87. *Loci e libro veritatum*, pp. 8, 9, 48, 103, 104, 206, 207.

88. Chastellain, *Chronique*, pp. 109-112; cf. D'Escouchy, *Chronique*, II, 324-328; and the report of Bernhard von Kraiburg, based on eyewitness accounts, summarized in Babinger, *Mahomet II*, pp. 176-177.

89. Pastor, *HP*, II, 405.

90. *Ibid.*, II, 408, 410-412.

91. A. Serra, *L'Albania e la Santa Sede*, pp. 37-45.

92. Hofer, *Giovanni da Capestrano*, pp. 687, 693.

CHAPTER III

Perfidious infidel

The new pope was a remarkable man who brought to his high office a rich background in humanistic studies and extensive experience in practical politics and diplomacy. For more than thirty years Aeneas Sylvius had been directly involved in the public affairs of Europe. He had seen service at half a dozen courts, attended important catholic councils and congresses, and traveled widely throughout Europe. Possessing a restless and inquiring mind he managed to continue to study and write during his active public life. "Few men", Creighton commented, "have combined the labours of practical politics with assiduous study and constant literary production to so great a degree as did Aeneas. His mind was perfectly encyclopedic; he seems to have had a perfect passion for seeing everything and writing about it...."[1] Among the many subjects which early attracted his attention and remained a matter of concern throughout his career the Turkish problem stands prominent. Long before he became pope, even before the fall of Constantinople he pleaded with the rulers of Christendom to take up the challenge of the Turks. Now all the skills of the humanist, the diplomat, and the ecclesiastical administrator were marshalled to bring pressure on princes and people. The continuance of Calixtus III's anti-Turkish policy was more than assured. "Among all the purposes he had at heart", Pius wrote of himself, "none was dearer than that of rousing Christians against the Turks and declaring war on them".[2] Soon after his coronation he announced in full consistory his intention of prosecuting the crusade above all else. He declared, "that nothing was more bitter to him than to behold the ruin of a Christian nation, that he was charged with the care of their most holy religion, and that he had decided to take the offensive against the Turks".[3] On the same day (October 13, 1458) he issued the bull *Vocavit nos Pius* in which he deplored the miserable condition in which he found the church and connected its troubles to the spread of Islam. He reviewed the course of Turkish conquests and the torments inflicted upon Christianity which resulted from the discord among Christian princes. Although elevated to the See of St. Peter in a time of great tribulation, the pope had not lost hope since all things were promised to those who repent. Pius recalled the recent victory over the Turks at Belgrade which showed that the infidels were not invincible and what might be accomplished if

Christendom were united. The Turks, he insisted, were aware of the divisions and rivalries among Christians and counted on them to insure their success— such were the sins of Christians. But the pope was determined to make every effort to reconcile the rulers and initiate the war against the Turks. He therefore called all princes to attend a congress to be held at either Mantua or Udine commencing June 1, 1459; and to set the exemple Pius planned to preside in person and leave Rome and the states of the church unguarded, thereby showing that he was more concerned with spiritual matters than temporal, with the well-being of the whole church than the patrimony of St. Peter.[4]

Those who insist upon clear cut and decisive answers for all the questions raised by history will not readily attain their hopes in dealing with the complex and troubled career of Pius II. Such was his misfortune that in the pope's own time his every word and deed were called into question and the gravest doubts were expressed concerning his motives and sincerity. Pius himself complained bitterly about the distrust and suspicion he met on all sides. To a group of cardinals he once revealed his disillusionment; reassuring them of his earnest desire to prosecute the war against the Turks, he insisted that the failure of his policy was not to be laid at his own door. All his attempts to implement it had been thwarted: "If we think of convening a council", he declared, "Mantua teaches us that the idea is vain. If we send envoys to ask aid of sovereigns, they are laughed at. If we impose tithes on the clergy, they appeal to a future council. If we issue indulgences and encourage the contribution of money by spiritual gifts, we are accused of avarice. People think our sole object is to amass gold. No one believes what we say. Like insolvent tradesmen we are without credit. Everything we do is interpreted in the worst way."[5]

How fortunate for Pius that he was unable to know that his acts and words were still to be the subject of intense debate five hundred years later. After all his speeches, the congresses and interminable negotiations, the aid actually sent to support the war against the Turks, and the pope's own death at Ancona, whence he had traveled to embark for the Levant as leader of the crusade, doubts are yet entertained regarding his intentions and his integrity. His enthusiasm for the crusade has been interpreted as a move to identify his name with a great idea and thereby win everlasting renown. He has been charged with using the crusade to counteract the particularist policies of the princes (much as the latter threatened the pope with a council), and as a means of reasserting the universal authority of the papacy. And even when he has been credited with having harbored good intentions he has been accused of undermining them through a conflict of interests.[6]

Since its restoration to Rome under Martin V the papacy had struggled to maintain its authority, indeed its very existence, against an imposing array of assailants. At one and the same time it had to combat constitutionalism within the curia, conciliar proposals from every quarter, the "pragmatics" of the northern princes, and the widespread heresy of Hus; and if it were to remain in Rome it was deemed necessary to recover control of the papal states and bring about the pacification of Italy. The prosecution of this program required, in addition to the necessary physical resources, highly qualified, energetic, and determined leadership. Among the popes of the fifteenth century Pius II was distinguished for his dedication to this program. The record speaks clearly regarding his plans to reestablish the authority of the See of St. Peter.[7] The waging of a successful crusade might have been expected to promote the pope's cause at home. Specifically it would have greatly enhanced the ideal of the *Respublica Christiana* and papal leadership over it. One can hardly believe that such a possibility, together with the opportunity to raise his own prestige, was lost on Pius II. A master publicist of long standing, he certainly appreciated the importance of influencing public opinion and of building the reputation and proper image of the ruler. But Pius was more than a skilled propagandist; and he surely was not a rank amateur (as he has sometimes been portrayed) in the practice of politics and diplomacy. Almost singlehandedly he had scored two major victories against the prevailing trend toward national churches when he won Germany over from the position of neutrality in the later days of the council of Basel, and more recently when he persuaded the king of France to renounce the Pragmatic Sanction.[8] He knew that in the raw, ruthless power politics of his day prestige or reputation did not stand long unsupported and that they conferred only a limited power upon the ruler who, in order to benefit from them, must possess as well, to use a modern phrase, "the realities of power". The point is that while a successful crusade (and Pius appreciated better than anyone the possibility of failure) would have raised the stature of the papacy, it was no substitute for a full treasure and a well-stocked armory which were utterly necessary for the defense of the church against the numerous enemies within Christendom.[9]

If Pius was seriously committed to the restoration of papal monarchy and yet knew that aside from certain ephemeral advantages attention to the Turkish problem would hardly guarantee the success of his policies at home (especially since to gain the adherence of the princes to the crusade inevitably meant making concessions in vital areas), how are we to understand his devotion to the crusade? And how did it stand in relation to his own commitments? Are we not in fact confronted here with the classic case of the statesman who in domestic affairs is every inch a realist but in turning to foreign policy becomes the visionary? With our knowledge of the larger currents of European history we may be inclined to assess all the chief ingredients of the pope's program—the peace and unity of Christendom, the restoration of the universal power of the papacy, and the crusade against the Turks—as impractical and idealistic. But then Pius did not share our advantage of hindsight. To him and many contemporaries they consituted very real and necessary objectives; and with Pius their formulation in terms of policy was tempered by his grasp of the realities of politics in his own time. Pius was not without his dreams but in the routine planning and execution of policy he was very much the practical ruler. In respect to the Turkish question it can be said that he was not without strong feelings for the subjugated Christians and the church in the East. But his crusade plans were not the expression of a visionary scheme for the recovery of the Holy Land. The defense of Christendom in the largest sense of the word was, he believed, the responsibility of the successor of St. Peter; but at that very moment it was Latin Christendom, indeed the West itself which was threatened. The pope's estimate of the crisis at the beginning of his pontificate is clearly stated in his address to the representatives of the duke of Burgundy who, appearing before him at Mantua, had urged elaborate but time-consuming preparations before marching against the Turks. Pius acknowledged the desirability of solving all problems at home before taking on the Turks: "But", he concluded, "all this would take a long time; ambassadors would have to be sent and the contestants would have to be sounded, persuaded, and skillfully handled; for how could the enmities of many years be dispelled in a few days? Meantime the Hungarians, who were by now nearly exhausted by war, would perish. The Turks were already threatening them and in the coming summer they would without doubt attack with all their might. Already the Rascians were on the side of the Turks and through the defection of the Bosnians they had taken Senderovia, where troops could easily be put across the Danube. If Hungary surrendered to the Turks, the door was wide open into Germany and Italy and their strength was almost doubled. There could be no doubt that if the Hungarians were deserted by the other Christians, they would be wiped out or would ally themselves with the enemy. Either event would be fatal. . . . since it was absolutely certain that the Turks were aspiring to the empire of the West."[10]

In his own account of the negotiations at Mantua Pius stated concisely the guiding principles of his policy decisions. In plain language he declared that "the greater evil is always the one to be faced first".[11] Although he entertained hopes beyond the immediate defense of Hungary, he was realist enough to admit that "we must do what we can, not what we wish".[12] At Mantua he called first for quick, decisive action to save Hungary. While the grand crusade to expel the Turks from Europe remained his ultimate objective, he acknowledged that: "Empires are won by perseverance, courage, and wisdom; by idleness, cowardice, and ignorance they are lost".[13]

In emphasizing expedience and decisiveness as essential to success in political undertakings and in stating his case in maxims of a general nature Pius bears a striking resemblance to Machiavelli.[14] When he writes: "No steel is so good as a sword for digging out gold"; or, "He is a fool who thinks people can be persuaded to noble deeds unless it is to their material advantage"; and, "It is arms that make king or captive"; or again, "In matters carried on from a distance there is abundant opportunity for deception and truth can seldom be discovered", we seem to have entered the thought world of the famous Florentine.[15] Yet Pius is no advocate of a secular doctrine of power politics. On this point he is most emphatic when he sternly rebukes the Florentine ambassador Otto Niccolini for suggesting that it would be to the advantage of all Italy if the Venetians and Turks were left alone to annihilate each other. "The princes of this world and governors of cities care not by what means they protect their power so long as they protect it", he exclaims, "and therefore they violate the law of nations and act contrary to honourable practices.... If their own state is safe they will let the Christian state go to ruin." Such behavior people would not tolerate on the part of the pope, he assures the envoy, who should not be surprised then, "if in regard to the matters at hand our opinion differs from yours and that of the Florentines". Pius does not doubt that the Venetians aspire to the mastery of all Italy: "It is a common fault that no one is satisfied with his lot. No state's lands are broad enough." But even Venetian domination is to be preferred to that of the Turks: "No Christian who deserves the name would prefer the rule of the Turks under which the sacraments of the Church must finally be doomed and the gate to the other life be closed.... The victory of the Turks means the overthrow of the Gospel, which we are bound to try with all our might to prevent".[16]

With these principles in mind we may now turn to the last and most blunt attack upon the integrity of Pius' crusade policy. Whereas formerly he was accused of opportunism or idealism he is here charged with defeating his own cause by cultivating what is called "nationalistic patriotism"; that is, he is alleged to have wrecked the chances for a crusade by subordinating the interests of Christendom to those of Italy.[17] Several examples are adduced to substantiate this claim but the main argument contends that he allowed his Italian sympathies to dominate his policies especially regarding France.

These were, it is claimed, the major considerations for his opposition to the restoration of Anjevin power in the *Regno* (in favor, it should be noted, of the Spanish dynasty of Aragon), and for seeking to thwart the direct intervention of France in the affairs of the peninsula.[18]

It is well known that Pius harbored strong emotional ties toward the land and ideals so fervently celebrated a century earlier by Petrarch in his *Italia mia*. He was passionately persuaded of the superiority of Italian culture, but so were most humanists, including some non-Italians. Such convictions no doubt entered into his political thinking. But it seems an oversimplification to explain the Italian orientation of the papacy in the *Quattrocento* in terms of an attitude which is better described as cultural patriotism. Certainly the record of past relations between the papacy and France—the introduction into the peninsula of Anjevin power in the time of Clement IV, the persecution of the church by Philip IV, the "Babylonian Captivity", and most recently the problem of the Pragmatic Sanction—were sufficient to recommend that the independence of the papacy was better assured by alliances with the powers of Italy and by a pope who was himself a native son. The fact remains, Pius can neither be credited with nor condemned for setting the course whereby the papacy was to be reduced to the level of an Italian principate.[19] Moreover, apart from the evident opposition of France to his plans for the reordering of Latin Christendom, it is clear that Pius expected little or nothing from her in support of the crusade. It was not "patriotic nationalism" alone then which led him to declare that "the salvation of Europe could be found only in Italy...". Once again it was the political realist speaking. Obviously the Turks were an immediate threat to Italy. Both at home and in the Levant the Italians were more directly involved and had more to lose than any other western power. Short of a miracle of the kind which had accompanied the preaching of Urban II, Peter the Hermit, or Bernard of Clairvaux, Pius was compelled to count mainly on those powers whose selfish interest forced them to deal with the Turkish threat.[20]

Both the proximity of the Turks and the adverse effects of their expansion upon the Leventine interests of the Italians were amply demonstrated during Pius' pontificate. In the eight years which followed the Christian victory of Belgrade during which Calixtus and Pius endeavored to arouse the West to the Turkish peril, the armies of the Conqueror campaigned in Europe and Asia, gained new victories and territories, and advanced steadily upon the heart of Christendom. Although a Turkish army under the command of Isa Beg was annihilated by Scanderbeg in the mountains of Albania in

September 1457, in the following spring (1458), led by Mahmud Pasha, the Turks marched into Serbia, ravaged the countryside and occupied several strong places. At the same time Mehmed II, at the head of another army, entered Greece. In the Morea he forced the Greek despots, Thomas and Demetrius Paleologus to cede to him the cities of Corinth, Patras, Vostitsa, and Kalavryta, and to guarantee payment of an annual tribute of 3000 pieces of gold. At the end of August 1458 the Grand Turk paid his historic visit to Athens where he stopped for four days and confirmed the privileges already granted to the Athenians by Omer Beg. After viewing Thebes and Negropont, Mehmed left Greece carrying with him an enormous booty and followed by a long train of unhappy captives. The sultan reached Adrianople by the autumn of 1458, where he passed the winter (1458-59).[21]

With the arrival of spring (1459), Mehmed II marched at the head of his army into Serbia. He advanced as far as Pirot, where the keys of Semendria, the capital city, were handed over to him. By the end of the year all Serbia was in the hands of the Ottomans. The ancient slavic state lost the last shred of its independence. Reorganized as the *sanjak* of Semendere it began its long history as a Turkish province which it was to remain for over four hundred years.[22] While the Grand Turk was thus occupied in Serbia another Turkish force commanded by Hamza Pasha, governor of Thessaly, penetrated the Morea. Despite all their losses to the invader and the ever present threat of complete extinction the Greek despots continued to fight one another over the pitiful remains of their territories. Hamza Pasha tried unsuccessfully in 1459 to quell the disturbances. In the spring of 1460 Mehmed II returned in person to the Greek peninsula. By mid-summer the independence of the despotate was at an end. When the sultan left the Morea at the end of the summer, among his captives and hostages was Demetrius Paleologus. Thomas, as we have seen, fled to Corfu (July, 1460), and from there to Italy. Omer Beg was appointed governor over their former possessions.[23]

In 1461 Mehmed II occupied himself with the affairs of Asia. He led his victorious forces against Kastamonu, Sinope, and Trebizond all of which capitulated to him without much resistance.[24] He returned to Europe in the next year, drove Vlad Dracul from Wallachia and invested Vlad's brother, Radu, with the lordship of the country.[25] In the course of the years 1461 and 1462, the sultan gave considerable attention to the construction of a large fleet and improved port facilities at Constantinople and Gallipoli. Immediately after his Wallachian campaign, he directed his new fleet against the island of Mitylene (autumn 1462). After a month-long siege the city of Mitylene surrendered to the Turks. Although Mahmud Pasha had promised the islanders clemency if they would yield to him, the sultan caused three hundred Italians to be sawed in two. He claimed that in so doing he was not violating his pasha's guarantee, which he had personally confirmed, since Mahmud had promised that the inhabitants would lose neither their heads nor their goods. The Turks enslaved a number of the island's inhabitants, and a short time after executed the lord of Mitylene, Niccolò Gattilusio.[26] Upon his return to Constantinople in October 1462, the Grand Turk began at once great preparations for a new expedition. At the end of March, 1463, he was already in the field leading his army westward. The objective of this new campaign was the kingdom of Bosnia. Deserted by the West, the kingdom quickly succumbed before the Ottoman onslaught, and King Stephen who made his submission to the Turks was beheaded. In June Mehmed led part of his army into Herzegovina, and though he ravaged the countryside, he withdrew without having defeated the defenders of this mountainous country. When the Ottoman sultan turned toward his capital, there marched in his train more than 100,000 Bosnians, now slaves of the Turks. Mehmed left behind as his first governor of the new Turkish province Isa, son of Ishiak Beg of Üsküb who was, however, soon replaced by Mehmed, son of Minnet Beg. [27]

It is unnecessary here to review in detail all the means by which Pius II sought to arouse Europe to the Turkish peril and to organize the crusade. From the moment of his election until his death at Ancona in 1464 he employed every method, seized every opportunity to gain support for his cause.[28] As his predecessor had done, Pius began by taking advantage of the presence in Rome of ambassadors, sent by the powers of Europe to congratulate him upon his accession to the papal dignity, to open negotiations with the separate states. He repeatedly addressed the papal curia on the subject of the crusade during the first weeks after his election.[29] Then he did what Calixtus III had believed would be of no avail, and what Pius had already seen fail miserably in the days of Nicholas V; he issued the call for a European congress, which in the next year (1459) was held at Mantua.[30] In the meantine he continued to write letters and deliver eloquent exhortations to the leaders of Christendom. Personally or through his representatives he pleaded and bargained with them, promised, harangued, warned, threatened, and condemned them variously in order to bring peace among Christians and carry the war against the Turks. Legates, preachers, and sellers of indulgences he dispatched throughout Europe, and when Europe failed to respond to his urgings the ever resourceful mind of Pius had recourse to other expedients. He entered into negotiations with Levantine princes, both Christian and pagan, who sent embassies to Rome. The pope received them with respect and had them travel about the West to stimulate interest. He received and employed in a similar fashion several Christian rulers whose lands had fallen to the Turks and who had fled to the pope for protection. Beyond these measures Pius gave what support he could to the Christian powers who were attacked by the infidels. He aided the knights of St. John at Rhodes, and initiated two new military orders whose specific mission was to oppose the Turks. He placed some hope in an alleged half-brother of Mehmed II, named Bayezid Tchelebi, who was under the protection of the Roman court. By advancing the dubious claims of this adventurer, the pope expected to embarrass Mehmed II, and sow dissension among the Turks when the Christian crusaders arrived in the East.[31] Finally when all else had failed, the infirm Pius, aged beyond his years, determined to lead the crusading army himself and thereby shame the princes of the West into joining him. On June 18, 1464, he took the cross in St. Peter's, and began the journey to Ancona where the crusaders were to assemble. He reached the port of embarkation on July 19, but proceeded no farther. On August 13, 1464, Pope Pius II died. In his last words, spoken to Jacopo Ammanati, Cardinal of Pavia, he charged his devoted friend to "keep the continuation of our holy enterprise in the mind of the brethren, and aid it with all your power. Woe unto you, woe unto you, if you desert God's work".[32]

From the letters, orations, official pronouncements, and the historical-literary works of the humanist-pope we may amply document his estimate of the Ottoman menace and his attitude toward the Turks. Many of these works, it is true, are of a publicist character and were written for the purpose of advertising the problem and arousing support for the crusade. But his view of the threat and of the Turks themselves is, with one exception, consistent throughout. The one exception is, of course, the troublesome letter in which Pius addressed Sultan Mehmed II in a benevolent tone for the expressed purpose of winning the Grand Turk over to Christianity. Studied apart from his other writings, not to mention the work of his pontificate, the letter has been cited variously as (1) an example of the willingness of the Renaissance papacy to negotiate and cooperate with the Turks and enemies of the Latin Christian princes; (2) as an expression of the highest aims of an orthodox catholic reform program based on the principles of Christian humanism (as opposed to the alleged paganizing tendencies of humanism); and (3) one of several temperate, cosmopolitan, and rational responses to the challenge of Islam, "a moment of vision", at the height of the Renaissance, but one allegedly preceded by and to be succeeded again by ignorance, prejudice, and bigotry.[33]

The letter is certainly a model of Renaissance eloquence, combining a felicitous style with a carefully structered argument in which its author achieved a rare synthesis of orthodox doctrine and humanistic values. But it hardly reflects Pius' true convictions. The whole thing is too contrived, too much an academic exercise to be convincing. The letter subsumes a recipient who shared with the author a knowledge of both Christianity and Islam and a common acceptance of humanistic values. It appeals to the wisdom, tolerance, and benevolence of the "caliph of the Turks". Nowhere else in the writings of Pius do we find such a benign sultan. On the contrary he is always described as the meanest, most vile, and impious barbarian. But more than this it is the very kind of impractical scheme the pope had little use for. Letters, most of them spurious, to and from the Turkish sultan were widely circulated in Renaissance Europe. Most were no more than fanciful compositions through which their authors satisfied a prevailing apocalyptic yearning; many were simply amateur literary efforts whose authors traded on current interest in the subject.[34] Some were the work of political propagandists and perhaps Pius had some hope of frightening the rulers of the West by proposing to legitimize the sultan's conquest of Byzantium in return for his conversion to Christianity. Some perhaps really thought or hoped to influence the sultan's policy much as do writers of letters to public officials today. Such I believe was the intention of the mystical theologian Paolo Giustiniani in an unfinished and unpublished letter addressed to the "emperor of the Turks" in which the author advised the sultan to follow the example of Constantine rather than that of Alexander.[35] Surely Pius entertained no such illusion as the latter. He was of course acquainted with the various schemes which recommended a conciliatory approach to the Turks. He had only recently received the suggestions of the Spanish Franciscan and historian of the Council of Basel, Juan de Segovia, and was certainly familiar with the ideas of Nicholas of Cusa, both urging peaceful conciliation as the best way to deal with the Turks.[36] The constructive approach of Cusa and Segovia may be seen in the letter especially where the pope stressed the doctrines upon which Christians and Moslems were in accord.[37] But I cannot believe that Pius took seriously the possibility of conversion, and certainly he did not consider Mehmed, as a recent scholar had suggested, "a man of brilliant intelligence". The letter, it will be recalled, was composed subsequently to the disappointing experience of the congress of Mantua. Tired, discouraged, and frustrated in his efforts to raise an army of crusaders, Pius no doubt found it refreshing to reflect for a moment on the approach urged by those he normally regarded as theoreticians. The matter ended there. No embassies were exchanged and no discussions were held. The notion was appropriate for idle speculation during a period of leisure while the pope was recovering from the exhausting trials of practical negotiations. It was never a part of the latter.[38]

Owing to Pius' preoccupation with the Turkish question we find the problem treated in nearly everything he wrote. Thus we are not dependent upon those sources which were composed especially to publicize the subject and gain support for the crusade for our assessment of his views. In addition to the crusade bulls, public speeches, and occasional reports on particular events such as his *De Captione urbis Constantinopolitane* there are lengthy discussions of the Turkish question included in his more scholarly works, for example the *Europa*, and the subject occupies as much space as any other in his correspondence.[39] The latter particularly affords us glimpses of the astute powers of observation, the sharp critical attitude, and the uncommon insight and judgment which established their author among the first rank of the humanists of his day. Even when writing about those affairs in which he was directly involved he sometimes attained a high degree of objectivity, and often revealed, though not always intentionally, the motives behind his own actions.[40] He was not, however, without prejudices and, when it suited him, he was capable of misrepresenting the facts to support his own views or interpretations. What has been said about his letters is equally true of the *Commentaries*, which are perhaps, for the historian of the *Quattrocento*, Pius II's most important work. Largely autobiographical, but including substantial historical and geographical sections, the *Commentaries* abound in colorful descriptive passages, piercing character analyses and snatches of information on the odds and ends of contemporary life which attracted the attention of the pope. Combining some of the best and worst features of humanistic historiography the *Commentaries* are dominated by their author's conception of the position and the purpose of the papacy in Christian society. The narrative of negotiations and military action which occupies considerable space in the thirteen books can only be understood in this context. And it is certain that Pius intended that the work of his pontificate was to be judged solely in these terms. The work, then, is above all a frank expose of the pope's role in the affairs of his time supported by a sustained justification which leaves no doubt about the values and assumptions which served as the springs of action. Since Pius never found time to edit the work beyond the first book, and since that assignment was taken lightly by his secretary Campano, the *Commentaries* have come down to us pretty much in the form of a hurriedly written first draft revealing much more than the pope realized or probably ever intended. More than in any of his other works we encounter here the unrestrained, even unsophisticated expression of feelings and thinking of the man himself.[41]

It is thus not surprising that considerable space is given to the Turkish problem; in fact the eastern peril and the proposed crusade constitute its central theme. Indeed, if we can judge by the *Commentaries*, no matter what task or detail occupied the pope's attention at a given moment, the plans for the crusade were never far from his mind. It is here that we see how he turned almost any incident or affair into an instrument for raising interest in his favorite project. In 1460, when Thomas Paleologus, brother of the deceased Emperor Constantine, fled from the Morea, he carried with him the head of St. Andrew the first apostle. Pius offered the fallen despot the protection of Rome and a pension, and urged him to bring the head there that it might rest "beside the bones of its brother, St. Peter, prince of the Apostles, and in the Apostolic See, the citadel of the Faith, the safe refuge for all who are driven from their own churches." When Thomas arrived at Ancona, Pius sent Alexandro Oliva da Sassoferrato, cardinal priest of Santa Susanna, to receive the head and carry it to the papal fortress at Narni for safekeeping.[42]

Plans were made to bring the head of St. Andrew to Rome during Holy Week of 1462. The events connected with this celebration are described in full detail comprising nearly one-half of Book VIII. It is obvious that the pope attached much importance to the occasion. The narrative merits our attention for the light it sheds on the character of the pope's religious beliefs and how they in turn colored his views of the Turks. The detailed description also reveals much about the nature of popular religion at the time, and finally it illustrates some means and techniques employed in mass communication and the cultivation of public opinion. The pope sent word through Italy promising plenary remission of sins to all who witnessed the event. Cardinals Bessarion, Sassoferrato, and de' Todeschini traveled to Narni to get the sacred relic. Returning on Palm Sunday (April 11, 1462), the cardinals deposited the head in the tower of the Ponte Molle, two miles from Rome, where it remained overnight guarded by two archbishops. On the next day Pius led the cardinals, the Roman clergy, the foreign ambassadors, the nobles, and the populace, all carrying palm branches, to a meadow close by Ponte Molle. Here the pope had caused to be built a high platform with an altar in the center. While Bessarion mounted the platform from one side bearing St. Andrew's head in a reliquary, the pope, cardinals and prelates, robed in their sacred garments, ascended from the opposite side. Bessarion reverently placed the casket in the center of the altar. When it was opened he took the head and offered it to the pope. Before receiving it Pius, supposedly weeping all the while, knelt and prayed aloud:

Take loving thought for all Christendom, that by thy intercession the mercy of God may be upon us and that, if He is angry with us for our sins, which are many, His anger may be transferred to the impious Turks and the barbarian nations who dishonor Christ the Lord. Amen

Then with all around him crying and sobbing and beating their breasts, the pope kissed the sacred head. The multitudes stood silently in the fields and watched as the cardinals and prelates followed the pope in kissing the relic. Pius prayed again and then took the relic and raising it high above his head walked around the platform so that the people below might see it. The valleys, we are told, echoed with the sound of their weeping and prayers. The choir intoned the *Te Deum*, and then sang a hymn, written at the command of the pope by Agapito da Rustici-Cenci, bishop of Ancona.[43]

When the hymn was finished the pope took the sacred bones in his own hands, descended from the platform, and led the clergy and the people back to Rome. He deposited it on the altar of the church of Santa Maria del Popolo, and appointed certain bishops to watch over it during the night. The next day the pope carried the relic in a grand procession through Rome whose buildings and streets were richly decorated for the occasion. When the procession reached the basilica of St. Peter's, the pope paused after climbing the stairs and exhibited the sacred head to the throng of people gathered there. Inside the church Pius and the prelates moved with difficulty through the great crowd of worshippers who carried lighted tapers. At last he reached the high altar upon which he placed the head of the holy apostle. The prelates then came forward and kissed it. Among them was Isidore, the cardinal of Russia who had escaped from the hands of the Turks and spread the alarm in the West. The year before the arrival of St. Andrew's head Isidore had suffered a stroke of apoplexy and the loss of his speech; but when he saw the holy relic carried past his house he arose from his bed and followed it on foot to St. Peter's.[44]

Cardinal Bessarion now stepped between the pope and the head of St. Andrew and delivered a long sermon which Pius copied into the *Commentaries*. Bessarion addressed St. Peter on behalf of his brother and proceeded to explain (for the benefit of those gathered in the church), the circumstances behind the event they were commemorating. He described the conversion of the Achaeans, the martyrdom of St. Andrew, and the long and peaceful residence of his sacred head in the Morea until the coming of the Turks. Speaking for the saint, Bessarion continued, "But when the Mohammedans (Ah, piteous and tragic tale!) following the son of Satan, the antichrist

Mahomet, after seizing the rest of Greece and the Orient... subjugated Achaia too and perverted it with infamous worship, then by God's aid I fled thence from the clutches of the heathen and I have come to thee, most holy brother...". The Greek cardinal has St. Andrew exhort his brother to smite the enemies of Christ as he did the high priest's servant, Malchus, in the garden of Gethsemane. "What wilt thou do now? Wilt thou be inert or slow," he inquired of St. Peter, "against the impious Turks, the bitterest enemies of the most holy cross of our salvation, through which He Who redeemed us by it gathers to himself both thee and me against barbarians who are savagely rending asunder Christ's limbs and continually assailing Christ Himself with blasphemy and insult? Wilt thou endure such deeds?" Bessarion still speaking for St. Andrew reminds St. Peter of his duty; he recalls his former deeds, and declares that now more than ever before his sword is needed for the defense of Christians. "For now are they beset with divers torments and calamities. Surely thou wilt raise them up from oppression and rescue them from the hands of the unrighteous." The sword must be wielded, "against the slaves of sin and unrighteousness, the bondsmen of vileness; now is the time with hands and teeth and all manner of torture to assail not only the betrayers of Christ but His tormentors and oppressors".

Still speaking for St. Andrew, Bessarion then turned to the pope and urged him to persevere in the holy cause of the crusade. He admonished him not to despair despite the poor response of the Christian princes. He assured the pope that "one day they [the princes] will come to reverence Christ, one day they will reverence Peter, and calling upon thee and me, they will put on the spirit of Christian kings. They will at last act as becomes them and by assaulting the most cruel foe will win everlasting fame...". Pius replied by promising Andrew that he would devote all in his power to recovering the Apostle's home now in the hands of the Turks. "For nothing is closer to our heart than the defense of the Christian religion and the orthodox faith, which thine enemies and ours, the Turks, are striving to trample under foot." At this the ceremony came to an end. The pope blessed the multitude and the Cardinal of Siena announced plenary indulgence.[45]

It remains only to summarize Pius' views on those matters which principally exercised the minds and imaginations of his generation: the origin of the Turks; the significance of the Ottoman advance for the Christian religion; and the actual threat to Europe including his estimate of the relative military capabilities of the Turks and Latin Christendom. Pius' treatment of the origin of the Turks was devoted mainly to refuting the current legend representing the *Teucri* as the descendants of the ancient Trojans. A close student of geography and ethnography he had, while still attached to the

Origo gentis turcoꝛ.

IV: Turkish warrior
(Hartmann Schedel, *Liber Chronicarum*. Nuremberg, 1493).

imperial court, sought authoritative opinion on this subject.[46] "This race," he explained, "which had once migrated from eastern Scythia, had subdued Cappadocia, Ponthus, Bithynia, and almost all Asia Minor. Soon after they crossed the Hellespont, seized most of Greece, and advanced their arms as far as the famous rivers Save and Danube." They were a crude and barbarous people whose occupation of the territories of the Greek empire was an act of unprovoked aggression. Pius had no time for the theories about the Turks avenging their ancestors or occupying a rightful inheritance.[47]

Once Mehmed II had captured Constantinople he "began to aspire to the sovereignty of all Europe...". The Grand Turk's intentions were demonstrated when he gathered a large force and marched into Hungary during the pontificate of Calixtus III. Although he was stopped at Belgrade by an army of courageous crusaders led by John Capistran and John Hunyadi, "Nevertheless he [Mehmed II] did not lose courage nor relax his hatred of the Christians, but recruiting fresh forces day by day, he proceeded to harry now the Albanians, now the Rascians, now other neighboring Christian peoples, resolved to trample down and utterly annihilate the Holy Scriptures and the Divine Law of Christ".[48] The head of Catholic Christendom, Pius II consistently represented the Moslem Turks as the natural enemies of the Christian faith. "As a nation," he wrote, "the Turks are the foes of the Trinity."[49] In his first oration before the congress of Mantua he proclaimed his intention of protecting the faith which the Turks were doing everything in their power to destroy.[50] Some years later in addressing a Burgundian embassy he praised Philip the Good above all other princes; for although he had less to fear from the Turks than anyone, the duke had promised to do more for the sake of the Holy Gospel.[51] Toward the end of his pontificate (September 23, 1463), in what we today would call a white paper setting forth the work of his reign, Pius defended before the cardinals in secret consistory his plan to lead the crusade personally: "We shall imitate our Lord and Master Jesus Christ. . . . We too will lay down our life for our flock since in no other way can we save the Christian religion from being trampled by the forces of the Turk. . . . An unavoidable war with the Turks threatens us. Unless we take arms and go to meet the enemy we think all is over with religion."[52]

In viewing the conflict in such terms we cannot be surprised to find the pope's opinion of the Turks' own religion to have been something less than informed and objective. Actually since the twelfth century scholars in the West had accumulated a fair knowledge of Islam which in Pius' own day was considerably amplified.[53] The pope was not unaware of the Latin studies on Islam; as we have seen he was personally acquainted with several of its leading authors. Although translations of the Koran and commentaries and treatises on Islam were ready at hand Pius made little or no use of them. His summary sketch of the rise of Islam and its main tenets, quoted here in full, was hardly the product of a critical and much less a generous spirit:

> They follow a certain false prophet called Mahomet, an Arab imbued with gentile error and Jewish perfidy, who listened to Christians infected with Nestorianism and Arianism. He advanced his fortunes by seducing an influential widow and became notorious for his intrigues; he collected a band of brigands with which he made himself lord over the Arabs. Acquainted as he was with the Old and New Testaments he perverted them both; he had the effrontery to say that he was a prophet and talked with angels and he cast such a spell over ignorant peoples that he was able to give them a new law and persuade them to abandon Christ, the Savior. For he made use of incantations and magic and by permitting lust and incest he easily won over to him the common people, who are prone to sensual pleasure. Except wine there was nothing he did not allow them, in order to persuade them to worship according to his law, which, though it admits that Christ was inspired of God, born of a Virgin, and able to perform miracles, yet denies that He was divine and that He suffered the agony of death for our redemption. It does not acknowledge the Prophets or heed the precepts of the Apostles or the Evangelists. The influence of this monstrous doctrine increased to such an extent that almost all Asia and Africa was infected with its poison; it made its way with the Turks into Greece and through the Moors took possession of Baetica in Spain; and although the Bishops of Rome have tried in many ways to combat this plague, nevertheless it has continued to gain strength gradually to this day and has penetrated our very vitals.[54]

Islam was according to Pius a pernicious force, incompatible at all points with Christianity and dedicated by its very nature to the overthrow of the Christian religion. The Turkish problem was regarded by the pope as fundamentally a religious struggle. The war between the two systems had been waged for centuries. It was the primary obligation of all Christians to oppose the infidel from whatever quarter he came. Now the menace, which had never disappeared since its inception in the seventh century, had become greater with the onslaught of the Ottoman Turks, the most recent and victorious of a succession of Moslem peoples![55]

While religious considerations were the very basis of Pius' arguments for opposing the Turks they were invariably elaborated in terms of the temporal situation. In the first oration at Mantua, mentioned above, he predicted that if aid were not rushed to Hungary, ". . .all Europe would be subdued, a calamity that must bring with it the destruction of our faith." Pius consistently viewed European society as a cultural unity; the conquest of Europe by the Turks meant the destruction of its peculiar culture the essential component of which was the Christian religion. Mehmed ", he believed, was determined to exterminate the latter and rule over the former. "Can we expect peace," he warned, "from a nation which thirsts for our blood, which has already planted itself in Hungary, after having subjugated Greece? Lay aside these infatuated hopes. Mehmed will never lay down his arms until he is wholly victorious or completely vanquished. Each success will be only a stepping stone to the next until he has mastered all the western monarchs, overthrown the Christian faith, and imposed the law of his false prophet on the whole world." For Pius the fate of Christian culture was at stake.[56]

The inclusion of both religio-ideological and practical arguments in the pope's appeals to the princes is indicative of his assessment of the temper of contemporary politics. On the one hand it was the responsibility of the priest to recall the princes to their duty as Christian rulers—and Pius doubted neither his authority to do so, nor, despite the reactions of the princes, the necessity of such appeals. In this respect he stood in the line of succession from Gregory VII, Innocent III, and Boniface VIII. "What authority is higher, what dignity more sublime, what power more exalted than that of Christ's Vicar?" he wrote of his office.[57] On the other hand, while he rarely missed an opportunity to speak to their consciences, he recognized the necessity of demonstrating that the unopposed Ottoman advance was an imminent threat to the temporal interests of the princes. There is no doubt that Pius was genuinely convinced that the Turks both aimed at the mastery of Europe and were bound to succeed if undeterred. He was persuaded by reports from the Levant that the sultan schemed "to win over the empire of the West", aimed at "the sovereignty of the seas", "often talked of Rome and has turned his thoughts thither," and that his "insatiable passion for power knows no limits".[58]

Probably no western prince had a wider view of the contemporary international scene than Pius II. He predicted that the subjugation of Bosnia would increase the vulnerability of Hungary and expose the Dalmatians, Croatians, Istrians, and the Italians to the Turkish raiders.[59] He foresaw that the defeat of Hungary would open the door to Germany and the very heart of Latin Christendom.[60] He understood that the Venetian fleet was the key to the sea passage to the West and that Italy was safe from attack in this quarter unless, as happened in 1480, Venice were found negligent.[61] In his appeals to the princes he stressed the continued progress of the Turks and rightly pointed out that each new victory enhanced the power of the enemy. But how well did he know the Turks themselves? Was he equally correct in his estimate of their strength and military capabilities and what it would take to halt them?

While he maintained that the Turks posed a serious and imminent threat Pius never doubted that a moderate Christian force was capable of stopping them. He admitted that the Turks were aggressive, courageous, and ready to die for their religion, but he vehemently countered those Christians who asserted that the Turks were invincible or too numerous to defeat. He was ashamed that their very name inspired terror in Christians and explained that though they were strong in troops and strategy, they were yet to be tested, for they had gained their reputation by overwhelming the Greeks who were cowardly, unarmed weaklings. He was certain that when they were confronted by an army of Latin Christians the result was going to be a different matter. He cited the example of the battle of Belgrade where a large and well-provided Ottoman army was defeated by a few, mostly unarmed crusaders. "The courage of Christians," he insisted, "had always been the terror of the Turks and they had never been worsted unless betrayed or overpowered by too great odds, when they were weary of conquest, or because our Lord God was angry at our sins." The success of the Turks he attributed largely to the divisions and dissensions among Christians who preferred spoiling one another to defending the faith.[62] Pius had little to say about the qualities of the individual Turkish warrior. In the fashion of the Renaissance historian he was content, as were his antique models, to write about rulers and generals. While he occasionally acknowledged the bravery of the Turks, he preferred to characterize them as weak and effeminate and he took an obvious delight in recounting the story of how a woman, bearing men's arms, saved the island of Mitylene during the pontificate of Calixtus III.[63]

In September of 1459 Pius claimed that the Turks were unable to put into the field more than 200,000 men. The majority of these were unarmed peasants, a rabble unaccustomed to fighting. The core of the Turkish military was to be found in the janissaries whom he numbered about 40,000 men. He also acknowledged that the sultan commanded a strong force of cavalry. But he felt that the Turkish navy was not of much account and that a fleet of 30 or 40 Christian galleys and supporting craft to be sufficient to prevent the Turks from passing between Asia and Europe. What the defeat of the Turks required then, beyond the spiritual acts of contrition and repentance, was not nearly so much as had been claimed. While the crusade was truly a task for the whole of Christendom, a smaller force was capable of halting the Turkish advance, and perhaps even driving them from Europe. He claimed that those who were acquainted with the Turks had assured him that an army of 50,000 or

60,000 men was sufficient. Besides, that number was certainly easier to raise and to command and coordinate than a larger force. [64]

Pius' account of one of the important conferences held on the subject at Mantua (September 27, 1459), affords some interesting insights into the thinking of the Italian governments represented. Francesco Sforza pleaded ignorance of the enemy's strength and therefore declined to say how large a force was needed. But he advised a combined land and sea operation. He believed that the actual fighting was the task of the Hungarians and other neighbors of the Turks who were acquainted with the enemy and were familiar with their tactics. The Italians and other western nations were to support the campaign with money. If the latter were to go in person it might lead to quarrels with the Hungarians, and it was certainly more expensive to send western troops and to maintain them in the field.[65]

While most of the participants in the conference were reported to have agreed with Sforza's ideas there was one outstanding exception. The veteran condottiere, Sigismondo Malatesta argued strongly in favor of sending Italians to do the fighting. He declined to comment on the matter of a fleet claiming that he had no competence in naval affairs. But he had no doubts about the outcome of the operation providing Italian cavalry and infantry were armed in sufficient numbers since the soldiers and captains of Italy were the best fighters of the time. Moreover, he protested reliance on Hungarians, Rascians, Wallachians, Bulgarians, Epirotes, and Greeks all of whom had been previously defeated by the Turks and dared "not look them in the face". He felt that ignorance of Turkish tactics was no particular liability since the enemy was also ignorant of Italian methods. He was certain that owing to the quick-wittedness of the Italians it would be easier for them to avoid the tricks of the Turks than vice-versa. "Therefore," he concluded, "I urge that the others contribute money and the Italians wage the war."[66] In response the pope agreed that it was good advice to fight the war with Italians who were without equal in the profession of arms. But he doubted that Italian captains were willing to lead the crusade (in Italy "they wage war without risk to their lives and with great profit; battles with the Turks are bloody and the only prizes to be won are souls"). The important consideration, however, was that if Italy failed to finance the war, there was no one else to count on, and the Italians were not to be expected to do both.[67] The Venetian ambassadors, Lodovico Foscarini and Orsatto Giustinian, protesting that they spoke only as private individuals (they had not yet received detailed instructions), proposed that 30 galleys and 8 saette were adequate for harrying the coasts of Greece and Asia. This action was calculated to force the sultan to spread his troops along the coasts to defend the towns. The Venetians, too, spoke in favor of the Hungarians and their neighbors carrying the burden of the attack on land. They felt that 40,000 horse and 20,000 infantry were needed. According to the pope, however, following the conference the Venetian representatives changed their tune and demanded many special concessions and a much larger force before agreeing to participate in the crusade. We know that Pius had a low opinion of merchants and republics in general and that he especially disliked and distrusted Venice. "Too much intercourse with the Turks has made you the friends of the Mohammedans," he charged the envoys of St. Mark, "and you care no more for religion."[68]

In point of fact the Venetians, who had already suffered much at the hands of the Turks and were alarmed at the possibility of new advances, were most unhappy to be regarded as friends of the Turks. In their initial instructions the Venetian ambassadors were urged to do whatever was possible to counter the bad press they were receiving owing to their relations with the Ottomans and their lack of enthusiasm for the crusade. With the pope they were to stress the importance of what they had done and currently were doing to stay the Turk by maintaining a fleet in the Levant. At the same time they were to plead the exposed position of their holdings in the Mediterranean as their reason for not wishing to be publicly associated with the pope's plans and propaganda for the crusade. In any event they were to do everything possible to prevent an ill-planned crusade and insist that only an expedition of major proportions be undertaken.[69] The detailed instructions which Foscarini and Giustinian received from the senate (dated October 3, 1459), were conceived with these objectives in mind. The Venetians concluded that the proposed expedition required a force of no less than 50,000 cavalry and 20,000 infantry which was to advance from Hungary to the waters of Greece, "and erase the Turkish name from the map of Europe". They insisted further on a fleet of 60 galleys and 10 *navi* with a force of 8,000 marines. The main expedition was to be supported by a diversionary action which involved an additional 6,000 cavalry and 4,000 infantry to cooperate with Scanderbeg in Albania and with other Christian lords of that area.[70]

Although these demands were to be slightly altered in subsequent negotiations, the Venetians never wavered in their main contention. The only expedition they were willing to support was a full-dress all-European offensive. In its instructions of October 11, 1459, the senate reiterated these points and insisted that the pontiff must be made to understand the vulnerability of the Venetian position which necessitated a cautious policy. Moreover, the Venetians emphatically countered the pope's estimate of Ottoman power. They recalled the defeat of the Christians at Varna by the forces of Murad II. Since that time the Turks had greatly increased their strength and the present sultan was much more ferocious and dedicated all his resources to military expansion. Whether wisely or not, the rulers of Venice, too, acted consistently on the matter of the crusade. Convinced that the rest of Europe would not respond to the pope's appeals, they were unwilling to become involved in a limited action in which they undoubtedly would bear the brunt of the fighting. First among the Latin powers to accept the establishment of the Ottomans in Europe as a *fait accompli*, they were determined to make the necessary adjustments in pursuit of a policy of peaceful coexistence.[71]

Pius, on the other hand, without neglecting the exigencies of practical politics—the selfish interests of princes, the actual strength of the enemy, the question of finances, the strategic importance of Hungary—in the last resort relegated the problem to the realm of religion. The crusade was not just the pope's war, it was God's will. In such matters the essential requirement was faith. Thus his decision to lead the crusade in person was more than a dramatic, sacrificial act; it was predicated upon a profound if misguided faith.[72] By it he hoped to fan the embers of religious devotion smoldering in the hearts of Christian princes. If the Venetians, who had wrecked his plans at Mantua, were beyond salvation, there were others who still recognized their duty to God. In taking the cross himself he was certain that other princes, particularly the duke of Burgundy, would be provoked to act. During the last months of his pontificate as he feverishly prepared to launch the crusade, Pius increasingly looked to *le grand duc d'occident*, as the one ruler who understood that the defense of the faith and the honor of the church were the chief concerns of the Christian prince. At Mantua Pius had proclaimed that if only Philip's fellow princes "were animated by a like zeal, Turks would not now be insulting Christians nor would Saracens be guarding the sepulchre or Our Lord". It was indeed one of the painful ironies of history that when the pope went to die at Ancona the much-lauded Burgundian remained home, and only the ships of the despised Republic of merchants ,who in Pius' words fought the Turks "not by any desire to defend the faith but by greed for power. . . seeking the Peloponnese not Jesus", came to support him.[73]

NOTES TO CHAPTER III

1. M. Creighton, *Historical Essays and Reviews* (London, 1902), pp. 77, 78.
2. *Commentaries*, II, 115.
3. *Ibid.*, II, 118.
4. Iorga, *Notes et extraits*, IV, 164, 165.

5. *Commentaries*, VII, 516.

6. For a review of the various arguments see J. G. Rowe, "The Tragedy of Aeneas Sylvius Piccolomini (Pope Pius II): An Interpretation", *Church History*, XXX (1961), 288-313.

7. Cf. H. Jedin, *The Council of Trent* (London, 1957), I, 62-71, 83-85; and Aubenas and Ricard, *L'Église et la Renaissance*, pp. 46-64.

8. See G. Kallen, *Aeneas Silvius Piccolomini als Publizist in der "Epistola de ortu et auctoritate imperii romani"*, (Cologne, 1939); C. Lucius, *Pius II und Ludwig XI von Frankreich* (Heidelberg, 1913).

9. Cf. R. Haubst, "Der Reformenwurf Pius des Zweiten", *Römische Quartalschrift*, XLIX (1954), 188-242; and on the failure of the reform work owing to the preoccupation with the crusade, H. Jedin, *Studien über Domenico de' Domenichi (1416-1478)* (Wiesbaden, 1958), pp. 185-197.

10. *Commentaries*, III, 213-216. He employed the same argument with the Venetians, *ibid.*, pp. 257-259.

11. *Ibid.*, p. 213.

12. *Ibid.*, p. 255.

13. *Ibid.*, p. 223.

14. See e.g. F. Chabod, "Machiavelli's Method and Style" in *Machiavelli and the Renaissance*, tr. D. Moore (Harper Torchbooks, New York, 1958), pp. 126-148.

15. *Ibid.*, III, 271; V, 374; XII, 776, 801.

16. *Ibid.*, XII, 813-817. Some material bearing on Otto's mission to Rome including several letters touching on the Florentine reaction to the affairs of the Levant are published by G. N. de Camugliano, *The Chronicles of a Florentine Family* (London, 1933), pp. 267-274; 341-344.

17. J. G. Rowe, *op. cit.*, pp. 292-300.

18. Cf. *Commentaries*, XII, 819, where he explained to the cardinals, "We must either yield Rome or fight the French.... Before attacking the Turks we must bring peace at home. To this all our mind, all our thoughts have been bent. We fought for Christ when we defended Ferrante. We were attacking the Turks when we battered Sigismondo's lands".

19. See R. Aubenas, "The Papacy and the Catholic Church", *NCMH*, I, 76-94, for a brief discussion of the trends in the fifteenth century after the struggles over the schism.

20. In his speech to the cardinals announcing his decision to lead the crusade in person Pius acknowledged that from the western peoples he expected help only from the Italians and Burgundy. *Commentaries*, XII, 826.

21. Babinger, *Mahomet II*, pp. 185-197. On the date of the Turkish occupation of Athens and the taking of the citadel see K. M. Setton, *Catalan Domination of Athens, 1311-1388* (Cambridge, Mass., 1948), p. 210.

22. Babinger, *Mahomet II*, pp. 199-201; Inalcik, "Mehmed the Conqueror", p. 422, adds that in the same year, inspired by his success in Serbia, Mehmed moved against Amastris, a Genoese castle on the Black Sea coast.

23. Babinger, *Mahomet II*, pp. 201-203, 210-215.

24. *Ibid.*, pp. 228-236; Inalcik, "Mehmed the Conqueror", p. 422. Among the sources on the taking of Trebizond see E. H. Wilkins, "The Harvard MS of Petrarch's *Africa*", *Harvard Library Bulletin*, XII (1958), 320-325; and F. Babinger, "La Date de la prise de Trebizonde par les Turcs", *Revue des études byzantines*, VII (1949), 205-207.

25. Babinger, *Mahomet II*, pp. 244-251.

26. *Ibid.*, pp. 253-257. For a contemporary report on the fall of Mitylene see *Leonardus Chiensis de Lesbo a Turcis capta epistola Pio Papae II*, ed. Karl Hopf (Königsberg, 1866).

27. Babinger, *Mahomet II*, pp. 262-271; Inalcik, "Mehmed the Conqueror", p. 423. See also A. Burmov, "Les Problems de la conquête de la péninsule des Balkans par les Turcs", *Études historiques à l'occasion du XIe congrès international des sciences historique* (Sofia, 1960), 135-142.

28. A great deal has been done on the subject but the following are basic: Pastor, *HP*, III; Rigomer Eysser, "Papst Pius II und der Kreuzzug gegen die Türken", *Mélanges d'histoire générale*, ed. C. Marinescu (Bucharest, 1938), II, 1-134; E. Hocks, *Pius II und der Halbmond* (Freiburg, 1941). Among the important contemporary sources are Pius' *Commentaries*; Leodrisius Cribellus, *De expeditione Pii II adversus Turcos*, ed. Giulio C. Zimolo *(RISS*, XXIII, pt. v, Bologna, 1950).

29. Pastor, *HP*, III, 21-23.

30. See *Commentaries*, III, 191-279; Cribellus, *De expeditione*, pp. 86-107. On the Burgundian embassy to Mantua see d'Escouchy, *Chronique*, II, 377-392, and the oration of Jean Jouffroy in *Chroniques relatives à l'histoire de la Belgique*, III, 117-206.

31. See F. Babinger, "'Bayezid Osman' (Calixtus Ottomanus), ein Vorläufer und Gegenspieler Dschem-Sultans", *La Nouvelle Clio*, III (1951), 349-388.

32. *Epistolae Jacobi Picolomini Cardinalis Papiensis* (Milan, 1521), fol. 28^r.

33. Cf. H. Pfeffermann, *Die Zusammenarbeit*, pp. 65-81; G. Toffanin, *Lettera a Maometta II* (Naples, 1953), pp. xxiv-lvii, with the text of the "Epistola ad Mahumeten", pp. 107-177; R.W. Southern, *Western Views of Islam in the Middle Ages* (Cambridge, Mass., 1962), pp. 98-103.

34. E.g. Laudivio Zacchia, *Epistolae Magni Turci* (Naples, 1473).

35. "Epistola ad Turcarum imperatorem", cited in J. Leclercq, *Un Humaniste ermite: le bienheureux Paul Giustiniani (1476-1528)* (Rome, 1951), pp. 76, 158.

36. John of Segovia's letter to Aeneas Sylvius pleading the conciliatory approach is printed in D. Cabanelas Rodríquez, *Juan de Segovia y el problema islámico* (Madrid, 1952), pp. 343-349. Pius, in fact, prompted Cusa to undertake his important study of the Koran, *Cribratio Alchorani*.

37. "Epistola ad Mahumeten", in Toffanin, *op. cit.*, pp. 126-129.

38. R. J. Mitchell, *The Laurels and the Tiara. Pope Pius II 1458-1464* (London, 1962), pp. 171-173.

39. E.g. in the *Opera omnia* (Basel, 1571), *Europa*, pp. 394-402; *Asia*, pp. 307, 383-386. See various orations in his *Orationes politicae et ecclesiasticae*, ed. J. D. Mansi, 3 vols. (Lucca, 1755-1759); and numerous letters in Wolkan, *Der Briefwechsel*, Abt. III, Band I.

40. Cf. the remarks of Creighton, *Historical Essays*, p. 80.

41. See the introduction to the *Commentaries* by Leona C. Gabel, pp. vii-xxxviii.

42. *Commentaries*, VIII, 523-525; cf. the pope's interpretation of the significance of the discovery of the Tolfa alum mines, *ibid.*, VII, 505-507.

43. *Ibid.*, VIII, 525-530. On September 23, 1964 in the midst of the proceedings of the Vatican Ecumenical Council, in solemn processions Pope Paul VI opened three days of special masses and prayers prior to the relic's being returned to Patras as a conciliatory gesture to the Orthodox church.

44. *Ibid.*, VIII, 531-537.

45. *Ibid.*, VIII, 537-541. On Bessarion's oration see "Discours pour la translation des reliques de St. André de Patras à Rome, 12 Avril 1462", *Neohellenomnenion*, X (1913), 59-63.

46. Iorga, "Notes", *ROL*, VIII, 288, 289.

47. *Commentaries*, II, 115; cf. his remarks in the *Europa* and his *Asia* both in *Opera omnia*, pp. 394, 395, 383-386.

48. *Commentaries*, II, 115; cf. Wolkan, *Der Briefwechsel*, Abt. III, Band I, nos. 112, 166, 171, 202.

49. *Commentaries*, II, 116.

50. *Ibid.*, III, 141.

51. *Ibid.*, XII, 810.

52. *Ibid.*, XII, 822.

53. Cf. Daniel, *Islam and the West*, pp. 275ff.; D. Cabanelas Rodríguez, *Juan de Segovia*, *passim*.

54. *Commentaries*, II, 116.

55. Pius' treatment of the subject in the "Epistola ad Mahumeten" (in Toffanin, *op. cit.*, pp. 27ff.) is on only a slightly higher plane. Daniel, *Islam and the West*, p. 279, does not see it as deserving of the praise which it has received.

56. *Commentaries*, III, 192.

57. *Ibid.*, VI, 417. Cf. III, 198, 199; Pius' understanding of the authority of his office was forcefully set forth on January 18, 1460 at Mantua in the bull *Execrabilis*, described by Aubenas as a "clear affirmation of pontifical absolutism". The bull was promulgated at this time to counter in advance the opposition of the "Nationals", to the new crusade taxes. See Aubenas and Ricard, *L'Église et la Renaissance*, pp. 52, 53.

58. *Commentaries*, II, 715; III, 214; IX, 576; X, 634; XI, 741; Cf. Wolkan, *Der Briefwechsel*, Abt. III, Band I, nos. 207, 211, 291.

59. *Commentaries*, XI, 741.

60. *Ibid.*, IX, 576.

61. *Commentaries*, X, 685.

62. *Ibid.*, III, 213-215.

63. *Ibid.*, X, 637.

64. *Ibid.*, III, 256.

65. *Commentaries*, III, 254. Sforza, as we have seen was none too enthusiastic about the crusade. His wife Bianca, however, contributed to the 300 soldiers sent to Greece. On the question of the relative importance of land and naval forces we read in a

report of Vincenzo da Scalona, Mantuan ambassador to Milan, dated August 18, 1459, that the Florentine advisor to Sforza, Agnolo Acciaiuoli "...conclude la imprexa da terra doversi fare et essere necessaria, ma non esserli expediente mandarli gente italica, allegendo la ragioni etc., quella de aqua non bisognare et, se pur per alcuni rispecti ch'el toca, se volesse fare armata, ogni poca armata basta a satisfare...." G. Picotti, *La dieta di Mantova e la politica de Veneziani* (Venice, 1912), no. xi, p. 413; cf. the opinion of F. Filelfo who thought it a waste of money to provide a large fleet, Raynaldus, *Annales*, ad an. 1464, no. 23.

66. *Commentaries*, III, 254, 255.

67. *Ibid.*, III, 255; cf. IV, 309, for an adverse assessment of Italian soldiers. On the question of finances and the extremely high estimate of the Venetians which caused a new clash with the pope see Picotti, *La dieta di Mantova*, pp. 245-253 and doc. xxx, pp. 467-470.

68. *Commentaries*, III, 256-258.

69. Picotti, *La dieta di Mantova*, pp. 172-177 and doc. xviii, pp. 425-430.

70. *Ibid.*, pp. 195-200 and doc. xxiii, pp. 446-449.

71. *Ibid.*, doc. xxiiii, pp. 450-457. See also Thiriet, *La Romanie vénitienne*, pp. 353ff.

72. In his oration to the cardinals, September 23, 1463 (*Commentaries*, XII, 822-824), Pius showed that he clearly understood the difference between the two approaches. After admitting that the papal treasury was empty, that the war would cost at least 3,000,000 ducats—and that the credit of the curia was low, he concluded: "we must change to paths long disused. ...Abstinence, purity, innocence, zeal for the Faith, religious fervor, scorn of death, eagerness for martyrdom have set the Church of Rome over the whole world".

73. *Commentaries*, III, 208; XII, 815.

CHAPTER IV

The chivalric ideal

Philip the Good succeeded to the Burgundian holdings in 1419, when his father, Duke John was murdered at the hands of the Orleanists on the bridge of Montereau-faut-Yonne. He was a prince with a vision—the creation of a kingdom of Burgundy, the restoration of the ancient Middle Kingdom.[1] There were formidable obstacles to be overcome. The establishment of a strong independent power demanded severance of all ties with France and the empire, and the consolidation of his diverse lands and peoples into a unified state with common interests and effective machinery of government. Convinced of his destiny, Philip labored with the passion of a reformer determined to construct an ideal society. The ideal in this case was to be accomplished in conformance with the code of knightly chivalry. Philip envisaged and sought to build a powerful Burgundian kingdom upon the foundation of knighthood, the practice of chivalry, and the Christian faith. Burgundy would illuminate the path of true virtue, and lead, by example, western Christendom out of the decay into which it had fallen.[2] In view of the magnitude of this mission and the sustained effort required to achieve its fulfillment, one might expect Philip the Good to be the least likely of all European rulers to interest himself in the affairs of the Levant and develop an active eastern policy. We know, however, the opposite to be true. More than the kings of England and France, or even the emperor of Germany, the duke of Burgundy agitated for a crusade. His efforts were both serious and prolonged; throughout his long reign (1419-1467), he repeatedly proclaimed his intention to go to war against the Turks.[3] Thus the praises and expectations voiced from every quarter, hailing *le grand duc d'occident* as the determined enemy of the infidel, were not the result of wishful thinking or solely the product of successful Burgundian propaganda.

Geographically, Burgundy was farther removed from the Turkish menace than most of the greater European powers. The political and economic fortunes of the duchy were not directly linked with any power in the immediate vicinity of the Turkish imperium. The motives behind Philip the Good's preoccupation with the crusade may be best explained in terms of his vision, and the program by which he sought to achieve it. Philip by no means ignored practical political considerations. A prince who was seeking a crown and recognition as an independent ruler had much to gain by assuming the role of champion of the faith. Popularity and prestige throughout Christendom and the support of the papacy were useful weapons with which to face any opponent. But it was not simply political opportunism which provoked the Burgundian prince to adopt the role of crusader; it was also his personal dedication to the chivalric ideal. The true knight was the protector of religion and the warrior against all enemies of the faith. In this connection, with regard to the crusade, Huizinga wrote, "...the chivalrous ideal was implied in the nature of the enterprise itself...".[4] The crusade occupied a prominent place in Philip's plans. "He saw himself as the pillar of western ideals"; Cartellieri wrote approvingly, "he longed to avenge the insults which had been showered on the Cross. The crusading fever left no rest to princes and people, to thinkers and poets...".[5] Both Cartellieri and Huizinga have emphasized the importance of the spirit of revenge in Burgundian history.[6] The course of action which Philip followed in the early years of his rule to avenge the murder of his father is well known. There was one insult, however, greater than all the others, which went unavenged. Philip's father, John, then count of Nevers, had been one of the leaders of the crusaders who had gone down in humiliating defeat at the battle of Nicopolis. Thousands of Christian knights had died in battle or were cruelly slain afterward by the Turks. A few, among them the count of Nevers, were led into ignominious captivity, and freed only upon the payment of a huge ransom.[7]

Nicopolis, however, was not the only blemish on the Burgundian record. This same house was guilty of two most grievous breaches of the code of knightly conduct. In the popular mind, the murder of Duke John had erased the memory of the assassination of Louis of Orleans, and perhaps retrospectively atoned for it. But John's son, the hero of the chivalric ideal, was not likely to forget that his father was responsible for the slaying of a prince of the royal house of France. Extreme devotion to idealism does not prevent inconsistencies and even infractions by its most eager proponents, and Philip was no exception. In 1420, when he signed the Treaty of Troyes with England, he placed himself in opposition to his own feudal lord. Cartellieri aptly observed, "...the principle of unqualified honour and allegiance received a blow from those who had set themselves up as its most passionate devotees".[8] By joining England, the enemy of France, Philip the Good preserved and strengthened the state of Burgundy, but he also violated the fundamental tenets of his knightly faith. Psychologically and theologically salvation might be found through atonement. As the haunting specter of the charred remains of Vitry drove Louis VII to the Holy Land in the Second Crusade, so might Philip of Burgundy find expiation in a similar enterprise.[9]

Long before the fall of Constantinople Philip demonstrated his intentions of aiding the Christians of the East and fighting against the enemies of the Catholic religion. His interest in the Holy Land led him to pay for the reconstruction of the church of Our Lady of Zion at Jerusalem. At Rama he purchased a house which he turned over to the Franciscans in Palestine to run as a hospice for pilgrims. He had wood shipped from Venice to Bethlehem for the rebuilding of the roof of the church in the town of Christ's birth.[10] The knights of St. John were indebted to him for funds which enabled them to carry on the work of reconstructing their fortifications on Rhodes.[11] In 1441 a small Burgundian squadron under the command of Geoffroy de Thoisy aided the knights in their struggle against the Mameluke forces of Egypt. Again in the year 1444, in concert with the crusade which ended in the bitter failure at Varna, Philip sent a naval expedition to the East. Part of this Burgundian force, under the command of Geoffroy de Thoisy, after scouring the coast of North Africa in search of Moslem ships, joined with the knights of Rhodes in driving from the latter's stronghold, an invading force from Mameluke Egypt. The rest of Philip's vessels, under the command of Walerand de Wavrin, with some other western ships, sought unsuccessfully to prevent the troops of Murad II from passing from Asia Minor to Europe.[12]

In the two years immediately preceding the Turkish capture of the capital of Byzantium, the duke of Burgundy, moved by the frantic appeals from the East, sent ambassadors to the courts of Europe to secure help in raising an army to relieve Constantinople. The ambassadors Jean Germain, Andrieu de Humières, and Nicolas le Jaul who went to France, and Jean de Croy and Jacques de Lalaing who negotiated at Rome and Naples were all prominent councillors and servants of the duke. Envoys were also sent to Poland and to the empire. In connection with the latter embassy Ludwig Pastor cites a work entitled *Tractatus seu propositio pro subsidio fidei catholicae contra Thurcum anno domni* 1451. It was composed by a knight named Petrus Visques and a Dominican called Nicholas Laqueri, who were Philip's ambassadors to Frederick III.[14] The knight Petrus Visques was undoubtedly Pedro Vasquez of Saavedra, one of the many foreign adventurers who sought his fortune at the court of Burgundy. His career, which has never been critically studied, illustrates the appeal and attraction which the Levant still possessed for the western knight and adventurer in the fifteenth century. Whether the objective was Jerusalem or Constantinople, for men like Vasquez the crusade and the Turkish threat were neither dead issues, nor simply subjects upon which to exercise one's imagination and rhetorical ability. Prior to his mission of 1451, the Spaniard had participated in the Burgundian expedition against the Turks in 1444 and 1445.[15] In 1447 he received the sum of 186 ducats for his service under Walerand de Wavrin. Sometime in the mid-fourteen forties he was made chamberlain to Duke Philip.[16] We find him at the Feast of the Pheasant in February 1454, where his courage in the jousting attracted the attention of Mathieu d'Escouchy.[17] Olivier de la Marche wrote that Vasquez accompanied Anthony of Burgundy on his expedition against the infidels in 1463-64, and that he remained one year after Anthony returned to Burgundy, and continued to fight against the Saracens.[18] There exists in a contemporary manuscript a portrait of Pedro Vasquez, and a brief description which says he was a noble knight, councillor, and chamberlain to Philip the Good and Charles the Bold; "...le quel chevalier a este en plusieurs batailles et rencontres contre les infidels et ailleurs, par mer et par terre...". It gives the year 1477 as the date of his death.[19]

The duke of Burgundy's appeals in 1451-52 produced no tangible results.[20] At the same moment, Philip himself was forced to turn his attention to a serious problem at home. He was busily engaged with a revolt in Ghent when Constantinople fell into the hands of the Turks.[21] The news of the Turkish victory reached Burgundy in late July or early August, 1453. By letters sent from Nicholas V and Frederick III, Philip was informed of the details of the tragedy. He viewed the seizure of Constantinople by Mehmed II as a direct challenge to himself. His honor and his faith hung in the balance.[22] He quickly resolved the problem of Ghent, and turned his attention to the challenge of the infidels. His immediate program involved arousing his people in favor of the crusade; getting the nobility to pledge their personal participation in a campaign against the Turks; securing the necessary financial support from the estates; and coordinating his plans with those of the other European powers. Once again letters and envoys were dispatched to the courts of Europe. Philip went, as we have seen, in person to the council of Ratisbon. The duke ordered his councillors and scholars to study the problem, and submit recommendations to him.[23] He called meetings of the estates to raise money, and held special feasts to bring pressure upon his nobility to enlist in the crusade.[24]

His efforts reached a dramatic climax at the much-publicized feast of the pheasant held at Lille in February, 1454. The festivities, especially the banquet given on Sunday, February 17, have fascinated yet perplexed historians of Burgundy from Olivier de la Marche to Otto Cartellieri.[25] Contemporaries of Philip the Good and historians writing in the nineteenth and early twentieth centuries have been equally overawed by the fantastic dimensions of the entertainment and ceremonies of the banquet, so much so that some scholars have had difficulty believing that Philip really took the affair seriously.[26] While overwhelmed by the extravagance of the celebration, these same historians have been repelled by the excesses and vulgarity of the display, especially in view of the fact that alongside and mixed in with the worst expressions of bad taste were to be found works of the finest artists and craftsmen of the day. The historian of just a generation ago arrived at the real meaning and significance of the feast of the pheasant only through the most strenuous exercise of his analytic and perceptive powers.[27] To today's observer with the evidence of what the most absurd forms of advertising can accomplish to mesmerize the public, it is not so difficult to believe that the duke of Burgundy shrewdly played to the tastes of his audience. Here was, as Huizinga has shown, the fullest expression of all the diverse tendencies of the age. Every form of art, and much that was not art, was employed to express the most varied motifs. The whole was loosely strung together by the single thread of what the court conceived to be the tradition of chivalry.[28] As entertainment it may have been crude and showy, but it fitted the mood of the day. Philip the Good got much pleasure and expected to profit from these affairs. He believed them to be grand and magnificent reproductions of the courts of love of an earlier era. For him they combined esthetic pleasure with religious worship, courtly behavior, and political expediency. His own devotion to the heroic ideal convinced him that concrete results would be attained by cultivating them. Philip knew well the nobility of his court, and knew how to enlist their support in his favorite projects.[29]

The feast of the pheasant was planned with the greatest care. Olivier de la Marche, Jean de Lannoy, and Jean Boudault made up the committee responsible for the plans and preparations. All the talents of the court were at their disposal, and their imaginations were not to be curtailed by financial restrictions. Two lesser banquets held on January 20, and February 5, preceded the main feast. On February 17, the celebrations opened with a joust. Dressed in their finest and most colorful garments, trimmed with furs and jewels, the ducal family and other high members of the court marched in procession to the place where the joust was held. The participants were splendidly arrayed, and performed their feats with much fanfare, according to the meticulous rules of the event.[30] The preparations for the banquet were accomplished with the strictest secrecy. The great hall of the Hotel de la Salle was richly decorated with brilliant tapestries. On the banquet tables and about the room *entremets*, grandiose floats, had been arranged. Some were contrived to depict some popular theme; others were simply huge and elaborate novelties. Here was a church wherein sat four musicians who played for the guests. There, on a table, twenty-eight musicians played their numbers from inside a large pie. Apparently only one of the *entremets* touched on the main theme of the feast; directly opposite the duke's table the figure of a woman stood on a high pillar. She wore one hat of gold, studded with precious stones, and another on top of the first garnished with flowers. Her blond hair fell loosely to her feet, and around her body was draped a veil with Greek letters painted on it. Throughout the banquet spiced wine flowed from her right breast. Next to her on a lower pillar was chained a live lion, described by d'Escouchy as a most beautiful beast. Against the column, upon which the lion stood guarding the woman, was a placard with the following words in gold letters: *Ne touchiés à ma dame.* The figure of the woman represented Constantinople, and the live beast, the Turk, who had captured and ravaged the capital of Byzantium.[31]

When everyone had inspected the *entremets*, they took their proper places and the banquet began. Jugglers, musicians, falconers, and mock animals vied with one another to win the favor of the company. A three act mystery, "The Adventures of Jason at Colchis", was performed.[32] Finally the moment for the grand finale arrived. All the entertainers and the *entremets* disappeared. The hall grew silent. Suddenly a great giant, alleged to be the largest man ever seen in Burgundy, entered the room. He was dressed in a long green-striped, silken robe, and wore a turban on his head. He carried in his left hand a huge battle-axe, and with his right hand he led an elephant. The beast was draped with silk, and on its back was a tower with a damsel inside poised in a religious attitude. She was dressed in a modest white robe, which revealed her high birth and noble stature, and she wore a black mantle, indicating that she was in mourning. On her head was the white coif of a Beguine.[33]

When the elephant had entered the hall the damsel, who symbolized the holy catholic church, commanded:

> Geant, je voeul cy arrester;
> Car je voy noble compaingnie,
> A laquelle me fault parler
> Geant, je voeul cy arrester.[34]

The giant who represented the Turk only glanced at the damsel, but paid no heed until he had led the elephant directly before the duke where he stopped. Holy Church then delivered a long lamentation in a high, piteous voice:

> Hellas! Hellas! moy dolereuse,
> Triste, desplaisant, annieuse,
> Desolée, las! peu eureuse
> La plus qui soit.
> Chascun me regarde et me voit,
> Mais ame ne me recongnoit,
> Et me laisse-on en cest endroit
> En tel langueur,

Qu'ame vivant n'eut onques tel doleur!
J'ay coeur pressé d'amertume en rigueur,
Mes yeux fondans, flatrie est ma coleur,
    Qui bien y vise.
Oez mes plaintes, vous tous, ou je ravise,
Secourez moy sans y faire faintise,
Plourez mes maulx, car je suis Sainte Eglise,
    La vostre mère,
Mise à ruyne et à doleur amère,
Pilée au pié par aspre vitupère,
Et ces souffrettes, porte, soeuffre et compère
    Par voz desertes.[35]

The losses to the church are evident everywhere, she proclaims! Her houses
and lands are deserted. Many of her children have perished, some in the
fields, others in captivity. The domain of the church is in the hands of infidels.
Thus does she cry for aid, burdened, constrained, and grieved—running from
place to place, begging succor! She has appealed to the emperor and the king
of France. She has informed other kings and princes of the evils she has suffered, and implored their help.

Aussy faiz-je à ceste compaingnie.
Pour mon ayde, l'un à l'autre s'alye,
Car Dieu le veult, qui nul bien fait n'oublie.
. . . .

O toy, o toy, noble duc de Bourgoingne,
Filz de l'Eglise et frère à ses enfans,
Entens à moy; si pense à ma besoingne,
Poins en ton coeur la honte et la vergoingne,
Les griefz remors qu'en moy je porte et sens.
Les infidelles par milliers et par cens,
Sont triumphans en leur terre dampnée,
Là où jadis solois estra honourée.

Vous autres princes, puissans et honorez,
Plourez mes maulx, larmoiez mes doleurs;
Ma joye est née, s'emprenre le volez
A moy vengier, que bien faire devez,
En servant Dieu et en querant honneur:
Par mes enfans je suis en ce malheur:

Par eux seray, se Dieu plaist, secourue,
Sy requiers Dieu de consel et d'alhue.

Vous, chevalliers, qui portez la thoizon,
N'oubliez pas le très divin service,
Aussi les autres nés de bonne maison,
O gentilz hommes! vecy belle occoison,
Pour acquerir de los je benefice:
Mon secours est pour jones gens propices;
Les noms croistront et l'ame enrichira
Du service que chascun me fera.

Donc en amour le Dieu premièrement,
En en faveur du nom et de noblesse,
Je te requier acertes et fermement,
Mon amé filz, pour toute gentillesse,
Par tout m'en voy, car mon oevre presse.
Mon fait piteux, hellas! qu'on ne m'oublie.
Soubz tel espoir Dieu vous doint bonne vie.[36]

At the end of the lament a number of heralds-at-arms came forward with the King-at-arms of the Order of the Golden Fleece. The latter carried a richly decorated pheasant, and was followed by two ladies of the court who were escorted by two knights of the Golden Fleece. When they had all arrived before the table of the duke of Burgundy, and bowed before him, Golden Fleece presented the pheasant to his master and the court. He explained that it was an ancient custom of kings, princes, and nobles to swear binding oaths upon some noble bird. Philip the Good rose, and glancing sadly at Holy Church, atop the elephant, addressed the assembled company: "Je voue à Dieu mon createur, à la glorieuse Vierge Marie, aux dames et au faisant, que je feray et entretenray ce que je baille par escript."[37]

The lengthy vow of Philip the Good that Golden Fleece then read aloud clearly set forth the conditions under which the duke would take the cross. If it pleased the Most Christian King, his lord, ". . .to take the cross and expose his body for the defense of the Christian faith, to resist the damnable menace of the Grand Turk of the infidels", Philip promised to join him. If the king of France failed to go in person, but gave command of the French forces to a prince of the blood, or another chief lord, Philip promised to render obedience to the king's deputy. And if the king of France had nothing to do with the crusade at all, but other Christian princes took the cross, Philip vowed to go with them providing his lands were at peace and their security guaranteed. If the Grand Turk desired to meet him in individual combat,

Philip, for the defense of the Christian faith, and with the aid of God and His Sweet Mother, was willing to oblige him. Holy Church, visibly pleased, thanked the duke and blessed him, then turned to the court and admonished the knights to follow the example of their lord.[38]

At this point the giant led the elephant and Holy Church from the hall. Some of the greater lords then swore their oaths aloud. The rest were ordered to submit them in writing to Golden Fleece. Most of the oaths followed along the lines of that made by Philip the Good. The lords of Burgundy swore on the pheasant and before God and His Holy Mother, and to the ladies of the court, to serve their lord in the defense of the Christian religion. Some of the oaths were brief and relatively modest. Some, in carefully contrived stipulations, revealed that the swearer had no intention of undertaking the crusade. Others made boastful claims and promises. Several vowed to maintain various ascetic practices until they had taken the field and met the enemy.[39] Anthony, the bastard son of Philip, vowed to meet a Turk, in any manner his enemy might choose, and to send his challenge to the enemy camp.[40] The count d'Estampes vowed to accompany his lord on the crusade for "...la deffence de la Foy crestienne, et resister à la dampnable emprinse du Grand Turcq et des infidelles...". He too, offered to challenge any of the "...grans princes ou seigneurs de la compaingnie dudit Grant Turcq et tenant sa loy, qui ait volenté de avoir afaire à moy corps à corps, deux à deux, trois à trois..."[41]. Hugh de Lannoy promised to join his lord, the duke of Burgundy on the crusade "...pour resister à puissance à l'encontre de l'empereur des Turcqs, ennemy de la saincte Foy crestienne...". If age and infirmities prevented his going personally, he vowed to send two men-of-arms and two archers, whose expenses he would pay for one year.[42] The lord of Honnelzin, Jean de Bos pledged that when they had joined battle with the Turks, he intended to cast the sultan's banner to the ground or die in the attempt.[43] Claude de Thoulongon swore to fight one of the Turk's people, on horse or on foot, either before his lord the duke of Burgundy, or if his opponent insisted, before the Grand Turk himself, and in his own camp.[44] The lord of Vaulx, Hugh de Longueval promised not to drink any wine until he had tasted the blood of an infidel and enemy of the faith.[45]

The question of the sincerity of the oaths has been answered by Huizinga.[46] While certainly some of the nobles had no intention of taking the cross, and were merely play-acting, others, inspired by the enthusiasm of the moment, were, or thought themselves to be, quite serious in their proclamations. For us, the chief interest in the oaths lies in what they reveal of the Burgundian nobility's conception of the crusade, and what they thought about the Turks. As for the crusade, there is little doubt; it was presented in terms of what was believed to have been the religio-chivalric expedition of the Middle Ages—a conception bred not of a knowledge of the true past but from reading the *chansons du geste*. It was an affair of honor, the work of men of noble blood, indeed the prerogative as well as the obligation of knighthood. There was one major departure from the customary projects for a crusade: the Burgundian nobility had learned that the Turks stood in the path to the Holy Land. The emphasis placed upon the Turks in the vows clearly indicates that Philip and his paladins recognized that the armies of Mehmed II constituted their chief problem. Despite the appeals to the memory of Godfrey of Bouillon, and the other trappings of the medieval crusade, they knew only too well that before the Holy Sepulcher could again be in Christian hands, the Turk must be defeated and driven from Europe.[47]

The influence of the heroic ideal did not stop here, however, but as in times past it led Christian knights to endow their opponents with their own ideals and characteristics.[48] Alongside the popular characterizations of the Turk as a primitive savage, there emerged from the vows sworn on the pheasant an Ottoman nobility imbued with the qualities of chivalry. Turkish society was construed to have had a social stratification comparable to the structure of western society. The Turkish soldiers were expected to accept and entertain in knightly fashion personal challenges. It was assumed that the Turks would govern themselves in these matters in accordance with the rules of conduct current in the West. In a moment of excited dedication to the heroic ideal, the Burgundian courtiers represented the Turks as the enemy of the Christian religion, but not of courtly chivalry. They credited the Turks with having a code of honor, and comparable rules of conduct. The noble Turk was viewed as a worthy opponent of the Christian knight.

Concern with the Turks and the world of the Levant was not, however, solely a matter of court politics. A heightened curiosity, even fascination, with things oriental was exhibited at numerous public celebrations and festivals. The citizens of towns saw fit to include among the displays and floats with which they decorated the routes of parades and processions, some dealing with Moslem subjects or the crusade. For the visit of Philip the Good in 1455 the people of Mons prepared such tableaux along the route of his entrance. One, for example, recalled the events of the fourth crusade and the successful capture of Constantinople.[49] At Louvain in the same year the duke was reminded of the Turkish peril and his duty to Christendom by similar representations including a scene which depicted the rulers of Islam already in defeat and in chains falling at the duke's feet.[50]

After the feast of Lille perhaps the most pretentious and elegant display of pomp and pagentry was held in conjunction with the wedding of Charles the Bold and Margaret of York in the summer of 1468. At such affairs it was the *pas d'armes* which absorbed the attention and energies of everyone. In a complicated and elaborate ritual a variety of currently popular themes and motifs were carried out in the rich if stilted imagery and symbolism. On this occasion it was the half-brother of the duke, the bastard Anthony, who defended an *arbre d'or*. One of the challengers, Jean de Chassa, drew upon levantine lore in the composition of his role as a knight errant. By way of explanation he bore a letter addressed to the ladies. The document revealed that he had been in the service of a *dame d'Esclavonie* who had spurned his supplications. He had then become an ascetic recluse until his lady, taking pity, had sent a maiden to cure him of despair and accompany him for one year in his travels. He now appeared in Burgundy, as the noble Saladin and other infidels before him had journeyed to France in search of adventure, and begged permission to joust with the knight of the Golden Tree. Having been granted his request he marched onto the field preceded by two Moors and a fool, escorted by the maiden in whose train were four noblemen with long beards dressed as Turks and bearing the legend, *Le Chevalier Esclave*.[51]

The oriental vogue, of course, was not peculiar to Burgundy; but it was prevalent especially in those societies in which the ideals of chivalry weighed heavily in the scale of values. Another participant in the *pas d'armes* of 1468, Anthony of Luxembourg, count of Roussy and Brienne, entered the lists locked in a make-believe fortress led by a dwarf who bore a key and a petition addressed to the ladies who alone had the power to release the prisoner. The dwarf, who had come from Constantinople, was borrowed by the count from the king of England. Whether the unfortunate creature was Greek or Turk we cannot be sure. But his successor, who no doubt provided similar amusement for the English court, was Turkish. He was seen by Sir John Paston who wrote in March 1470: "Ther is comen a newe litell Torke, whych is a wele vysaged felawe, off the age off xl. yere; and he is lower than Manuell by a hanffull, and lower then my lytell Tom by the schorderys, and mor lytell above hys pappe; and he hathe, as he seyde to the Kynge hymselffe, iij. or iiij sonys, chyldre, iche one off hem as hyghe and asse lykly as the Kynge. . ."[52]

The chronicler Jean Molinet described how the marriage arrangements between Charles of Austria and Claude, the daughter of the French king, Louis XII were celebrated at Lyons, August 12, 1501. An unusual dance was performed by the members of the court. One couple attired as a French shepherd and spouse were followed by three other couples dressed in the distinctive garb of Germany, Spain, and Italy. Each pair performed a dance typical of their country. With the completion of these routines there appeared an unaccompanied male. He was very tall, with a stern countenance, and richly but strangely dressed. "Il se forcha de querir dame ou damoiselle pour faire son debvoir comme les aultres, mais il fut du tout refusé", continued the chronicler; "dont, par grant despit qu'il concheut, en son corage, rua sur le pavé ung sceptre qu'il tenoit en sa main, sy le brisa en plusieurs pièces et retourna mortelement confus". Molinet explained that the stranger represented the Turk who menaced France, Spain, Germany, and Italy. The dancers, who remained united against him, signified the union, peace, and accord of the Christian nations. A unity which the marriage was to strengthen so that the Turk might never assail them.[53]

Courtly chivalry, the holy war, and the Ottoman peril were the stock-in-trade of the authors of contemporary romance literature. As the medieval crusade had given rise to the *chansons du geste*, the Turkish advance and the efforts to oppose it now inspired the literary proponents of a chivalric revival. Medieval legends and the new knowledge of the Levant were combined and adapted by these writers to fit their own didactic and moralistic purposes. Their Turks were often conventional types which bore little resemblance to reality. The author of *Le Petit Jehan de Saintré* sent his hero on the sacred crusade into Prussia. There he opposed the mightiest Saracen host encountered by Christians since the days of Mohammed! The Saracens were led by the soldans, kings, and princes of India, Persia, Syria, Egypt, Assyria, and Asia. The description of the enemy's order of battle reveals the imaginative character of the whole account:

> Now in the first company Abzin chose to be, which was at that time the Grand Turk of Persia and bore on his banner *gules, with a great Turkish sword, in bend, argent, hilted azure, crossed and pommelled or;* and in the great pride of his might, which was thirty of two-score thousand horse and upwards of an hundred thousand foot, he held the Christians as naught.
>
> In the second company rode Zizaach, that called himself Emperor of Carthage, and bore on his banner *sable, two horses' heads endorsed or;* and Almoch, Soldan of Babylon, who bore a banner all *or* with no other charges; and Azahul, Soldan of Mabaloch, attended by sixty thousand horsemen; and after them, an hundred and sixty thousand foot.
>
> In the third company were the Kings of Greater Armenia, of Fez, and of Aleppo, and Bagazul, Lord of Wallachia; who had two-score thousand horse and three hundred or four hundred thousand footmen, out of Armenia, Barbary, Russia, Samara, and Tartary; so many that all the face of the land was covered with them.[54]

Le Petit Jehan—"all armed upon his right puissant courser, both he and his courser richly caparisoned with cloth of gold painted with his arms, and

93

upon his basinet a passing fair plume, shewing high above all others"—directly challenged and slew the Grand Turk; and personally struck down the banner of the Turks. Although the triumph of the Christian host was never held in doubt, our author did not fail to credit the enemy with putting up a courageous and valiant defense. But their valor earned them neither victory nor mercy; for on the morning after the battle while searching for their fallen comrades the victors "found many Saracens stricken but not yet dead, lying beneath their horses and stretching out their hands for to yield them; but all were put to sword".[55]

Romanticized accounts of the early crusades provided the perfect frame for elaborating the lessons on chivalry. The wonder-working power of knightly behavior was illustrated in countless ways; but perhaps the most telling was its alleged effect upon even the Moslem opponent. In this connection the legends of Saladin were particularly favored. Thus Ghillebert de Lannoy, councillor of Duke Philip the Good, concluded his *L'Instruction d'un jeune prince*, with a chapter entitled "Cy parle de l'ordre et estat de chevalerie et comment on le doit entendre". Here he demonstrated the character and influence of chivalry as a moral force by a tale in which the Christian hero, Hugh de Tabarie, has fallen into the hands of the mighty Saladin. When Hugh protested his inability to pay a ransom, fixed at the huge sum of 100,000 besants, the Turk replied: "Vous la payerez bien. . . car vous estes bon chevalier et hardy, et les preux et vaillans hommes vous donront assez". Arrangements were then made for Hugh to depart for a year in order to raise the ransom; but before dismissing the knight Saladin made one request: "Hues, dist le roy, je voeul que me moustrés la manière comment l'en fait chevaliers en la cristienté". Hugh replied, "Sire, sur qui le moustreray?" "A moy mesmes", was the sultan's response. The rest of the story relates how the Christian hero inducted the Moslem ruler into the orders of knighthood with the miraculous, yet expected, result that Saladin then showed him the highest honors and courtesy. In the conclusion Hugh was richly rewarded, and accompanied by other Christian knights whom Saladin had freed, and an escort of twenty Sarracen warriors, he was safely returned to his own lands.[56]

Levantine lore and Turkish themes were no less favored by the authors of those works of a less edifying character which were intended for a wider public. One of the best known is *Les Cent nouvelles nouvelles*. Without departing from his favorite theme of marital infidelity, the author of the sixty-ninth *nouvelle*, entitled, "L'honnête femme a deux maris", expressed his views on the Turks.[57] The tale deals with a knight who was captured at Nicopolis, and his loyal and loving wife who waited nine years for his return, but finally married anew. Of the Christians captured by the Turk, the writer declared many were killed and persecuted, ". . .les autres furent enchartes a perpétuite, les autres condammez à faire office de clerc d'esclave. . .". The hero of the sixty-ninth *nouvelle* fell in the last category, and bore a miserable servitude for nine years. At last, with the aid of some Christians he was freed and returned to his home in Flanders. His wife, who had only married the second time when convinced by her friends that her husband was dead, learning of his return, fell into remorse, refused nourishment and died within three days.[58]

It is from the popular literature that we get some indication that not everyone felt the Turk to be such a grave menace as the court made him out to be. The anonymous versifier of the following lines seems to have been unconvinced of the necessity of the crusade, and saw it as a scheme devised by Anthony, the lord of Croye to enhance his own power.

> Le voiage de Turquerie
> Fut machiné par ton conseil,
> Et cuida par ta triquerie
> Que ce puissant duc imparel
> Deust preparer son apparel
> Pour aller mectre le Turcq jus;
> Mais Jhesus Christ le vray consel
> Le vault preserver de telz jus![59]

An anti-Burgundian Tournaisien seized the occasion of the collapse of the expedition of 1463-64 to satirize Anthony the Great Bastard, and the crusade. In the sixth verse of his *Ce sont les souhais de Tournay fais en l'an mil iiii^c et LXVI*, we read:

> Le quint fut homme de fachon:
> Il souhaida a mains ung pattart,
> D'autant que vailli la renchon
> Du turcq à monsieur le bastard.
> S'eust autant d'escus pour sa part
> Pour avoir plus grande sacquie,
> Que ceulx de dessoubz son estandart
> Tuerent des gens de Turquie.[60]

But a pro-Burgundian minstrel in his *Les Menestrels pleurent cette mort*, has the departed Philip the Good reminding the same Anthony of his promise to fight the Turks:

> Mon fils bastard, vaillant et preu
> Je te supplie au départir,

De tenyr foi, promesse, et veu,
A ton seigneur, sans foy partir.[61]

The lines of Jean Wauquelin in his *Cronicques des faiz de feurent Monseigneur Girart de Roussillon*, appropriately summarize the more widely held view of Duke Philip:

Sa banniere par tous pays
Est cogneute tres grandement,
Car par elle sont envays
Et Turs et Sarrasins souvent:
Sa valeur, plus rade que vent,
Vole par tout en grant cremeur
Renommer se fait vaillamment
Phelippe de Bourgoingne seigneur.[62]

For the better part of Philip's reign the Turkish problem was the cause of feverish activity and lively debate at the court of Burgundy. The duke participated personally or sent representatives to the succession of diets and congresses held in Germany and Italy. Envoys to and from Naples, Rome, France, the empire, Portugal, and Hungary regularly appeared before the court, received their instructions or reported on their missions. A voluminous correspondence supported these efforts and kept Philip informed of the latest events affecting the prospects of the crusade. Embassies from the East, refugees, travelers, adventurers, and even Turkish prisoners, excited the imagination of court and countryside with their exotic dress and customs and sensational stories.[63] But the problem was also the object of much sober and critical study. However idealistic his devotion to the crusade may have been, in his planning Philip was practical and business-like. Ardent prosecution of a visionary policy, in this case the crusade conceived of as a chivalric enterprise, but executed with scrupulous regard for pragmatic and temporal considerations, was characterictic of princely behavior in the Renaissance. While he may have expected the Turks to comply with his own knightly principles of warfare, and indeed was prepared to meet the Grand Turk in personal combat, the duke of Burgundy harbored no illusions about the Ottomans' military capabilities. Nicopolis was not only a blot on the honor of his house, it was a harsh reminder that more than courage and dedication were necessary to defeat the Turks. Philip recognized the need for thorough planning and adequate preparations. Thus in addition to his diplomatic negotiations in search of allies and material aid he gave particular attention to the matter-of-fact problems of finance, military intelligence, and strategy.

Success depended not only upon the enthusiasm of the Burgundian nobility. Such a costly venture required the financial support of all his subjects. In order to realize the highest returns it was necessary to appeal to the estates. But were the merchants and tradesmen of the Lowlands likely to be sympathetic to appeals such as that issued at the feast of Lille? It may have been, as Arthur Ferguson has said of their fellowtownsmen across the channel, that the commoners ". . .had as yet no other measure of worldly sophistication than that provided by the forms of chivalry".[64] Unquestionably they were much moved by the spectaculars staged by the court; and the wealthier among them endeavored to emulate the habits and manners of the nobility to whose estate they sometimes aspired. In matters of high policy or questions which did not touch their daily lives, their opinions ". . .were largely fashioned in the castle rather than the cottage. . .".[65] But in such sensitive areas as taxation and increased government control we know that the common folk were the source of significant reform impulses—that the traffic in ideas was ascending as well as the reverse. When it came to the matter of financial support for the duke's ambitious programs, his subjects had some thoughts of their own, as the people of Ghent had so forcefully demonstrated. It is in this context that we must place the appeal, preserved in Chastellain, delivered in the name of Philip by Louis du Chesne before the estates of Holland and Zeeland at La Haye in November 1455.[66] Chastellain has given us a word-picture of the meeting worth quoting: "Sy y vinrent au jour ordonné les prélas du pays, samblablement les barons et nobles d'Hollande et Zeelands, avecques les bonnes villes en députation notable. Et le duc", the chronicler continued, "soy veuillant abrégier en ses affaires, et assis en dais richement paré, leur fit dire et remonter droit-là par la vouche d'un maistre Loys du Chesne la cause de leur mand, et pour quoy droit-là les avoit fait convenir."[67] In the name of Philip, du Chesne greeted the assembly. He apologized for the duke's long absence from Holland, but explained that many problems had kept him away. He assured them that they had not been forgotten, and thanked them for their continued obedience and loyalty. Turning at once to the main problem, du Chesne described briefly the growing menace of the Turks, how they had occupied Greece, attacked the church, and forced Christians to submit to their will. For many years the Turks had done great damage, and perpetrated evils which affected all Christianity.[68] Within three or four years past, a new Grand Turk had ascended the throne, a cruel enemy of God, full of arrogance, and aspiring to temporal glory. Usurping the prerogatives of God, even as Lucifer, he intends to invade and to subject to his power all the kingdoms of the world. He claims that he is greater and

97

more powerful than Alexander, and to demonstrate his prowess he has seized Constantinople.[69]

Du Chesne described the horrors of the sack of Constantinople, the insults sustained by the Catholic religion, the suffering of the emperor and the Greek people. He continued, explaining that when the emperor Frederick III heard the unhappy news, he wrote to Duke Philip, as one of the first princes of the empire, and requested him to attend a council at Ratisbon. Philip responded to the emperor's summons, went to Ratisbon, and before the collected assembly declared his intention to offer resistance to the cruel tyrant, the Grand Turk with all the power at his command. The duke now appealed to the estates for their support, that he might fulfill his holy vow. Du Chesne recalled the exploits of the noble Baldwin of Flanders, to whose glorious name and reputation the Turkish conquest was a direct insult. He declared that Duke Philip felt compelled to follow in the steps of his glorious predecessor, and to avenge this insult to his name. At the same time the duke was moved to fight in the name and sign of the Cross, against the enemies of Christendom; and to this end he had sent embassies to the pope in Rome, to the emperor, and to other princes to secure their unity, accord, and assistance in the project. He informed the king of France of all that had transpired at Ratisbon, and of his intention to take the cross. Philip, du Chesne continued, has requested Charles VII's leave to go against the Turks, and has asked the king to guarantee his safety and the protection of his lands in his absence. Having received the king's permission and blessing, Duke Philip now desired to inform the people of Holland and Zeeland, as well as their neighbors in Flanders, of his plans. He pleaded for their aid and assistance in this holy work, which was the responsibility of all Christian people. For the expedition he needed much money and many men. He appealed to the pride of the citizens that they might not be disgraced by a force insufficient in strength and arms, and he prayed that they would be generous in their support of this campaign which sought to relieve Christianity from the grave peril.[70]

In his quest for information and what was required for a successful expedition, Philip virtually transformed the Burgundian court into a seminar for Turkish studies. All available materials were collected and carefully examined. The duke's secretaries, Guyot d'Angers, David Aubert, de Hesdin, Droin Dueret, and Jean Miélot, were ordered to copy and translate descriptions of the East, accounts of the Turks, and crusade plans. Several contemporary miniatures portray Miélot, a monk of Saint Pierre de Lille, presenting the duke with books he had translated into French. Among his many works two at least dealt with the eastern question. One was the *Description of the Holy Land* by the German Dominican, Burchard of Mount Zion. Chiefly an account of the land and people of Syria and Palestine, the book was originally written in 1280, but was well-known in the fifteenth century and was printed for the first time in 1475 in the *Rudimentum noviciorum* (Lübeck: Lucas Brandis).[71] Miélot also probably translated the *Advis de Messire Jehan Torzelo*, a crusade plan first published at the council of Florence, March 16, 1439. Its author, described as "serviteur et chambellan de l'empereur de Constantinoble", claimed he had spent a dozen years at the Grand Porte and regarded himself as an authority on Turkish affairs. The *Advis* contains an estimate of the Turkish forces as well as a detailed discussion of the size and composition of the crusading force and an overall plan of operations. Torzelo called for a Latin army of 80,000 men. They were to proceed by the land route through Hungary after which they were to be divided into three contingents to move against the Turks by way of Vidnic, Belgrade, and Pedra. With the help of Albanians, Greeks, Serbians, and Wallachians, he predicted victory over the Turks in less than a month! Torzelo was equally optimistic about the recapture of the Holy Land. All this was to be accomplished with little reliance on sea power. He allowed for a fleet of twenty galleys to support the campaign but felt it was not essential to the success of the expedition.[72]

The pragmatic side of Philip may be seen by the fact that he was not taken in by Torzelo's optimism, nor was he ready to risk his resources in an expedition based on dated information and the chance reports of self-styled experts. Together with the establishment of a more permanent and professional diplomatic service, Renaissance princes now gave considerable attention to gathering accurate and timely information on friend and foe alike. Merchants and diplomats regularly doubled as spies.[73] And when the occasion demanded special espionage agents were dispatched to accomplish specific missions. Less than two years after coming to power, Philip joined with Henry V of England in sending Ghillebert de Lannoy to the Levant to gather the necessary information for a crusade. The evidence found in Lannoy's own account of his journey suggests that he was charged with a double task: to visit the East-European Christian rulers and inform them of the willingness of the sovereigns he was representing to participate in the crusade, and to urge them to compose their differences. Clearly, he was instructed to travel through the Mediterranean territories under Moslem rule, and to observe and report his findings.[74]

Ghillebert de Lannoy's report has little in common with most of the numerous plans for a crusade produced during the fourteenth and fifteenth centuries. It is a careful intelligence study, a sober and factual description of proposed areas of operation. Its author includes detailed information about harbors, port facilities, fortifications, demography, and political, social and, economic conditions. It is almost completely free from the fanciful notions that the majority of his generation held. His tales about Prester John, and his placing the source of the Nile in India and in the Earthly Paradise are notable exceptions.[75]

He begins with an account of the port of Alexandria as one approaches it from the sea, describes its configuration and its position in relation to the city, and gives exact figures on the depth of the harbor. Lannoy enumerates the walls, brays, fosses, and towers on the seaward side of the city, and points out that between the old and new ports, there is a strip of land about a mile in length, on which are located mosques and cemeteries, and which, he suggests, might be used as a beach-head. He depicts Alexandria as a very large and impressive city, enclosed with high walls bristling with many towers. The city, he writes, is seated on firm soil, conducive to successful mining operations. But the fortifications and houses are all constructed of a soft stone that crumbles easily. He explains how the city is supplied with water once a year by a canal from the Nile. Although many people are to be seen in the narrow streets, the place is largely depopulated and many of its buildings are in ruins. Lannoy concludes with a note on the Christian community and its treatment by its Moslem rulers.[76]

Rosetta, Damietta and Cairo he treats in a similar fashion. The latter city, unlike Alexandria, is heavily populated, and a great center of international trade. After giving an account of the lay-out of Cairo and its defenses, he turns to the government of the Mamelukes and its military organization, analyzes the rigid class structure of Egyptian society and tells of the wretched condition of the native population, of the warlike nature of the Arabs in the countryside, and of the plight of the Christian minority groups. Next he contrasts the topography and peoples of Egypt with those of Syria. He then provides a careful survey of the Nile, from above Cairo to Damietta. In Syria and Palestine he describes the terrain, harbors, and fortifications of Jaffa, Acre, Sur, Saida, and Beirut, and inland the town of Rama, and the cities of Jerusalem and Damascus.[77]

Since he had been prevented from visiting Turkey, Lannoy includes little information about the Ottoman military regime; but he explains the causes of the civil war then being fought among the relatives of the deceased Mehmed I, and the role that the Greeks played in it. Having passed Gallipoli on his way to Rhodes, he is able to say something of its fortifications and harbor facilities, and notes that it was the Turks' main naval base. He also describes the fortress opposite Gallipoli on the Asian shore which controlled the passage to and from the two continents, commenting that, if an enemy held it, the Turks would have "no sure passage from one to the other".[78]

Less than ten years after Lannoy's return, Philip the Good charged another of his court councillors with a similar assignment. Like his predecessor, Bertrandon de la Broquière was knowledgeable in military and civilian affairs. His official report, entitled *Le Voyage d'outremer*, shows its author as a spirited, daring, and resourceful personality, possessing extraordinary powers of observation and judgment. La Broquière sailed from Venice aboard a pilgrim galley on May 8th, 1432. He went to the holy places in and about Jerusalem and traveled extensively in Palestine and Syria, visiting Acre, Nazareth, Beirut, and Damascus. It was at Damascus that he gained the confidence of a Turk named Khodja Baraq, the leader of a Moslem pilgrim caravan traveling from Mecca to the old Turkish capital of Brusa. The Turk allowed La Broquière to join the caravan; and he disguised himself in Turkish dress—vermilion boots with spurs attached, fustian drawers, a linen girdle, a long white robe, and a white turban. He purchased a horse, *tarquais*, Damascus blade, which he greatly prized, and a kettle drum. In Damascus, too, where he met Jacques Coeur, La Broquière obtained a makeshift Turkish vocabulary from a Jewish merchant; and, on his first night out, he read from his list the appropriate phrases for obtaining barley and straw, much to the amusement of his Ottoman companions. These fellow travelers befriended him and began teaching him their language; so that, by the time he reached Brusa, he no longer needed his vocabulary. He notes that from Antioch on to Brusa the natives all spoke Turkish, which, he adds, is "a very beautiful language, concise and easy enough to understand".[79]

Of the Turks themselves, La Broquière has much to say. He observes that they are accustomed to a rough life, subsisting on little and disregarding physical comforts. Yet they maintain a pleasant disposition, entertaining themselves with songs that commemorate their past history and the deeds of native heroes. They are also generous and willingly share their food with strangers, a thing that Christians never do! They are a handsome people; the men bearded and of medium height and strength. He adds, however, that the common saying, "as strong as a Turk", is not accurate; for he believes that most Christians were more than their match. They are, none the less, diligent, well disciplined and practical. La Broquière discusses their religion, but acknowledges that the Turks do not always live up to it. He tells an amusing story of a drinking party he attended with five Turks at the home of a Greek in Hamah, the ancient Epiphania, which almost ended in a brawl.[80]

At Kutahieh his career as an intelligence agent nearly came to an end. A Turkish official from the court of Alaeddin Ali, son of Sultan Murad II, and governor of the province of Amassia, recognized La Broquière as a westerner and accused him of being a spy. The Turk declared that if he were a pilgrim or a merchant, he would have returned home by ship from Syria. La Broquière gave the excuse that the Ventians and Genoese were at war, and that the sea-route was unsafe. Apparently the Turk was reassured; and, when he learned that La Broquière came from Burgundy, his interest was aroused; for he declared that he himself had been to the West, visited Paris, and served under a mercenary captain named Barnabo; at which the astonished Burgundian conjectured that "he was one of those who had been taken prisoner in the battle of Hungary, when my lord Duke John was prince".[81]

From Kutahieh the caravan moved on to Brusa, which La Broquière described at some length. He was particularly impressed by a large castle belonging to Murad II. He learned that the Sultan housed some fifty wives there and came often to amuse himself by boating with them. He also visited a market place where Christian slaves were sold, and lamented the pitiful sight of Christian men and women squatting in rows on benches waiting to be purchased. Traveling in the company of Genoese merchants, he continued to Pera, where he met a Milanese ambassador named Benedetto Folco da Forli, on his way to the Sultan's court to negotiate a peace between Hungary and the Turks, who allowed La Broquière to accompany him. After a short stay in Constantinople, they set out for Adrianople where they appeared before the sultan.[82]

La Broquière draws a vivid picture of the Porte of the Grand Turk. He describes Murad as short and stocky, having the face of a Tartar, with high cheek bones, dark complexion, a large crooked nose, little eyes, and a round beard. The sultan's pleasures include hunting, women, boys, and, especially, wine. But he is a kind, generous, and peaceful ruler, which is lucky for Christendom; if the sultan were to mobilize all his forces, he would have no trouble in seizing much of Europe. La Broquière praises the sultan's government, and discusses the administration of justice, the system of taxation, the rules of the pashas, the organization of the Porte, its officials and its protocol.[83]

Thence he proceeds to an analysis of the Turkish army, its composition, weapons, and tactics. The sultan could raise in Greece an army of 120,000 men, which included 4,000 or 5,000 of his own slaves. About half this force, or 60,000 men, La Broquière considered to be effective and well armed, each man having a horse, *tarquais* and sword. The rest were not worth much, poorly armed and unhorsed, in some instances carrying no more than a club. To muster this force, the sultan must pay eight aspers to each cavalryman and five aspers to the foot soldiers. La Broquière also showed great interest in the condition of the sultan's finances. The ruler collected annually 2,500,000 ducats in rents and tribute, and according to one source, had then a treasure of 1,000,000 ducats, but, according to another, only half that much. The

V: Turkish troops
(Guillaume Caoursin, *Obsidionis Rhodiae descriptio*. Ulm, 1496).

wealth of his slaves and his women our agent estimated at 1,000,000 in gold; his plate he valued at the same figure. He concluded that, were the Grand Turk to give nothing away for a single year, he would save 1,000,000 ducats. As for the troops of his household, numbering 5,000, both cavalry and infantry, he merely paid them their wages. Beyond these forces, there were 30,000 men in Greece, holding land from the sultan, who were ordered to hold themselves ready to fight wherever he led them. Similarly, he had awarded a number of great seigniories in Turkey, whose owners occupied them on sufferance and were bound to serve him with a certain number of men. In time of war, the troops raised from such sources cost him no more than in peace time. Indeed, when the sultan mobilized he made money, because the troops from Turkey, when crossing to Greece, had to pay the comarch five aspers per horse and three per man. If they crossed the Danube, they paid similar sums. The sultan also had the right to claim one-fifth of all prisoners of war. Finally, La Broquière noted that a large part of the army, which had been recently in Greece, was made up of Christians from Serbia, Albania, Bulgaria, and elsewhere, and that many Christian slaves fought in the Turkish ranks.[84]

In Greece La Broquière witnessed several mass conversions of Greek Christians to Islam. The Turkish soldiers turned out in full dress, and paraded through the towns with loud fanfares. On these occasions they wore handsome coats of mail made of tiny links, and, to our Burgundian traveler, they resembled pictures he had seen of the soldiers of Julius Caesar. Their armor reached half way down the thigh, and had attached to it a piece of silk cloth which fell to the calf of the legs. They wore pointed white head pieces, half a foot in height, to which were secured four pieces of metal, or *clinques*, on the front, back, and two sides, designed to ward off sword-blows. Over these helmets they usually wore another head piece made of iron wire. Many were richly decorated and cost from forty to fifty ducats, while others cost only a ducat or two, but were strong enough to resist the cut of a sword.[85]

The richer Turkish soldiers carried a bow, *tarquais*, and sword, the last an excellent weapon. Some also carried a large mace, a brutal instrument, especially when used against an unprotected shoulder of arm. Some Turks had small wooden bucklers, which covered them well on horseback when they used the bow, at which they were most expert. The Turkish soldier, he reported, was highly obedient to his commander, for disobedience might be punished by death. La Broquière, who was much impressed with the high degree of discipline maintained in the sultan's army, attributed the better part of the Turks' successes to this fact: ". . .it is one of the things to which they owe their greatest triumphs and conquests in war, far surpassing, alas, those of the kingdom of France". Turkish military intelligence, like their discipline, was superior to that of western armies. They always knew in advance, wrote the Burgundian, when any Christian power was going to attack them. With this foreknowledge, the Grand Turk assembled his forces two or three days' journey from the place where he expected to meet his enemy. Meanwhile, his scouts watched the enemy's movements. Then, suddenly, in a surprise maneuver, the Turks sprang upon them. In executing this action, such secrecy was maintained that one hundred Christian soldiers made more noise than ten thousand Turks. They began their movement from an assembly area, then proceeded to a line of departure from which they launched their attack. To the beating of a kettle-drum, the leading troops marched off and were followed by the rest in continuous file. Their horses were especially trained for this type of action. Being lightly armed, the Turks were able in one night of forced marching to cover the same distance they would normally cover in three days.[86]

When they arrived at the place selected to meet the enemy, they divided into several groups. The number and size of the groups depended on how numerous they were, and on the condition of the terrain. They then prepared an ambush. Scouts mounted on swift horses were sent out to determine the enemy's disposition. If the enemy were found to be in disorder, the Turks seized the initiative and assaulted at once. If they found the enemy to be drawn up in battle order, they would skirt the edges of his line, riding swiftly, but all the while firing their arrows with deadly accuracy. They would continue firing with great intensity for a long time, until they had thrown the enemy into disorder. If their opponents attempted to counter-charge, the Turks would fall back and disperse, still using their bows effectively against their pursuers. As soon as the enemy pursuing them had broken formation, the Turkish commander gave three raps on his kettledrum. The other Turks responded in like manner, and re-formed around their leader. If the enemy were sufficiently disorganized, the Turks stood their ground, and received his assault. If, however, the enemy were still well constituted in one body, the Turks divided once again into groups and assulted their opponents at different points. One means by which they disorganized the enemy's troops was to throw fire among their horses. Another tactic was to station camels or dromedaries in front of their line. Driven into the enemy's cavalry, they stampeded their mounts.[87]

By such methods, La Broquière declared, the Turks had defeated Christian armies in the past. Although they usually achieved victories with armies of 100,000 of 120,000 or even 200,000, these numbers were not so impressive as they might seem. Many Turkish soldiers were poorly armed; and a con-

VI: Sultan mounted
    (Joerg von Nuremberg, *Anzeygung*. Nuremberg, 1500).

siderable element of the Turkish army was always made up of Christians, who, La Broquière insisted, would defect, if they witnessed the appearance of a respectable Christian force. La Broquière admitted that he had found the Turks a frank, loyal, and valiant race; but, he asserted, they were not invincible. A well-ordered army from the West, only half the size of the Turkish army, acquainted with their manner of fighting had every reason to expect victory.[88]

It was sometime shortly after the feast of Lille that Philip ordered La Broquière to put in writing his findings on the Levant. At the same time he was asked to criticize Torzelo's recommendations, and to submit his own plan of operations. La Broquière agreed in general with Torzelo's estimate of the Turkish military though he revised some of the Greek's figures concerning the size of the several components of the Ottoman army. He questioned the multiple routes into Turkey and was skeptical about the aid to be gotten from the Christians of the Balkans. He criticized Torzelo for failing to inform the Latin princes of the Turks' methods of fighting and emphasized the necessity of maintaining security at all times since the Ottomans were masters at surprise tactics. He cautioned Duke Philip that the defeat of the Turks and the recovery of the Holy Land were not so easily achieved as Torzelo had suggested.[89]

On the basis of his own experience among the Turks and with a knowledge of the disastrous mistakes made by the western knights at Nicopolis, La Broquière submitted his own plan which included the following significant recommendations: (1) combatants were to be recruited from England, France, and Germany and they were to consist of men-of-arms, crossbowmen and archers; (2) the army was to be paid regularly for their services; (3) they were not to be allowed to take anything from the lands through which they traveled without paying for it; (4) they were all to be lightly armed, and he detailed just what weapons they should carry; (5) the army was to remain in one compact unit and under no circumstances was it to be divided; (6) when the Christians engaged the Turks in battle, their advance and rear guards were to take up new positions to protect their flanks; the archers were to be mixed throughout the main body, and used as skirmishers; the knights were not to be permitted to skirmish; lightly armed troops were to be placed in front of and on the flanks of the main body; and the Turks were not to be allowed to make a breach in the main body, or all would be lost; (7) finally, when the Turks drew back, or feigned retreat, if the Christians pursued them, it must be accomplished in one body, and in good order, ready at all times to receive and repel a Turkish counter-attack. With the army advancing always in mass, the Turks would be forced to flee before it, and retreat from

Europe leaving everything behind, or risk a decisive engagement at their disadvantage, and be defeated.[90]

Perhaps not so knowledgeable as La Broquière, though certainly far more experienced in actual combat with the Turks, Geoffroy de Thoisy must also be counted among the Burgundian experts on the Levant. Councillor and chamberlain to the duke, he had first traveled to the Levant with La Broquière in 1432. It was de Thoisy who commanded the small squadron which was sent to defend the knights of Rhodes against an attack from Mameluke Egypt. In command of three galleys and one galeote, he participated in the expedition of 1444-1445, in conjunction with the crusade of Varna, and saw action off North Africa, Rhodes, in the waters around Constantinople and in the Black Sea. He was, as we might expect, among those who took the crusade vow in 1454. In 1456 and again in 1464 he was sent to discuss the expedition at Naples and Rome. In light of all this we can believe that de Thoisy spoke his true mind when he addressed Philip in the following words: "j'ose dire que Julius Sezar, quant il ala combatre Pompei en Thessaille, ne fist pas plus grande antreprize que ceste sera, se Dieu plaist."[91]

Geoffroy de Thoisy was an active participant in the planning and discussions which by 1463-64, in preparation for the crusade of Pius II, reached a feverish pitch. The author of two plans, de Thoisy, in contrast to La Broquière, was committed exclusively to a naval compaign. He proposed as intermediate and final objectives, Gallipoli and Constantinople, whose capture he declared would paralyze the Turks. He had reservations about cooperating with Venice. He recommended the ports of southern Italy, Ragusa, or the Ionian islands as probable staging areas the use of which would keep the Turks guessing about the destination of the fleet. Most important, however, de Thoisy, whose experience must have lent great weight to his counsel, urged caution and careful preparations before embarking upon the seas. Time and adequate forces, together with peace, and assurances from Burgundy's neighbors were absolutely essential to the success of the enterprise.[92]

In this advice de Thoisy was firmly seconded by another of the duke's Turkish authorities, the former commander-in-chief of Philip's fleet in 1444-45, Walerand de Wavrin. Although he too favored a naval campaign, he claimed that the ships then being outfitted at Ecluse would not be ready in time. Moreover, the proposed force he held to be insufficient to transport the knights and their horses, let alone attack a strong port such as Gallipoli defended perhaps by 20 or 30,000 Turks and much artillery, or Constantinople which was three times as strong. He declared that more time was required. The forces agreed upon with Venice and the pope were not adequate. He urged the construction of a larger fleet including sixteen or twenty large ships to carry archers, artillery, and provisions. He disagreed with de Thoisy and believed the support of Venice to be essential to success and discussed at length the plans for a rendezvous with the Italian vessels and common action. But like de Thoisy he was opposed to any hasty measures. A firm peace between England and France was imperative and the two kings were to provide, at their own expense, a large and powerful army to accompany the duke. He was convinced that if the proposed force of Burgundy, Venice, and the papacy went alone the result would be disastrous and concluded: "Et se l'armée se rompt, sans conquester Constantinoble, ce sera ung grant orgueul aux Turcs, et fort en seront encouraigez les ennemys de la foy, car ilz tiennent monseigneur le duc, par renommée, l'ung des plus puissans princes des chrestiens, et que craingnent plus". [93]

The cautious approach based on a realistic assessment of the military capabilities of both sides was, to be sure, not shared by all the duke's councillors. At the Burgundian court the advice of few men was more highly regarded than that of Jean Germain (d. 1460). Theologian, diplomat, councillor, and administrator, he had represented the duke at the councils of Basel and Florence, was confessor of the duchess, Isabel, first chancellor of the Order of the Golden Fleece, president of Philip's council, and successively bishop of Nevers and Châlon-sur-Saône. Concerned primarily with the principles and practice of religion and chivalry, Germain never doubted the wisdom of the enterprise.[94] In his correspondence with Juan de Segovia, the Franciscan advocate of a peaceful policy toward Islam, he defended the crusade by citing the authority of Scripture, the pronouncements of the popes, and the historical record of Christian chivalry. In view of the imminent peril to the West he declared that the militant approach offered the only positive guarantee against continued Turkish aggression.[95]

In 1452 Germain had taken part in the mission to France which sought to enlist the support of Charles VII in the crusade which at that time might have saved Constantinople. The bishop of Châlon prepared for the occasion, *Le Discours du voyage d'oultremer au très victorieux roi Charles VII.* He described the rise of Islam, and the present state of the Moslem world in the 1450's, emphasizing that most of their conquests had been accomplished in Christian lands. It was the deepest humiliation of Christendom that the sultan of Egypt ruled over the Holy Land. Germain recalled to the memory of Charles VII the past glories of French kings, who had led armies against the foes of Christ. The time had come again when a French king must fight to preserve Christendom. At that moment the Turks were endeavoring to exterminate Christianity from Greece! The Grand Turk had decreed that all his Christian subjects, of whatever rank and station, were to give up their third son to become a Turk; "...c'est à dire circonciz et renyra son baptesme et sa foy, s'il est d'age". In his gross arrogance and conceit the Grand Turk, Germain continued, had named Asia Minor, his first conquest, Old Turkey. Greece, his more recent conquest, he called New Turkey. For twenty years he had not ceased to assault Hungary. If God and the Christian princes did not stop him, he would continue victorious, and Constantinople would be his (one year later this prediction came true). From there it would be an easy matter for him to go on to Old Rome, and in Italy he would find many people ready to aid him! He intended to call himself emperor of the East and of the West, and all Christian princes were to become his tributaries. Having set forth "les doleances du petit estat de la chrestienté en Orient", and predicted what would happen if the Turks and Mamelukes were not stopped, Germain proceeded to outline those conditions which made it propitious to undertake the crusade at that moment. The time was ripe, he declared, "...porter un grant dommage au Turcq et au souldan d'Egypt et faire ung grant secours à la Chrestienté".[96]

While Jean Germain contributed his share to the literature of crusade exhortations, his true forte lay in the refutation of Islam. He was in possession of a copy of the Koran and a Life of Mohammed. The books had been acquired by La Broquière from the chaplain of the Venetian bailo in Damascus and turned over to the bishop of Châlon at the request of Philip the Good.[97] Germain is credited with having written three works in Latin dealing with the subject: Adversus Turcarum Alcoranum: Adversus Mahometanos et fideles; and De Saracenorum legis falsitate tractatus. The problem also found its way into his work dealing with the art of tapestries, Deux pans de la tapisserie chrétienne. But judging from the number of extant manuscripts his best known work was Le débat du Crétien et du Sarrazin. Employing the popular form of a dialogue between a Christian and a Moslem, held allegedly in the palace of the emperor of the Saracens, Germain attacked the folly of Islam, reviewed the evidence supporting the authenticity of Christ and other arguments in favor of Christianity, and, to his own satisfaction, exposed the falsity of the motives commonly cited for abjuring Christianity in favor of Islam. Arguing from the assumed authority of Scripture and of the superiority of Christianity, Germain produced but another work of Christian polemic and contributed nothing new to the West's knowledge of Islam nor a more constructive approach to the Moslem world.[98]

Although Germain was not alive to take part in the court conferences of 1463-1464, the arguments of the conservative theologian were forcefully upheld by others who were similarly less worried than the duke's lay advisors about such matters as the state of finances at home and the lack of an adequate force to engage the Turks. The reform-minded ecclesiastics of this camp were unswerving in their adherence to the orthodox formula: as the defender of Christ's church the Christian prince must forego his selfish interests and desist from shedding the blood of fellow Christians; let him follow the pope's lead and take up the cross; he cannot but succeed, for *Deus vult!*[99] In the end Philip faltered in the gap between intent and reality: the chivalric policy was incompatible with requirements of practical politics. A token force under his bastard son Anthony sailed to the Mediterranean but accomplished little.[100] Philip was able to assemble an impressive list of excuses: troubles with his son and impatient successor, Charles; the duke himself was old and not in good health; his suzerain, Louis XI, demanded that the expedition be postponed and threatened dire results if Philip failed to heed him. [101] But probably the most telling of all was the advice of his experienced councillors who made him face the realities of the situation. The duke of Burgundy did not abandon the idea of a crusade (nor indeed did his lay councillors), but he had to relinquish the old idea of a grand expedition and accept the contemporary policy of an occasional show of force and limited engagements—in short a policy of coexistence and containment.

NOTES TO CHAPTER IV

1. See Otto Cartellieri, *The Court of Burgundy*, translated by Malcolm Letts (London, 1929), pp. 11, 14, 15; cf. A. Kleinclausz. *Histoire de Bourgogne* (Paris, 1909), pp. 154, 155.

2. Cartellieri, *Court of Burgundy*, pp. 12-16; cf. Huizinga, *Waning of the Middle Ages*, p. 94, and Kleinclausz, *Histoire de Bourgogne*, pp. 184-187.

3. On the question of Philip's sincerity with regard to the crusade, and the attitude of the authorities see Henri Pirenne, *Histoire de Belgique*, I (3rd ed., Brussels, 1928), 389, n. 79; cf. Cartellieri, *Court of Burgundy*, p. 12.

4. Huizinga, *Waning of the Middle Ages*, p. 95.

5. Cartellieri, *Court of Burgundy*, p. 12.

6. *Ibid.*, p. 9; Huizinga, *Waning of the Middle Ages*, p. 20, wrote: "In writing the history of the house of Burgundy, the *leitmotiv* should constantly keep before our minds the spirit of revenge".

7. See Cartellieri, *Court of Burgundy*, p. 135; and Charles Schefer (ed.), "Le Discours du voyage d'oultremer au tres victorieux roi Charles VII, prononcé en 1452, par Jean Germain, évêque de Châlon", *ROL*, III (1895), 310; cf. A. S. Atiya, *The Crusade in the Later Middle Ages* (London, 1938), p. 462, who believes that except by Philippe de Mezieres the failure of Nicopolis was quickly forgotten in the

West. On the reaction to Nicopolis see T. G. Bulat, "La Croisade de Nicopolis dans la littérature du temps", in *Mélanges d'histoire générale*, edited by Constantin Marinescu, I (Cluj, 1927), 101-123. Aeneas Sylvius, writing about Philip's presence at Ratisbon, showed himself well acquainted with the reasons for the duke of Burgundy's enthusiasm for the crusade. He counted as one possible motive the duke's desire to avenge his father. Pius II, *Commentaries*, I, p. 69. The emblem of the Order of the Golden Fleece, connected with the legend of Phrixus and Helle, was chosen in memory of John the Fearless's treatment at the hands of the Turks. See D. Vaughan, *Europe and the Turk*, p. 286.

8.   Cartellieri, *Court of Burgundy*, p. 91.

9.   *Ibid.*, 9, 10.

10.   Schefer (ed.), "Le Discours", *ROL*, III, 303.

11.   See Albert Gabriel, *La Cité de Rhodes*, MCCCX-MDXXII, I (Paris, 1921), 79.

12.   See the narrative of the Burgundian expedition written by the uncle of Walerand de Wavrin, Jehan de Wavrin, *Anchiennes chronicques d'Engleterre*, edited by Mlle. Dupont, II (Paris, 1859), 12-162. Jehan de Wavrin's account is one of the longest, most interesting, and best informed reports on any Turkish-related topic to be found in any western chronicle of the fifteenth century. It deserves to be studied more carefully. Cf. N. Iorga, "Les Aventures 'sarrazines' des français de Bourgogne au xvᵉ siècle", *Mélanges d'histoire générale*, I, 7-12. Cf. references in Adrien de But, *Chronique*, pp. 276-280.

13.   See Schefer, "Le Discours", *ROL*, III, 312; Barante, *Histoire des ducs de Bourgogne*, VII (7th ed., Paris, 1854), 148. Cf. Jean Germain, *Liber de virtutibus Philippi Burgundiae et Brabantiae Ducis*, edited by Kervyn de Lettenhove (*Chroniques relatives à l'histoire de la Belgique*, III, Brussels, 1867), 77, 78.

14.   Pastor, *HP*, II, 302.

15.   See de Wavrin, *Chronicques*, II, 51, 52; cf. Iorga, "Les Aventures", p. 17.

16.   See notes of Dupont in her edition of de Wavrin, *Chronicques*, II, 37.

17.   D'Escouchy, *Chronique*, II, 129. D'Escouchy recorded the vow of Vasquez (*ibid.*, p. 203): "Je veue aux dames et au faisant, que, s'il y a bataille dedens ung an à l'encontre du Grant Turcq, que pour l'amour et reverence de Dieu nostre Sauveur Jhesus-Crist, se il me garde d'encombrement, je y seray; et pour le jour je sievray le bon chevallier le seigneur de Halbourding de tout mon pooir, pour lui aidier à acomplir son veu; ou de moy aborder à la banière du ensaingne dudit Grand Turcq, en tel manière que je l'abaisseray ou y laisseray les ensaingnes, se en la voie pour l'acomplir ne suis mort, ou en tel manière navré que je ne peusse furnir, ou que mon cheval me fausist enchemin."

18.   De la Marche, *Mémoires*, II, 41.

19.   Extract in Dupont, *op. cit.*, II, 51, 52, cited from A. Dinaux, *Archives historique*, 3rd series, III (1852), 166.

20.   See G. du Fresne de Beaucourt, *Histoire de Charles VII*, V (Paris, 1949), 229.

21.   See J. Calmette, *Les Grand ducs de Bourgogne* (Paris, 1949), pp. 221, 222, 228. Cf. the letter of the Franciscan preacher, John Capistran to Philip the Good, March 19, 1453, exhorting Philip to conclude peace at home and take up the defense of the faith, in Chastellain, *Chronique*, II, 342-345.

22. In general see Jules Finot, *Projet d'expedition contre les Turcs préparé par les conseillers du duc de Bourgogne Philippe-le-Bon* (Lille, 1890), who gives a series of crusading plans projected in Burgundy during the decade following the Turkish victory in 1453. Cf. remarks of Chastellain, *Chronique*, III, 73, 74.

23. G. Doutrepont, "A la cour de Philippe le Bon. Le Banquet du faisan et la littérature de Bourgogne", *La Revue générale*, LXX (1899), 799.

24. Chastellain, *Chronique*, III, 12-14, 71-77.

25. Cartellieri, *Court of Burgundy*, pp. 135-163, and references, pp. 263-265.

26. Even Huizinga wrote in *The Waning of the Middle Ages*, p. 250: "We find it difficult to regard these entertainments as something more than exhibitions of almost incredible bad taste."

27. E.g. Georges Doutrepont in *La Revue générale*, LXX (1899), 787-809; LXXI (1900), 99-118.

28. Huizinga, *Waning of the Middle Ages*, pp. 89-93, 250-252.

29. Cf. d'Escouchy, *Chronique*, II, 113-245, and Olivier de la Marche, *Mémoires*, II, 340-394; and see Georges Doutrepont, *La Littérature française à la cour des ducs de Bourgogne* (Paris, 1909), p. 106, n. 4.

30. De la Marche, *Mémoires*, II, 341-348; d'Escouchy, *Chronique*, II, 118-130; Cartellieri, *Court of Burgundy*, pp. 137-139; Doutrepont, "A la cour de Philippe le Bon", pp. 787, 788.

31. De la Marche, *Mémoires*, II, 348-354; d'Escouchy, *Chronique*, II, 130-138.

32. *Ibid.*, II, 138-152; de la Marche, *Mémoires*, II, 354-361.

33. *Ibid.*, II, 361, 362; d'Escouchy, *Chronique*, II, 152, 153.

34. *Ibid.*, II, 153, 154; de la Marche, *Mémoires*, II, 362. The quatotions are from the text of d'Escouchy. Slight variations are to be found in de la Marche.

35. D'Escouchy, *Chronique*, II, 154, 155; de la Marche, *Mémoires*, II, 363.

36. *Ibid.*, II, 363-366; d'Escouchy, *Chronique*, II, 155-159.

37. *Ibid.*, II, 159-160; de la Marche, *Mémoires*, II, 366, 367.

38. D'Escouchy, *Chronique*, II, 160-163.

39. *Ibid.*, pp. 165-222; de la Marche (*op. cit.*, pp. 381-399), lists the vows at the end of his description of the banquet, and gives the texts of only twenty-three. D'Escouchy gives 102 vows. In addition to the vows of the feast at Lille, see those taken at Arras, Mons, Bruges, and Holland in the same year in a manuscript published in part by Georges Doutrepont in "Notice sur le manuscrit français 11594 de la Bibliothèque nationale: La croisade projetée par Philippe le Bon contre les Turcs", *Notices et extraits des manuscrits de la Bibliothèque nationale*, XLI (Paris, 1923), 9-28.

40. D'Escouchy, *Chronique*, II, 169.

41. *Ibid.*, p. 167.

42. *Ibid.*, pp. 170, 171.

43. *Ibid.*, pp. 184, 185.

44. *Ibid.*, pp. 189, 190, "...je porterai une emprinse pour faire armes à pié ou à cheval contre d'ung des gens dudit Turcq, laquelle je feray seigniffier, se je puis, en son ost; et tout par le bon gré et license de mondit seigneur ou commis de par lui, je l'iray combattre devant ledit Turcq moiennant que je y puisse avoir bonne seurté".

45. *Ibid.*, p. 192.

46. Huizinga, *Waning of the Middle Ages*, pp. 89, 92, 93.

47. E.g., see the vow of Hugh de Longueval, where it is made quite clear that Constantinople is the principal objective of the crusade (d'Escouchy, *op. cit.*, p. 192).

48. See Dana C. Munro, "The Western Attitude Toward Islam During the Period of the Crusades", *Speculum*, VI (1931), 318, 339.

49. L. Devillers, "Les Sejour des ducs de Bourgogne en Hainaut", *Bulletin de la Commission royal d'histoire*, 4th series, VI (1879), 351.

50. Doutrepont, "A la cour de Philippe le Bon", pp. 804, 805.

51. Cartellieri, *Court of Burgundy*, pp. 124-134.

52. *Ibid.*, pp. 130, 131; J. Gairdner, ed., *The Paston Letters* (London ,1858), V, 69-70.

53. Molinet, *Chroniques*, II, 486, 487.

54. Antoine de la Sale, *Le Petit Jehan de Saintré*, ed. and tr. I. Gray (London, 1931), pp. 231-235. Some idea of the extent and character of the literature in this area may be gained from G. Doutrepont, *Les Mises en prose des épopées et des romans chevaleresques du XIVe au XVI^c siècles* (Brussels, 1939); on the continuity of the tradition see A. Vovard, *Les Turqueries dans la littérature française* (Paris, 1959); and C. D. Rouillard, *The Turk in French History, Thought and Literature* (Paris, 1938).

55. De la Sale, *Le Petit Jehan*, pp. 236-239.

56. *Instruction d'un jeune prince* in Lannoy, *Oeuvres*, pp. 417-425. For more on Saladin see Suzanne Duparc-Quioc, *Le Cycle de la croisade (Bibliothèque de l'école des hautes etudes*, CCCV. Paris, 1955), pp. 170-205.

57. *Les Cent nouvelles nouvelles*, edited by Le Roux de Linay, II (Paris, 1841), 143-146. Other references to infidels in this work may be found in volume I, pp. 135, 153.

58. *Ibid.*, I, 143-146.

59. Le Roux de Linay, *Chants historiques*, p. 68.

60. *Ibid.*, pp. 114, 115. Concerning the Tournaisiens at the time of the death of Charles the Bold, Molinet *(Chroniques*, I, 217), wrote, "Nul ne scaroit ymaginer les joyes et les festoyemens que les Tournisyens menèrent pour la perte de ce très noble duc. Ilz firent feus, chansons et danses et, comme s'ilz eussent assommé le Grant Turcq. .". Charles' unpopularity also caused him to be compared with the Grand Turk. Landucci wrote in his *Diary* (p. 13), "This Duke of Burgundy was considered to be a most cruel man, it being a common report that he in the West and the Grand Turk in the East delighted in men's blood, and that they caused people to be slaughtered in a barbarous fashion. The Lord sometimes frees the world of such men." On Antoine's campaign in 1464 see J. Finot, *Projet d'expédition contre les Turcs*, p. 21; de Wavrin, *Chronicques*, II, 321, 322; le Huen, *Le Grant voyage*, fols. clxxv^r-clxxvi^v.

61. *Chants historiques de la Flandre*, 400-1650, edited by Louis de Baecker (Lille, 1855), p. 209; cf. G. Doutrepont, "A la cour de Philippe le Bon", p. 804.

62. Jean Wauquelin, *Cronicques des faiz de feurent Monseigneur Girart de Roussillon*, edited by L. de Montille (Paris, 1890), p. 519. Quoted by G. Doutrepont, *La Littérature française*, p. 381.

63. See Chapters II and III above, *passim* on councils and diplomacy. A number of in-

teresting notices on the appearance of Turks and other eastern people in Burgundy and France may be found in the following: J. Aubrion, *Journal*, p. 59; d'Escouchy, *Chronique*, II, 305; le Huen, *Le Grant voyage*, clxxiv^r-clxxv^r; cf. Pius II, *Commentaries*, V, 371.

64. A. Ferguson, *The Indian Summer of English Chivalry*, p. 21.

65. D. Hay, *The Italian Renaissance*, p. 4. Certainly the last word has not been said on this.

66. Chastellain, *Chronique*, III, 71-77; cf. pp. 12-14, for his account of a meeting of the estates of the Franche Comté at Salins.

67. *Ibid.*, p. 71.

68. *Ibid.*, pp. 71, 72.

69. *Ibid.*, pp. 72, 73. Constantinople is described as "... la plus redoutable cité des autres, clef et bastille de la cristienté vers Orient...".

70. Chastellain, *Chronique*, II, 73-77; cf. *ibid.*, p. 13, for the terms in which Philip made his plea to the estates of the Franche-Comté.

71. See Baron de Reiffenberg, "Jean Miélot, calligraphe et secrétaire du duc Philippe le Bon", *Bulletin du bibliophile belge*, II (1845), 381-386.

72. *L'Advis de messire Jehan Torzelo*, in Reiffenberg, *Monuments pour servir à l'histoire des provinces de Namur, de Hainaut et de Luxembourg* (Brussels, 1848), V, 541-544.

73. In respect to Philip the Good see the reports sent by the Florentine Antonio del Palagio in N. Iorga, "Les Aventures 'sarrazines' des Francais de Bourgogne au xve siècle", *Mélanges d'histoire générale*" (Cluj, 1927), I, pp. 48-56; and my article "Western Spies in the Levant", *History Today*, XIII (1963), 747-756. Venice was unquestionably the best informed power in the West. See e.g. the documents relating to the war of 1463-79 in C. N. Sathas, *Documents inédits relatifs à l'histoire de la Grece au moyen âge (Monumenta historiae hellenicae, VI, Paris, 1855), 1-92; the mountain of material scattered throughout the volumes of M. Sanuto, *Diarii*, ed. F. Stefani, 58 vols. (Venice, 1879-1903); and for the later period E. Albèri, ed., *Le relazioni degli ambasciatori Veneti al Senato durante il secolo decimosesto*, 15 vols. (Florence, 1839-1863). Most of this material, however, never filtered beyond the lagoons and little affected western views of the Turks outside Venice.

74. Ghillebert de Lannoy, *Rapports sur les voyaiges de pluisiers villes, ports et revières que je fis en l'an vingt-deux, tant en Égypte comme en Surie* in *Oeuvres*, pp. 52-56, 65.

75. *Ibid.*, pp. 113, 130.

76. *Ibid.*, pp. 99-110.

77. *Ibid.*, pp. 110-159.

78. *Ibid.*, pp. 65-67, 160, 161. In 1446 Lannoy was sent on another mission to the Levant, but except for a brief itinerary we know nothing more about it; *Oeuvres*, pp. 174-178.

79. *Le Voyage d'outremer de Bertrandon de la Broquière*, ed. C. Schefer, (Paris, 1892), pp. 7-65, 100, 101.

80. *Ibid.*, pp. 72-80, 96, 97, 216, 217.

81. *Ibid.*, pp. 128, 129; cf. A. S. Atiya, *Crusades in the Later Middle Ages*, pp. 443, 444, on Turks captured by the crusaders enroute to Nicopolis.

82. *Le Voyage*, pp. 132-136, 141, 142. On the Milanese embassy see G. Romano, "Filippo Maria Visconti e i Turchi", *Archivio storico lombardo*, XVII (1890), 585-618 and D. Vaughan, *Europe and the Turk*, pp. 49-51.

83. *Le Voyage*, pp. 181-198. Cf. description of Murad and his court by Tafur, *Travels and Adventures*, pp. 127-137.

84. *Le Voyage*, 182-185. For details on ranks and the pay scale see the *Ordo portae*, ed. and tr. Şerif Baştav (Budapest, 1947); and Jacopo de Promontorio de Campis, *Stato del Gran Turco*, ed. F. Babinger in *Sitzungsberichte der Bayerischen Akademie der Wissenschaften*, Heft 8 (1956).

85. *Le Voyage*, pp. 219, 220.

86. *Ibid.*, p. 222. In the sixteenth century the English author of *The Policy of the Turkish Empire* (London, 1597), still felt "...that the chiefest cause of their sodaine and fearefull puissaunce, hath beene the excellencie of their Martial discipline ioyned with a signgular desire and resolution to aduance and enlarge both the bounds of their Empire and the profession of their Religion".

87. *Le Voyage*, pp. 220-224.

88. *Ibid.*, pp. 224, 225.

89. *L'Advis et advertissement* in Reiffenberg, *Monuments*, V, 544-546.

90. *Ibid.*, pp. 546-549.

91. On de Thoisy's activities see C. Marinescu, "Philippe le Bon, duc de Bourgogne et la croisade (première partie, 1419-1453)", *Actes du vi^e congrès international d'études byzantines*, I (Paris, 1950), 154-165.

92. Text in M. le Glay, "Sur la croisade projetée en 1453", *Compte rendu des séances de la commission royale d'histoire*, 3rd series, II (1861), 213-228; but given the wrong date by the editor. Cf. C. Marinescu, "Philippe le Bon, duc de Bourgogne, et la croisade (deuxième partie, 1453-1467)", *Bulletin des études portugaises et de l'institut français au Portugal*, new series, XIII (1949), 17-19.

93. *L'Advis de monsr de Waurin touchant le voyaige de Turquie* in Reiffenberg, *Monuments*, V, 549-553. Cf. Marinescu, "Philippe le Bon (pt. 2)", 19-21.

94. Abbé Bugniot, "Jehan Germain, évêque de Châlon-sur-Saône (1436-1460)", *Mémoires de la société d'histoire et d'archéologie de Châlon-sur-Saône*, IV (1863), 377-401. Cf. his views in his *Liber de virtutibus Philippi Burgundiae*, Chaps. 40-57, and a sermon he preached before the Order of the Golden Fleece at Mons in 1450, de la Marche, *Mémoires*, II, 486.

95. Cabenalas, *Juan de Segovia*, pp. 329, 330.

96. *Liber de virtutibus Philippi Burgundiae*, pp. 77, 78; "Le Discours", in *ROL*, III, 314-338.

97. *Le Voyage*, pp. 260, 261.

98. Paulin Paris, *Les Manuscrits français de la bibliothèque du roi* (Paris, 1836), I, 83-86. *Catalogue des manuscrits français: Ancien fonds* (Paris, 1868), I, 5, 162; nos. 69, 70, 947, 948. Cf. Bugniot, "Jehan Germain", pp. 394-401; Cartellieri, *Court of Burgundy*, p. 136; R. W. Southern, *Western Views of Islam*, pp. 94-98; and Doutrepont, *La Littérature française*, p. 252.

99. Doutrepont, "L'Épitre à la maison de Bourgogne sur la croisade turque projetée

par Philippe le Bon (1464)", *Analectes pour servir à l'histoire ecclésiastique de la Belgique*, 3rd series, II (1906), 144-195; H.-V. Sauerland, "Rede des burgundischen Gesandten und Bischofs von Tournay Wilhelm Filastre in Sachen eines Kreuzzugs gegen die Türken, gehalten zu Rom am 8. October 1463 im öffentlichen Consistorium vor Papst Pius II", *Römische Quartalschrift*, V (1891), 352-363.

100. C. Marinescu, ".Philippe le Bon (pt. 2)", pp. 22, 23.

101. *Ibid.*, pp. 24-28.

CHAPTER V

Chivalry in action

While the western princes moved gradually, if reluctantly, toward a policy of containment and coexistence with the Turks, there were still many proponents of the chivalric tradition who espoused a more aggressive approach. Among those who believed that the code of chivalry required unremitting warfare against Islam, particularly prominent were the members of the military-religious orders.[1] Devotion to the ideals of knighthood—of courage, renown, honor, fidelity, and the defense of religion—still found its most complete expression in the institution of knightly orders. At the end of the fourteenth century the passionate promoter of the crusade, Philippe de Mezieres, believed that the only hope for Christianity in the Levant was to be found in the creation of a new chivalric society. He labored through the better part of a lifetime to enlist support for his *Novo Religio Passionis Jhesu Christi*.[2] By far the most distinguished of the new creations in our period was that of the Golden Fleece. The symbol of Burgundian power and glory, among its statutes one required its members to serve in defense of the Christian faith and the Holy See of Rome. An exclusive and elegant fraternity of the Burgundian court, the Order of the Golden Fleece was not conceived of as essentially a crusading order, though its individual members were encouraged to participate in the holy enterprise and its convocations served as a means of promoting the crusades.[3] Two new orders whose specific purpose was that of fighting the Turks, were Our Lady of Bethlehem and the Society of Jesus, both founded by Pius II. The first of these was to be based on the island of Lemnos but was short lived. The second, the Society of Jesus was long believed not to have materialized at all but to have served its chief promoter, Gerard Deschamps, as a means of advancing his own interests.[4]

The principal source for this censorious judgment was none other than the pope who had commissioned the order. According to Pius' account in Book XII of the *Commentaries* Gerard was a Frenchman who had acquired some wealth as the owner of a brothel in the city of Bologna. But after the fall of Constantinople he was converted by the sermons of crusade preachers who promised salvation to those who took the cross. During the reign of Calixtus III, Gerard had used his money to collect a band of 300 men but apparently got no encouragement from the pontiff. Pius wrote that he first learned of the matter while enroute to the congress of Mantua when Gerard came to him with a petition asking to be allowed to enlist 10,000 men in a society bearing the name of Jesus and for the purpose of going against the Turk. The pope granted the request, owing, he was careful to add, to the pleas of Cardinal Bessarion, and with the stipulation that only those able to support themselves during one year of campaigning be permitted to join. Armed with the pope's commission Gerard went off to France presumably to recruit followers. Pius complained that he heard no more of the man until four years later when a messenger from Gerard appeared before him at Pienza. The messenger reported that 4000 men had already enlisted and that his master expected soon to have more than 10,000; but money was needed to carry on the work, and a sum of 200 ducats was specifically requested to enable Gerard to secure the release of his son from his creditors. Gerard also asked the pope to provide him with a papal standard. At this point in the narrative Pius explained that although Bessarion still favored the society he was himself convinced that Gerard was a fraud. He therefore sent an agent, a Dalmatian named Luca to investigate. The latter found Gerard in Savoy where, Pius admitted, "a number of excellent men" had actually enrolled in the society and the duke's own son, Philip, planned to enlist if the pope were willing to make him general of the order. But in Burgundy Luca claimed to have found no evidence of the 4000 men and numerous arms which Gerard said he had gathered there. Moreover, the pope's agent accused the dubious organizer of setting traps which he narrowly escaped enroute to Brussels where again he found no troops. He learned, however, that shortly after receiving his commission Gerard had gone directly to the French court. There he had sought to persuade Charles VII to permit him to raise an army in France, ostensibly for the crusade, but to be used in Italy to fight for the Anjevin claimant to the throne of King Ferrante the pope's own ally. Pius concluded his account with the comment that once Gerard realized that his deception had been discovered, "he took care to disappear completely".[5]

It is unnecessary here to deal with all the discrepancies in the above account. We may note, however, that Pius spoke much more favorably of the society and its promoter in the bull *Dilectis filiis* announcing its formation at Rome on January 13, 1459, that is, before the pope's departure for Mantua. In this document he referred to Gerard as the *orator* and *nuntius* of a numerous company of men, of great piety "et probitate praestantissimos", whom he predicted would render great service in Hungary or other places menaced by the Turks.[6] Similarly in a bull cited by Raynaldus and published at Mantua, June 29, 1459, Pius acknowledged awarding many privileges to the society which he commended to the support of kings and princes.[7] In a letter to

Charles VII of October 30, 1459, he requested that the king release from royal service one Guillaume de la Tourette, then stationed with the French garrison at Asti, and whom Pius intended to appoint captain of the new order.[8] On the other hand, in the unfavorable account in the *Commentaries*, Pius would have us believe that from the time of Gerard's departure for France in 1459 until the arrival of his messenger at Pienza, a period of four years had passed during which he had heard nothing of the society. The fact is that if the messenger came to him at Pienza it must have been sometime during the autumn of 1462. It was then that Pius visited the place of his birth, the former Corsignano, which he caused to be renamed Pienza and upon which he had spent considerable money in a program of urban renewal.[9]

Of far greater significance than Pius' errors in chronology, however, was his unqualified denunciation of Gerard as a fraud and his assertion that the plans for a Society of Jesus were a complete failure. For these conclusions from the pen of the founder of the order and the chief advocate of the crusade were not only long accepted without question, but served as prime evidence for discrediting the crusading efforts of the period. Was this not proof, and from the best authority on the subject, of contemporary indifference to the whole question and of the shallowness of the chivalric protests and vows? And was not the bankrupt state of the holy enterprise clearly revealed by the fact that it now attracted such schemers and adventurers, confidence men, like Gerard, who were equally able to serve as the head of a brothel or an agent of the church?

Whether the product of ignorance (Pius did not live to see the completion of Gerard's enterprise), misinformation, or willful distortion of the facts, the pope's account did not render justice to Gerard Deschamps. On the basis of documents from the archives of Besançon and Geneva we know that in addition to the nobility of Savoy, there were others from France and the Lowlands who enlisted in the Society of Jesus. The order, for example, received the support of the bishop of Besançon whose chapter agreed on February 11, 1463, to hold solemn processions at St. Stephen's on the following Sunday when the suffragan bishop, Anthony, was to deliver a sermon "Pro bullis super Societate Jesu contra Turchos concessis publicandis...".[10] Owing to such assistance, his own recruiting efforts, and those of the preachers assigned to promote the society, Gerard was successful in raising a moderate force. Though greatly handicapped by the lack of funds and difficulties put in his way by inhospitable cities such as Geneva, Gerard led his troops to Hungary by way of Germany continuing to enlist new members along the way. He joined forces with King Mathias Corvinus and participated in action against the Turks at Jaicza which the king of Hungary had laid under siege

October 1, 1463. On December 16, the Turkish garrison capitulated. For his part in the battle, the leader of the Society of Jesus received a share of the Turkish prisoners, including one captain, whom together with a Turkish banner, he took back to the West as tangible evidence of the order's participation in the war against the Ottomans. Gerard himself was enobled by the king of Hungary and from the emperor, Frederick III, he received the title of count palatine.[11]

The value which these two monarchs attached to the services of the order was further witnessed by arrangements concluded with Gerard whereby he was to raise a new force in the West and return to Hungary to take part in a proposed expedition against the Turks in the spring of 1466. In a letter bearing Gerard's signature over his new title, as well as that of captain of the Society of Jesus, and addressed to the government of Geneva, December 8, 1465, we read that the emperor and the king of Hungary had provided him with twenty-eight "paire de lettres closes adrechantes à rois, à princes et à communities", to facilitate the accomplishment of his new project.[12] Three of these letters praising the conduct of the society and in particular that of its leader, and requesting the cooperation and aid of the addressees are extant and serve to corroborate the fact that the society and its leader did fight against the Turks.[13]

We must not exaggerate the importance of the order's role in defending Europe against the Turks, though, as suggested before, the cumulative effect of successive minor expeditions was probably greater than has usually been granted. But within the context of this chapter the brief history of the Society of Jesus is significant as further confirmation that the spirit of chivalry went farther than the festivals and tournaments of princely courts and the moralizing romance literature of the age. If it was incapable of restoring knighthood to the full measure of its former glory it continued to influence the behavior of those who aspired to its ideals and standards. The pursuit of adventure and renown, the defense of honor and faith, combined no doubt with less exalted motives to move men to band together under the discipline of a semi-religious code and cross the frontiers of Christendom. Moreover, their promotion and recruiting efforts, their experiences abroad, and the tales and trophies which they brought home further stimulated the imagination and added to Europe's knowledge of the world of Islam.

Judged both in terms of the military resistance it offered the Turks and the attention which its efforts attracted in the West, no order was comparable to the knights of Rhodes. Its skirmishes with the Ottomans on the coast of

Asia Minor, the islands of the Aegean, and at sea were publicized by pilgrims, merchants and diplomats, and, of course, the knights themselves. While its headquarters was still in the Levant, the order recruited its members from among the nobility of Europe. It maintained priories and commanderies in many western countries where its knights and officers were often influential at court. Although its reputation had at times suffered from its involvement in western politics and owing to the wealth and luxury of its European establishments, the order's unique role in resisting the Ottoman menace now contributed to restoring its ancient glory. Offspring of the first and most successful of the crusades, and the perpetual opponent of the Moslems, the knights of St. John enjoyed a special distinction among the military orders of the fifteenth century. Convinced that the sultan would sooner or later attempt to drive them from their island, the grandmaster and his subordinates were tireless in addressing appeals for aid and situation reports to the pope, the Latin princes, and the officers of the order stationed in the West. A dispatch of July 1477, from the grandmaster, Pierre d'Aubusson to the priors in Europe is characteristic of these appeals. The heritage for which their ancestors fought, he wrote, was threatened by the tyranny of the infidels and would be lost unless all members of the order came to its aid. Everyday the haughty sultan grows more powerful, more redoutable. He is a thunderbolt which nothing can stop and which carries with it the terror and desolation of all. His army is beyond numbering and it obeys him blindly at the slightest sign. His ships are captained and manned by skilled sailors. He has the best engineers, the finest machines of war, and a full treasury. He has vowed to drive all Christians from the Levant, and regardless of treaties or bad seasons, he strives continually to subdue all Christian lands and especially those possessed by the knights.

D'Aubusson reported that he had learned from spies and those in his pay at the Porte, that the Grand Turk was preparing to attack Rhodes with the most fearful force ever raised. The conqueror of Constantinople and Trebizond was determined to crush the knights who presented an obstacle to his boundless ambition. At this very moment, the grandmaster declared, the sultan is preparing his fleet and building up his forces on the mainland opposite Rhodes. He urged the brothers in Europe to reflect upon the certain disaster which would befall the order unless they came at once to its aid. Rhodes was surrounded by fire and would surely perish without the support of every member. He reminded them of their vows to fight in the defense of the faith. He begged them to succor the order which had nourished them, and not to abandon it to the fury of the barbarians.[14]

Contrary to d'Aubusson's expectations Mehmed II's forces did not strike

Rhodes in 1477 or in the following year of 1478. In fact in the summer of 1479 a Turkish envoy came to Rhodes with the mission of concluding a permanent truce between the knight sand the Porte. D'Aubusson believed this move to be a ruse to throw the knights off guard. He nonetheless signed a truce with the Turks, but at the same time speeded up his preparations in anticipation of a major attack. The knights did not have long to wait.[15] On January 25, 1479, sixteen years of war between Venice and the Turks had come to an end when the two powers concluded peace at Constantinople. Although the Republic's Italian enemies might rejoice over her losses, the West in general could take no comfort in a peace which increased the size and strength of the Ottoman giant. The permanent acquisition of places like Croia, Skutari, Negropont, and Lemnos by the Turks meant that the enemy of Christendom was not only more firmly established in the Balkans and the Aegean Sea, but had made strategic gains which would facilitate new aggression.[16] The Ottoman sultan left no doubts in the minds of western Christians as to his future intentions. Immediately in the summer of 1479 he ordered Ghedik Ahmed Pasha, sandjak-bey of Valona to attack the Ionian islands. Leonardo III Tocco, despot of Arta, count of Santa Maura, and duke of Cephalonia and Zante, unable to resist the Turks, fled with his family and some of his followers to Naples. The islands were left to the mercy of the Turks who were said to have massacred the servants of the duke and transported many of the inhabitants to Constantinople. Meanwhile Turkish raiders had penetrated Hungary and the lands of the Hapsburg, pillaging and ravaging the countryside.[17] The raiders were followed by a large Turkish army which invaded Transylvania. Stephen Bathory, voivode of Transylvania, and the colorful Paul Kinizsi, ban of Temesvar, hastily raised a Christian army of Hungarians, Saxons, Serbs, and Vlachs. They met the Turks between Broos and Mühlbach on October 13, 1479. When the day ended the Christians occupied the field from which the Turks had fled after one of the bloodiest and hardest fought battles of the period.[18]

Neither the knights of St. John nor the Latin West found much time for rejoicing over this victory. For while his troops were thus occupied Mehmed II remained in his capital completing preparations for the campaigns of the following year which brought the long awaited attack on Rhodes and the much feared invasion of Italy. Already in December 1479, a Turkish fleet under Mesih Pasha, a Greek renegade of the Paleologus family, appeared before Rhodes and off the island of Tilos. But finding both places stoutly defended the Turks retired to the bay of Physcos to await reinforcements the following spring. Finally at the end of May 1480, the Turkish fleet, now numbering more than one hundred vessels, returned, and on May 22 or 23, the sultan's troops debarked under cover of artillery fire and landed on the west coast of the island. The battle for Rhodes had begun.[19]

The siege of Rhodes in 1480 attracted more attention in the West than any battle between Christians and Turks in the half-century after the fall of Constantinople. The Ottoman failure was regarded as a significant set-back and it was widely publicized by the knights and their proponents in the West. But in a larger sense the mounting pressure of the Turkish advance, which reached a climax in 1480-1481, caused not only fear and alarm, but stimulated Latin curiosity. The result was, in some cases, a more searching and critical examination of the enemy, his history, institutions, and customs. As the ancient Persian conquest of Ionia had once conditioned the rise of Greek historiography, the Ottoman subjugation of a significant portion of Christian Europe had a similar effect on the development of historical thought and practice in the Renaissance.[20] Evidence of this new historical interest is to be seen in the works selected for publication by the early printers who at once capitalized on prevailing tastes while contributing to their further cultivation. No less than three histories of the siege were almost immediately printed in the West. Of these the *Obsidionis Rhodiae urbis descriptio* of Guillaume Caoursin, vice-chancellor of the order and a participant in the events he described, was printed ten times in the three years 1480-83, appearing in Latin, Italian, German, and English.[21] *De urbis Collosensis obsidione anno* 1480 *a Turcis tentata* of Giacomo de Curti and *Le Siège de Rhodus*, by Mary Dupuis, both eye-witnesses, were also printed in 1480, the former at Venice and the latter at Lyons and Audenarde.[22]

These historical narratives are, to be sure, still written from a distinctly Christian point of view and addressed to a Christian audience. The battle is cast in the context of the continuing struggle between the true faith and the infidel. The sultan is portrayed as the unequivocal foe of the religion of Christ, and his purpose in attacking Rhodes is to further his diabolical design of persecuting and ultimately exterminating the flock of St. Peter. The knights on the other hand are the defenders of the faith whose virtue and fidelity, courage and obedience, with the help of God, bring victory to the Christian cause. Indeed, divine assistance is not restricted to the indirect sort, but at the critical moment in the final assault appears in the persons of St. John the Baptist and the Virgin with the cross of Christ and accompanied by a heavenly host.[23]

But these conventional pious explanations are interspersed with interpretive passages betraying a critical and analytical facility. The Grand Turk also desires Rhodes for perfectly sound strategic reasons—its location, strength, economic importance—and for reasons of prestige, since all the world knows that the knights have successfully defied and resisted his previous designs on their island.[24] Moreover, the bulk of the text in each of the three works is devoted to the events of the siege which is reconstructed in a straight-forward factual narrative. Considerable attention is given to the composition of the opposing forces, their weapons and armament (especially the Turkish employment of artillery), to tactics (the accounts are invaluable for the detailed information on the amphibious aspects of the operation), and to matters of logistics. Although the hero of the story is the grandmaster, Pierre d'Aubusson, as the villain is the Turkish commander, Mesih Pasha, the deeds of individual warriors on both sides are recounted and even the role of the citizens of Rhodes is duly acknowledged.[25] In structure and content the three histories are characteristic of that genre of Renaissance historical writing which contemporary humanistic scholarship recognized as something less than true history but as factual histories worthy of being read and employed in the composition of the former.[26]

In the following pages the struggle for Rhodes has been reconstructed primarily on the basis of Caoursin, Dupuis, and de Curti. Additional sources such as diplomatic dispatches have been used only to clarify a few particulars and to render the account more intelligible. Otherwise the narrative reproduces substantially, though in abridged form, what literate contemporaries now for the first time were able to read only a few months after the event about a major battle with the Turks.[27]

Following their successful landing the Turks concentrated their forces on and about a hill called St. Stephen's due west of the city of Rhodes near the northern tip of the island. From St. Stephen's they were able to survey the entire city and its harbor defenses. After the initial landings, their ships continued to ferry reinforcements from the Turkish mainland until their forces numbered perhaps 70,000.[28] While the main body was consolidating its position under the protection of St. Stephen's hill, the Turks placed three large cannon near St. Anthony's church, not far from the harbor. They opened fire on St. Nicholas's tower, the key to the harbor defenses and the approach to Rhodes from the sea.[29] Mounted patrols scouted the walls of the city, but were prevented from getting too close by the defenders who sallied from behind the walls and drove them off. In one of these brushes, however, the Turks surrounded a small band of defenders and a knight was killed and decapitated. Although the Christians recovered his body, the Turks fixed his head to a lance and rode back to their camp carrying it aloft.[30]

Mesih Pasha fully appreciated the strategic importance of the tower of St. Nicholas, which denied him use of the harbor in an assault upon the city. From the first then, his strongest efforts were aimed at the reduction of the tower. Day and night the Turks bombarded it with the cannon around St. Anthony's church, but the knights delivered counter-battery fire against the Turkish positions, and somewhat hampered their activities. The Turks, nevertheless, fired three hundred stones at the tower, and succeeded in damaging a large part of the western wall. D'Aubusson sent working parties to repair the damage with stones and trees. He strengthened the garrison within the tower, stationed men under the walls in that section of the city, and under the wall which ran from the tower of St. Peter to the Mandrakee. At this last point, the Turks were to be permitted to land, because, when the tide was out, the knights had strewn the bottom with casks and planks full of spikes to make it impassable. Small craft were fitted out with gunpowder and other combustibles to serve as fire ships. D'Aubusson emplaced the artillery within the city to achieve the utmost firepower against the Turkish ships. Finally, when all preparations had been made, the grandmaster took personal command of the garrison in the tower of St. Nicholas.[31]

In the early morning hours of June 9, fifty Turkish ships loaded with troops and weapons slipped from their moorings behind the hill of St. Stephen. Under cover of darkness they sailed around Sandy Point, the northeast end of the island, and headed toward St. Nicholas. As they came near to the mole and the tower, the pre-dawn silence was shattered with wild shouts, blasting trumpets, crashing tambourines, and other loud noises. The defenders replied with artillery. The knights drove the ships back from the mole, sinking several of them. Led by the grandmaster they engaged those Turks who managed to land. A fierce struggle ensued. Many Turks met death on the mole, at the breach in the tower, or by drowning in the sea. After a short time it was all over; the Turks withdrew from the first assault on St. Nicholas leaving behind seven hundred dead.[32]

During the action against the tower, the Turks were busy against other parts of the city. Mesih Pasha had ordered a continuous bombardment of the walls, especially in the sections defended by the tongues of Italy and Provence, hoping to draw off defenders from St. Nicholas. With the failure of the amphibious assault upon the harbor, however, he now determined to destroy the walls and storm the city from that quarter. A tremendous cannonade followed. The buildings within the city were shaken as though by an earthquake. Large parts of the walls as well as the houses within crashed to the ground. The deafening reports from the guns were heard for miles around.[33] The grandmaster responded to this challenge as he had to the threat against

VII: Rhodes
   (Hartmann Schedel, *Liber Chronicarum*. Nuremberg, 1493).

the harbor. He ordered prayers, and devotions, and religious processions. He had all the buildings in the Jewish quarter behind the walls of Italy and Provence torn down. Everyone within Rhodes was kept busy repairing the damaged walls, digging hasty defenses as a secondary line of defense, or preparing fagots with sulphur or other combustibles to be hurled down on the Turks in the fosses.[34] The Turks, nevertheless, under cover of artillery fire advanced to the banks of the ditch immediately before the wall near the tower of Italy. Here they dug gun emplacements and brought forward some of their cannon. Seeing the danger a band of defenders moved silently along the ditch until they reached the spot where the Turks had prepared their positions. With the help of ladders they sprang from the trench and threw themselves upon the enemy. They took the Turks by surprise, killed ten and drove off the rest. The knights wrecked the abandoned artillery and threw in into the ditch. They beheaded the ten dead Turks, put their heads on the ends of lances, and mounted them on the wall for all to see.[35]

Meeting such stubborn resistance before the walls, the Turkish commander decided to assault a second time the tower of St. Nicholas. The Turks built a pontoon bridge out of casks with planks nailed to them, wide enough for six mounted soldiers abreast, and long enough to stretch from the bank under their control to the tower.[36] When the battle began, the bridge was to be towed by rowboats to the mole. Aware of the Turks' preparations, d'Aubusson again strengthened the garrison in the tower and on the mole. A thousand laborers were employed in digging ditches around the tower in which soldiers were stationed. A strong contingent of knights was also posted in the damaged section of the tower.[37]

The expected assault came shortly after midnight on June 19. Thirty Turkish galleys shielded the barges which towed the bridge toward the mole. Picked troops in small boats sailed directly for the tower. Others debarked from the galleys which all the while supported the landing operation with cannon fire. As the Turks' leading elements approached the tower, they once again filled the air with shrieks and cries and other noises. The defenders opened fire, showering the fleet and advancing soldiers with missiles from the guns within the tower and from the town. Four ships were sunk; others were set afire; and others, their cables severed by the cannon fire, capsized later at sea and were lost. With great effort the Turks rowed the bridge into position, only to see it destroyed by the knights' cannon, and many of their men drowned. Those who reached the mole were engaged by the Christians and driven back into the sea. The battle raged over the control of the mole through the early morning hours. The Turks, however, despite their overwhelming numbers, were unable to establish a beachhead, let alone seriously threaten the tower.

Around 10:00 in the morning, with the momentum of their assault long since dissipated, the Turks withdrew. They had suffered a costly defeat. Twenty-five hundred of their number were reported slain; many more were wounded, and the losses in weapons and equipment were beyond measure. Mesih Pasha, disheartened over his losses and his inability to take the tower by storm, spoke with no one, we are told, for the space of three days. The assault against the harbor defenses was not renewed.[38]

The Turks now settled down to a more systematic siege. While all parts of the city were subjected to artillery fire and harassing activities, Mesih Pasha focused his attention upon the eastern section, the walls around the Jewish quarter in the neighborhood of the tower of Italy.[39] Some accounts of the daily activities of besieged and besiegers during this period are found in the eyewitness reports. There are detailed descriptions of the Turks' conduct of the siege—the continuing bombardment, mining operations, skirmishes and the like.[40] There are also tales describing the Turks' nature, cruelty, and duplicity. Mary Dupuis describes a skirmish during which the Turks captured a knight and a citizen of Rhodes, who, along with another Christian, were impaled and exhibited above the fosses. Impaling, Dupuis explains, was the special method reserved by the Turks for the execution of Christians, "...pour les faire morir plus angoisseusement, et a plus grant martir". In an approving manner Dupuis records that the grandmaster retaliated on the following day by impaling five Turks. They were raised high on the wall, in view of all the enemy, "...en leur demontrant que pour ung Chrestien quils y mectroyent, il y en mectroit deux Turcs".[41]

Caoursin relates an incident which shows that the Ottomans had some knowledge of psychological warfare. He writes that just before the final assault, Turks came to the fosses in the evenings in groups of two and three. Accompanying themselves with taborettes, they sang gay and boasting songs predicting a Turkish victory over Rhodes. They said that their commander had promised them the riches of the city. They proclaimed their intentions of enslaving all children under the age of ten and of converting them to Islam. Everyone else was to be slaughtered; those under twenty by having their throats slit, those over twenty were to be impaled. The Turks sharpened for this purpose eight thousand long stakes which they carried with them in the final charge.[42] In the end, however, these threats seem to have stiffened the defenders' spirit of resistance. De Curti testifies that since God was their protector, "...neither death nor the vindictive sword, nor pales sharpened before our eyes, nor most cruel torments affected to abate us".[43]

Apparently the Turks' attempts to further their cause through plots and intrigues met with no better success. The eyewitnesses all dwelt at length

VIII: Siege of Rhodes 1480.
(Johannes Adelphus, *Die Türkische Chronica*. Strasbourg, 1516).

on the deceitful character of the Turks—their efforts to misguide the knights through traitors, to eliminate d'Aubusson by assassination, and to undermine the resistance of the defenders through false negotiations. It was common knowledge that Mehmed II regularly employed Greeks, Jews, and Latin Christians for political, diplomatic, and military purposes. Indeed, they played important parts in many of his ventures. His ability to use others for his own purposes, regardless of their origin, creed, or original allegiance, was indisputably one of the sultan's greatest gifts; but the practice was of course vehemently condemned by the defenders of Rhodes and the Latin narrators of the siege. The tale of treason goes back to the planning stages of the campaign when Mehmed II called upon three renegades to advise him. One was a former Rhodian nobleman named Anthony Meligalas, who, according to Caoursin, not only provided the sultan with much technical information about the city but enthusiastically urged him to attack the island. Another was Demetrius Sophianos, who, after the fall of Negropont, renounced Christianity in favor of Islam and entered the service of the Turks. He had been in Rhodes as a Turkish envoy and therefore possessed some intelligence concerning the disposition of the city.[44]

A more significant and sustained role was played by a renegade named George, who with his family had made his home in Constantinople. He was an expert in the making and employment of artillery and had been in the service of the sultan for some time. George, too, had visited Rhodes and therefore advised Mehmed during his preparations for the siege, and accompanied the Turks when they attacked the island. Shortly after the beginning of the battle George appeared before the walls of the city and begged to be permitted to enter. He was led before the grandmaster where he confessed the evils he had done to Christianity; but, for the love of the true faith, and his soul's salvation, he now desired to repent. In order to demonstrate his faith, he answered the grandmaster's questions about the strength of the Turks. Nevertheless, many knights counseled against trusting a man who had forsaken Christ and had fought on the side of His enemies. Others, struck by his speech and bearing, believed he was truly repentant and wished to use his skills for the Christian cause. Within a few days, however, informers in the Turkish host shot arrows into the city, bearing notes which warned the defenders to beware of the treason of George. D'Aubusson assigned six knights to watch his movements, yet continued to consult him on matters of the defense. During the last days of the siege, the grandmaster at George's suggestion placed a cannon near the damaged section of the wall in the Jewish quarter, but succeeded only in drawing increased fire from the Turkish guns. Convinced of George's treachery, d'Aubusson had him tortured, whereupon the renegade confessed that he had been sent by the Turks to spy and to mislead the Christians in their conduct of the defense. He also admitted that, in like manner, he had assisted in the capture of many Christian places in Greece, for which crimes the knights condemned and executed him.[45]

According to our Latin accounts a number of Moslems and renegade Christians deserted the Turkish camp and fled to the city professing their desire to become Christians. D'Aubusson and the knights were, with good reason, very suspicious of these alleged converts. Some undoubtedly were sincere, for when the siege was lifted sixty of them sailed aboard a vessel bound for Italy to appear before the pope. Others, however, like the renegade George, were clearly spies and saboteurs. On one occasion, two Turks sought to enter the city in the guise of deserters, with a secret mission of poisoning the grandmaster. The Christians easily discovered the plot, and while one escaped, the other was executed by the knights who threw him into the sea with a large stone tied around his neck.[46]

The defenders did not deceive themselves by underestimating the Turks' strength. While they described the Turks as infidels and savages, depraved, treacherous, and brutal, our narrators did not refrain from praising their power and ability. The Christians were outnumbered more than ten to one. Mesih Pasha's fleet covered the waters around Rhodes. The Turks had accomplished no mean task in gathering this huge force, but had performed a spectacular feat in ordering, controlling, transporting, landing and supplying an army of such proportions in an amphibious operation. The Christians marveled over the Turks' skill in tactics and engineering. They were most impressed with the Turks' artillery—in its numbers, size, accuracy, and effectiveness.[47] The Rhodians feared and admired the artillery above all else. The three cannon emplaced in the churchyard of St. Anthony's at the start of the siege made short work of the west wall of the tower of St. Nicholas. The renegade George told the grandmaster, according to Caoursin, that the Turks had sixteen such pieces, all of them twenty-two feet in length, and firing stones the least of which measured four spans in circumference. Even the most experienced soldiers were astonished by the size and effectiveness of these weapons; George declared that there were none to equal them anywhere in the world.[48] Eight of these big guns bombarded the wall around the Jewish quarter. The bombardment was so intense in the days immediately preceding the final assault that the defenders were unable to remain at their posts, and were prevented from raising their heads above the wall. Altogether the Turks fired more than three thousand stones at the wall, much of which was destroyed. The stones also demolished the secondary defenses, behind the breach, and filled up the fosses before the wall. In the face of such artillery the walled city had become obsolete.[49]

One hour after sunrise, on the morning of July 28, the main body of the Turks charged the weakened wall around the Jewish quarter. With little effort, they passed through the breach and several thousand of them mounted the wall and planted their banners before the Christians could sound a general alarm. Some of the attackers, climbing down a ladder inside the wall, entered the city. Within a matter of minutes, however, all Rhodes was alerted. One body of defenders led by the grandmaster, and another commanded by his brother, Antoine d'Aubusson, ascended the wall and engaged the Turks. Others destroyed the ladder by which the Turks were passing into the city, and killed those who had reached the ground. As the battle raged atop the wall, shouts and cries invoking the names of Jesus and Mohammed rose above the clash of weapons and bodies. For two hours the conflict continued. Pierre d'Aubusson was several times wounded, but remained in the press. The knights contained the penetration, seized the Turkish standards and planted in their place banners bearing the effigies of Christ, His Holy Mother, and St. John the Baptist, patron of the order. The Turks on the wall were unable to break through the line of the defenders and could not jump to the ground because of the height of the wall. Behind them thousands more swarmed over the fosses and into the breach, but while the Christians held fast, they could go no farther. The defenders above hurled boiling oil and burning fagots upon the enemy under the walls and in the fosses. Before long the Turkish ranks fell into disorder; and in their efforts to withdraw they stumbled over one another in utter confusion. The knights, led by Antoine d'Aubusson pursued them outside the city and prevented them from regrouping before the wall. The rout was complete.[50] The battle was over. The Turks had suffered tremendous losses. In the final assault alone more than 3,000 died, and in the whole campaign, Caoursin recorded that 9,000 Turks perished, while twice that number were wounded. Less than three weeks after the final assault, the entire Turkish force withdrew to its ships and returned home. With a numerically superior navy and army and the best artillery of the day, the Turks had endeavored unsuccessfully for three months to take the city of Rhodes.[51]

First reports of the Turkish siege of Rhodes reached Italy late in June and early in July 1480. Alberto Cortese, envoy of the duke of Ferrara at Venice, wrote on June 18, that news had arrived of the Turks' descent upon the island of Rhodes.[52] On July 3, Antonio da Montecatino reported that an account of the siege and the battle over the tower of St. Nicholas was discussed in Florence.[53] According to Battista Bendedei, the representative of Ferrara in Rome, letters reached the papal court on June 29 and July 2 describing the Turkish attack and appealing for immediate aid from the West. The first request was forwarded to Rome by King Ferrante of Naples who urged the pope to join him in sending ships and supplies to the knights.[54] On July 3, Sixtus IV announced his intention of preparing several ships for the immediate relief of Rhodes, and of soliciting the support of the Christian powers to raise a large fleet by mid-August.[55] On July 5, the pope called upon the princes of the West to assist him in raising a fleet of forty-eight vessels to relieve Rhodes and inflict a major defeat upon the enemies of the name of Christ.[56] The pope announced the grant of indulgences to anyone who would contribute to the cause of the holy work.[57]

Sixtus IV's efforts to raise a large fleet to drive the Turks from Rhodes were to be interrupted by more pressing demands in Italy itself. Some aid from the West, however, did reach the besieged island. Giacomo de Curti mentions the arrival of a vessel from Sicily on the morning of June 1. It carried food, supplies, and many soldiers. The defenders were amazed by the passage of the ship through the Turkish fleet, and praised God and St. John for the miracle. Early in August two more ships came to Rhodes.[58] They were sent by Ferrante of Naples and brought men and supplies and the promise of additional help from Sixtus IV. Although the Turks tried to prevent their reaching the island, the Christian vessels successfully braved the enemy's cannon and entered the harbor amidst cheers and shouts of encouragement from those in the city.[59]

At about 9:00 on a September evening less than a month after the siege had been lifted, the pilgrim galley on which Felix Fabri sailed arrived before Rhodes. As they prepared to enter the harbor, Felix tells us, the Rhodians created much commotion, lighting fires on their towers, and firing a cannon at the approaching vessel, thinking it to be one of the Turks'. When the pilgrims had convinced them otherwise, he continues, the people from all over the city flocked to the wall carrying lighted torches anxious to greet the first Christian vessel to enter their port after the departure of the Turks.[60] As they entered the harbor the next morning the pilgrims passed by the shores which were covered with the bodies of dead Turks. The city itself was almost completely ruined, and the stone cannon balls fired by the Turks were everywhere. Felix's party remained at Rhodes for four days during which our pilgrim tells us they spent much money, for everything was expensive owing to the plundering and destruction accomplished by the Turks. When they left the island there embarked with them some knights of the order of St. John, and some who had spent many years as captives of the Turks and who deserted the Turkish army during the siege. There also sailed with them some Jews who had fought valiantly in the defense of the city.[61]

IX: The final assault on Rhodes, 1480
(Johannes Adelphus, *Die Türkische Chronica*. Strasbourg, 1516).

With the arrival in Europe of the pilgrims, ex-captives of the Turks and those who had fought at Rhodes, the news of the Christian victory spread throughout the continent. On November 29, 1480, Louis XI, king of France, addressed a letter to the citizens of Angers announcing the great triumph. By the grace of God, the Blessed Virgin, and St. John, Louis wrote, the siege of Rhodes by the cruel enemy of the Christian faith has been lifted. The knights killed 10,000 or 12,000 Turks! All good Christians should rejoice and return thanks to God and His Holy Mother; therefore, Louis commanded that the victory should be announced to the people. He ordered celebrations to be held, ". . .et en faire feuz de joye, processions solennelles, sonner cloches et chanter loanges à Dieu, acostumées à faire en saincte eglise pour telles grandes et miraculeuse nouvelles".[62]

Before Europe had received the welcome news of the Christian victory, however, it had experienced its own Turkish invasion. Only a few weeks after the first reports of the descent of the sultan's troops upon Rhodes reached the West, a fleet of 140 vessels under the command of Ghedik Ahmed Pasha appeared off southern Italy.[63] On July 28, 1480, the very day on which the Christians of Rhodes triumphed over the Turks, an estimated 18,000 Ottoman soldiers landed on the shore of Apulia near the city of Otranto.[64] Panic spread through the Italian peninsula. King Ferrante was at Aversa when he learned that the Turks had invaded his kingdom. He began feverish preparations to raise a force to relieve Otranto.[65] On August 2, he wrote to his son Alfonso, duke of Calabria, ordering him to halt his campaign in Tuscany and to march at once for the south. On the same day Ferrante addressed letters to the pope and to the rulers of Urbino and Ferrara, requesting immediate aid.[66] In the days which followed the king sent similar letters to other Italian governments warning them that unless they joined him in expelling the infidels the latter would soon overrun their own states.[67]

Meanwhile the troops of Ghedik Ahmed Pasha ravaged the countryside in the vicinity of Otranto, pillaging and burning everything in their path and killing or enslaving the peasants. The stout garrison of Otranto counter-attacked the Turks before they had established their camp and defenses, and luckily freed some of the captives. The Ottomans, however, far out-numbered the defenders, who lacked not only men but also adequate weapons, and soon contained them within Otranto which they then placed under siege. The Turkish commander promised the citizens of Otranto their lives and freedom if they would submit peacefully. When the Christians refused, the Turks commenced an intensive bombardment of the city. Although the people of Otranto resisted stubbornly, on August 11, 1480, the enemy forced an entrance through a breach in the wall made by their cannon, and easily took command of the city. The Turks had at last acquired a foothold in the Italian peninsula.[68]

The disturbing news that Otranto had fallen struck terror in the hearts of the Italians as reports of the Turks' savage treatment of the Otrantini became known. The invaders led 800 innocent citizens to a nearby hill, called since that time the hill of the martyrs. There, at the order of the pasha, the Christians were offered the choice of embracing Islam, or submitting to a most barbarous slaughter. According to Pietro Colonna, one man replied: "Scegliamo piuttosto di perire per Christo, con qualsiasi di morte, anzichè rinegare la sua fede". Galatino proudly recorded, "uno ha dato la riposta per tutti, sciamo pronti a subire qualsiasi morte, anzichè rinunziare a Christo, figlio di Dio, e alla sua fede".[69] The Turks then butchered the martyrs; some were beheaded, others impaled. They were reported to have fed the remains to dogs. The aged archbishop, Stefano de Agercula Pendinelli was celebrating the mass when the Turks seized him at the holy altar and, we are told, sawed him in two. A similar fate befell the captain of the garrison, Francesco Zurlo, and his son. Altogether the Turks were said to have slaughtered 12,000 people. Those who remained alive they herded into boats and sent to Valona to be sold into slavery.[70]

News of the massacre of Otranto spread quickly through the peninsula. On August 14, Niccolò Sadoleto sent to his government "la mala novella che Otranto e perduto, cum altre castelle. . .". King Ferrante requested Sadoleto and the ambassadors from Milan and Florence to inform their respective governments of the Turkish victory and the impending danger to all.[71] The king sent his own messenger to Rome with an account of the tragedy and an urgent appeal to the pope. Battista Bendedei wrote that news of Otranto's fall reached Rome on the night of August 12, and that the pope and cardinals were greatly disturbed and consulted at once on the matter.[72] Sigismondo de' Conti recorded that the Romans were so alarmed, one might believe that the Turks were already at the city gates. "Terror had taken hold of all minds," he declared, "even the pope meditated flight."[73]

Sixtus IV, however, remained in Rome and did all he could to muster aid to repulse the Turks. De' Conti admitted that the pope would have watched with indifference if any Christian power had attacked his faithless ally the king of Naples. "But it was a very different matter when the common foe of Christendom had actually got a footing on Italian soil", he observed, "and speedily the papacy and Rome itself were threatened with utter ruin, unless he were promptly expelled."[74] The pope demanded immediate assistance from the princes. "If the faithful, especially the Italians, wish to preserve their lands, their homes, their wives, their children, their liberty, and their lives," he declared, "if they wish to maintain that faith into which we have been baptized and through which we are generated, let them at last trust in our accord, let them take up arms and fight."[75]

On August 14, the pope held a consistory where it was decided to devote all energies to expelling the Turks from Italy.[76] On August 18, Sixtus appointed Gabriele Rangoni cardinal legate to Naples, and on August 23, he sent an appeal to the Italian powers to send representatives to a congress to be held in Rome in November.[77] The pope labored tirelessly to bring about peace among the Italians. He set an example by settling his own troubles with Florence, and got the Republic on the Arno to pledge fifteen galleys. On December 4, he dispatched Cardinal Savelli to Genoa to settle the strife in that city and to oversee the outfitting of the papal fleet.[78] Twenty-five galleys were being constructed, some at Genoa and the rest at Ancona.[79] To finance the undertaking the pope levied a tax of a gold ducat upon every hearth in the states of the church, and a tithe for two years upon every ecclesiastical establishment in the same territory.[80] Also, on December 4, 1480, Sixtus appointed the Franciscan, Angelo Carletti, to the post of nuncio and apostolic commissioner for the crusade.[81] The pope charged Carletti with preaching the crusade to the Christian people. He ordered the Minorite to collect money for the same cause and remit it to the Franciscan convent of Santa Maria of Aracoeli in Rome. He empowered Carletti to commission others to aid him in the preaching, and to grant plenary indulgences to those who contributed a sum equal to that which they spent in maintaining their families for one week.[82]

In the meantime envoys from the Italian governments arrived in Rome and discussed measures to meet the emergency. In a letter to Bologna on January 3, 1481, Sixtus IV explained that he and the cardinals had decided to contribute 150,000 ducats to the war against the Turks. They intended to send 50,000 ducats to Hungary and to use the rest of the money in outfitting 25 galleys. In addition to the troops already sent to Ferrante, the papacy planned to raise a force of 3000 soldiers for the recovery of Otranto. The envoys at Rome had agreed that a fleet of 100 galleys should be gathered, and that 200,000 ducats should be sent annually to the king of Hungary. Sixtus urged all the princes to follow the example of the papacy and to contribute their share. [83] On March 8, 1481, the pope wrote to the Italian powers proclaiming a general peace in Italy and demanding immediate support of the campaign against the Turks. He declared that France had agreed to participate in the war and that Germany would be invited to do the same. The papacy intended to furnish 25 galleys, Naples 40, Genoa 5, Ferrara 4, Siena 3, Bologna 2, and Lucca, Mantua, and Montferat 1 each. Milan had promised 30,000 ducats and Florence 40,000 ducats.[84] On April 8, 1481, the pope wrote to all the Christian princes calling upon them to take the cross. He granted indulgences to all who contributed to the defense of Christendom.[85] On April 9, he levied a tenth on all ecclesiastical revenues in France and the Dauphine and appointed Cardinal della Rovere collector general.[86]

The Italians responded slowly, but during the spring of 1481 a fleet was prepared and on June 30 it was commissioned by the pope. Under the command of Cardinal Fregoso it sailed to Naples and on to Otranto which was finally recovered from the Turks on September 10.[87] The northern powers —Germany, France, and England—played no part in driving the Turks out of Italy. Internal dissensions occupied the Germans. Louis XI of France only used the occasion to attempt to wring privileges from the pope and to gain papal support for his opposition to Ferrante of Naples.[88] Edward IV of England wrote to Sixtus that although he desired to join the war against the Turks his troubles at home prevented him from doing so. He reassured the pope that he would have "preferred being associated with the other sovereigns of Christendom in an expedition against the Turk", to making war upon Christians as he was forced to do to maintain his throne.[89]

We must not conclude that the English were uninformed or unconcerned with the problems of the Levant. The view that life in England in this period was wholly disrupted by the ravages of the so-called Wars of the Roses and that the nation was mostly cut off from the wider currents of European history is no longer tenable. The works of Paul Murray Kendall, George Parks, R. J. Mitchell, and Roberto Weiss show that at the same time that the nation was in the throes of finding itself, individual Englishmen were involved in international affairs.[90] By letters and reports from the continent and through foreign residents and travelers the doings of the Turks were regularly publicized. English chroniclers recorded the details of all the important battles with the Ottomans—the fall of Constantinople, and the sieges of Belgrade and Rhodes. English pilgrims and adventurers brought home first-hand reports of the East and the much-feared enemy of the faith. Although the creation of the Levant Company was still in the distant future English merchants were attracted by the lucrative markets of the eastern Mediterranean. We read of a trader by the name of Nicholas Jone who in 1443 returned from Turkey leading three camels and an ostrich as presents for his king. In 1446 and again in 1456 ships put out from Bristol to carry on trade in Turkish waters. Commerce in the Mediterranean was no less dangerous for Englishmen than for their counterparts on the continent; and in 1514 we hear of the capture of an English vessel by Turkish pirates.[91] The contacts between English merchants and Moslems were at least sufficient to provoke King Edward IV to rationalize the practice in a letter to the pope. In his view it was "advantageous to the Christian religion that wealth and other things precious from their natural excellence should be drawn into its power from the hands of infidels", and therefore Edward "willingly permits his subjects to pass over to any part of Africa for traffic, and the exchange of baser merchandise for nobler, provided this be sanctioned by the pope's authority".[92]

Papal emissaries, crusade preachers, and collectors of crusading taxes were active throughout the British Isles. In the manner of his predecessors, Pope Paul II directed the attention of Thomas, Archbishop of Canterbury, to the grave danger threatening Christendom which was only to be resisted by the unified strength of the Christian princes. He therefore implored the archbishop "to request and exhort the king and the natives of the said realm [of England] in his city, diocese and province, to undertake the crusade", and "to publish, in his own person or by fit preachers appointed by him the said [pope's] letters, and to stir up the faithful of his province, of both sexes, secular and regular, to devotion and to an expedition so holy, or at least to induce them to contribute aid". For this purpose the archbishop was granted authority to grant dispensation to those who assumed the cross, or to those who were sick or otherwise unfit for fighting, but who contributed money, and to commute vows into almsdeed for the defense of the faith.[93]

A score of entries in the *Calendar of Papal Registers* testify to the activities of papal commissioners in the British Isles. On February 17, 1473, the archbishop of St. Andrew's was appointed papal nuncio with the power of legate *de latere* to secure with the help of the king of Scotland support for the crusade. In 1476 the same prelate was given the faculty "to dispense a hundred men and women related in the simple third and the third and third, and the simple fourth, and the fourth and fourth degrees of kindred and affinity, to marry, or, in the case of those who have married to contract anew and remain in their marriages. . .". The letter instructed the legate to make a money composition with those involved, "for the preparing of a fleet against the Turks and [to] send such money to the *camera* within six months after the dispensation". On May 24, 1476, the abbot of St. Mary's ,Abingdon, in the diocese of Salisbury, was appointed papal nuncio and commissioner to King Edward and his people, and collector in England ". . .especially of the offerings of those who have not been able to go to Rome in person in order to gain the indulgences of the Jubilee; the said offering to be used for the maintenance of a fleet and army against the Turks". On April 1, 1476, Giovanni de Giglis, a subdeacon and nuncio of the pope was appointed collector of the apostolic *camera* in

England. In December 1478, the pope empowered de Giglis to grant plenary remission of all sins and the Jubilee indulgence to those who "being contrite in spirit and truly confessed" contributed as much money as they would have spent going to Rome. The money was to be used for the defense of the Christian religion against the Turks. On September 29, 1481, the pope granted Richard Lessi, a priest of the diocese of York, commutation of his vows to make pilgrimages to Rome and the Holy Land, into a sum of 100 gold ducats, "which he has paid to the pope's datary in aid of the crusade and in aid of the fleet which with a great number of triremes the pope has prepared against the Turks".[94]

Although England was not a prominent participant in the crusades of the Middle Ages, the ideal of the holy war was, together with the other accepted values of Christian chivalry, espoused by her aristocracy and continued to be so through the fifteenth century. Commenting on the English authors and translations of our period Arthur Ferguson observes: "All agree, and moreover, constantly reiterate, that the knight's duty is to defend Holy Church, protect the widow and orphan... maintain justice, and repel aggression".[95] What is more, individual Englishmen, and Scots too, responded to the appeals of churchmen and contributed not only money but went in person against the Turk. On April 20, 1455, Calixtus III awarded a special grant and provision to one Alexander Preston, a canon of Glasgow, "...who went lately with a notable company to the Holy Land to fight against the infidels, and whose father and many other of his kinsmen have fought against the infidels in the lands of the infidels and been made knights...". The same pope provided letters of safe conduct for Robert and Thomas Garnet and Robert Allerton who with their servants passed through Rome on their way to fight the Turks.[96] In 1458, Pius II made a grant to Alexander Preston, who had been "...engaged for about a year with 12 archers and more in fighting against the infidels", and the pope issued a safe conduct to him and his retinue to the numner of 12. On February 19, 1460, Pius II granted remission of a year and forty days of enjoined penance to all who made gifts to Richard Morray and Patrick Hunter, laymen of the dioceses of St. Andrew and Glasgow. The pope explained that the two men had "for more than six years fought in Turkey for the defense of the Catholic faith against the Turks, exposing their bodies to bloodshed", and having exhausted their money and supplies they were so poor that they were unable to return to their homes without help.[97] Others who are mentioned by name—John Sayntone, William Atwode, Hugh Johnnis, Sir Robert Curson, Robert Champlayn—received credentials and letters of permission to go and fight the Turks, but of their activities we have no further information.[98]

136

X: Turkish attack on Otranto, 1480
(Johannes Adelphus, *Die Türkische Chronica*. Strasbourg, 1516).

Englishmen, too, were prominent members of the Order of St. John and in this capacity were active in publicizing the Turkish threat in England as well as resisting the Turk in the Levant. English archers participated in the defense of Rhodes in 1444. An English sailor, one Roger Jervis, has been credited with helping to foil the second assault of the tower of St. Nicholas by diving under water and detaching an anchor to a cable by which the Turks had planned to fasten a pontoon bridge to the mole where the tower was situated.[99] Sir Hugh Middleton, Turcopolier at the time of the siege in 1444, and Sir John Langstrother and Sir John Weston, both grand priors in England, played important roles in the affairs of the order at home and in the East.[100] The career of Weston's successor as grand prior, Sir John Kendall, further illustrates the involvement of Englishmen in the affairs of the Levant as well as the efforts prosecuted by English members of the order to arouse their countrymen to the Ottoman peril. It is also indicative of the continuing importance of knights and officers of military and chivalric orders who participated in the public life of the time. At different periods Kendall served as representative of his order to Rome, Venice, France, and England, as papal envoy to various countries in the West, and as English ambassador to France and Austria.[101] In 1479 he was charged with the important mission of alerting the pope to the impending Turkish attack on Rhodes. He remained in the West to raise money and supplies for its defense. Sixtus IV appointed him papal commissary and deputy at large with authority to distribute indulgences to those who contributed to the defense of the faith. For this purpose he had standard forms printed on parchment to which he affixed his seal. He received the support of his own king, Edward IV, who in a document of April 29, 1480, commanded all persons in Ireland to assist Sir John Kendall in raising aid in money and men to fight the Turks.[102] He apparently achieved some success. An indulgence bearing his seal and the date April 22, 1480, was issued to Dame Joan Plumpton, wife of Sir William Plumpton and is published in the correspondence of that Yorkshire family. [103] With the money he raised Kendall was able to provision a ship in which he sailed for the Levant. But the vessel never reached Rhodes, nor, contrary to the official historian of the order in England, was Kendall able to assume command of the English knights during the siege. From a decree of the Venetian senate dated April 19, 1485, awarding restitution for losses incurred, we learn that enroute to Rhodes Sir John Kendall and his ship were seized by the Venetian naval captain at Modon. His cargo was plundered and Sir John himself lost a horse and 80 ducats.[104]

In conclusion we cannot dismiss the response of King Edward IV to the pope's appeal as nothing but a weak attempt at dissimulation. Remote as the Turkish threat was from the British Isles, it was still a problem for all Christians and especially Christian rulers. The crusade can hardly be described as a major issue in the foreign policy of fifteenth-century England; but, here too, it was considered a moral obligation of the Christian prince. Behind the ruthless, dynastic, and materialistically oriented power politics of Lancastrian, York and Tudor, lurked a conscience impregnated with the ethical norms of Christian chivalry. However short of the ideal they may have fallen in performance, knighthood remained their one real measure of princely aims and attainment. Thus Henry IV before mounting the throne had both journeyed to the Holy Land and "crusaded" in Prussia. His brother, Sir John Beaufort, fought the Moslems at the siege of Mahdia. If Henry failed to produce the men and arms requested by the Byzantine emperor, Manual Paleologus, he extended the hospitality of the realm to the visiting monarch and at least felt constrained to promise support. And in the very last year of his reign the matter was still discussed in council held at the White Friar's in London where it was agreed that galleys and other provisions were to be made for the expedition which the king planned to lead to the Levant. The campaign, we know, never came off. But, if the poet Thomas de Elmham may be believed, the king's conscience was slightly eased, when, as he lay dying, he was moved to a room called the chamber of Bethlehem, since he had sworn to enter Bethlehem before his death.[105]

Similarly Henry V, Henry VI, and Edward IV all proclaimed their intentions to take the cross while at the same time pleading that their troubles at home prevented their doing so. All three monarchs, however, agreed with the principle of the crusade, gave token aid, and endorsed the papal efforts to raise men and money in England, and in particular supported the efforts of the knights of Rhodes. Henry V joined with the duke of Burgundy in dispatching the reconnaisance agent Ghillebert de Lannoy to gather information in the Levant. The king died in the same year; but in his last moments protested the sincerity of his plans to take the cross if only France had not interfered and God had granted him more time.[106] In 1454, Henry VI, too, proclaimed his willingness "to risk the whole strength of his realm on behalf of the catholic faith". The chronicler of London speaks favorably of the reception accorded in his reign to papal collectors who were sent by the Holy Father "...to mayntayn hys warrys agayne the Turke, that was fulle cruelle unto Cristen men and thoroughe thys londe of Ingalonde every man was fayne to do and gyffe after hyr power".[107] A curious report, allegedly based on the conversation of a Milanese ambassador with a servant in the royal household and pertaining to Edward IV's personal habits, represented that king as devoting "himself to his pleasures and having a good time with the ladies", but without completely neglecting his duties as a Christian prince; for he was also believed to be "making preparations to send the Earl of Rocimonte across the sea against the Turk with 3000 combatants".[108] Although he failed to join Sixtus IV in driving the Turks from Italy in 1480, Edward had only one year earlier anticipated the Turkish invasion. At that time he expressed the opinion that the pope ought to have pacified Italy "owing to the great perils... for the Christian religion, when the Turk is at the gates of Italy and so powerful, as everyone knows".[109]

Finally English kings also revealed a sense of obligation for the protection and succor of Christendom by their grants of aid and subsidies to refugees fleeing the Turks. The issue roles of the exchequer show, for example, that in the year 1456, money was given to four Greeks who visited the island kingdom, among them the prominent humanist, John Argyropolos. In 1467, Edward IV granted two Greeks the right to collect alms from his subjects for two years. The king's license named the pair, Demetrius Crisasius and Theodore Guias, and explained that they had been taken prisoner together with their wives and families "by the cruell Turk enemye of þe chirch and x̄pen faith and putt to gret and excessive finance for the which thair plegge lien still in the handes of þe subjectȩ of þe said Turke in gret miserie and dureis of enprisonement likely to pisshe wᵗouten the charitie of trewe x̄pen people be to thaim imparted...".[110]

NOTES TO CHAPTER V.

1. In connection with the Turkish threat, the most important order was the Knights Hospitallers of Rhodes. The standard work for the preceding period is J. Delaville le Roulx, *Les Hospitaliers à Rhodes jusqu'a la mort de Philibert de Naillac, 1310-1421* (Paris, 1913). C. Marinescu, "L'Ile de Rhodes au xvᵉ siècle et l'ordre de Saint-Jean de Jerusalem d'après des documents inédits", *Miscellanea Giovanni Mercati* (Rome, 1946), V, 340-382; and N. Iorga, *Rhodes sous les hospitaliers* (Paris, 1931), are helpful but restricted. Baron de Belabre, *Rhodes of the Knights* (Oxford, 1908), is thin and unreliable and the conclusions of V. J. Flynn, "The Intellectual Life of Fifteenth-century Rhodes", *Traditio*, II (1944), need to be revised.

2. See A. S. Atiya, *The Crusade in the Later Middle Ages*, pp. 140-154.

3. Kervyn de Lettenhove, *La Toison d'or* (Brussels, 1907).

4. Pius II, *Commentaries*, X, 790-792; cf. J. Philippe, *Guillaume Fichet, sa vie ses oeuvres* (Annecy, 1892), p. 86; and E. de Moreau, *Histoire l'église en Belgique* (Brussels, 1949), IV, 296.

5. Pius II, *Commentaries*, X, 790-92.

6. In H. Prutz, *Pius II Rüstungen zum Türkenkrieg und die Societas Jesu des Flanderers Gerhard des Champs, 1459-66 (Sitzungsberichte der Koniglich bayerischen Akademie der Wissenschaften. Philosophisch, philologische und historische Klasse* (Munich, 1912), pp. 60-63.

7. Raynaldus, *Annales ecclesiastici*, ad an. 1459, no. 83; see also Pius' comments to Nicholas of Cusa, *ibid.*, ad an 1459, no. 10.

8. In D'Achery, *Spicilegium*, III, 806.

9. See Pius II, *Commentaries*, bks. IX and X.

10. "Delibération du chapitre métropolitan de Besançon", in M. Castan, "Rapport sur trois documents rélativfs à la Société de Jésus au xvᵉ siècle", *Revue des sociétés savantes*, 6th ser., II (1876), 480.

11. See the account given by Gerard in his letter to the council of Geneva, December 8, 1465, in C. le Fort, "Une Société de Jésus au quinzième siècle. Documents inédites des archives de Génève", *Mémoires et documents de la société d'histoire et d'archéologique de Génève*, XX (1879), 109-113.

12. *Ibid.*, p. 110.

13. *Ibid.*, pp. 107, 108; and M. Castan, "Rapport", pp. 480-482.

14. In D. Bouhours, *Histoire de Pierre d'Aubusson, grandmaistre de Rhodes* (2nd ed., Paris, 1677), pp. 94-98.

15. On the preparations of d'Aubusson leading up to the siege in 1480 see Vertot, *History of the Knights Hospitallers of St. John of Jerusalem, Styled Afterwards the Knights of Rhodes, and at Present the Knights of Malta*, English translation (Edinburgh, 1757), III, pp. 37-50. For the negotiations with the Turks see L. Thuasne, *Djem-sultan fils de Mohammed II, frère de Bayezid II (1459-1495)* (Paris, 1892), pp. 12-17; cf. Babinger, *Mahomet II*, p. 466.

16. Babinger, *Mahomet II*, pp. 452-456; Thiriet, *La Romanie vénitienne*, pp. 390, 391, 435, 436.

17. See the documents in Iorga, *Notes et extraits*, V, 45-50; and "Die Stände von Krain an Kaiser Friedrich IV. über die Türkennot", in K. Haselbach, *Die Türkennoth im xv. Jahrhundert* (Vienna, 1864), pp. ix-xv; and *Anschlag wider die Türken* (Augsburg, 1474); see *GW*, nos. 2028-2030.

18. Iorga, *GOR*, II, 181, 182; Babinger, *Mahomet II*, pp. 458-461.

19. *Ibid.*, p. 467.

20. Cf. A. D. Momigliano, "Herodotus in the History of Historiography", *Studies in Historiography* (New York, 1966), pp. 137-141, who observes that the discovery of America and the increasing knowledge of the Turks had the effect of bringing contemporary scholars to a true appreciation of Herodotus and through him a better understanding of their own world: "he [Herodotus] seems to have been appreciated especially because in his quiet way he had understood the Persians, and through him the Turks could be seen more objectively". For the impact of the Persians on Greece as it pertained to the rise of historiography see J. B. Bury, *The Ancient Greek Historians* (London, 1909), pp. 15-18, 33-35.

21. In Latin: Venice, 1480, Parma, 1480, Bruges, 1480, Passau, 1480, Barcelona(?), 1481, Rome, 1482, Odense, 1482; in German: Passau, 1480-1481; in English: London, 1483; in Italian: Venice, 1480. See *GW*, VI, nos. 6004-6013.

22. *GW*, VII, no. 7860; and nos. 9097, 9098. The text of Dupuis was published by Vertot in his *History of the Knights* (London, 1728), I, 91-103, under the title *Rélation du siège de Rhodes en* 1480; citations here are to this edition. De Curti appeared in an Italian translation under the title *Relazione* and was printed in E. F. Mizzi, *Le Guerre di Rodi* (Turin, 1934), pp. 68-87, which is the text used here. See also Pierre d'Aubusson, *De obsidione urbis Rhodiae* (Mainz, 1480; Nuremberg, 1480; Strasbourg, 1480), *GW*, nos. 2773-2775. For a report of the capture of Negropont (1470), in humanistic style see the letter of the grandmaster, Girard Duhem edited by F. Mollard in *Bulletin historique et philologique du comité des travaux historiques et scientifiques* (Paris, 1891), pp. 65-68.

23. Cf. Caoursin, *Descriptio*, fols. 9ᵛ-11ᵛ; Dupuis, *Relation*, pp. 99, 100, 102; De Curti, *Relazione*, p. 86.

24. Caoursin, *Descriptio*, fols 2ʳ-4ʳ.

25. E.g. Dupuis, *Relation*, p. 96.

26. See F. Gilbert, *Machiavelli and Guicciardini*, pp. 223-226, esp. n. 41. Thus Mary Dupuis, *Relation*, p. 91, ". . .gros et rude de sens et de entendement je veuille parler et descripre au plus brief que je pourray et au plus pres de la verite selon que je peu voir a lueil. . . . Mais seulement en gros le descrips selon que je le peu savoir pour en advertin ceulx les quieulx en vouloront savoir des nouvelles, et aussi les quieulx y prendront plaisir de loir lire".

27. The important sources, after the three histories, are three letters of the grandmaster Pierre d'Aubusson: (1) a final appeal to the knights in the West written May 28, 1480, just after the Turkish siege began, published by Pauli, *Codice diplomatico*, II, no. CXXV, 148, 149; (2) letter of d'Aubusson to Frederick III, September 13, 1480, in *ibid.*, no. CXXVI, 149-153; and (3) d'Aubusson to Sixtus IV, September 15, 1480, in J. Ludewig, *Reliquiae manuscriptorum omnis aevi diplomatum ac monumentorum*, V (Frankfort, 1723), 290-299. A number of documents touching on the siege of Rhodes were published by C. Foucard, "Fonti di storia Napoletana dell' archivio di stato di Modena—Otranto nel 1480 e nel 1481", in *Archivio storico per le province Napoletane*, VI (1881), 74-176. See especially the letter of Gabriele Pisitillo from Rhodes, June 3, 1480, *ibid.*, pp. 135, 136; "Relazione di Ser Bernardo Donato, Padrone di Nave, venuto da Rodi, al capitano di Candia, June 21, 1480", *ibid.*, pp. 137, 138. In addition to the works of the eyewitnesses and participants in the siege there is much material on the battle in the accounts of the pilgrims and scattered throughout the western chronicles.

28. Cf. Caoursin, *Descriptio*, fol. 3ʳ; Dupuis, *Relation*, p. 92. De Curti, *Relazione*, pp. 68-70, on the landing of the Turks. On the size of the Turkish force d'Aubusson, in his letter to the knights, May 28, 1480 (in Pauli, *Codice diplomatico*, II, 148) said there were about 70,000; Battista Bendedei, representing the house of Este at Rome, wrote in a dispatch of June 29, 1480, that a letter written by d'Aubusson was sent to Rome by the king of Naples which described the descent of the Turks on Rhodes, ". . .cum circa septanta milla persone, et è li cum CLX velle, fornito de victualia, artegliaria, macchine, et altri instrumenti bellici da expugnare città" (in Foucard, "Fonti", p. 103). The envoy of the Este at Florence wrote on July 3, 1480: "Hozi, parlando pure con questi Signori Octo, dicevano dela armata era a Rode del Turcho, et che ci era adviso como li era a campo, cum 160 vele, tra galee et palandete, et eragi 60 milia turchi" (in Foucard, "Fonti", p. 118). Gabriele

Pisitillo ("Lettera" in Foucard, "Fonti", p. 135), gives a much smaller number, but mentions how the Turks continued to ferry reinforcements from the mainland. According to Caoursin (op. cit., fol. 3ᵛ), the renegade George told the grandmaster that the Turkish army numbered 100,000.

29. Caoursin, *Descriptio*, fol. 3ʳ; Dupuis, *Relation*, p. 92; d'Aubusson to Frederick III, September 13, 1480, in Pauli, *Codice diplomatico*, II, 150; Gabriele Pisitillo, "Lettera", in Foucard, "Fonti", p. 135.

30. Dupuis wrote that the knight who was beheaded was a Calatan named Pierre de Bourges (in *Relation*, pp. 92, 93). De Curti (*Relazione*, p. 70), said he was a Portuguese. J. Bosio mentions the incident, but I do not find the knight's name in his list of casualties (*Dell' istoria della sacra religione et illustrissima militia de San Giovanni Gierosolimitano*, II, Rome, 1602, 321, 341).

31. Caoursin, *Descriptio*, fol. 3ʳ; Dupuis, *Relation*, pp. 93, 94; d'Aubusson to Sixtus IV, in Ludewig, *Reliquiae manuscriptorum*, V. 291, 292; d'Aubusson to Frederick III, in Pauli, *Codice diplomatico*, II, 150.

32. Caoursin, *Descriptio*, fols. 3ᵛ-4ᵛ; Dupuis, *Relation*, pp. 94, 95; De Curti, *Relazione*, p. 75; Ser Barnardo Donato, *Relazione*, p. 138. Cf. report of Antonio da Montecatino from Florence, July 3, 1480, in Foucard, "Fonti", p. 118, and that of Alberto Cortese from Venice, July 15, 1480, ibid., p. 131.

33. Caoursin, *Descriptio*, fols. 4ᵛ-5ʳ; Dupuis, *Relation*, p. 95. De Curti (*Relazione*, pp. 71, 72), wrote: "Non si erano mai tanti e cosi fatti ne erano usciti da Costantinopoli. In fede mai, io credo che egli abbia recato contro l'Ordine del Santissimo Precursore le più belle artiglierie: certo è che egli collocò sedici grandi bombarde nell' intenzione di circondare la città, senza contare quelle che erano capaci di trasportare ciascuna cinque massi di marmo. Che poteva egli escogitare di più feroce? Se tu avessi sentito la terra tremare sotto i piedi, come noi la sentimmo, ti saresti rifugiato in una caverna".

34. *Ibid.*, pp. 75, 76; Caoursin, *Descriptio*, fol. 5ʳ; Dupuis, *Relation*, p. 96.

35. Dupuis, *Relation*, p. 97.

36. *Ibid.*, p. 97; Caoursin, *Descriptio*, fol. 6ʳ.

37. Caoursin, *Descriptio*, fol. 6ʳ; d'Aubusson to Frederick III, pp. 150, 151.

38. Caoursin, *Descriptio*, fol. 7ʳ; Dupuis, *Relation*, pp. 97, 98. De Curti, *Relazione*, p. 77; Ser Bernardo Donato, *Relazione* in Foucard, "Fonti", p. 138.

39. D'Aubusson to Sixtus IV, in Ludewig, *Reliquiae manuscriptorum*, V, 294; d'Aubusson to Frederick III, in Pauli, *Codice diplomatico*, II, 151; Caoursin, *Descriptio*, fol. 7v.

40. Cf. De Curti, *Relazione*, pp. 80-83; Dupuis, *Relation*, pp. 98, 99; Caoursin, *Descriptio*, fol.s 7ᵛ-10ᵛ.

41. Dupuis, *Relation*, p. 99.

42. Caoursin, *Descriptio*, fol. 10ʳ.

43. De Curti, *Relazione*, p. 83.

44. Caoursin, *Descriptio*, fols. 1ᵛ-2ᵛ; cf. Babinger, *Mahomet II*, pp. 483, 484.

45. Caoursin, *Descriptio*, fols. 3ʳ, 8ᵛ, 9ʳ; Dupuis, *Relation*, pp. 93, 94, 99; De Curti, *Relazione*, p. 71.

46. Dupuis, *Relation*, p. 96; Caoursin, *Descriptio*, fol. 5ᵛ.

47. Cf. Dupuis, *Relation*, pp. 94, 95; De Curti, *Relazione*, pp. 71, 72; Casola, *Pilgrimage*, p. 205; Schefer (ed.), *Le Voyage de la saincte cyté*, pp. 115, 116.

48. Caoursin, *Descriptio*, fols. 3ᵛ, 4ᵛ; cf. Dupuis, *Relation*, p. 93.

49. *Ibid.*, p. 100; Caoursin, *Descriptio*, fol. 10ʳ; De Curti, *Relazione*, pp. 81, 82.

50. Caoursin, *Descriptio*, fols. 10ᵛ-11ᵛ; Dupuis, *Relation*, pp. 100-102; De Curti, *Relazione*, pp. 84, 85; d'Aubusson to Frederick III, September 13, 1480, in Pauli, *Codice diplomatico*, II, 152, 153.

51. Caoursin, *Descriptio*, fols. 11ᵛ-12ᵛ; Dupuis, *Relation*, pp. 101-103; d'Aubusson to Frederick III, September 13, 1480, in Pauli, *Codice diplomatico*, II, 153.

52. Letter of Alberto Cortese, Venice, June 18, 1480, in Foucard, "Fonti", pp. 129, 130. See also letters of July 15, and September 7, *ibid.*, pp. 131-134.

53. Letter of Antonio da Montecatino, Florence, July 3, 1480, in Foucard, "Fonti", p. 118. See also the letter of July 14, *ibid.*, pp. 119, 120.

54. Letter of Battista Bendedei, Rome, June 29, 1480, in Foucard, "Fonti", pp. 103, 104; and letter of July 2, *ibid.*, pp. 104, 105.

55. Letter of Bendedei, Rome, July 3, 1480, in Foucard, "Fonti", p. 106.

56. Letter of Bendedei, Rome, July 5, 1480, in Foucard, "Fonti", pp. 106, 107. For further negotiations see Bendedei's letters of July 8, July 12, and July 24, *ibid.*, pp. 107-110.

57. Raynaldus, *Annales*, ad an. 1480, no. 2; Volaterranus, *Diarium Romanum*, cols. 105, 106; *Diarium Parmense* (*RISS*, XII, Milan, 1733), cols. 343-345; cf. Pastor, *HP*, IV, 333 and notes.

58. De Curti, *Relazione*, p. 73.

59. Cf. Dupuis, *Relation*, p. 102, and Caoursin, *Descriptio*, fol. 12ʳ.

60. Fabri, *Evagatorium*, I (ed. Hassler), 46, 47.

61. *Ibid.*, I, 47, 48.

62. *Lettres de Louis XI*, edited by Vaesen et al. (Paris, 1903), VIII, 318, 319.

63. As early as the middle of May 1480, the Italians heard that the sultan was concentrating his forces in the vicinity of Valona for an attack on southern Italy. See the letter of Niccolò Sadoleto, May 14, 1480, Naples, in Foucard, "Fonti", p. 80. Cf. his letters of May 18, June 10, and July 1, *ibid.*, pp. 80, 81. See also the letters of Antonio da Montecatino, from Florence, June 9, and June 14, in *ibid.*, p. 119.

64. The Turkish invasion of Italy in 1480 has been the subject of considerable scholarly inquiry. Among recent works on the subject Antonio Antonaci's *Hydruntum* (Galatina, 1954), while not definitive, is a highly readable and engrossing survey. Antonaci has compiled an attractive and useful companion volume of sources and illustrations, *Otranto, testi e monumenti* (Galatina, 1955). Other works of significance are: S. La Sorsa, *Lo Sbarco dei Turchi in Puglia e le guerre* (Rome, 1945); G. Panarco, "In terra d'Otranto dopo l'invasione turchesca", *Rivista storica salentina*, VIII (1913), 35-56; P. Coco, *La Guerra contro i Turchi in Otranto. Fatti e persone, 1480-1481* (Lecce, 1915). The reaction and response of the Aragonese has been studied by Palumbo, "Gli Aragonesi alla guerra di Otranto", *Rivista storica salentina*, III (1907), 357-378; and Ferrante's politics by Pietro Egidi, "La Politica del regno di Napoli negli ultimi mesi dell' anno 1480", *Archivio storico per le province napoletane*, XXXV (1910); that of Milan by V. E. Fossati, "Dal 25 luglio 1480 al 16 aprile 1481: l'opera

di Milano", *Archivio storico lombardo*, XXXVI (1909), 1-71. The controversial role of the Venetians has been clarified by the study of Alessio Bombaci, "Venezia e la impresa turca di Otranto", *Rivista storica italiana*, LXVI (1954), 159-203.

65. Letter of Niccolò Sadoleto, August 1, 1480, from Naples in Foucard, "Fonti", p. 81.

66. Letter of Niccolò Sadoleto, August 2, 1480, from Naples in Foucard, "Fonti", p. 82. The Florentine Landucci viewed the Turkish attack on Naples as a blessing to his city. The duke of Calabria had intended to do much evil against Florence but "...by a great miracle it happened that on the 6th August (sic), the Turkish army came to Otranto and began to besiege it; so it was necessary to leave our neighborhood, at the king's command, and return to defend the kingdom. The Turks were encamped in three places, being at Rodi, and with the Hungarians, besides at Otranto". *Florentine Diary*, p. 30.

67. Letter of Niccolò Sadoleto, August 3, 1480, from Naples in Foucard, "Fonti", pp. 83, 84.

68. A vivid description of the action is given by Giovanni Michele Lagetto in his *Historia della città di Otranto* edited by Antonaci in *Otranto, testi e monumenti*, pp. 54-66; cf. Antonaci, *Hydruntum*, pp. 159-164, and Babinger, *Mahomet II*, pp. 478, 479.

69. Pietro Colonna, *In Apocalypsin Johannis libri decim*, extract in Antonaci, *Otranto, testi e monumenti*, p. 135.

70. Cf. Giovanni Lagetto, *Historia* in Antonaci, *Otranto, testi e monumenti*, pp. 63-73; Antonio de Ferrariis, *De situ Japigiae* in Antonaci, *Otranto, testi e monumenti*, pp. 132, 133. The canonization of the martyrs under Clement XIV in 1771 provoked the production of a host of commemorative volumes which include some useful information, e.g. Francesco Antonio Capano, *Memorie all' posterita delli gloriosi e costanti confessori di Giesu Christi, che patirono martiro nella città d'Otranto l'anno* 1480 (Lecce, 1770); cf. the later works of G. Scherillo, *Archeologia II: Dei beati martiri d'Otranto* (Naples, 1874), and Cosimo de Giorgi, *Otranto ne 1480: Commemorazione civili dei difensorie martiri di Otranto* (Lecce, 1891).

71. Lettera of Niccolò Sadoleto, August 14, 1480, Naples in Foucard, "Fonti", pp. 85, 86.

72. Battista Bendedei, August 12, 1480, Rome, in Foucard, "Fonti", pp. 111, 112.

73. Quoted in Pastor, *HP*, IV, 334. De' Conti was at that time in the service of cardinal legate Giuliano, who was ordered to ready Avignon for the coming of the pope. The German humanist Peter Schott who was in Italy at this time rushed from Ferrara to Rome "...ut si a Turcis sit capienda prius eam viderim". "Letter to Johann Geiler von Kaysersberg, 1481", in *The Works of Peter Schott*, ed. M. A. and M. L. Cowie (Chapel Hill, 1963), I, 27.

74. Pastor, *HP*, IV, 335.

75. *Ibid.*, IV, 335, 336; cf. Raynaldus, *Annales*, ad an. 1480, nos. 20-28.

76. Niccolò Sadoleto, August 17, 1480, Naples, in Foucard, "Fonti", p. 98.

77. Pastor, *HP*, IV, 336.

78. *Ibid.*, IV, 336; cf. the remarks of Vespasiano da Bisticci *(Lives of Illustrious Men*, p. 151), who says that the pope did everything that was necessary for the safety of the church. Vespasiano described the mission of cardinal Giovanni de' Margheriti

to Venice, and vehemently condemned the Republic of St. Mark and other powers for not supporting the efforts of the papacy. *Ibid.*, pp. 150-152.

79. Pastor, *HP*, IV, 337. Volaterranus, *Diarium Romanum*, pp. 115, 116.

80. Raynaldus, *Annales*, ad an. 1480, no. 28.

81. See Mario Viora, "Angelo Carletti da Chivasso e la crociata contro i Turchi del 1480-81", *Studi francescani*, XI, n.s. (1925), 323.

82. *Ibid.*, p. 324. Viora quotes a passage from Marco da Lisbona *(Cronache degli ordini istituti dal. S. Padre Francesco*, Rome, n.d.), on Carletti's prosecution of this work *(ibid.*, p. 324); and on pp. 326-329, gives in its entirety a work written by Carletti to explain the meaning of Sixtus IV's bull to his assistants.

83. Pastor, *HP*, IV, 337, 338; cf. the documents in Iorga, *Notes et extraits*, V, 74-77, 79-81. For the diplomatic relations of the Italian powers concerning the organization of opposition to the Turks see the documents published by G. Grasso, "Documenti riguardanti la constituzione di una lega contro il Turco nel 1481", *Giornale ligustico di archeologia, storia e belle arti*, VI (1879), 321-494.

84. Pastor, *HP*, IV, 340; Raynaldus, *Annales*, ad an. 1481, no. 4.

85. *Ibid.*, ad an. 1481, nos. 19, 20.

86. Pastor, *HP*, IV, 341.

87. *Ibid.*, IV, 342-344; Antonaci, *Hydruntum*, pp. 179-188. On the recovery of Otranto and the Christian reactions cf. Infessura, *Diario*, col. 1148, Volaterranus, *Diarium Romanum*, cols. 146, 147; Iorga, *Notes et extraits*, V, 103.

88. On the pope's negotiations with Louis XI see J. Combet, *Louis XI et le saint-siège (1461-1483)* (Paris, 1903), pp. 185-188.

89. *CSPVen*, I, 142, 143.

90. Paul Murray Kendall, *The Yorkist Age* (New York, 1962); G. B. Parks, *The English Traveler to Italy*, Vol. I (Stanford, 1954); R. J. Mitchell, *John. Free* (London, 1954); R. Weiss, *Humanism in England During the Fifteenth Century*, 2nd ed. (Oxford, 1957).

91. *Cal. Pat. Rolls*, IV (1441-1446), 166; *CSPVen*, II, 173; E. M. C. Wilson, *Studies in English Trade in the Fifteenth Century* (New York, 1933), pp. 226ff.

92. *CSPVen*, I, 142.

93. *CPR*, XII, 229.

94. *CPR*, X, 95, 262-66; XI, 19-21, 32, 59, 80, 387, 401-403, 417, 418; XII, 229-232; XIII, pt. i, 159, 198, 199, 203-206, 208, 254, 255; XIV, 50, 52, 53, 57. Cf. J. Gairdner, ed., *Gregory's Chronicle of London* (London, 1876,) p. 197.

95. A. Ferguson, *The Indian Summer of English Chivalry*, p. 107.

96. *CPR*, XI, 158.

97. *Ibid.*, XI, 519, 590, 661.

98. Rymer, *Foedera*, II, 683, 733, 773; H. Nichols, ed., *Proceedings and Ordinances of the Privy Council* (London, 1837), VI, 165, 381; *Cal. Pat. Rolls. Henry VII*, I, 188; H. T. Riley, ed., *Chronica Monasterii S. Albani (Chronicles and Memorials of Great Britain and Ireland*, London, 1871, XXVIII), VI, pt. 2, 191, 192.

99. Babinger, *Mahomet II*, p. 485; E. J. King, *The Knights of St. John in the British Empire* (London, 1934), pp. 86, 87.

100. *Ibid.*, pp. 70-74.

101.   *DNB*, X, 1295, 1296; King, *The Knights of St. John*, pp. 74, 75; Rymer, *Foedera*, XII, *passim*; *CPR*, XIII, 177, 178. *CSPVen*, I, 148, 153, 154, 164, 167, 169, 172.

102.   *CPR*, XIII, 254; cf. Rymer, *Foedera*, XII, 112.

103.   T. Stapleton, ed., *Plumpton Correspondence* (London, 1839), 118, 119.

104.   *CSPVen*, I, 153.

105.   L. T. Smith, *The Expedition of Henry, Earl of Derby*, 1390-1, 1392-3 (London, 1894); J. J. Jusserand, *English Wayfaring Life in the Middle Ages* (London, 1889), p. 227; on Manuel II's visit to the West see A. A. Vasiliev, *History of the Byzantine Empire*, pp. 633, 634 and the literature cited there. Holinshed's *Chronicles*, pp. 101, 102; T. Wright, ed., *Political Poems* (London, 1861), p. 118.

106.   Lannoy, *Oeuvres*, p. 161.

107.   *CPR*, X, 263-266; J. Gairdner, ed., *Gregory's Chronicle of London*, I, 197; W. Lunt, *Papal Revenues in the Middle Ages* (New York, 1934), II, 465; H. Nichols, ed., *Proceedings and Ordinances of the Privy Council of England*, VI, 298, 299, 302.

108.   *CSPMilan*, pp. 222, 231; Wilkins, *Concilia*, III, 598.

109.   *CSPMilan*, p. 266; *CSPVen*, pp. 142, 143.

110.   See H. L. Gray, "Greek Visitors to England in 1455-1456", *Anniversary Essays in Medieval History to Charles Homer Haskins*, ed. C. H. Taylor (Boston, 1929), 81, 116; S. Bentley, ed., *Excerpta historica* (London, 1833), p. 392.

CHAPTER VI

The new barbarian

The failure of Renaissance popes to organize the grand crusade resulted in no diminution in either the quantity or ardor of appeals for the holy war. The lack of action on the part of princes was rarely regarded as a reflection of fundamental changes in the structures and patterns of political and social life. Sin, the unwillingness to do God's bidding, and the neglect of one's Christian duty, was seen, often by the princes themselves, to have been the source of the problem. With only minor variations the main theme of this argument was faithfully copied into the tracts of both lay and ecclesiastical publicists through the remainder of the fifteenth century and well into the next. Convinced of the logic of the orthodox formula these authors were incapable of analyzing or reconciling the contradiction between the ideals they professed and the altered conditions of Renaissance society. Unable to understand their own milieu we can hardly expect them to offer anything new concerning their Moslem opponents. What Norman Daniel has written about the medieval polemicists' view of Islam was no less true of their fifteenth-century counterparts: "There was a Christian picture in which the details (even under the pressure of facts) were abandoned as little as possible, and in which the general outline was never abandoned. There were shades of difference, but only within a common framework. All the corrections that were made in the interests of increasing accuracy were only a defense of what had newly been realized to be vulnerable, a shoring up of a weakened structure. Christian opinion was an erection which would not be demolished, even to be rebuilt."[1]

Thus through the crusade appeals the view of Islam developed in the Middle Ages was carried over to the Ottomans and perpetuated even after the main lines of the medieval world view had crumbled. One can understand the disinclination or inability of the conservative defenders of church and chivalry to take a new look at the matter. But it is not so easy to explain the fact that so many humanists were or appeared to be committed to the crusade and the medieval conception of the Moslems. Advocates of a cultural and educational program based essentially on the moral precepts and teachings of the ancients, the humanists were the authors of the new morality for their time. But while they were able to shape a code of behavior which took account of the *vita activa* and even the pursuit and possession of wealth, they were, with few exceptions, unconcerned to breech the barriers of orthodoxy in reorienting the attitudes of contemporaries toward non-Christians. It was precisely at this point that their favorite antique models failed them; for few among the ancient Greek or Roman historians had been able to view objectively the so-called barbarians of their day.

Here the case of Herodotus is instructive. Recognized as the father of history and among the most distinguished of ancient Greek writers, Herodotus was duly prized by those Italian humanists who first gained an acquaintance with his work. But Herodotus had not worn well with the historians who were his successors in the ancient world. Both his choice of subject and his method had come under attack by a distinguished line of critics from Thucydides to Plutarch and Cicero. The father of history was condemned for not sticking to political history; he had transcended the bounds of local or national history and had delved into the remote past of distant countries; accused, on the one hand of partiality toward Athens, he was denounced for not sufficiently extolling the glories of Hellas. As the Italian humanists became aware of this body of criticism they appropriately backed off. The assault by Plutarch was the most telling—among other faults, Herodotus had shown too much sympathy for the barbarians.[2]

We must not press this argument too far; regarding the Ottomans, as for many other subjects, there were significant exceptions in the views of the humanists. If only to serve as a basis for condemning the Turks, Aeneas Sylvius had, as we know, asked Sagundino to provide him with an account of their origins.[3] The Greek humanist, Theodore Gaza, wrote for Francesco Filelfo a similar work entitled *De origine Turcarum*.[4] It was to be expected that the humanists would emphasize the parallel between the Turks and the barbarians of the ancient world and would take up the task of finding a connection between the two. The identification of the Turks with the Trojans, or in Latin *Teucri*, was, of course, not a humanist invention. During the later Middle Ages the fictitious Trojan genealogy, which provided Turks, Franks, and Italians with a common ancestry, found favor with anti-Greek polemicists in the West. Critical humanist historians, however, had already discarded such myths connected with the origins of Italian cities; and after the destruction of Byzantium, proponents of the crusade attacked the *Teucri* thesis and preferred to identify the Turks with the ancient Scythians who were regarded as an especially cruel and barbaric people.[5]

Still the Trojan origin of the Ottomans was not abandoned altogether and some effort was made to justify the Turkish conquest of Greece on the basis of the legend.[6] In an epic piece of more than four thousand verses entitled

Amyris, Giovanni Mario Filelfo described the career and conquests of Mehmed II. Conscious of having opened himself to criticism in his choice of a subject he defended the work on the basis of antique precedent and claimed that his topic was worthy of historical consideration, as formerly the deeds of Hannibal, Pyrrhus, Cyrus, and Philip of Macedon had been recorded.[7] The main body of the poem deals with the capture of Constantinople and the sultan's campaigns in Greece. The author, who was born in Constantinople (his mother was a member of the Chrysoloras family), and studied there in the years 1440-1442, blamed the Greeks for their own defeat and was no less scornful of the inability of the Latins to unite against the conqueror. He was, however, uncommonly strong in his praise of the sultan whose personal qualities, he asserted, showed that he was anything but a barbarian. Through the mouth of Bellona the profession of arms and the path of conquest which the sultan pursued were extolled for the immortal glory and renown they conferred upon the victorious. Filelfo made much of the Trojan ancestry of Mehmed and represented his subjugation of Greece as a triumph of justice. At last the aggressive conquest of Troy by the Greeks had been avenged![8]

A preface in prose written by Othman Lillo Ferducci and addressed to Mehmed II indicates that the *Amyris* was intended as a panegyric in honor of the sultan. Originally merchants from Ancona, the family of Lillo, whose given name was taken from the founder of the Ottoman dynasty, had been established at Gallipoli and was on good terms with the Porte during the reign of Murad II. Mehmed II showed his favor for the Ferducci when he willingly freed Lillo's brother-in-law, Angelo Boldone, who had been seized at the capture of Constantinople. The *Amyris*, according to Lillo, was composed so that he might offer it as a token of his gratitude and devotion to the sultan, and, we might add, with the hope of obtaining new favors. If such in fact were the conditions which inspired the poem, we are justly entitled to doubt the sincerity of Giovanni Mario Filelfo's protestations in favor of the sultan. But the credibility of the work, as an indication of changing attitudes toward the Turks, is wholly demolished by the further fact that in book four, apparently added later, the *Amyris* was rededicated to Galeazzo Mario Sforza, duke of Milan, and cast in the form of a crusade exhortation![9]

If the antics of opportunists like Giovanni Mario Filelfo have raised doubts about the integrity of the humanist appeals for the holy war, the conformance of these same writers to the current fashion in political oratory and their response to the demands of patronage have all but wholly discredited their anti-Turkish utterances. At diplomatic congresses, the reception of ambassadors, the elevation of a pope, the marriage of a prince, or almost any public occasion an orator trained in the new rhetoric might step forward and deliver an *Exhortatio ad bellum contra barbaros*. One gets the impression that the composition of an oration against the Turks was 'the thing to do' and that every self-respecting man of letters kept several in his repertory for the appropriate occasion and included them in his *Opere* whether or not he had delivered them. That the Turkish threat was considered an appropriate topic for an exercise in the rhetorical training of students is suggested by the *Declamationes* of Benedetto Colucci. The author represented Ficino as assigning the composition of an appeal for a crusade to five of his pupils. Then on three consecutive days he had them win the approval of the Platonic Academy by parading their erudition and saying the right things about unity, harmony, responsibility, patriotism, learning, and the faith.[10]

What, to some modern historians, has appeared as the ambigious, if not ambivalent, attitude of the humanists toward the crusade and the Turk, is perhaps best illustrated by the father of Giovanni Mario, Francesco Filelfo. Accused, in his own time, of crass opportunism, of duplicity, and ingratitude and disloyalty to his benefactors, he was a favorite with nineteenth century historians who emphasized the amoral, egocentric individualism of the Renaissance. Certainly few humanists of the fifteenth century wrote so frequently over so long a time span about the Turkish problem. As is well known, Filelfo had studied Greek while still a young man in Constantinople with John Chrysoloras. In the course of a seven year stay in the Levant he learned a good deal about the Turks. He even participated in an embassy to the court of Sultan Murad II. Soon after he had returned to the West he wrote from Bologna (July 3, 1428), to his Greek friend George of Trebizond concerning Turkish affairs. He acknowledged receipt of George's book, *Against the Turks*, and informed his correspondent that he had discussed the work with the learned men of Bologna. All agreed that now was the time to strike back. With prophetic insight Filelfo observed that if the Turks were to build a navy as strong as their army it would be difficult for anyone to stop them; and if Constantinople were seized then all Italy would be imperiled.[11]

It was in 1451 that Filelfo addressed his famous appeal to Charles VII of France. The danger to Constantinople was mounting daily. Greek envoys were hastily dispatched to the capitals of Italy in a frantic bid for last minute aid. In view of his strong attachments to Byzantium there is no reason to doubt that Filelfo honestly desired her rescue. At the same time we know that he was planning a trip to Paris, and it is clear that in this way he hoped to earn the recognition and good will of the French king. At any rate the exhortation was a model of humanist crusading rhetoric. It was known to the next generation of French humanists who at least credited its author with being one of the few Latin champions of Byzantium in her hour of need.[12] But while Constantinople, nearly unsupported, faced her final ordeal, Filelfo's attention was directed to Rome and Naples whence he journeyed to be honored by Nicholas V and crowned poet laureate by Alfonso the Magnanimous. It was only upon his return to Milan in the autumn of 1453 that he learned of the captivity of his mother-in-law and her daughters. Seized in the taking of Constantinople they had been sold into slavery. Filelfo took what was for him the obvious course. He wrote the Turkish sultan and requested the release of his wife's family. For good measure he included a Greek ode celebrating the Conqueror's deeds and virtues. He appealed to Mehmed's desire for fame (which only the poet was able to make immortal); to his courage and power (God had made the sultan an instrument of His vengence against the Greeks whose sins had caused them to lose their empire); to his justice (Filelfo's relatives had offended neither God nor Mehmed); to his propriety (Manfredina Chrysoloras was chaste, pious, and of noble birth); and to his sense of shame (only the Jews would demand the highest price). He offered to pay a reasonable ransom concerning which the sultan's secretary, Kyritzis, was informed of the details. The court humanist did not neglect to mention his own patron, Francesco Sforza, whom he described as the most skilled and successful captain among the Latins. He assured Mehmed that the duke of Milan was anxious to maintain good relations, that he was one of his best friends, and like the sultan was an enemy of Venice. We have only to add that Filelfo was granted his request. The captives were freed without a ransom. But the combination of a traditional friendship between Milan and the Turk and the humanist's own influence at the Porte was not likely to improve his reputation at home.[13]

Yet in the years immediately after the fall of Constantinople Filelfo was active in assisting other Greeks in escaping Turkish rule and resettling in the West. A number of letters survive in which he introduced needy refugees to influential people.[14] Moreover, he returned to the project of a crusade. At the Congress of Mantua, it is true, he spoke in the name of Sforza. And although Pius II praised the speech and hailed the orator as an Attic Muse, we know how Sforza really felt about rescuing Venetian galleys from Turkish pirates. Filelfo's ardor for the crusade momentarily cooled when he broke with Pius over the matter of a pension.[15] In a letter of December 23, 1463, he warned Bessarion that while the cardinal legate was busy tending the affairs of the crusade in Venice the ". . .ruse of Renard had another object". And in a letter to Paul II he charged the pope's predecessor with having spent on himself and his family all the money Calixtus III had raised for the Holy War. It was in fact during the attack on Pius II that Filelfo himself was accused of planning to turn Turk. Although he vehemently denied it he had written to Cardinal Ammanati that if Pius failed to pay his pension, ". . .he would move to a place that would greatly displease the pope. For all the world was the fatherland of the scholar. . .", and he regarded ". . .as barbarians only those who showed it in their actions". An idle threat, no doubt, but Filelfo was not noted for either his constancy or his loyalty. Alarmed and indignant Ammanati censured the ingrate and ordered him to consult his conscience. Such a move, he wrote, would simply confirm the opinions of his enemies. The response to the cardinal's letter was an offer by the unpredictable humanist to march with the army of Pius II.[16]

Filelfo continued for many years to write on the subject of the war against the Turks. In fact, upon the accession of Paul II he sent the pontiff his most ambitious and practical plan for a crusade.[17] He continued to correspond with his Greek friends urging them to promote the project and demanded news of the Turks and of the fate of Greece under Ottoman domination. He severely denounced those who went back or were planning to seek their fortune among the Turks, and he rejoiced when they returned or remained in the West; for Greece, he wrote, ". . .had been wholly barbarized and completely enslaved after so many years ruled by the Turks, the most barbarous and wretched race on earth". In a letter of May 30, 1477, to Demetrius Chalcondyles, Filelfo defended his lifelong dedication to the cause of the war against the Turks. For years he had appealed to the emperor, to the kings and princes of Europe to take up the war against the enemy. They had remained indifferent and preoccupied with spilling the blood of fellow Christians so that now the Turks were the most redoubtable foe of Christendom. Although he was himself growing old (he was 79), and had lost his physical vigor, his soul was still consumed with concern for the well-being of Europe. He took Chalcondyles to task for his apathy and for busying himself solely with scholarship. It was vain, he warned, to enlist the support of princes in the cause of liberal arts when all were soon to fall into the hands of the Turks.[18]

A list of fifteenth century Latin humanists who wrote orations against the Turks or who in one way or another promoted the crusade would include the names of many of the most distinguished men of learning. Whether they were motivated by serious concern or political expediency, or both, the result was the same. The causes of the liberal arts and that of the crusade, however incongruous, were advanced by the same pens. The Turks were denounced in humanist orations, in their letters, and in the prefaces and conclusions appended to their scholarly works and editions of classical authors. Thus the image of the Turk as the enemy of faith and culture, endorsed by the founders of the new classical literary studies, was transmitted to the heirs of this tradition in succeeding generations.[19]

Of no small consequence in the crystallization of Latin humanist conceptions about the Turks were the propaganda activities of Greeks who had fled Ottoman domination. Greek scholars, ecclesiastics, and diplomats made their way west in growing numbers during the fifteenth century. Byzantine missions were present at the councils of Constance and Basel. To the council of Ferrara-Florence a delegation of some seven hundred accompanied the emperor John VIII Paleologus. In the years immediately preceding the fall of Constantinople a rash of embassies traveled to the courts of Latin princes vainly seeking aid for their doomed capital. Many who came never returned home. Some, accepting the decree of church union, entered the papal service, though few rose to positions of prominence as did Isidore of Kiev or Bessarion. Others found a place at one of the secular courts. Taking full advantage of the hellenic proclivities of the Renaissance, Greek scholars sought and found teaching and other scholarly occupations. The coveted chair of Greek language and literature, founded in 1361, was at Florence; but similar endowments were created in 1455 at Bologna and in 1463 at Padua. In Rome Cardinal Bessarion opened his house to talented youths from his native land, provided patronage, found them jobs, and in general served as unofficial leader of the refugee community in the West.[20]

The fall of Byzantium and the consolidation of Turkish power in Greece and the islands of the Archipelago resulted in swelling the ranks of the exile communities in the cities of Italy. By 1478 more than four thousand Greeks were settled in Venice alone. Representing now all strata of Byzantine society and drawn also from the Venetian possessions in the Levant, they entered a variety of occupations. For example in the late fifteenth century Greeks comprised a significant part of the military forces of Venice and fought in the Republic's wars against Turks and Christians. At the end of the sixteenth century members of the Paleologi family were still serving Venice in this capacity.[21] But it is with the intellectuals that we are here primarily concerned. Their scholarly activities have been the subject of extensive study for some time and we know a good deal about their contributions as teachers, translators, copyists and editors for the early printers, and as authors of original works. We are however much less informed regarding other aspects of their life in exile not the least significant of which, both from their point of view and ours, were their labors as anti-Turkish propagandists.[22]

The fall of Byzantium closed, for the time being, the question of union between the Latin and Greek churches and many exiles made their peace with Rome. The Turkish conquest, moreover, worked toward ameliorating the intense hostility which the Greeks felt toward the Latins. But the life of exile was not easy; nor did it always engender a harmonious relationship between the two peoples. In Venice the Greeks lived in their own ghetto and in the main held to their own religion. But only after protracted negotiations gave rise to new misgivings did the Venetian government permit the organization and building of an Orthodox church.[23] From the correspondence of Greek scholars and sympathetic Latins we learn of the desperate straits which drove many to the lands north of Italy in search of money for their own support and to pay the ransoms of relatives still held by the Turks. Forced by necessity to peddle their learning as itinerant merchants even the better scholars complained of poor treatment and exploitation. In a letter to a friend, the humanist Constantine Lascaris bared a sense of despair and futility – the common properties of the psychology of the displaced person. A native of Constantinople Lascaris was only nineteen when he fell with the capital into the hands of the Turks. After gaining his freedom he wandered first to Rhodes where he copied manuscripts and then to Corfu. His career in the West began at Milan where between 1460 and 1465 he taught Greek. By royal commission he was appointed professor at Naples but found his lot there so intolerable that in less than a year he departed with the declared intention of returning to occupied Greece. He actually got no farther than Messina where he again took up teaching. Comparing his life in exile to one in bondage he complained that for the scholar there was no sure refuge, for while Greece groaned under the yoke of the savage tyrant the West was held in the grip of barbarism. He decried the cities of Lombardy and Naples; and Rome, which he labeled the New Babylon, he described as the mother of every vice. The Latins, he declared, valued neither scholars nor ancient learning![24]

Allowing for an understandable tendency to depict only the distressing aspects of refugee existence, it was none the less true, as Constantine Lascaris claimed, that Greek men of learning died in neglect and poverty. Even at this distance one cannot but be moved by the accounts of the hardships and indignities which they suffered. The insatiable quest for recognition and reward, the romantic yearnings for the recovery and restoration of Byzantium, the obstacles encountered in pursuing their profession in a strange land combined with countless minor but daily frustrations to produce a socio-psychological type only too familiar to our own strife-ridden world. Preoccupied with compensating for the insecurities born of a complete disruption of their established mode of life, the refugee view of contemporary politics and particularly the problem of the Turks was inevitably colored by intensely personal considerations. Yet, in the case of the Greek scholar, owing to his first hand experience and his status as a man of classical learning, his pronouncements on the affairs of the Levant carried much weight. In the eyes of his Latin colleagues he qualified as an expert on the Turks.

Though it cannot be cited as typical, the career of Michael Apostolis reveals how the needs and pressures of exile conditioned the work of the publicist. A native of Constantinople, Apostolis as a youth fell under the spell of Gemistos Pletho's neo-platonism and studied with John Argyropoulos whom he later succeeded as professor of Greek literature at the higher school of Byzantium. Captured by the Turks in 1453, less than a year later he was established at Candia (Herakleion), on Venetian Crete, where in the course of the next thirty years he was twice married, raised a family, and earned a living doing some teaching but mostly by copying manuscripts. Apostolis was distressed not by the barbarism to be found in the West, but by his failure to find a desirable position. He visited Italy perhaps as many as four times, and for nearly two decades was preoccupied with schemes for settling in the peninsula.[25]

Commissioned by Bessarion, he scoured the libraries of Crete and other places, twice visiting Turkish Constantinople, searching for the works of Greek writers. Apostolis was, however, no mere copyist or purveyor of manuscripts. Sensitive to the intellectual problems of Greeks and Latins alike, he plunged enthusiastically, if recklessly, into the bitter controversy over the relative merits of Plato and Aristotle. He wrote several works supporting Bessarion's defense of the former. With the hope of enhancing his reputation and attracting the attention of those who might secure him a professorship in Italy, he wrote a provocative treatise on how to teach Greek to foreigners. In contrast to the prevailing method of teaching by comparing the Greek text with a Latin translation, he advocated presenting all instruction in Greek. By means of his own journeys and his correspondence he managed for a quarter of a century to keep in touch with the world beyond Crete. A forlorn and disappointed representative of the last generation of Byzantine scholars marooned between Latin Christendom and the Ottoman empire, his views on the events of his time were a curious mixture of stark realism and mystical yearnings.[26]

If for some the hope of recovering Byzantium for the Greeks died hard, Apostolis was not long deceived about the fate of his country. The Turk was now master of the Greek empire whose inhabitants were incapable of freeing themselves. The fears he frequently expressed that Crete too would soon succumb were certainly not feigned. Yet it is clear that his appeals to Latin princes on behalf of his country were no less intended to bring his own case or that of a friend to the attention of a potential patron. His oration to Frederick III (ca. 1468), was prompted by a Greek in the emperor's service, one John Staurkios, in whose name Apostolis saluted the emperor of the Romans and of all Christians. Following the customary flatteries, the author turned to the problem of the Turks, reviewed the record of their victorious rise, but assured Frederick that in the end victory was to be his. He based his prediction upon a threefold argument involving the philosophic principle of necessity, the historical theory of cyclical change, and the authority of oracles. Apostolis stressed especially the latter and played upon the emperor's alleged knowledge of astronomy which he claimed would reveal to Frederick that the time for action had arrived. He appealed to the emperor to free the Greeks and enslave the Turks; to recall from diverse countries the miserable exiles and restore to them their native land; and to avenge in the name of Constantine those who had died fighting the Turk. Apostolis proposed that Frederick appoint his own son Maximilian as the new emperor of the Greeks and share with him dominion over Byzantium and the whole East. From this novel suggestion he passed on to request a special favor for his friend Staurkios and to offer his own services to the emperor.[27]

A eulogistic and self-promoting rhetorical oration, yet the appeal to Frederick was the work of a frightened and desperate man who was both moved by the fate of his countrymen and apprehensive about the continued advance of the Ottomans. In light of his own personal experience there is no reason to doubt the fear of the Turk Apostolis revealed here and in his other works. In a prayer written shortly after his release from Turkish captivity and appended to a eulogy celebrating the lost glory of Byzantium, Apostolis implored Christ the emperor to halt the advance of the Turk whom God had permitted to become sated with Greek blood and who having destroyed Byzantium was preparing to subjugate all Europe: "stop him, stay his violence and deflect his knife and spear", he prayed, and "remove from us the bitter executioner and enemy". Comparing the scattered exiles to the lost drachma, he appealed to Christ to gather them together and to restore their homeland. But the *leitmotiv* of the petition, and of those addressed by Apostolis' compatriots to both the prince of heaven and his temporal vicars, was the plea for Christian unity and harmony; "even if this has hitherto been impossible", wrote Apostolis, "now let them enjoy concord because of the Turks, who commit evil acts without ceasing. . .".[28]

As an apostle of unity and advocate of the holy war Michael Apostolis was, however, but a pale reflection of his sometime patron, the most distinguished among the Greeks in the West, Cardinal Bessarion. Bessarion's career and his activities relating to the Turkish problem are too well known to require extensive treatment here; and yet he is too important in the context of this chapter to be left out altogether. For a quarter of a century Bessarion was the head of the dispersed community of Greeks in the West, as well as its most influential member in Latin circles. To him the refugees looked for spiritual guidance; and to him they turned for protection from Latin intolerance and for aid for their poor and needy including those yet to be freed from Turkish bondage. The eminent scholar served as schoolmaster to young exiles and devoted much time and great sums of money to the preservation of Greek culture, especially the recovery of books.[29] His concern over the advance of the Turks was of long standing. No doubt, when in 1438 he had first come to Italy to attend the council of Ferrara-Florence, along with most of the pro-unionists among the Greeks, he had been moved to support the union because of the Turkish threat and the need for western assistance to save Byzantium.[30] Certainly he welcomed his elevation to the dignity of cardinal, the reward for successful leadership at the council, as enhancing his opportunities to work for consolidation of the union and the crusade against the Turks. Although the needs of the Roman curia were to engage his talents and energy in other directions, it can readily be shown that the Turkish question and the suffering of his compatriots were never long absent from his mind.[31]

His letters, public speeches, and orations, and even his scholarly writings are strewn with references to what was for Bessarion the foremost problem facing Christendom. The fall of Constantinople and the subsequent victories of Mehmed conditioned all his thoughts and activities. Bessarion was keenly aware of the fact that in his lifetime the Turks had absorbed Greece, captured its capital, and founded a new empire. More than most publicists, Bessarion based his arguments on an intimate knowledge of the historical record of events and a clear comprehension of its meaning. A Byzantine patriot as well as a strong supporter of the conservative program of the Renaissance papacy, Bessarion was not deceived about the fate of his country nor its significance for Latin Christendom. The pragmatic cast of his thinking can be seen in a letter dated May 20, 1459, to the Franciscan preacher Jacopo Picentino in which Bessarion discussed the significance of the Ottoman invasion of the Morea. He noted that the land was rich in agriculture and natural resources, and that it was strategically located between Italy, the islands of the Archipelago, and Asia Minor. He urged that it was to be held by Christians at any cost since it was unequalled as a base for further operations against the enemy. He then outlined in a practical vein what measures were needed in order to prosecute a successful campaign.[32]

Among the myriad pamphlets, letters, addresses, and treatises exhorting Christians to unity and the crusade one scarcely finds a more convincing appeal than Bessarion's *Orationes* published in 1471 by the first press of Paris. Now neglected by all but students of the early history of printing, the work was composed subsequent to the Turkish conquest of Negropont, the key to the Venetian empire in the Levant, and a critical victory which Bessarion fully appreciated.³³ Written in polished humanistic style, but based on a careful analysis of the facts, the *Orationes* reveal that Bessarion understood the structure and mechanics of the Ottoman military state, and, more than most curialists, sensed something of the immense changes which had been wrought in the practice of Renaissance statecraft. Clearly he recognized that to enlist the support of the princes it was not sufficient to appeal simply to their Christian consciences. Drawing upon his knowledge of the historical development he recounted the obscure and humble origins of the Turks. To sharpen his readers' sense of perspective he emphasized that only 130 years had passed since these same Turks first entered Europe. But now, he exclaimed, they occupied no small part of the continent. Their conquests, moreover, had been accomplished by overcoming great obstacles; neither the depths of the Danube nor the heights of Illyrium were able to restrain them. He recalled how critical the last seventeen years of the present sultan's reign had been; and declared that at that very moment the Turks were preparing to throw themselves against Germany and Italy. Who, he demanded, was to stop them? Bessarion then described briefly the composition and strength of the Turkish forces and explained the conditions which favored the sultan whose personal prowess and martial talents he readily acknowledged. In support of his claim that Mehmed planned to invade Italy he again fell back upon his store of historical knowledge, in this case that of ancient Rome, and showed how Italy had always aroused the cupidity of foreign powers. He recalled the examples of the Gauls, of King Pyrrhus, of Hannibal, the Huns, and several Germanic tribes.³⁴

Following this impressive display of erudition, though characteristically Renaissance use of history, Bessarion moved on to an analysis and explanation of the sources and motives of the Turks' aggressive behavior. Like many of his Latin contemporaries Bessarion was perplexed and awed by the novel practice of a ruler's maintaining a large standing army. Certainly he was not the first to point out that Mehmed's permanent force cost him as much in time of peace as in war. From this, however, he argued that Mehmed could ill-afford to remain at peace. Indeed, he rightly observed, it was not just costly, but peace was dangerous to the sultan since the janissaries were a threat to internal security if they remained idle for very long. Therefore, Bessarion concluded, to preserve his empire the Turk had constantly to expand it; and to do that he required subservient allies and needed to keep his enemies weak and divided. The very existence of the Ottoman empire was dependent upon his maintaining a powerful military force which in turn he was obliged to employ against his neighbors. To the Turks, treaties were but convenient pauses in a permanent struggle; and if, he warned, the sultan adopted a passive attitude it behooved the Italians to watch him more closely. Such a state, Bessarion declared, was a constant threat to the peace of all nations; founded on conquest, war was its very lifeblood.[35]

In the second discourse of his *Orationes* to the Italian princes the Greek cardinal turned to the problem of Christendom's failure to meet the Ottoman challenge. With the tragic history of his own people fresh in mind he warned the West against the sad consequences of disunity and internecine strife. In a letter written just after the news of the Turkish capture of Negropont had reached him, he revealed to a friend who also bore the name Bessarion, his deepest feelings about warfare among Christians. Writing in a fit of despair he sharply upbraided those rulers whose discords, he claimed, had permitted and encouraged new Turkish conquests. The princes of the West, he deplored, had remained blind to each successive advance. And when Constantinople was threatened not one of them had come to its defense since they did not consider it a danger to themselves. Alas, how many disasters had now followed because aid was not forthcoming! In the strongest language the aging champion of the crusade confided to his friend his own bitterness and disillusionment over the sad state of Christendom led by such selfish and shortsighted princes.[36]

If in the second discourse to the princes Bessarion was more guarded and impersonal, his condemnation of fighting among Christians was no less sweeping. Bringing to bear the full weight of his learning in classical literature, history, and Neo-platonic philosophy he demonstrated that civil strife was the most damaging kind of warfare and that no positive results were ever obtained by it. The Turks, he asserted, fully understood the help which the wars in the West lent to their successes and in their prayers they petitioned for peace at home and discord among Christians. Bessarion then described the ideal of harmony and by various means showed it to be the essential condition for achieving the true existence of the Christian in this world.[37] Bessarion concluded with an estimate of the enemy and a plan for defeating him. In short, he stated that the Turks were no better than savages. Despoilers of all that was worthwhile, inhuman barbarians, fiercest of wild beasts, they were guilty of every vile and debased deed. Their behavior at Negropont recalled the horror of the rape of Constantinople. Their heinous treatment of non-combatants, of old men, women, and children and the corpses of the deceased was beyond belief. He recounted, for example, how at Negropont Mehmed's soldiers stuffed the bodies of Christians into vases and hurled them by catapult against the camp of the defenders.[38] But despite his huge forces and his unspeakable cruelty, the enemy was not invincible. Among the sultan's weaknesses he mentioned the untrained condition of the bulk of his forces, his difficulties in prosecuting a sustained campaign, and his financial problems. On the other hand, he pointed to the advantages which the Latins possessed, including a well-trained cavalry and unlimited wealth. But most important of all, it was the will of God that Christians halt their internal strife and join in a common effort against the infidels. Despite his grasp of the political realities and his recognition of the need to appeal to the princes in terms which they understood, Bessarion, in the end, recalled them to what he regarded as a higher commitment. Neither his knowledge of the ancients nor of recent and contemporary events had altered his belief in the sovereign role of Providence in history. As the instrument of Almighty God, a united Christendom could not fail to overcome His enemies.[39]

Despite a lifetime of disappointments and frustrations in his own efforts to implement what he regarded as the will of God, Bessarion held fast to his faith. Though he gave evidence of doubts and despair he was not to be numbered among those devotees of antiquity who had recourse to *fortuna* or fate as the author of history. Worn down by years of exacting labor in the service of the church, his countrymen, and scholarship, he was reluctant to undertake a final mission to France to patch up the troubled and complicated relations between Louis XI and the pope. Ill and apparently in much pain, but conforming to the habit of a lifetime, he set out, encouraged by the hope of enlisting the king's support for the crusade. His meeting with Louis was unhappy and unrewarding. Bessarion never returned to Rome. He crossed the Alps in a litter and traveled by boat from Turin to Ravenna where he died November 18, 1472.[40]

Neither the failure of Bessarion's last mission nor his death, which deprived the Greeks of their most influential spokesman, resulted in any reduction in the anti-Turkish activities of the Byzantine refugees. The younger scholars, though they were infants when Constantinople fell to the Turks, preserved in exile not only the heritage of Greek scholarship but were passionate patriots who nursed an intense hatred for the Turks. Addressing their appeals to any prince or influential person who might possibly render assistance, they were often disheartened but none the less persistent. Toward the end of the fifteenth century, as the political situation in Italy became less stable, the Greeks turned increasingly to the transalpine rulers. Recognizing long before the Italians the growing power of the dynastic monarchs, they pinned their hopes particularly on the kings of France. Thus despite Bessarion's bitter experience with Louis XI, it was from the latter's successors—Charles VIII, Louis XII, and Francis I—that the younger generation of exiles received the most encouraging signs. It has long been emphasized that the French invasions of Italy resulted in a political upheaval which encouraged the flight of letters to the north. In the case of the Greeks, however, it should be noted that together with the possibility of brighter scholarly opportunities, French power and subsequently that of the Hapsburg rulers offered the best promises for the fulfillment of their schemes for the destruction of the Turks.[41]

The career of Janus Lascaris, scholar, diplomat, and anti-Turkish publicist illustrates the new direction taken in the appeals of the Greek exiles; it also documents the means and methods by which humanistic scholars kept the image of the Turk as the infidel barbarian before the eyes of sixteenth-century Europe. Born in Constantinople about the year 1445 Lascaris was still a child when the armies of Mehmed II swarmed over the walls of the capital. Fleeing before the Turks first to the Morea and then to Crete, he followed the refugee route west arriving in Venice in 1463 or 1464. From here he moved to Padua where Demetrius Chalcondylas was professor of Greek; and when the latter was appointed to the chair at Florence Lascaris followed. At Florence Lascaris gave private lessons and delivered public lectures in the Greek language. In the twenty years (ca. 1475-1495) that he was established in Florence the city was the unrivalled center of Renaissance culture. Together with the most prominent Italian scholars, Florence boasted the flower of Greek learning including Chalcondylas, John Argyropoulos, Lascaris, and the soldier-poet Michael Marullus Tarchaneiotes. Here too a younger generation of Greek scholars pursued their studies. Among Lascaris' students the best known were Michael Trivolis from Arta and the Cretan Mark Musurus.[42]

Although we possess few details concerning Lascaris' life during his stay in Florence we know that he attracted the attention of Lorenzo de' Medici who appointed him director of his library. While in Lorenzo's service Lascaris made two journeys to the Levant during the years 1489-1492. In a document written many years later, the Greek scholar recalled that he had been provided with the title of ambassador and armed with credentials addressed to the sultan Bayezid II. Charged with collecting books for the Medici library he visited Corfu, Salonika, Mt. Athos, Constantinople, and Pera. Lascaris revealed, however, that he had also been instructed to observe and report on the state of the Ottoman military and that while traveling through the lands of the Turk he was to take note of all things which had any bearing on the proposed crusade.[43]

For nearly forty years after returning from his journeys to the Levant Lascaris endeavored to arouse the West to action against the Turks. Combining an active and productive life of scholarship with extensive tours in the diplomatic service of France and the papacy he seized every opportunity to write or speak in favor of the crusade. His hopes were undoubtedly lifted when he learned of the proposed expedition of Charles VIII of France to recover

Byzantium. He was on hand to greet the king as he rode into Florence (November 17, 1494), and assisted in translating a letter from Bayezid II to the pope which at that time had fallen into Florentine hands. Despite the disastrous results of Charles' expedition to Italy in 1494-1495, Lascaris followed the king back to France in the latter year.[44] He found favor with Charles' successor, and was employed in the negotiations which preceded the descent of Louis XII on Milan in 1499—an action which Lascaris construed as a necessary step toward the crusade and one which seemed justified in light of the crusade bull promulgated by Alexander VI (June 1, 1500), and the subsequent French naval expedition to the Levant in 1501. During the first decade of the sixteenth century Lascaris journeyed as a French envoy twice to Venice and once to Rome. His diplomatic career, however, was temporarily ended when France joined the League of Cambrai (1508) in which Louis XII, Ferdinand of Spain, the emperor, and the pope, together with Mantua and Ferrara combined against Venice. Although the league was concluded for the immediate purpose of solving disputes between the powers and Venice in Italy, the allies had some common interest in uniting against the Turks. Certainly the Turkish question was much discussed by the powers who reassured themselves by claiming that their enemy Venice was friendly with the Ottomans. At any rate Lascaris responded to the discussions about a crusade by preparing a planning paper, *Informatione ad impresa contro a Turchi*, in which he urged the powers to act while the time was ripe.[45]

Since the *Informatione* was written as propaganda in support of a crusade, Lascaris tended to emphasize the weaknesses of the Turks, and failed to give a balanced and objective estimate of their power. The greater part of the work involves an examination of the conditions which the author believed favored an expedition at that time, and a comprehensive plan of operations. Lascaris included, however, some important items of information based upon his own observations in Turkey and his discussions with Greek refugees more recently arrived in Italy. He begins with a brief history of the Turks from their origin down to the fall of Constantinople. He then analyzes the conditions which contributed to the internal weakness of the Turkish empire at the time of his writing. He cites the growing antagonism between the renegades and the native Moslem population. The government, he declares, is in a state of chaos owing to this conflict and the fact that the sultan is "...molto intermazo et molto fiacco de animo et di corpo". Bayezid is an old man of peaceful temperament who might as well be retired. In fact, Lascaris observes, his sons are already quarreling over the succession, an additional source of weakness since it is not fixed by Turkish law. He who has the strongest forces is able to make himself sultan.[46]

Lascaris' description of the Turkish military is brief and superficial. He states at once that they are not equal to their reputation. He notes that there are at the Porte 3000 knights who call themselves slaves. They are limited to a maximum strength of 5000 and are recruited from the most powerful families. The janissaries number 7,000 to 10,000, the latter when they are at full strength. He describes their dress and their weapons which vary considerably from one man to the next. The spahis are assembled only with difficulty. They are poorly armed. Some carry a lance, but others only a sword and a bow. They are not in a state of combat readiness. The army is weak, moreover, because the Turks have lost most of their experienced commanders in the war against Egypt. Except for a squadron of corsairs there is no navy to speak of, and most of their ships are rotten. In regard to logistics there is a severe shortage of artisans, and the Turkish artillery is definitely inferior to that of the western powers. The vast stretches of the interior are poorly guarded and the fortresses are undermanned.[47]

Lascaris includes some information on the pay of the soldiers and the sources of Turkish revenue. The knights, he explains, are paid a ducat for four or five days; higher salaries are paid only to the 200 who are called "proprii de Signore", and who accompany the sultan wherever he goes. The infantry-men receive a ducat for ten days, and are paid quarterly. The major tax is an impost on the hearths of more than 300,000 Christian families. Those who pay it are sometimes able to retain their horses and even carry a scimitar as the Turks do. Many Christians are exempt from the tax since they serve in the territorial guard, especially along the coasts and rivers. Lascaris is certain that they will all flock to the Christian standard when the time arrives. The villagers, especially the mountaineers, moreover, are hardy souls who hate the Turks. The Turks are afraid to venture into many places in the mountains and are able to collect the *kharâj* only if it is voluntarily offered. Often they are greeted instead by an attack from a hostile Christian band.[48]

Indeed, Lascaris, like many of his exiled compatriots, is optimistic about the aid a western force would receive from the Greek subjects of the sultan. He cites the cruelty of the Turks and their ill treatment of the Christians, partic-ularly the practice of seizing children and turning them against their faith and their parents. He recommends that agents be sent in advance of an expedition to arouse the people, and distribute weapons, including swords inscribed with the word "liberty" in Greek. But it is necessary to act quickly while there are still men in Greece who are able to recall their former liberty and who still hold fast to the Christian faith. The younger generation, unhappy with the lot of a subject people and tempted by not having to pay the *kharâj*, is succumbing to the conqueror and turning Turk.[49]

It is unnecessary here to examine in detail the plan of operation which Lascaris proposed for the western forces. He called for the employment of a combined land and sea force under a unified command. He outlined the composition of the forces, their different routes of approach and overall scheme of maneuver. Constantinople was the ultimate objective, but he also indicated intermediate objectives such as the fortresses in the vicinity of the capital and Gallipoli, the seizure of which would deny the sultan reinforcements from Asia. He discussed the financing of the expedition and its logistical support. Throughout Lascaris emphasized the need for surprise and the maintenance of good security, for he admitted that the Turks were swift and crafty. The Venetians were to carry out a diversionary action by invading the Morea. Every precaution was to be taken to keep the plan a secret, and he suggested that a rumor be circulated that the objective of the expedition was to be the Holy Land![50]

The League of Cambrai, as we know, merely opened a new phase in the struggles for Italy which now involved all the major states of Europe. Instead of the crusade it led to the Holy League in which the powers, including Venice and the Swiss, turned on France and drove her, temporarily, from Italy. In the subsequent diplomatic negotiations which punctuated the military actions prosecuted by the League, or by France, Lascaris played a prominent role. Representing the interests of Louis XII in Rome he passed into the service of the papacy with the accession of his long-time friend Giovanni de' Medici as Pope Leo X in 1513. Concerned with reestablishing relations between France and the papacy he was also encouraged by the pope's interest in the plight of the Greek exiles, which resulted in the founding of a Greek college in Rome in 1516 in which Lascaris and Mark Musurus were appointed professors.[51] He was no less active in pressing Leo X to organize a crusade and when in 1517 the sultan of Egypt, faced with an Ottoman invasion, appealed to the West for aid, Lascaris was appointed the pope's ambassador to Cairo. The mission failed to materialize since Egypt fell to the Turks before Lascaris ever set out. The conquest of the Mameluke empire by the Turks, however, was the occasion for renewed interest in the crusade on the part of the pope and the western powers.[52] In support of the pope's efforts Lascaris returned to France. Here and in subsequent trips to Milan and Venice Lascaris continued to work for the establishment of a Greek college, now under French auspices and to urge Francis I and the successors of Leo X, Adrian VI and Clement VII, to organize the crusade.[53] The rivalry between Francis and the new emperor, Charles V, however, took precedence over all. Lascaris' last important mission followed the fateful battle of Pavia (1525) when the French were defeated and their king was carried off to Spain as the prisoner of Charles V. A member of the embassy sent by Clement VII to Spain to bring about an equitable settlement for Francis I, Lascaris used the opportunity, as was his custom, to represent the cause of peace and unity and to appeal to the victorious emperor to take up the struggle against the Turks.[54].

In the "Harangue de Lascaris à Charles-Quint après la bataille de Pavie", we have an intensely personal document in which the aged humanist, now about 80, recapitulated the lifetime labors of an anti-Turkish publicist. Beginning by establishing his credentials as an authority on the Turks, Lascaris introduced himself as a native of Greece and member of an ancient and noble family. Although driven from his home by "the tyranny of the infidel Moslem", Lascaris claimed that from his childhood he had studied the affairs of the Levant. He recalled his journeys in the service of Lorenzo de' Medici, when he had lived for two years in Turkey. In addition to his own firsthand experience he claimed to have studied the history of the Ottomans from their origins to the present tracing all their campaigns on land and sea, in Asia as well as in Europe. Moreover he had supplemented his studies by interrogating the Christian subjects of the sultan and had even talked with janissaries. He was convinced that no one alive knew more than he about the customs of the Turks, their military forces, order of battle, tactics, command structure, discipline, and weapons.[55]

Lascaris then reviewed his own attempts to arouse the Latin princes declaring that "he had not ceased to work for peace among Christians in order that they would undertake a general war against the infidels". He recounted his relations with five popes, three kings of France, the various powers of Italy, the king of Spain, Emperor Maximilian and Charles' own father, Philip, all of whom he had admonished to provide assistance to their Christian brethren and to give serious thought to the tumult which he predicted would one day fall on their own heads. Now he implored Charles, in the name of the pope, to seize the opportunity presented by his victories to conclude peace with all Christians and turn his might against the Turks and all evil infidels. But he spoke, Lascaris affirmed, not on behalf of the Holy See alone. It was "l'ancienne Grece et les reliques de la presente" who prostrated themselves before the emperor begging him to have compassion on those whose children were torn from their arms and taken to be converted to a law contrary to that of Jesus Christ and to serve the tyrants even to the point of returning to war on their own parents. By secret messages smuggled out of Greece they appealed to Charles, promising to rise up themselves, whatever the cost, if only he would come to their aid. He concluded by reminding the emperor that war among Christians played into the hands of the infidels; and that it was for this that the "mophty et autres ministres de la loy alcoranique" prayed three times daily since they recognized that only a divided Christendom had permitted the establishment and continuance of their power.[56]

Among those who aided in disseminating and perpetuating the conception of the Turk as the bloodthirsty foe of Christ and Plato, a crucial role was played by the scholar-publishers—pioneers of the first half-century of printing. Combining a sharp eye for business, a passion for scholarship, and some spirited concern for the moral issues of the day, they quickly weilded their presses in defense of the faith. Publishing news and reports of the Ottoman advance, the tales of travelers, histories, and a wide variety of publicistic pieces, the printers kept the Turkish peril before the eyes of an ever-expanding reading public. Although it cannot be said that the *Türkenfurcht* was mainly the product of their publishing ventures, it was certainly true that their printed texts, often accompanied by pictoral illustrations, further stimulated the sense of crisis. The large volume of works made available for the new reading public of the Renaissance presented the eastern peril in terms and proportions inconceivable in the Middle Ages. Thus in the fifteenth century the Turk became a more immediate threat owing not alone to his geographical proximity, but as the result of the technological revolution in printing.[57]

One of the earliest extant specimens of modern printing is the indulgence granted by Nicholas V in 1451 to raise money for the relief of Cyprus. King John II of Cyprus appointed one Paulin Chappe to receive the money in Europe. Chappe's agents obtained a license from the bishop of Mainz, and in that city in 1454 had numerous copies of the indulgence reproduced.[58] *Türkenablässe* continued to occupy a prominent place in the inventories of printers throughout the fifteenth century. Much more than the question of the crusade was involved here. The printers' responsiveness to the financial needs of the church on the one hand, and the insatiable quest of the populace for spiritual assurance on the other, was good business. But we must not forget that the indulgence was granted in return for support for a specific purpose—in this case the war against the Turks. Thousands of copies distributed especially in Germany, but also in the Lowlands and in England, reminded the faithful that the Turks were the enemy of Christ and were determined to subjugate all Christendom.[59]

The Turkish peril also figured prominently in a variety of experiments by early printers who, sensitive to the possibilities of turning a quick profit, pioneered in journalism. News of military actions by and against the Turks provided the subject for numerous broadsides and newssheets, prototypes of today's newspaper. An early and enterprising example was *Eine Mahnung der*

Christenheit wider die Türken, a crusade appeal cast in the form of a calendar in 1455. Prefaced by a prayer to "almächtiger König auf des Himmels Throne" the appeal was addressed to the various powers—the pope, the emperor, etc., each under a different month. Thus for "Herbstmant" we read:

Alle hertzogen von oisterich vnd beyerlant,
Von sassen, brunswig wol erkant,
Von gulch, geller vnd von cleue,
Von dem berge, slesier vnd auch ander me,
Marggrauen von brandenburg vnd baden
Sollen alle den von myssen laden;
Darzu der lantgraue von hessen vnd toringen
Sollen alle vil folkes brengen,
Dem türken zu leide vnd zu gruwe;
So kommet vns dz x nuwe
Uff samstag vor sant gally
Des morgens dem funfften nahe do by.[60]

The name newspaper itself appeared in German, apparently for the first time in print, in a broadside, *Newe zeytung von orient und auffgang*, of 1502, reporting the struggles of the Venetians with the Turks.[61] In the choice of subject material for the newssheets the printers were unquestionably influenced by contemporary interests and tastes. But mass printing, in turn, had the effect of sharpening public awareness and concern, and helped to shape the opinions of contemporaries toward the Turks and all other subjects treated by the new medium.[62]

One incident in the early history of the first press of Paris and in the career of its principal sponsor, Guillaume Fichet, will illustrate the use of the new invention for the express purpose of influencing public opinion against the Turks. For the background to our example we must return for a moment to the end of 1470. In that year Europe was again stunned by the news of a major Turkish victory. The bastion of Negropont had been considered the mainstay of Venetian possessions in the East and therefore a buttress to the crumbling structure of Levantine Christianity. The fall of Negropont renewed all the fears and memories of Turkish savagery on the occasion of Constantinople's capture. Once more the cry of alarm sounded from the bell-towers and pulpits of cathedrals and churches throughout the West. Mendicant preachers called on the people to repent and contribute according to their sins to the pope's war against the infidel. The pens of publicists were sharpened and put to writing the appeals and projects which make up the huge corpus of *Turcica*. The new scare provoked the veteran promoter of the crusade Cardinal Bessarion to marshal his failing resources for a last attempt at arousing Christendom. In this effort he concentrated upon enlisting the aid of the princes of Italy and the king of France. He knew that Fichet shared his desire for the reform of Christendom and that they agreed upon some important particulars. He knew that as a royal diplomat Fichet had recently pleaded before the court of Milan the causes of peace and unity among Christian princes and the crusade. He was also aware of Fichet's efforts to introduce humanistic studies and the benefits of classical culture at the University of Paris. And it is likely that he had heard of the founding of a press in the precincts of the Sorbonne. Bessarion was, therefore, not just conforming to correct usage when he addressed Fichet as his dear friend in his letter dated December 13, 1470. In the opening sentence he acknowledged the French scholar's learning in philosophy and the Holy Scriptures and particularly in rhetoric. He wrote that in these matters he had nothing worthy to offer his correspondent; however, he was sending his *Orationes*, which dealt with the danger then threatening Italy and all Christianity. He admitted that his purpose in forwarding the work was not so much to provide Fichet with an example of inspired discourse or pure style, but rather to lay bare the terrible misfortune which plagued Christendom and to urge him to bring it to the attention of the king and other responsible people.

It took about six weeks for the *Orationes* to reach Fichet. Upon receipt the latter immediately prepared the work for the press. In mid-April 1471, the first printed copies were turned out—only the fifth book to be produced by the new firm. Fichet sent copies to the king of England, the dukes of Burgundy and Savoy, and a number of lesser lords both lay and ecclesiastical. For some of the volumes he wrote and had printed special letters of dedication addressed to the person for whom the book was intended. The letter of dedication to Cardinal Rolin, Fichet's longtime friend and principal backer of the press, is dated April 23, 1471. In March of the following year he was able to report to Bessarion that he had distributed at his own cost forty-six copies. The dedicatory letters show our Paris theologian as no mean propagandist. To the various notables he introduced himself as the servant of the Cardinal of Nicea on whose authority he was acting. He commended Bessarion to them, reminded them of their duty, recalled the precedents established by their ancestors, cited the example of their lords or peers who were devoted to the crusade, and enumerated the particular obligations of each. The central idea which ran through all the letters and linked them to the *Orationes* was the appeal for the cessation of fighting among Christians and the pressing need for the holy war.[63]

As well as in books dealing specifically with the Turks or the religion of

Islam, publishers and their learned colleagues frequently touched upon the subject in the prologues or conclusions to scholarly works, editions of classical writers, and other texts. The Turkish peril was never more dramatically characterized nor the Turks themselves more thoroughly excoriated than in the "Hymn to Plato" prefixed by Mark Musurus to his Greek edition of Plato's works published by Aldo Manuzio in 1513. A native of Crete, a distinguished teacher of Greek who counted among his students Gasparo Contarini, Girolamo Aleandro, John Conon, Germain de Brie, and Erasmus, Musurus was associated with the Aldine press and the humanist program to produce accurate printed editions of Greek texts. An ardent patriot Musurus was also preoccupied with the fate of Greece under Turkish domination, and like most Greek refugee scholars, he actively, and simultaneously, prosecuted the causes of Greek culture and the crusade. The mingling of concern for the fatherland, scholarship, and the crusade may be illustrated by a few verses from the impassioned preface to his Plato. Addressing first the ancient philosopher, author of "the sacred work" in which "...full displayed, we may trace the mighty hand of him, the one great Architect...", Musurus turned to Pope Leo X and bade him accept the book in the name of Aldo, and in return prayed:

But that thy hand [the pope's] might dash the fiend of war,
　　That now relentless o'er Eugania's plain
Roams uncontrolled, and drives his iron cur
　　Thro' scenes of horror and o'er heaps of slain.
What heart so hard, that would not melt to hear
　　The orphan's wail, the widow's piercing cry?
Antiphates himself might drop a tear,
　　And Polyphemus heave a pitying sigh;
Temples and domes a common ruin share;
　　The crackling harvests in the flame expire;
Whilst fierce barbarians, all unused to spare,
　　Glean the last relicks of destructive fire:
Calm thou their fierce contentions mighty chief;
　　To peace, to love thy erring sons restore;
From thee, let suffering nations find relief;
　　And bid contending monarchs rage no more.
Deep hid within his cavern's dark recess,
　　Too long has Mars the goddess Peace confined;
Thou lead her forth, to harmonize, to bless,
　　And with her bounteous gifts, enrich mankind.

Then turn the tide of war on Turkey's shores,
    And curb the wolf-like, unbelieving band,
Whose tyrant empire fainting Greece deplores;
    Whilst hovering now o'er Iapygia's strand,
They threaten in degrading chains to bind
    Thy sons, and banish the Redeemer's name;
But let them first thy ready vengeance find;
    On Asia's shores let warlike myriads gleam.[64]

Then citing in turn the role to be played by each of the European powers (wherein the Cretan scholar shows some acquaintance with their particular skills), Musurus envisioned a victorious outcome:

Then o'er Byzantium's towers, if once again
    The light of freedom dawn; if then represt
By thy victorious arms, on Graecia's plain
    The poisonous dragon low'r his fateful crest,
Tis—all achieved—for then, from bondage freed,
    Achaia's sons their ancient fires shall feel;
Beneath their hands the barbarous foe shall bleed,
    Or fly before their swift avenging steel.

The defeat of the Turks, he prophesied, was to usher in a new age of peace and sacred justice under the scepter of the pope. Until then, Musurus concluded by urging Leo to lend his support to "drooping science", and be generous with his aid to the learned but neglected poet.[65]

Publication of a particular volume was sometimes rationalized as appropriate to recalling a faltering Christendom to its duty. In the preface to the *Epistole de Sancta Catharina da Siena* (1500), Manuzio remarked how the letters seemed to be addressed to the popes of his time as well as those of the preceding century, and he urged that His Holiness and the cardinals hasten to oppose the pagans by arms, "for we are in great danger of becoming the slaves of the infidels".[66] Translations were especially justified as providing examples of past achievements and valor and for the purpose of inspiring Christians to march against the Turks. Such, we are told, was the reason for William Caxton's publication of his *Godeffroy of Boloyne*.[67] To the French rendition of Quintus Curtius Rufus *De la vie et gestis dalexandre le grant*, the translator, Vasco de Lucerna, added a conclusion in which he endeavored to demonstrate to Charles of Burgundy the advantages which the duke enjoyed over Alexander who singlehandedly and without the help of Christ had conquered the whole orient.[68]

We may conclude with one further illustration, a preface by John Kay, self-styled poet of Edward IV of England, to the English translation of Caoursin's *Siege of Rhodes*, published in 1483. Commemorating the victory over the Turks, the poet revealed the sense of relief and expectation which followed the succession of events in 1480-1481, culminating in the death of Mehmed II: "the turkes", he wrote, "hane vexed the crysten partyes, & hane preuayled, and had of the crysten men the ouerhande". Indeed, the Turks have advanced to the shores of Italy and occupy territory in the realm of Naples, "in pre-iudyce & horryble terrour to the court apostolyque & to al crystendome". The Grand Turk, the late Mehmed, raised a strong force with which he intended to seize the holy city of Rome, and to subject all Italy, and ultimately to overcome and oppress the rest of Christendom. "But Jhesu cryste our redemptour wold not his crysten people to be put into lenger peyne, or to more trybulacion: he hath retrayte & withdrawen hys rodde: as a kynd father to his dere children contente with grete menasses & lytil punycyon". Because of the sins of Christians God had allowed the Turks in the past to be victorious; but now owing to the prayers and repentance of the pope, the cardinals, the Christian princes and people, He has granted His pardon: "through the grace of the blessed Jhesu: this grete turke in his moste pryde, & his moste hope hath made be sodeyn deth an ende of his lyue: and ys the cruel generacyon of the turkes foreuermore, with goddes grace deiecte, & caste out of Italye. And all the turkes among them selfe in grete werres, whiche thyng ys token to all crysten prynces here after to recouer the partyes crysten".[69]

NOTES TO CHAPTER VI

1. Daniel, *Islam and the West*, p. 260.

2. See A. D. Momigliano, "The Place of Herodotus in the History of Historiography", in *Studies in Historiography*, pp. 133-139.

3. Nicolaus Sagundino, *De turcarum origine* (Viterbo, 1531).

4. Theodore of Gaza, *De origine turcarum* in J. B. Migne, *Patrologia series Graeca*, CLXI, cols. 997-1006.

5. See especially Aeneas Sylvius, *Europa* in *Opera*, p. 394, and in his *Cosmographia*, *ibid.*, p. 383; cf. Andrea Cambini, *Della origine de' Turchi* (Venice, 1538), fol. 2ʳ. Particularly strong in denouncing this tradition was Jean Lemaire de Belge who, however, quite seriously put forward the theory that the Trojans were the common ancestor of the French and Germans who ought therefore to join together and recover their heritage seized by the Turks. See *Oeuvres*, ed. Stecher (Paris, 1882-1885), I, 15;

II, 473, 474. On this see T. Spencer, "Turks and Trojans in the Renaissance", *Modern Language Review*, XLVII (1952), 330-332; and A. Eckardt, "La Légende de l'origine troyenne des Turcs", *Körösi Cosma Archivum*, II (1926-1932), 422-433. I have not seen the latter. Cf. D. Hay, *Europe: The Emergence of an Idea*, pp. 108-110.

6. See below Chapter VIII, p. 204, cf. L. Chalcondyles, *De origine ac rebus gestis imperatorum Turcarum*, in J. B. Migne, *Patrologia series Graeca*, CLIX, col. 397.

7. *MHH*, ed. Dethier, XXII, pt. i, 280-283, 291, 292.

8. *Ibid.*, pp. 292-294, 308-319, 400-406.

9. *Ibid.*, pp. 267-279.

10. *Scritti inediti di Benedetto Colucci da Pistoia*, ed. A. Frugoni (Florence, 1939), pp. 1-47. Francesco Filelfo's student, Lapo Birago da Castiglionchio, dedicated a crusade plan, *Strategetica*, to Nicholas V (see G. Tiraboschi, *Storia della letteratura italiana*, Milan, 1824, VI, ii, 1206, 1207); cf. the student exercises on the Turkish threat published by L. Thuasne in *Djem-sultan, fils de Mohammed II, frère de Bayezid II, 1459-1495* (Paris, 1892), pp. 434-437. For Ficino's own anti-Turkish orations see *Opera omnia* (photographic reprint of the Basel edition of 1576, Turin, 1959), I, ii, 721, 722, 808-810. Excellent examples of humanist orations against the Turks which were actually delivered and which may be readily consulted are the following: "Petri Paschalici Veneti oratoris ad Hemanvelem Lvsitaniae regem oratio", fascimile edition with English translation in D. Weinstein, *Ambassador from Venice, Pietro Pasqualigo in Lisbon*, 1501 (Minneapolis, 1960); "Oratio Reverendi in christo domini Joannis de Margarit Episcopi Gerundense", before the Venetian senate on May 10, 1481, in Robert B. Tate, *Joan Margarit I Pau. Cardinal Bishop of Gerona* (Manchester, 1955), pp. 142-145; and the address of Robert Gaguin before the English court in *Roberti Gaguni epistole et orationes*, ed. L. Thuasne (Paris, 1904), II, 291-299.

11. Letter to George of Trebizond, July 30, 1428, in *Cent-dix lettres grecques de François Filelfe*, ed. E. Legrand (Paris, 1892), no. 3, pp. 5-8.

12. Letter to Charles VII, February 15, 1451 in *MHH*, ed. Dethier, XXII, pt. i, no. 10, 503-533; mentioned by R. Gaguin, *La Mer des croniques et miror historial de France* (Paris, 1530?), fol. clxiv.

13. Legrand, *Cent-dix lettres*, no. 32, pp. 63-68; no. 11, pp. 211-214.

14. *Ibid.*, nos. 33, 37, pp. 68, 69, 73, 74.

15. "Oratio ad sacrosanctum ecclesie Romanae pontificem Pium II. Mantuae congregato Consistorio publico, assistentibus Duce Mediolanensi, et oratoribus regnum et principum 1459", in G. B. Mitarelli, *Bibiotheca codicum manuscriptorum monasterii S. Michaelis Venetiarum* (Venice, 1779), cols. 888-893; cf. Pius II, *Commentaries*, III, 225.

16. Legrand, *Cent-dix lettres*, no. 60, p. 109; *Francisci Philelfi epistolarum familiarum libri. XXXVII* (Venice, 1502), fols. 157^v-158^r; *Epistolae Jacobi Picolomini*, fols 468^r-469^v.

17. Iorga, *Notes et extraits*, IV, 234ff.

18. Legrand, *Cent-dix lettres*, no. 74, pp. 127, 128; no. 98, pp. 169-171; no. 110, pp. 190-194.

19. On the importance of the humanist exhortations in influencing both officials and public opinion cf. remarks of C. Marinescu, "Le Pape Nicolas V et son attitude envers

l'empire byzantine", p. 339; and J. G. Rowe, "The Tragedy of Aeneas Sylvius Piccolomini", p. 311, n. 89; and P. O. Kristeller, *Studies in Renaissance Thought and Letters* (Rome, 1956), p. 112, n. 51.

20. There is a vast literature on the subject but in addition to special studies cited in the following notes, I have depended heavily on E. Legrand, *Bibliographie héllenique ou description raisonnée des ouvrages publiés en Grec par des Grecs au XVe et XVIe siècle*. 4 vols. (Paris, 1885-1906). See also the articles cited in notes 4 and 6, Chapter II above.

21. Geanakoplos, *Greek Scholars in Venice*, pp. 53-70; and N. Iorga, *Byzance après Byzance* (Bucarest, 1935), p. 18. The case of Michele Marullo Tarcaniota is especially interesting; a native of Constantinople, he studied Greek and Latin in Venice, philosophy at Padua, wrote poetry and supported himself as a condotiere. Many of the poems are dedicated to his suffering compatriots and appeals for their relief. See B. Croce, *Michele Marullo Tarcaniota* (Bari, 1938); A. Persoa, *Michaelis Marulli Carmina* (Zurich, 1951).

22. Geanakoplos, *Greek Scholars in Venice*, gives some attention to sociological matters but is mainly interested in intellectual problems. B. Knös, *Un Ambassadeur de l'hellénisme, Janus Lascaris, et la tradition greco-byzantine dans l'humanisme français* (Uppsala, 1945), appreciates more than most scholars the importance of the anti-Turkish activities of Greek scholars; see e.g. p. 30.

23. Geanakoplos, *Greek Scholars in Venice*, pp. 61-67.

24. Legrand, *Bibliographie héllenique*, I, lxxi-lxxxvii.

25. On Apostolis see H. Noiret, *Lettres inédites de Michel Apostolis* (Paris, 1889); Geanakoplos, *Greek Scholars in Venice*, pp. 73-110.

26. *Ibid.*, pp. 79ff.

27. "Oratio acclamatoria, ad religiosissimum et serenissimum Romanorum imperatorem. . .Fridericum III", *Rerum germanicarum scriptores*, ed. B. G. Struve (Strasbourg, 1717), II, cols. 47-50.

28. Quoted in Geanakoplos, *Greek Scholars in Venice*, pp. 109, 110.

29. The standard work on Bessarion is that of L. Mohler, *Kardinal Bessarion als Theologe, Humanist und Staatsmann*, 3 vols. (Paderborn, 1923-1942); but see also L. Bréhier, "Bessarion", *Dictionnaire d'histoire et de géographie ecclésiastique*, VIII, cols. 1181-1199.

30. See his opening speech at Florence, October 8, 1438 in G. Hoffman, ed., *Acta Latina concilii Florentini* (Rome, 1955), pp. 34-38.

31. Bréhier, "Bessarion", cols. 1185, 1186.

32. *Ibid.*, cols. 1186, 1187.

33. On the first printing of the *Orationes* see pp. 167, 168.

34. The text used here is in J. B. Migne, *Patrologia series Graeca*, CLXI, cols. 651-653.

35. *Ibid.*, cols. 653-659.

36. *Ibid.*, cols. 647-651.

37. *Ibid.*, cols. 660-664.

38. *Ibid.*, cols. 665-667.

39. *Ibid.*, cols. 667-669; cf. L. Mohler, "Bessarions Instruktion für die Kreuzzugspredigt

in Venedig (1463)", *Römische Quartalschrift für Christliche Altertumskunde und für Kirchengeschichte* XXXV (1927), 337-349, for the more traditional approach as applied to the masses.

40. See P. Ourliac, "Louis XI et le cardinal Bessarion", *Bulletin de la société archéologique du midi de la France,* 3rd ser., V (1943).

41. For the activities of Greek scholars outside of Italy see R. Weiss, "Learning and Education in Western Europe from 1470 to 1520", *NCMH,* I, 102ff.

42. On Lascaris see B. Knös, *Un Ambassadeur de l'hellénisme, Janus Lascaris,* pp. 20-25, for his early life.

43. "Harangue de Lascaris à Charles-Quint, après la bataille de Pavie", Legrand, *Bibliographie héllenique,* I, cliii-cliv.

44. Knös, *op. cit.,* pp. 74-80.

45. *Ibid.,* pp. 90-121; "Informatione ad impresa contro a Turchi data per Jane Lascari nel MDVIII", in Iorga, *Notes et extraits,* VI, 45-55.

46. *Ibid.,* pp. 45, 46.

47. *Ibid.,* p. 46.

48. *Ibid.,* p. 47.

49. *Ibid.,* pp. 51, 54, 55.

50. *Ibid.,* pp. 47-54.

51. Knös, *op. cit.,* pp. 132-142.

52. *Ibid.,* pp. 155-157.

53. *Ibid.,* pp. 171-186.

54. See also *Monumenta saeculi XVI, historiam illustrantia,* ed. P. Balan (Innsbruck, 1885), I, 157, 158, for letter of Clement VII to Charles V urging the crusade.

55. "Harangue de Lascaris", cliii-cliv.

56. *Ibid.,* clv-clvi.

57. There is no catalog of fifteenth-century printed materials bearing on the Turkish crisis. But for the sixteenth century see C. Göllner, *Turcica: Die europaischen Türkendrucke des XVI. Jahrhunderts, I:* 1501-1550 (Berlin, 1961), which, however, is not complete.

58. G. Zelder, *Die Mainzer Ablassbriefe der Jahr* 1454 *und* 1455 (Mainz, 1913), pp. 1-13.

59. See the discussion of indulgences in Rudolf Hirsch, *Printing, Selling and Reading,* 1450-1550 (Wiesbaden, 1967), pp. 122-124.

60. *Türkenkalender auf das Jahr* 1455, ed. A. Bieling (Vienna, 1873), p. 20; cf. C. Wehmer, *Mainzer Probedrucke* (Munich, 1948).

61. *Newe zeytung von orient und auffgange,* ed. H. H. Bockwitz (Leipzig, 1920); cf. K. M. Setton, "Lutheranism and the Turkish Peril", p .137, n. 3; and in general K. Schottenloher, *Flugblatt und Zeitung* (Berlin, 1922).

62. For the use of the press as an instrument in molding public opinion see the discussion in H. S. Bennett, *English Books and Readers,* 1475 *to* 1557 (Cambridge, 1952), pp. 135-145.

63. The Bessarion-Fichet correspondence is in Legrand, *Cent-dix lettres,* nos. 1-12, pp. 223-251; seventeen of Fichet's dedicatory letters comprise nos. 15-31, pp. 256-289.

64. Translation in W. Roscoe, *The Life and Pontificate of Leo X*, II, pp. 243, 244.

65. *Ibid.*, p. 245.

66. See A. Firmin-Didot, *Alde-Manuce et l'hellénisme à Venise* (Paris, 1875), pp. 142-144.

67. *Godeffroy of Bologne*, ed. M. N. Colvin (London, 1893), pp. 1-5.

68. Quintus Curtius Rufus, *De la vie et gestes dalexandre le grant*, tr. Vasco de Lucerna (Paris, 1500?), fol. 239^{vr}.

69. Guillaume Caoursin, *The Siege of Rhodes*, tr. John Kay (London, 1483); quoted here from reprint in *Verbatum Reprints* (London, 1870).

CHAPTER VII

Travelers' tales

Among the various sources and media which provided Renaissance Europe with information and contributed to shaping the western image of the Turk, the reports of pilgrims who journeyed to the Holy Land must be assigned an important place. From the fourth century voyage of Helena, mother of Constantine the Great, until the Ottoman conquest of Syria and Palestine early in the sixteenth century the stream of pilgrims never completely subsided. Difficult, hazardous, and costly, the pilgrimage to Palestine ranked among the highest aspirations of successive generations of Latin Christians. Although the pilgrim need claim but spiritual motives, and indeed was admonished to harbor none other, clearly the journey was undertaken for a variety of reasons. Together with the desire for the assurance of salvation, there were the opportunities for adventure and worldly acclaim, the possibility of material profit, or the necessity of commuting a severe punishment for some crime.[1] Surely there is no figure more familiar to readers of late medieval or Renaissance literature than the stalwart pilgrim. With his staff and pouch and his letter of safe conduct, and if he had successfully reached his destination and was homeward bound, his supply of indulgences and sacred relics, he was a familiar sight in the public life of his times. The town chroniclers recorded his departure and return: "Item, tantost le lendemain de la S^{nt} Vincent, s'en allit le s^r Jehan de Heu, filz Collingnon de Heu, l'amant, visiter lez sainct lieu de Romme, de sainct Nicollais du Van, et de Jherusalem. En enmenit avec luy Joffroy Papperel, filz s^r Nicolle Papperel...", noted Jehan Aubrion, a citizen of Metz, in his journal under the date 1465. And in the following year he dutifully reported that on February 10, Jehan de Heu returned from his voyage to Jerusalem, St. Catherine's, and St. Nicholas du Vau, and related many tales of strange things that he had seen and of the countries which he had visited.[2]

Chiefly churchmen and nobles took up the pilgrim's staff, yet there were not a few commoners who left labors and home to visit Christ's birthplace and tomb. Thus the records of pilgrims representing every country of Europe and every walk of life provide a cross-section of public opinion quite unique among the sources of our period.[3] Although thousands of western pilgrims who went to Palestine failed to commit their experiences to writing we can be sure that like Jehan de Heu they passed them on to relatives and neighbors by word of mouth. Such accounts, repeated over and over, cannot for the most part have been distinguished for their accuracy or objectivity, especially where they involved Moslem affairs. Yet tales transmitted in this manner constituted a significant share of the common stock of Europe's knowledge of the East; and in a society still largely illiterate they weighed heavily in the formation of western attitudes toward the Ottoman Turks. For countless common folk the returned pilgrim served as the single, direct link with the mysterious and frightening world of the Levant. His meagre fund of half-truths regarding the Turks gave rise to exaggerated and bizarre concoctions among his fellow citizens. Only a few lines following his notice of the pilgrim's return to Metz, Jehan Aubrion related how the marshal of Burgundy had, on March 12, passed through the city on his way to attend a council called by the duke "pour déterminez d'une bien mervillouse chose. . .". Aubrion then disclosed, without further comment or question, that the Grand Turk had sent the duke "une tres grant et noble enbaxade, et moult richement adornes, et moult belle grande et saige. . ." to propose a marrige between the two houses. And the Grand Turk promised that when the alliance was concluded he and all his people were to be baptized![4]

The association of pilgrims with Turks or other Moslems in the minds of Latin Christians was carried over into the popular literature. The author of the French farce, *Colin et Thevot*, however, found it useful to reverse the normal sequence. Thevot, the mayor of a French town, is hearing the case of a woman whose chickenyard has been raided, when suddenly the proceedings are interrupted. The mayor's son, Colin, is introduced as having just returned from a journey to Italy and announces boldly that he has brought with him a "Sarazin" whom he captured on the road between Naples and Rome. As the coarse humor of the dialogue is developed we learn that the prisoner was seized while sleeping "au pié de la croix", that he carries "ung grant baston ferré", and that the likes of him had never before been seen in those parts. Thevot proceeds to examine the "Sarazin" who, though he speaks a strange tongue, finally produces a letter which Thevot snatches from him and attempts to read:

> Uni, uni, universis,
> Que je ne scay où j'en suis:
> Inspect, inspect, inspect. . . .

"Inspecturis", Colin queries? Thevot exclaims:

> A tredame, tu l'as trouvé!
> Ma foy, j'estoye fort troublé,

Je la lisoye a revers;
Mais il est tant de mauvais cleres!
Pensez que vecy mal escript.
Je cuide que la lettre dit
Qu'il s'en va en pelerinage.

The unfortunate victim, a pilgrim mistaken for a Saracen, can only reply, "Quel! Quel!"[5]

On occasion it appears that travelers to the Levant went beyond the mere spinning of yarns to stimulate the imaginations of the stay-at-homes and affected some habit or custom of the Turks. More than one voyager returned home attired in Turkish dress complete with turban. In the case of Robert Tiptoft, Earl of Worcester, the affectation involved a much more serious Turkish custom. Having served as Lord Treasurer (1452-54) and Keeper of the Sea (after 1454), he was appointed in August 1457 envoy of Henry VI along with Robert Flemming and Philip Wentworth to the court of Calixtus III. Tiptoft used this opportunity to make the pilgrimage to Palestine. Upon his return to Italy he was named as one of the English ambassadors to the Congress of Mantua, which he seems not to have attended. While he did not leave any written record of his pilgrimage or his opinion of the Turks it is certain that he was more than a little influenced by them. A few years later Tiptoft, Earl of Worcestor, earned for himself the title "Butcher of England" when, as Grand Constable under Edward IV he dispatched some Englishmen involved in a plot against the throne by having them executed in the peculiar Turkish manner of impaling.[6]

The extant pilgrim narratives, while somewhat similar in form, vary greatly in length, substance, and reliability. Many are fragmentary. Some consist of a bare itinerary of a few lines. Others are of considerable length; the relation of Felix Fabri numbers 1493 pages in a modern Latin edition.[7] Some of the fuller accounts give a good deal of detailed information, describe each place visited, note historical or mythological facts, and include many interesting incidents of the voyage. For the most part, the accounts may be divided into five sections: (1) an introduction, sometimes including biographical notes, a description of preparations and the first stage of the journey as far as the port of embarkation; (2) a description of the port city (generally Venice in the fifteenth century); (3) the journey from Venice to Palestine; (4) the Holy Land, usually the most detailed part of the account; (5) the return voyage and journey back to the pilgrim's home. Although many accounts are not this complete, some are even more extensive. The narrative of the well-known English pilgrim, William Wey, who twice went to Palestine, is prefaced with a treatise on the rates of monetary exchange from England to Syria; a "Preusysoun" listing all the necessities for the voyage; a metrical account of the pilgrimage; a "memoria technica", specifying the time required in traveling to the holy places; and a statement of purpose for visiting the shrines. By way of appendices, William Wey added after the description of his second voyage a Greek vocabulary, and an interesting map of the Holy Land.[8]

To the pilgrim from England, France, or Germany, it might have seemed, as he arrived in Venice for the first time, that he had already reached the Orient. The docks and markets of the city were filled with the products of the East. Embassies from Turkey, Persia, and Egypt were often there and Moslem merchants were not uncommon. An anonymous French pilgrim, on his way to the Holy Land in 1480, wrote that he saw in Venice a Turkish ambassador who had come to collect the tribute which Venice paid to the Turks.[9] In December of the next year, a German Franciscan, Friar Paul Walter, on his way to Palestine, was much disturbed by the things he saw and heard about the Turks in Venice. According to his report, there was then in the city a military mission, sent by the Grand Turk to advise the Venetians in their wars. Paul Walter saw the Turkish captain and his group. He was indignant over the favorable treatment accorded the Turks. The Venetians, he lamented, venerated the evil enemies of Christ. What was worse, the Venetians gave "those dogs and enemies of the sacrament" a place in the holy procession of the feast of Corpus Christi. When all Christendom should have grieved, the whole city calmly sat by and observed the Turks' irreverence and blasphemies.[10]

It seemed to Paul Walter that Venice was guilty of compromising with the Turks on all points—trade, politics, and now religion! He wrote that he had heard from a good source, that the Turks and the Venetians had made a common banner. The image of St. Mark the Evangelist was depicted along with the moon and the star of the Ottoman Turks. He concluded: "from this it was felt that St. Mark and Mohammed, the Turk and the pope, the Venetians and the infidels were united and allied". In these remarks, Paul Walter reflected the antagonism of German ecclesiastics toward Italy and the papacy in the fifteenth century, and he anticipated a favorite theme of Martin Luther's a generation later, linking the pope and the Turks together. Friar Paul pursued the subject further, saying that he had heard at Venice that there was considerable discord and turmoil in Rome over the relations of Christians and Turks. He was told that the cardinals and the Roman citizens were not at all reconciled to aiding Venice since the Republic sided with the Turks against other Christians. "Lamentabile hoc super lamentabile omnibus veris catholicis Christianis", he bewailed.[11]

Anti-Venetian sentiments, like those expressed by Paul Walter, ran high, especially after the peace of 1479. Before this time, however, and again at the end of the century, pilgrims from western Europe were loud in their praises of the Republic of St. Mark. In the eyes of many Christians Venice, having engaged the Turks single-handedly, had protected Europe from the Ottoman onslaught. Pilgrim visitors, impressed with the canals, the vast number of ships, and other signs of Venetian opulence—countless churches and monasteries, magnificent palaces and buildings of state—were carried away in their lavish descriptions.[12] A Milanese pilgrim, Canon Pietro Casola, realizing the extent of his own description of the city, was somewhat embarassed: "...I must make my excuses to the readers of this my itinerary, if it should seem to them that I have overpraised this city of Venice. What I write is not written to win the good will of the Venetians, but to set down the truth. And I declare that it is impossible to tell or write fully of the beauty, the magnificence, or the wealth of the city of Venice. . . . It will be incredible to anyone who has not seen the city."[13]

With the threat of the Turks hanging over their heads, the pilgrims were naturally interested in Venice's state of military preparedness. Each in turn extolled the might and prowess of St. Mark, and especially the abundance of armaments stored in the arsenal. The most detailed description of the arsenal is found in the relation of Arnold von Harff, a German pilgrim who was taken on a guided tour of it in 1496. The arsenal housed the facilities for construction and manufacture, testing and storage, maintenance and provisioning of the ships and ordnance. Von Harff was shown the sheds where ships were constructed, with canals running through their center into which new vessels were launched. He saw the shops where rigging was made; here 100 women were employed in making rope, and 50 more in sewing sails. He saw the forges where anchors and cannon were turned out; and he saw twelve powder mills turned by horses. In the new arsenal, which had a capacity for 100 galleys, there was a proving ground where cannon were fired into a huge wall. The small arms and equipment were stored in large halls; coats-of-mail, swords, daggers, spears, helmets, and shields were arranged on either side the lengths of the walls in three rows, one above the other. Other weapons by the thousands were stored there; crossbows were to be found in the lofts six rows deep. Altogether, there were five such halls, with two floors each, all arranged in like manner. The heavy ordnance was stored in separate buildings. Von Harff saw cannon twenty-four times a man's foot in length, which fired projectiles of one thousand pounds. Here, too, were stored slings, half-slings, carthouns, and chamber guns used on ships, and mortars. When at the end of a four-hour tour von Harff registered astonishment at what he had seen, he was assured that this was only a small part of Venice's military equipment. Every burgher and gentleman, he was informed, was able to outfit himself and many other men, and every town under Venetian domination was similarly equipped.[14]

The sight of all this must have been reassuring to the defenseless pilgrim. Indeed, a tour of the arsenal, mentioned by several pilgrims, may well have been a calculated effort on the part of the Venetians, pioneers in all the arts of modern salesmanship, to prepare psychologically the uneasy voyager.[15] Certainly it was of additional comfort to know that the dominion of Venice was not limited to the area of the lagoons, but that her possessions were strung across the Mediterranean like a mighty chain, as Christendom's first line of defense. This show of strength seems to have dispelled at least one voyager's fear of the Turks. William Wey, native of Devonshire, fellow of Eton College, a religious of the monastery of Edyngton, and who might be called a professional pilgrim, went first to the Holy Land in 1458, only five years after the fall of Constantinople. In the company of 197 pilgrims, aboard two galleys, he sailed from Venice on May 18, 1458. The ships arrived at Jaffa exactly one month later, and the pilgrims entered Jerusalem on June 24. After a brief stay, Wey's party left Jaffa on July 3, and was back in Venice only sixteen weeks from the time of departure. William Wey's account of this voyage is exceedingly short, and he mentioned the Turks infrequently. He did relate one interesting tale on the activities of Mehmed II who, Wey reported, was then in the Morea where he rounded up 30,000 men, women, and boys to resettle in and around Constantinople.[16] At Durazzo he heard stories of the battle of Belgrade (1456), where, it was alleged, 50,000 infidels had died. After this failure, the Turks were reported to have sent a fleet against Negropont. Wey does not betray any apprehension over the reported strength of the Turks on the sea. Undoubtedly the news, also learned at Durazzo, that the Venetians had sixteen armed galleys stationed in the Adriatic Sea to protect their possessions, cancelled any fears the pilgrims harbored.[17]

Despite the evident strength of the Republic of St. Mark, most travelers to the Levant during our period were acutely conscious of the danger from the Turks. The sea route from Venice to Palestine ran uncomfortably close to the Turkish mainland. All along the way, the voyager was hardly ever out of sight of lands ruled directly by the Turk, or paying tribute to him.

In Christian ports of call, Turkish merchants, sailors, and officials walked about the streets in broad daylight. At any moment, from the port of Parenzo to the harbor of Jaffa, a Christian vessel was likely to encounter a Turkish man-of-war or Turkish pirates. The immediate danger of the Turks, therefore, was never far from the minds of the pilgrims as they crossed the Mediterranean, where there were constant reminders of the Ottomans' progress.[18]

Returning from his second pilgrimage to the Holy Land, William Wey stopped at Rhodes on August 19, 1462. News had reached the island of a series of Wallachian victories over the troops of Mehmed II, of which Wey gave a detailed account.[19] The knights, he reported, were elated by the Christian successes, and there was rejoicing throughout Rhodes. The joy, however, was short-lived. According to Wey, the Grand Turk heard of their celebrating his defeat and vowed immediate vengeance. A cloud of anxiety descended upon the island. The pilgrims hastily departed, as the knights feverishly prepared for the expected onslaught. The apprehension of Wey's party was heightened when they arrived at Crete on September 5. They encountered a Venetian, fresh from Constantinople, who informed the pilgrims that the Turks were on the sea, bound for Rhodes with a fleet of 300 ships. William Wey fortunately escaped harm. He arrived safely in Venice on October 11, and was in Dover, England, on the first of December.[20]

Of their many ports of call nowhere were the pilgrims more likely to be regaled with stories about the Turks and the imminent threat which they posed than at Rhodes. The activities of its defenders and their constant clashes with the Turks evoked much comment from our western travelers. From the descriptions left by contemporary visitors we can get a fair picture of Rhodes and its inhabitants during the years immediately preceding and following the great siege. Mary Dupuis described it as, ". . .une belle et bonne et grant Isle moult bien fertille et habundante de biens du couste du soleil levant. . .". The city was large and beautiful, with an excellent port and mercantile facilities. Outside its walls were many gardens, and the houses and chapels of the Greeks. In short, it was ". . .lung des plus grans passaiges de tout le Levant".[21] When the cosmopolitan canon of Milan, Pietro Casola, visited Rhodes in 1494, commercial and other civilian activities seemed to have declined in face of military considerations. Casola found the island rather sterile, and everything excessively expensive. There was, he explained, merchandise, but it was all brought from other places, such as carpets from Turkey, and cloths from Italy. Yet there were merchants, he wrote, from ". . .every nation under the sun", especially many wealthy Jews who carried on the silk trade. "I saw", our careful observer further remarked, "some very beautiful women there of every nation." The Rhodians themselves, he tells us, were Greeks, and they lived extraordinarily long lives, "...either because the air is excellent or because they eat sparingly. Men are to be found there aged a hundred years, a hundred and ten and a hundred and twenty in excellent health and spirits...".[22]

The military fortifications were a marvel to all who beheld them. During the grandmastership of Pierre d'Aubusson (1476-1503), work on the defenses never ceased. Arnold von Harff, who toured the island for eight days in the year 1497, described Rhodes as a "...small but strong town surrounded by forts, ditches, walls, and gates". He must have surveyed every foot of the fortifications, for he left a very detailed account of them. Concerning the inhabitants, he wrote that 500 knights of the Order of St. John lived on the island along with the Greeks. The latter, he tells us, could be distinguished from Turks by the manner in which they wore their beards, the Turks shaving the beard off beneath the chin, and the Greeks cutting theirs the breadth of a finger. Both Turks and Greeks allowed the hair above the mouth to grow long, which they twisted like the tusks of a boar.[23]

From the pilgrim accounts we can also gain some idea of the day to day activities of the knights. Mehmed II's repeated warnings kept them constantly agitated—strengthening their defenses, storing up supplies, recruiting troops and money from Europe. Their appeals for aid met with some success. We read in the *Diary* of Jörg von Ehingen, a German knight and adventurer, that a large body of soldiers left Europe for Rhodes in the spring of 1454. At his father's behest, Jörg joined this group with instructions to participate in the defense of the island, and then to proceed, if still alive, on a pilgrimage to the Holy Land. His companions were mostly knights from France and Spain. Not one nobleman from the court of Duke Albert of Austria, where von Ehingen was serving, would go with him, he lamented; nor, indeed, did anyone from upper Germany accompany the expedition. The grandmaster welcomed von Ehingen, who remained at Rhodes for eleven months; but when the expected attack did not materialize, he continued on to Palestine and returned to his native land in 1455.[24]

Although the Turks did not attack the island in force until 1480, the knights fought limited engagements with them throughout the Aegean Sea during our period. For many years the knights did not trouble themselves to take prisoners. They slaughtered their captives indiscriminately and unmercifully. This policy was softened during the fifteenth century as a result of reciprocal action by their enemies, and because of increased opportunities of obtaining revenue from ransoms.[25] William Wey saw 250 prisoners led into the city when he was at Rhodes in 1458. He described the procession: "Christian boys, once captives of the Turks, dressed in white and carrying white crosses, preceded the Turks, who were dragged along by ropes, some pierced through the nostrils and others bound by the hands, behind their backs. . .".[26] Paul Walter saw, in 1482, many Turks engaged in rebuilding the city most of which had been destroyed in 1480, and by an earthquake the year after. He wrote that the prisoners wore heavy fetters on their legs, and performed the hardest and most contemptible tasks. "They carried stones and cement for the walls destroyed by their master", he explained, "and received food and drink not fit for beasts."[27]

In view of their dangerous position the knights were obliged to maintain a constant guard at all their stations. Several voyagers mentioned seeing signal fires ignited by the inhabitants of the Christian islands when a vessel approached. These fires could be seen on neighboring islands, and thus the warning spread abroad. Paul Walter recorded that the Turks practiced the same technique for reporting the approach of Christian vessels, and when his ship arrived at Rhodes, the Turks lighted such fires on the mountains along the coast.[28] The knights devised another type of warning system at a fortress which they maintained on the Turkish mainland. Here they kept and trained large dogs which were put outside the fort at night to look for Turks. According to William Wey these dogs were able to tell a Turk from a Christian. If, during the course of their vigil, they found no Turks, they came barking to camp in the morning; but, when they discovered Turks in the area, they returned to camp immediately and in silence. Any dog falling asleep, while on duty, was at once killed by the others.[29]

Despite the growing strength of the Turks, on land and sea, the knights of St. John, relying on such precautions, and occasional aid from the West, maintained their positions through the end of the century, and continued to aid other Christians in the East. As late as 1494 we hear of the fleet of the order pursuing Turkish pirates. Pietro Casola wrote that the pilgrims of his company were greatly alarmed when they heard that the Turks had seized two merchantmen, with cargoes valued at 60,000 ducats, between Rhodes and Cyprus. The Turks were led in this attack by the hated pirate captains Arigi and Camalio, the scourge of Levantine waters. Casola's party was somewhat reassured before they sailed from Rhodes. Brother Furiano, captain of the order's fleet, reported to the grandmaster that he had met and engaged the pirates. Although he was unable to destroy them, he had recovered the two merchant ships, and caught Arigi's boy, whom he cut into pieces.[30]

The fifteenth-century pilgrim, much as the modern tourist, was concerned to note the distances between the cities and countries along his route. This habit had the effect of emphasizing how near the Turks really were to the Latin West. A pilgrim of the year 1470, Anselm Adorne, calculated that with a good wind it took only one day to cross from the promontory of Otranto to the Peloponnesus. "The Turks", he exclaimed, "are much closer than one thinks! What keeps us then from uniting our efforts and attacking these barbarians with a force equal to their furor?" Somewhat better informed than most pilgrims, Anselm Adorne attributed the military success of the Turks largely to their discipline. He noted that there was in their army one special corps of twenty to thirty thousand men. They were well-trained in all the stratagems of war and often struck at night and in complete silence.[31]

The relation of another Englishman, the chaplain of Sir Richard Guylforde, who accompanied his master to Palestine in 1506, illustrates the fear and anxiety felt by most pilgrims. Sailing from Venice on July 4, the travelers reached Corfu July 18. Here they heard that a number of Turkish ships were lying in their path. The patron of the galley, and all aboard, armed themselves in preparation to defend the ship, but we read of no encounter. As the galley passed the southern coast of the Morea, our author remarked that they did not stop at Modon, ". . .for fere of the Turks". The galley's next stop was Crete where our anonymous chaplain mentioned seeing an ambassador from Egypt, with many Mamelukes in his company, who were on their way to Venice. He seizes this opportunity to reveal his knowledge of Cretan antiquities: "In Candia siue Creta was musyke firste founde, and also tourneys and exercyse of armes on horsebacke. There was lawe firste put in wrytynge; armour was first ther deuysed and foude, and so was ye making of remys and rowynge in boote. In Candy be ye caues called Labor Jutus; there growe grete wynes, and specially Maluesy and Muskadell. They speke all Greke, excepte the Venycyans, that be lordes and gouernours there. In ye same yle was Saturnus borne; 'Prymus Creteis Saturnus venit ab orbis,' etc."[32]

The pilgrims with whom the anonymous chaplain sailed reached Jaffa without serious mishap. But on the return voyage they experienced a succession of near tragedies. At the end of October, off the island of Longo, they ran into a severe storm which drove them toward the Turkish mainland. The vessel was ". . .almoste dryuen vpon the rok, whiche was hydyous and ferefull to loke vpon," the chaplain wrote, "and vpon the costes of Turkey, which caused vs to by the more in fere, in so moche every man made hym redy to Almyghty God. . .". When the storm subsided, the harried voyagers made their way to Crete. They learned there that the infamous Turkish admiral, Camalio, was somewhere between Crete and Corfu; he had a large fleet and had recently attacked several Christian vessels. Frightened by this news, the pilgrims remained at Crete for eleven days.[33] When they resumed their voyage, the adverse weather, which had accompanied them all along, worsened. They were unable to make progress, and were in danger of sinking. To complete the pilgrims' miseries, "...our moste noyannce and ferefull grefe was that we had no porte nor hauyn to flee to for socoure and harborowe", the chaplain lamented, "but into Turkey or Barbary, into the handes of the Infidels and extreme enemyes of our Cristen fayth". The inclement weather so lengthened the voyage that provisions began to run out. On Friday morning, December 18, about thirty miles from Modon, the patron informed the pilgrims of their plight. He offered them the choice between continuing toward Venice, and the possibility of being altogether without food, or putting in at Modon. Although the town was now inhabited by Turks, the patron was certain that provisions might be obtained. Since Venice was at peace with the Turks, the patron explained, he and his galley and crew would not be harmed, but he could not guarantee the safety of his passengers. The pilgrims, our author assures us, strongly opposed entering the harbor of the city. The patron, nonetheless, under pressure from his sailors, decided not to heed them. Late on that same Friday, the galley came before Modon. In the evening a small boat brought from the shore supplies and a message from the Turkish governor inviting the visitors into the town. No one left the ship, the chaplain recorded, and, the next day, as soon as a wind came up, the Christian vessel cleared Modon. As the pilgrim galley sailed up the Adriatic Sea, at last aided by fair winds, the exhausted voyagers were somewhat comforted. "We were also nowe passed yᵉ londes of the Infideles, as of Turkes and Sarrasyns, and wore comen into the londes of Christendome," wrote the chaplain, "whiche also increased our joye and gladnesse right moche."³⁴

Not all travelers to the Levant were successful in eluding the Turks. The Venetian pilgrim galley making the voyage in the spring of 1497 was one that did not. Hans Schürpf, a pilgrim from Luzern, was among its passengers and lived to tell of the hair-raising experience. Off Modon the galley was attacked by the Turks. The pilgrims, including Schürpf and two Swiss companions, together with groups from Danzig, Austria, and Pommerania, the latter led by their duke, Bogislaus X, joined in the defense. Seizing planks and mattresses for shields and improvising weapons, they were, Hans assures us, ready to die fighting rather than be taken prisoners by the Turks. In a long but lively passage he described the action which followed: the Turkish bombardment and their maneuvering to board the ship, the fierce hand to hand fighting, and the fate of the Turks who attempted to climb aboard: "Denselben hüwen wir die finger an den ruoden ab, das sy jn das mer fielent und all ertrunckent". The Turks then fired flaming arrows igniting the galley's sails which were destroyed. Finally the pilgrims were forced to surrender, but only, it is made clear, after their firing was restricted by the Turks who had suspended over the sides of their ships some Venetian sailors stripped naked whom they had pulled up from the sea. As it turned out in this case the villain was not the Turk but the Venetian captain. The latter had violated the custom observed by Venetian craft in Turkish waters and had failed to identify his galley or allow it to be searched when first sighted by the Turks and had foolishly precipitated the attack. In the end he took full responsibility and agreed to pay a penalty of a hundred ducats, after which the pilgrims were allowed to continue on their way.[35]

Apart from the very real danger from Turkish raiders, our travelers' apprehensions stemmed largely from their preconceived notions about the Turks as the sworn enemies of all Christians, or, in the words of the anonymous chaplain, the "extreme enemyes of our Cristen fayth". For the pilgrims, like most Christians, viewed the struggle between Europe and the Turks as essentially a religious conflict. The Turk was an infidel, a follower of the profane Mohammed, and a pernicious force dedicated to the destruction of Christendom. Some pilgrims gave considerable attention to the religion of Islam. The analysis of George Lengherand, mayor of Mons in Hainault, who visited Palestine and Egypt in 1486, is typical. In justifying his elaboration on the topic, Lengherand revealed the customary Christian bias; he justifies examining the religion of the Moslems at some length in order that Christians might come to hold it in greater disrespect.[36]

Mohammed, he stated, was born in 612 and descended from the nation of Agar, a concubine of Abraham. A diabolical heretic and opponent of all truth, he wrote a book called the Alcoran, which was full of heresies. Nonetheless, the Saracens observed it as do the Christians the Evangels. They denied, he continued, the Trinity, and asserted that by no means could God have a Son because he had no wife. Furthermore, they declared that it would be a great folly if God had a Son, and the world would be in grave danger. Some would follow the Son and others the Father, and the Son would turn against the Father. Indeed, they insisted that Christ himself claimed not to be the Son of God. They did confess that Christ was the Son of Mary, and was a holy prophet inspired by God. They honored Him and His Holy Mother, but denied He was crucified. They said God took Christ to Himself, and He promised to return at the end of the world to slay the anti-Christ, and then to die Himself. Mohammed, Lengherand explained, promised his followers material rewards in heaven. In fact, they believed blessedness consisted of food, drink, luxuries, and in all sensualities, and pleasures which excite the body, even sodomy. Mohammed, he asserted, decreed that those who did not live in such pleasures would perish. His Alcoran was full of such errors. "I believe it is the greatest horror in the world," the mayor of Mons concluded, "the way they live in such luxury, without conscience, and holding it to be virtue."[37]

Not all the pilgrim narrators misrepresented Islam to this degree. Arnold von Harff, with less passion, but greater accuracy, described in detail the practices and beliefs of the Moslems. He dealt with their worship habits, religious leaders, burial practices, marriage customs, and many other subjects. He was critical in his observations, and scorned the Moslems' failures to live up to their own laws. He did not, however, distort the facts to fit a preconceived picture of all Moslems as degenerates. Referring to the Moslems in Egypt, he declared that they knew nothing of Jesus Christ and His Holy Mother. He speculated that if preachers were sent among them, they would all be converted to Christianity, because they were so credulous. Von Harff was better informed than many travelers, and was less subjective in all his observations.[38]

The signs of the Turks' material progress greatly distressed the pilgrims. It would be extravagant to claim that the course of Turkish conquest in Greece, and the Aegean, Ionian, and Adriatic Seas could be reconstructed from the pilgrim relations. Nonetheless, their numerous, though admittedly subjective and often misinformed observations on the rise of Ottoman power add to our knowledge of western reactions to the Turks. Several of our narrators sought to explain the origin of this menace. The chaplain of Sir Richard Guylforde, commenting on the subjugation of Greece, wrote that beyond Greece lay Asia "...wherin, almoste at thentre standynge Troia, with the chyef porte the yle of Tenedos, that stondeth the see. And all the countre of Troya is the Turkes owne countre by inherytance", he emphasized, "and that countre is properly called nowe Turkey, and none other. Neverthelasse he hath lately vsurped Grece, with many other countreys, and calleth theym all Turkey".[39]

Once again the Trojan legend was invoked to identify the Turks and assign them their place in history. The anonymous chaplain, adapting the legend to his own persuasion, countered the argument of such humanists as Giovanni Maria Filelfo who attempted to justify the conquests of Mehmed II on the basis of his Trojan ancestry.[40] The Turks, descendants of the Trojans, rightfully possessed Asia Minor. They had no right in perpetuating the Trojan war—their seizure of Greece was unwarranted. The German religious and pilgrim, Felix Fabri, outdid the humanists in his search for the antique origins of the Turks.[41] In an uncritical but studied fashion, he traced their genealogy back to the time of Laomedan, king of Troy, the father of Priam. Felix explained that in his day many people believed that the Turks took their rise from a certain Teucer, son of the Greek Telamon, and the Trojan princess Hesione. Telamon, the friend of Hercules, was the first to ascend the walls of Troy. He won as booty Hesione, daughter of King Laomedan; and she bore him Ajax and Teucer. After the Trojan wars, Teucer went to Cyprus, where he founded Salamis, and dwelt the rest of his life. According to some authorities, Felix continued, the Teucri, that is the Turks, were descended from this Teucer. There was, he declared, another Teucer who lived in Trojan times. He was one of the many sons of Priam, and was not to be confused with the son of Telamon; he was mauled by a bear and died without progeny before the outbreak of the Trojan war.[42]

Felix, however, did not accept Teucer as the source of the Turks. He traced the Trojan origin of the Turks from a certain Turcus, a son of Troyas who was the son of Priam. In 1190 B.C., he wrote, when Troy fell, the distressed inhabitants fled in two groups. One was led by Franco, son of Hector. Franco's people settled first, he thought, in furthermost Germany, remaining there for a long time, and gave their name to the area Franconia. Later many crossed the Rhine and established themselves in the territory which they still held, calling it France. The remaining refugees from Troy, led by Turcus, settled in Asian Scythia. There they lived like beasts; they forgot the use of arms and took up herding sheep and cattle. Because of their primitive way of life, Alexander of Macedon shut them up, together with the Jews, in the mountains. Later one part broke away and settled in Persia, remaining there for many years as unhappy guests. They grew strong and numerous. The Persians, fearing their strength, treated them cruelly. Finally after much strife the Persians drove them out. Around the year 900, when the doctrine of Mohammed was flourishing, they chose from among themselves a king. He led them back to Persia. After defeating and subjecting the Persians, they attacked the Medes and the Arabs and descended into Syria and Egypt. They conquered the entire kingdom of the Orient. They subjected to their rule Cappadocia, Pontus, Cilicia, Greece, and Constantinople. At that moment, Felix wrote, their power extended right up to the limits of Germany. Felix believed that there was little disagreement among his sources, except in the matter of chronology. He concluded, therefore, that the Turks were truly Trojans, converted to Islam, and the very enemies menacing Christendom at that time.[43]

Most pilgrims were understandably more concerned with describing the

Turkish advance in their own time than with investigating the backgrounds of the problem. George Lengherand, writing about 1486-1487, recalled the fall of Constantinople. He did not elaborate on its significance, but echoed the common claims that the arrogance of the Greeks and their obstinancy toward church union, together with the negligence of western Christians, led to the city's fall.[44] Several travelers, including Peter Rot of Basel, were, as we have seen, in the Levant when Byzantium fell to Mehmed II and noted the event in their accounts.[45] Descriptions of the Turkish victories of Constantinople (1453), Negropont (1470), and Otranto (1480), and of the unsuccessful siege of Rhodes (1480), are all included in the famous compilation of Bernhard von Breydenbach.[46] Breydenbach was one of 150 pilgrims who went to the Holy Land in the summer of 1483. The canon of the cathedral of Mainz (who, after his return from Palestine became its dean), and his company departed Venice on June 1, 1483, and arrived at Jaffa at the end of the same month. Along with seventeen companions he journeyed on to Mt. Sinai to visit the relics of St. Catherine, and from there he traveled to Egypt. He sailed from Alexandria on October 26, and arrived in Venice on January 8, 1484.

Breydenbach's *Peregrinationes in Terram Sanctam* is no ordinary pilgrim account. The text of his itinerary which comprises only a small part of the work was written by Martin Roth of the Dominican convent of Pforzheim. The rest of the volume consists of descriptions of the Holy Land and the religions of its inhabitants, drawn largely from well-known medieval authors such as Jacques de Vitry and Vincent de Beauvais. There is an exhortation to the Christian princes, probably the work of Roth himself, a list of the islands between Venice and Rhodes and the distances between them, and a vocabulary of 228 Arabic words with translations. The section entitled "De Constantinopolitane urbis expugnatione" is the account of Mehmed II's conquest of Constantinople written by Isidore, the cardinal of Russia. The description of the siege of Rhodes, "De Rodis urbis obsidione", is the work of Guillaume Caoursin. The account of the fall of Negropont ("De Nigroponti captione") and that of the capture of Otranto ("De captione ciuitatis Ydruntine") are anonymous. Breydenbach included a summary of remedies for sea sickness and against vermin.[47]

In all this there is very little that is original; in fact the work suffers from the absence of those personal and down-to-earth comments and observations which distinguish and enrich many of the pilgrim accounts. It is true that the sum total of the various selections represents a kind of epitome of contemporary knowledge of the world of Islam, thus setting the work apart from the customary pilgrim narrative. More important, however, is the fact

XI: Janissaries
(Breydenbach, *Peregrinationes*. Mainz, 1486).

that Breydenbach introduced into his compendium graphic illustrations of the places and peoples described in the text. The woodcuts were the work of Erhard Reuwich of Utrecht. Made from sketches drawn at the places portrayed, they are the most authentic contemporary reproductions of Levantine scenes and people available. There are several woodcuts depicting Turks in various costumes, and one of a group of mounted Turkish soldiers complete with drum, horn, and iron staffs. The reader of Breydenbach's account need no longer depend upon his imagination to visualize what a Turk looked like.[48] In one other respect Breydenbach's work deserves special attention. First published at Mainz in 1486, it went through twelve editions by 1522. It was translated into German and printed at Mainz (1486), Augsburg (1488) and Speier (ca. 1505). A Flemish translation was also printed at Mainz (1488). In French it was printed at Lyons (1488, 1489), and Paris (1517, 1522) and in Spanish at Saragossa (1498). In addition to the original Latin edition (Mainz, 1486), it appeared in that language two more times at Speier (1490, 1502). All twelve of the above editions appeared complete with Reuwich's woodcuts.[49] Certainly Breydenbach's *Peregrinationes*, produced in several thousand copies in a little more than a generation, with its descriptions of the East, its refutation and condemnation of Islam, its accounts of the great Christian-Turkish battles, its appeal to the Christian princes, and its portraits of eastern figures, brought the world of the Levant into the homes of its readers.

No pilgrim accounts reflect any greater awareness of the Turks than those describing a voyage to the Holy Land in 1480. In the apology with which an anonymous French cleric, a pilgrim in that year, introduced his work, he explained that one of his reasons for writing was to acquaint the prospective pilgrim with the danger of the Turks.[50] Describing his experiences at Venice, where he saw a Turkish embassy, he lamented that the infidels had acquired a tributary as far west as the Italian peninsula! Venice, after a long struggle, and the loss of many islands, cities, castles, and galleys, had promised to render them an annual tribute. The Turks had, he continued, recently taken from the Venetians a large part of Slavonia and Albania, which were Christian lands.[51] As our pilgrim passed along the coasts of Dalmatia and Albania, he saw many evidences of the Turkish advance. On the island of Curzola he found the inhabitants all gathered within the city, because the Turks had harassed them. Ragusa, he wrote, was a strong city, but had lost its holdings, and was a tributary of the infidels.[52] On the coasts of Albania, he observed, there were great forests from which the Turks obtained each year enough lumber to build one hundred ships. "This is," he asserted, "a great evil, for the Turk would not be able to make war on Christians without a large fleet."[53]

The Venetian sailors informed the pilgrims, as they approached Valona, that the Ottomans maintained there a large army, and countless ships and galleys. To the anonymous French cleric and his companions, such information would have been disquieting at almost any time. At that moment it was particularly disturbing, for off Valona, our author's galley was becalmed. The pilgrims expected to be attacked at once:

> At nightfall there were on a high hill above the town several large fires which the said Turks made; because of which we were well dumbfounded, and all night we were in great fear and danger; and the pilgrims remained on watch all night with the sailors, fearing that the said Turks would come to assail our galley. All the cannon and artillery were readied and charged for our defense, in case they came.[54]

The pilgrims, unmolested by the Turks, put to sea again, only to be blown off course. After some difficulty, they arrived at Corfu on June 23, 1480. Here they learned that they had narrowly escaped a huge Turkish fleet, carrying a strong landing force, on its way to assault Apulia. The Venetians on the island urged them not to go on. They warned them that the Grand Turk had sent men to spy on the pilgrim galley in the ports where they had been. The Turk, they said, knew of the presence of some great Christian lords on board, and he intended to seize the vessel.[55] Felix Fabri, who also went to Palestine in 1480, reported how the Venetian captain of the sea, Vittore Soranzo, admonished the pilgrims at Corfu for so foolishly exposing themselves to such risks of both body and soul, of life and property. Soranzo insisted that the sea was covered with cruel Turks, from whose hands there was no chance of escaping.[56] Our anonymous cleric reported that twenty pilgrims, fearing the Turks, returned home, but the rest continued.[57] Everywhere there were signs of the Turks' destructive activities. All along the coast of Albania the pilgrims saw wrecked buildings. The Turks had demolished a castle on Zante, and had killed all the Christians, when the year before (1479), they had taken the island from the Venetians.[58] The strong fortifications of Modon were a comforting sight to the pilgrims, but from the city's walls, one looked out upon lands ruled by the infidels. While the pilgrims rested at Modon there occurred an incident which confirmed their opinions that the Turks were cruel and inhuman barbarians. Three Turks had come to the city to negotiate with the Venetian council. The principal Turk was dressed in black velvet with figures and leaves of gold cloth. In the evening, after the pilgrims had retired to their galley, a crowd of citizens gathered before an inn. The Turkish embassy, they discovered, had come to arrest a poor Christian man, claiming he was a subject and tributary of the sultan. The Turk declared, that if the man did not return and render obedience, he would seize his wife and children and all his goods.[59]

When the pilgrims arrived at Crete, the surprised citizens all came out to meet them. They could not believe that the pilgrims had reached the island since they had seen Turkish ships prowling the waters off Crete. Because there was no other place available, Felix tells us that the pilgrims stayed in a house of ill-fame, kept by a German. He assures the reader that his host cleansed the dwelling and sent away his courtesans, before the pilgrims took up residence. Across from the house where the pilgrims stopped there was an inn for Turkish merchants. Felix remarked that ". . .there were actually in it many rich Turkish merchants from Constantinople. . .". The Turks joined the Cretans in admonishing the pilgrims for continuing their voyage. "Some of these Turks even came into our house", Felix wrote, "and advised us not to put to sea for the present, because we should certainly be taken." Despite warnings and dangers, the pilgrims left Crete. They stopped briefly at Cyprus, and arrived at Jaffa, July 20, 1480.[60]

When a pilgrim galley neared its destination, a sailor mounted the masthead, and signaled as soon as he sighted the Holy Land. The pilgrims sang the *Te Deum*, and thanked God for his guidance and care. The recorded experiences of the pilgrims in Palestine, and of those who went on to Mt. Sinai and Egypt, are extensive and interesting. Before the Ottoman invasion of the Mameluke empire in 1516-17, however, there was little to provoke the pilgrims to write about the Turks in this part of their narrative. We find frequent references to the Mamelukes and Arabs, or to Saracens and infidels. The pilgrims complained about the rapacity of the Arabs. They waxed indignant over the humilating treatment received at the hands of the Moslem guides. The complaint of Sir Richard Torkington, who visited the Holy Land at the end of our period in 1517 when the area was already in the hands of the Ottomans, echoes that of his predecessors: ". . .the Turkes constreynyd vs to tary by the space of iiii howers, and ther we lay in the sande, and the sonne bornying excedyngly hoote, whiche was gretly to our payne. And ther we war ryght evyll intreated by the Turkes and Sarrasyns in many weys, and in grett fere. . .".[61] Their relations are full of advice and warnings to future pilgrims regarding their behavior in the company of the infidels.

The pilgrim travelers we have followed to this point have all skirted along the edges of the Ottoman empire. They saw many evidences of Turkish power, and in such places as Modon, Crete, and Rhodes, they came face to face with Turks. Only the most venturesome pilgrims journeyed beyond the Holy Land, and of these, but a handful penetrated Turkey.[62] The travels of Arnold von Harff in Turkey, and especially his tour of Constantinople in the spring of 1499, therefore, are of particular interest and significance.

Von Harff did not journey to the Levant by the usual pilgrim galley, but as he tells us, he chose to travel in the company of merchants, for they knew the language and the routes, and protected themselves by hiring escorts. Before leaving Venice, he engaged to accompany him a dragoman named Master Vincent, a Spaniard, and, as von Harff discovered later, a renegade, who knew Latin, Italian, Spanish, Wendish, Greek, Turkish, and Arabic.[63] Having visited the Holy Land, Mt. Sinai, Egypt, and perhaps Mecca, our pilgrim traveled overland from Damascus to Antioch, to Adana, then through Karamania to Brusa, and from there to Constantinople.[64] In Karamania, von Harff and his company were assigned an escort by the ruling Ottoman prince, described by our author as the eldest son of the Turkish emperor, a comely young man of twenty-four years of age.[65] From Konia to Brusa, von Harff traveled for seven days through mountains and deserts, where the only cultivated crop was cotton. He found Brusa to be a large, strong city, with a population ten times that of Cologne, and a teeming market of silks, satins, camlet, gold, silver and crimson cloths.[66]

Three days' journey from Brusa, von Harff reached Constantinople. In the harbor he saw 800 Turkish war galleys, and countless other vessels. He described Constantinople as an invincible city which fell to the Turks, he believed, only because of the foolhardiness of the Greeks. He was surprised to find two Franciscan monasteries where the mass was still celebrated. Many Christian churches, he explained, had been converted into mosques or were used as menageries to house the sultan's wild animals. The church of the Holy Wisdom was now the sultan's mosque, but von Harff was able to visit it. The Turks had destroyed its altars and icons, he wrote, and installed 500 lamps which were lit daily.[67]

Shortly after his arrival in the Turkish capital, von Harff was alarmed when Bayezid II summoned him to appear at court. Escorted to the Grand Seraglio by a Christian renegade, originally from Bresberg in Steiermark,[68] von Harff prostrated himself three times and kissed the ground before the sultan. Bayezid closely interrogated him through the German renegade. The Turk was especially interested in the activities of Charles VIII, who had partially justified his invasion of Italy as a prelude to a crusade against the Turks.[69] He asked von Harff about himself, his origin, and his activities, and offered him a position in his service with a salary of 200 ducats a month and the right to retain his religion. Our pilgrim, who had passed himself off as a Venetian merchant, feared to reveal his true identity as a German knight and soldier. He replied to Bayezid that he must return to Venice and report to his master concerning his trade; otherwise, he indicated his desire to try his fortune at the Turkish court, and promised to return. Bayezid was satisfied with his response, granted him a safe-conduct, and offered an escort for the remainder of his journey through Turkish territory. He presented von Harff with presents and commanded the renegade from Steiermark to show him all he wished to see in the city. At this, our author concluded, " . . .we parted from this mighty lord, being obliged to go out of this hall backwards, so that I did not turn my back to him".[70]

Arnold von Harff's tour began in the New Palace (*Yeni Saray*, popularly named, *Top-Kapu Sarayi*, Palace of the Cannon Gate, by the Turks, and called the Grand Seraglio by the westerners.) His description of it, and also of the Old Palace (*Eski Saray*), is one of the oldest known.[71] He saw three courts in the New Palace, and estimated that the sultan's household staff, which he described in some detail, numbered 60,000. This figure did not include the men-at-arms stationed permanently on the frontiers, but who were also in the sultan's pay. The army he numbered at 200,000. There were 32,000 footmen (janissaries), whom he compared to the bowmen in France, who always followed or ran after the sultan. There were also 600 knights, called *Salofftar* weapons-bearers, mostly renegade Christians, and 700 *Spagalan* youths on horseback, who were his body guards. Von Harff reported that there were always 700 or 800 young boys at the court who had been captured in Christian countries and who were trained to be his knights.[72]

He saw near the palace splendid stables with spaces for 1200 horses. With his guide, von Harff walked through the palace gardens where there were many rare trees and fruits, and unusual animals running loose. The sultan's treasure was stored in a castle built, he wrote, by Mehmed II. It had high walls and a tower at each of its four corners, and a higher one in the center. There was but one entrance into the building. Von Harff next visited the Old Palace, which he called the Women's Garden. Here, he declared, lived 101 legal wives of the deceased Mehmed II. Bayezid II, he recorded, had but 72 legal wives, many of whom did not live in the Old Palace, but in other residences of the sultan. He described the Old Palace as a pleasant building, where each wife had her own apartment, with windows opening on the gardens, and her own servants. There was only one entrance, and the women, he discovered, were closely guarded by eunuchs, mostly renegade Christians, who " . . . go about in their gold dresses, and are all stout and fat like beer casks, so that they can do no harm".[73]

Von Harff's remarks on Turkish life and customs beyond the royal court are rather meager. He mentioned visiting the great market square in the center of the city, where the criminals were punished. He said that every day while he was in the capital five or six people were executed by hanging, quartering, or beheading. He asserted that the sultan's justice was strict through-out the empire, and that the penalties for assault and homicide were exceedingly severe. Moreover, great nobles as well as commoners were subject to harsh punishment carried out in public. He described the dress of Turkish women he saw in the streets. They wore veils which obscured their faces, and both maidens and older women wore breeches down to their knees, made of leather, linen, or silk. Before they sleep with their husbands, he added, the women go to the bath before midday, for which purpose their husbands, who go to the bath after midday, give them three aspers. Von Harff included in this section of his work a long Turkish vocabulary, of which most of the words are identifiable.[74]

Few pilgrims shared Arnold von Harff's opportunity of observing the Ottomans at such close range. In most ports of the Levant they met Christians, and sometimes Moslems, who readily filled their ears with news and rumors about the Turks' latest moves, their future plans, and various snatches of information about their customs and culture. In the main the knowledge of the Turks carried home by the pilgrims was neither very complete nor accurate and no doubt it was further distorted as time and distance separated the story-teller from his source. But the body of facts mixed with imaginative recon-structions brought home by the Palestine pilgrims further stimulated Latins to think about the Turks and what they thought was inevitably colored by the tales of the travelers.

NOTES TO CHAPTER VII

1. The literature on the subject is voluminous. Notices of pilgrims and some texts have been published in the following works: Reinhold Röhricht, *Bibliotheca geo-graphica Palestina* (Berlin, 1890); and with H. Meisner, *Deutsche Pilgerreisen nach dem Heiligen Land* (Innsbruck, 1900); P. Girolamo Golubovich (ed.), *Biblioteca bio-bibliografica della Terra Santa e dell' Oriente francescano*, 1st series, 5 vols. (Florence, 1906-1927); 2nd series, 14 vols. (Florence, 1921-1928); 3rd series, 2 vols. (Florence, 1928-1948); Geoffrey Atkinson, *La Littérature géographique français de la renaissance: Répertoire bibliographique* (Paris, 1936); and the same author's *Les Nouveau horizons de la renaissance* (Paris, 1935); and his *Supplément au répertoire* (Paris, 1936); Charles Schefer (ed.), *Recueil de voyages et de documents pour servir à l'histoire de la géographie;* the volumes of the Palestine Pilgrims Text Society; and The Hakluyt Society; the publications of the Société de l'Orient latin; and some volumes of the *Bibliothek des literarischen Vereins in Stuttgart.* Other texts of pilgrim narratives are to be found, scattered helter-skelter, in independent volumes, scholarly journals, and the pub-

lications of local and national historical societies. A substantial number of pilgrim narratives remain unpublished, preserved in manuscript in the archives of Europe.

2. L. Larchey (ed.), *Journal de Jehan Aubrion avec sa continuation par Pierre Aubrion*, 1465-1512 (Metz, 1857), pp. 3, 14; for notices of the departure and return of other pilgrims see pp. 39, 40, 42, 91.

3. On the volume of the pilgrim traffic and its composition see Röhricht and Meisner *Deutsche Pilgerreisen*, pp. 1-26; and the informative study of Venetian legislation pertaining to the pilgrim trade which comprises the lengthy introduction by Margaret Newett to her edition of *Canon Pietro Casola's Pilgrimage to Jerusalem in the Year* 1494 (Manchester, 1907), pp. 1-113.

4. Jehan Aubrion, *Journal*, p. 15.

5. In Gustave Cohen (ed.), *Recueil de farces français inédites du xve siècle* (Cambridge, Mass., 1949), pp. 35-39.

6. See R. J. Mitchell, *John Tiptoft (1427-1470)* (London, 1938), pp. 41, 42, 46, 47, 61, 132.

7. C. Hassler (ed.), *Fratris Felicis Fabri evagatorium in Terre Sanctae, Arabiae et Egypti peregrinationem*, 3 vols. (Stuttgart, 1843-1849).

8. *The Itineraries of William Wey, Fellow of Eton College, to Jerusalem, A.D. 1458 and A.D. 1456; and to St. James of Compostella, A.D. 1456*, published by the Roxburghe Club (London, 1857). It should be noted that contemporaries of William Wey were not limited to the accounts of pilgrims of their own generation. Travel accounts from earlier times were popular with the new printers and, one may conclude, also with their customers; e.g. the fourteenth-century pilgrim Ludolphus de Suchen, *Iter ad Terram Sanctam*, appeared twice at Strasbourg, in Latin and German, in the years 1475-1480, and twice at Augsburg in the same period. By 1484 the work of John Mandeville's imagination, *Itinerarius* had been printed four times in Germany, and also appeared in a unique publishing adventure by the Dutch printer Gerard Leeu of Gouda in a matched set together with Ludolphus de Suchen and Marco Polo in the years 1483-85. The *Reisebuch* of the German Schiltberger who had been captured at the battle of Nicopolis was printed at Augsburg sometime before the end of the century. For a fascinating study of the early printed literature connected with the Portugese expeditions see Francis M. Rogers, *The Quest for Eastern Christians* (Minneapolis, 1962), especially chapter IV, "Early Latin Chapbooks and the Christians of the Indies".

9. C. Schefer (ed.), *Le Voyage de la saincte cyté de Hiersalem avec la description des lieux portz, villes, citez et aultres passaiges fait l'an mil quatre cens quatre vingtz* (Paris, 1882), p. 21. Cf. Malipiero, *Annali Veneti*, pt. I, pp. 122, 123.

10. M. Sollweck (ed.), *Fratris Pauli Waltheri Guglingensis itinerarium in Terram Sanctam et ad Sanctam Catharinam* (Tübingen, 1892), pp. 58-59. In contrast to Paul Walter's reaction was that of Commines who also met a Turkish ambassador in Venice in 1495. The Frenchman had the Turk visit him in his apartments where they talked for four hours about the possibility of establishing friendly relations between their two masters. See J. Calmette (ed.), *Philippe de Commynes: Mémoires* (Paris, 1925), III, 131, 132.

11. Paul Walter, *Itinerarium*, p. 59.

12. E.g. the impressions of an anonymous English pilgrim in the following verses:

> And Venice stondes alle in the See,
> And Yles about hit gret plente;
> And Lordez thei ben of diversez placez,
> To telle her Lordship I have no space;
>
> But I dar hit so discry,
> Hit is a riche toun of spicery:
> And of alle other marchandise also,
> And right well vitelet ther to.

In Samuel Purchas (ed.), *Hakluytus Posthumus or Purchas His Pilgrimes Contayning a History of the World in Sea Voyages and Lande Travells by Englishmen and Others* (Glasgow, 1905), VII, 542. See also E. S. de Beer, "An English Fifteenth-century Pilgrimage Poem", *Notes and Queries*, CLXXXVII (1944), 244-248.

13. Casola, *Pilgrimage*, p. 125.

14. M. Letts (ed. and tr.), *The Pilgrimage of Arnold von Harff* (London, 1946), pp. 59-62; cf. Casola, *Pilgrimage*, p. 139.

15. Venice, always concerned with the well-being of her trade with western Europe closely regulated the pilgrim trade for the protection of the pilgrims. Magistrates *(cattaveri)* were charged with direct supervision, and empowered to pronounce judgment on infractions of the law. Official guides *(tholomarii)*, were licensed to assist pilgrims upon their arrival in Venice in making preparations for the voyage. A decree of the Great Council, passed in June 1392, required the registration of ship captains *(patroni)*, in the offices of the *cattaveri*, who issued their licenses. Contracts between patrons and passengers were required to be registered in the ships' books and a copy sent to the *cattaveri*. The galleys were required by the Senate to carry certain weapons, armament, and defenders. These and many other requirements were set up in the fourteenth and fifteenth centuries with an eye to protecting the pilgrims from unscrupulous Venetian merchants and captains, and thus preserving friendly relations with the countries represented. See Newett's introduction to *Canon Pietro Casola's Pilgrimage*, pp. 23ff; and Röhricht, *Deutsche Pilgerreisen*, pp. 1-26.

16. William Wey, *Itineraries*, p. 78.

17. *Ibid.*, pp. 56, 57, "...habent in mari Adriatico sexdecim galeas subtiles, armatas, ordinates ad custodiendum civitates, villas et terras, quas habent in partibus illis".

18. See e.g. R. Röhricht and H. Meisner (ed.), *Das Reisebuch der Familie Rieter* (Tübingen, 1884), pp. 43, 44, 46, 47. Sebald Rieter came from a family which was particularly devoted to the pilgrimage to the Holy Land; his grandfather, Peter, and his father, Sebald, had both made the trip in 1436 and 1471 respectively. On the voyage of 1479, Sebald was accompanied by another citizen of Nuremberg, Hans Tucher whose *Reise zum heiligen Grab*, very quickly found its way into print (Nuremberg, 1482 and Augsburg, 1482, and again at Augsburg, 1486).

19. Wey, *Itineraries*, p. 93. On the activities of Vlad Dracul see Babinger, *Mahomet II*, pp. 244-251.

20. Wey, *Itineraries*, pp. 101, 102.

21. "Relation du siège de Rhodes en 1480 par Merri Dupui, temoin oculaire", in

R. A. Vertot, *The History of the Knights of Malta*, I (London, 1728), 91, 92. Clavijo, when he visited Rhodes in 1403, on his way to the court of Timur, observed: "The city is a great mart for merchandize, which comes from many countries; for no ships go to Alexandria or Jerusalem, or Syria, without touching at this island. . .". C. R. Markham (ed. and tr.), *Narrative of the Embassy of Ruy Gonzalez de Clavijo to the Court of Timur at Samarcand, A.D.* 1403-6 (London, 1859).

22. Casola, *Pilgrimage*, p. 208. Lengherand *(Voyage,* p. 105), also mentioned the beautiful women of Rhodes; he wrote: ". . .et sont femmes de tres beau taint; et tiens qu'il en y a largement qui vendent amour en detail".

23. Von Harff, *Pilgrimage*, pp. 84, 85, 88. Cf. Roberto da Sanseverino, *Viaggio in terra santa*, edited by G. Maruffi (Bologna, 1888), pp. 58-60.

24. Jörg von Ehingen, *Reisen nach der Ritterschaft* (Stuttgart, 1842), pp. 11-13.

25. Baron de Belabre, *Rhodes of the Knights* (Oxford, 1908), pp. 16-18.

26. Wey, *Itineraries*, p. 78. Wey explained (p. 94), how a certain duke of the island of Symi, subject to the knights, ". . .venit cum suis ad Rodys nudis tibiis, et multos capit de Turcis, et bene et fideliter custodit illam insulam ab omnibus inimicius; quod si contingat illum ducem esse vercordem et nolentem ire contra Turcos, ipsum occident et alium in loco ejus eligent".

27. Walter, *Itinerarium*, pp. 87, 88; cf. Dietrich von Schachten who mentioned seeing Turks laboring at Rhodes when he visited the island in 1491, in Röhricht and Meisner (eds.), *Deutsche Pilgerreisen*, p. 182, and Lengherand *(Voyage,* p. 105), who complained that the Turks lived in Rhodes with their wives and children.

28. Walter, *Itinerarium*, p. 85.

29. Wey, *Itineraries*, pp. 94, 95; cf. Walter, *Itinerarium*, p. 84.

30. Casola, *Pilgrimage*, p. 210.

31. E. de la Coste (ed.), *Anselme Adorne, Sire de Corthy, pèlerin de terre-sainte* (Brussels, 1855), p. 145.

32. H. Ellis (ed.), *The Pylgrymage of Sir Richard Guylforde to the Holy Land, A.D.* 1506 (London, 1851), pp. 11-15.

33. *Ibid.*, pp. 59-61.

34. *Ibid.*, pp. 68-70, 78.

35. J. Schmid (ed.), *Luzerner und innerschweizer Pilgerreisen zum Heiligen Grab in Jerusalem vom* 15. *bis* 17. *Jahrhundert* (Luzern, 1957), pp. 8-10. The Venetian accounts of this incident, which apparently involved an entire squadron of nine Turkish ships under the command of the much-feared "ex-corsair" Arigi, vary considerably from Schürpf especially in the matter of the patron's behavior. Schürpf not only blames him for having caused the trouble but claims that when the battle was over the pilgrims found him in hiding. *Ibid.*, p. 9. Cf. Sanuto, *Diarii*, ed. F. Stefani (Venice, 1879), I, col. 702, and summary from the patron, Alvise Zorzi, col. 728; Sanuto's pages are filled with notices of the activities of Arigi and Camalio.

36. Charles Denys, Marquis de Godefroy-Menilglaise (ed.), *Voyage de Georges Lengherand, mayeur de Mons en Haynaut, à Venise, Rome, Jerusalem, Mont Sinai et le Kayre* (Mons, 1861), p. 181. For other pilgrim discussions of Islam cf. Fabri, *Evagatorium*, III, 83-92, 94-101; Walter, *Itinerarium*, pp. 120-130; R. Pernoud (ed.), *Un Guide du pèlerin de Terre Sainte au* xve *siècle* (Mantes, 1940), introduction and *passim ;* and the lengthy

section in Bernhard von Breydenbach, *Peregrinationes in Terram Sanctam* (Mainz, 1486), fols. 50ʳ-76ʳ, which includes a life of Mohammed the prophet and an analysis of the Koran, based principally on Vincent of Beauvais, *Speculum historiale*, bk. 23. For the *corpus* of medieval knowledge and understanding of Islam see the study of Daniel, *Islam and the West*.

37. Lengherand, *Voyage*, pp. 181-182.

38. Arnold von Harff, *Pilgrimage*, pp. 116-119. Von Harff in these pages described the practices of the Moslems in Egypt. Later when he wrote about his stay in Constantinople he praised the orthodoxy of the Ottomans: "...the Turks are Mahometans and keep the law in all things, as I have described before concerning the heathen". *Ibid.*, p. 244.

39. *Pylgrymage of Sir Richard Guylforde*, p. 41.

40. Giovanni Maria Filelfo, *Amyris*, in Dethier (ed.), *MHH*, XXII, pt. i, no. 9, 308-319, 405, 453.

41. Fabri, *Evagatorium*, III, 236-239.

42. *Ibid.*, III, 236, 237.

43. *Ibid.*, III, 237-239.

44. Lengherand, *Voyage*, p. 67.

45. Bernoulli (ed.), *Pilgerreisen der Basler Hans und Peter Rot*, p. 90; see also E. Travers (ed.), *Deux pèlerinages en terre sainte au xvᵉ siècle. Les Princes d'Orange, Louis et Guillaume de Châlon* (Paris, 1869), p. 6.

46. Bernhard von Breydenbach, *Peregrinationes in Terram Sanctam* (Mainz, 1486), fols. 135ʳ-147ʳ.

47. See the study by H. M. Davies, *Bernard von Breydenbach and His Journey to the Holy Land, 1483-4. A Bibliography* (London, 1911), pp. vi-xi.

48. *Ibid.*, pp. xxi-xxv.

49. *Ibid.*, p. xviii.

50. Schefer (ed.), *Le Voyage de la saincte cyté*, p. 2.

51. *Ibid.*, p. 20.

52. *Ibid.*, pp. 35, 36; cf. Rieter, *Das Reisebuch*, p. 43; and Walter, *Itinerarium*, p. 74.

53. Schefer (ed.), *Le Voyage de la saincte cyté*, p. 39.

54. *Ibid.*, pp. 39, 40.

55. *Ibid.*, pp. 40-42.

56. Fabri, *Evagatorium*, I, 36, 77.

57. Schefer (ed.), *Le Voyage de la saincte cyté*, p. 43.

58. *Ibid.*, pp. 44, 45.

59. *Ibid.*, pp. 46, 47.

60. *Ibid.*, pp. 49, 50; Fabri, *Evagatorium*, I, 39, 40.

61. W. J. Loftie (ed.), *Ye Oldest Diarie of Englysshe Travells* (London, 1885), p. 55. Cf. the complaints of two other English pilgrims: *Pylgrymage of Sir Richard Guylforde*, p. 16, and an anonymous, *Information for Pilgrims unto the Holy Land*, ed. E. Gordon Duff (London, 1893). A contrary opinion, also that of a compatriot of Torkington's,

may be found in *The Book of Margery Kemp*, 1436, ed. W. Butler-Bowdon (London, 1936), p. 116; but Margery, who took a contrary position on most matters, was mainly concerned to show how anyone treated her better than her own countrymen with whom she traveled to the Holy Land.

62. A Russian merchant named Basil passed through Turkey on his way to Palestine in 1465-66, but unfortunately gives little more than a bare itinerary. See *Pèlerinage du marchand Basile*, tr. B. Khitrovo in *Société de l'orient latin, série géographique*, V (1888), 241-256. For two fourteenth century comments see Friar Jordanes, *The Wonders of the East*, tr. H. Yule (London, 1863), p. 58, and an anonymous *Voyage d'outremer*, extracts in J. Senebier, *Catalogue raisonné des mss conservés dans la bibliothèque de la ville et republique de Genève* (Geneva, 1779), p. 360. An early fifteenth-century pilgrim, Jacopo Sanseverino, *Viaggio* (Lucca, 1868), p. 27, gave a brief description of Turkey.

63. Arnold von Harff, *Pilgrimage*, pp. 4, 5, 69.

64. *Ibid.*, pp. 229, 237.

65. This was Sahinsah, born in 1460, the second of Bayezid II's eight sons, but the oldest at 'that' time since Abdullah, the sultan's first born had died in 1483. Von Harff is mistaken about his age. See A. D. Alderson, *The Structure of the Ottoman Dynasty* (Oxford, 1956), table xxviii, "Bayezid and his family".

66. Arnold von Harff, *Pilgrimage*, p. 237.

67. *Ibid.*, pp. 238, 239, 242; cf. J. Ebersolt, *Constantinople byzantine et les voyageurs du levant* (Paris, 1918), pp. 68, 69.

68. Von Harff gives the renegade's name as Franck Kassan, p. 239.

69. Charles VIII had died (April 7, 1498), the year before von Harff's visit to the Porte.

70. Von Harff, *Pilgrimage*, pp. 239, 240.

71. On this see Barnett Miller, *Beyond the Sublime Porte. The Grand Seraglio of Stambul* (New Haven, 1931), esp. p. 25. Miller claims, however, that the description of the New Palace by Angiolello *(Historia turchesca*, ed. J. Ursu, Bucarest, 1910), is the oldest known. She was apparently unacquainted with von Harff.

72. Von Harff, *Pilgrimage*, p. 241.

73. *Ibid.*, pp. 241, 242.

74. *Ibid.*, pp. 242-245.

CHAPTER VIII

The Turk as a Turk

The Ottoman assault on Rhodes followed by the invasion of Italy and the seizure of Otranto by the forces of Ghedik Ahmed Pasha caused a new wave of excitement and alarm in the West. In the years 1480-1481 it appeared that the prophecies of the crusade publicists were coming true and that their claims regarding the sultan's plans to subjugate the West were more than so much sabre-rattling. But before the pope's efforts to organize a counter-offensive had gone very far the news of Mehmed II's death was announced in the West amidst great rejoicing and a deep feeling of relief. It now appeared to many observers that the prayers of the faithful had been answered. Once again, it was asserted, Christendom had been saved by divine intervention; and once again, it was explained that the undeserving rulers had been granted another chance to make amends. The sultan's death had plunged the Turkish empire into a chaotic civil war. Mehmed's son Bayezid had seized the throne but his authority was contested by his brother, the popular Djem. The latter had the support of a considerable following among the Turks and was able to win as an ally the Mameluke sultan of Egypt. Here was repeated an opportunity similar to that missed at the beginning of the century when the fearful Timur had defeated and captured Bayezid I, and had sown destruction and confusion among the Ottomans. Proponents of the crusade made the best of the situation and urged immediate action before the Turks recovered and resumed their march on the West.[1]

Exhortations were issued, plans projected, and negotiations prosecuted; but, beyond the recovery of Otranto, there was no crusade. Such was to be the case, too, a dozen years later when Charles VIII of France, preparing for his invasion of Italy, proclaimed and widely publicized his intention of recovering Byzantium. And the same sequence of publicity, plans, and promises, but no crusade, was to be repeated in 1507-1508 when the League of Cambray was formed, and again at the end of our period in 1517-1518 as the Ottoman forces overran the Mameluke empire.[2] The relaxation of pressure on the West, occasioned first by the civil war in Turkey, was welcomed by the Latin powers as an opportunity to pursue more vigorously not the crusade but their own more immediate interests. The last two decades of the fifteenth century was, indeed, a crucial period which saw the intensification of rivalries in Italy, the consolidation and strengthening of the transalpine monarchies, and the French invasion which ushered in a new era in the relations of the European powers.[3]

Both sides, the Turks and the Latins, were in the generation following the death of Mehmed II, generally more disposed to negotiate than fight. Even after putting down the civil war and defeating Djem, who fled for refuge to Christian hands, Bayezid II found it desirable and profitable to maintain diplomatic relations with the Latin powers. Believed by western observers to have been a man of pacifistic temperament, he was in fact preoccupied with consolidating his power and creating an effective administration throughout the empire founded by his father. Quite content to pay his brother's keepers (successively the knights of Rhodes, the pope, and the king of France), to keep Djem out of his hair, the sultan certainly had no scruples about achieving his aims by peaceful or military means. The Latin powers, by the same token, enjoyed the greater freedom accorded by the abatement of Turkish aggression. Increasingly preoccupied with the rapidly changing political scene in the West, they remained sensitive to the Turkish question, continued to think in terms of the crusade, but found it convenient to carry on diplomatic relations with the Grand Porte. Even the papacy was not adverse to becoming a party to the negotiations over the question of Djem and for a time kept the unhappy Turk in Rome itself.[4]

Contemporary denunciations of diplomatic relations between Christian rulers and the Ottomans were to be echoed by modern historians who concluded that the crusade policies of the western powers were insincere and merely a matter of propaganda. Without denying the propaganda value of the publicity attendant upon the crusade plans of Renaissance princes we cannot agree that they were wholly without a serious basis. In the first place negotiations and even alliances between Latin powers and the Turks were nothing new in our period. An accommodation between Genoa and Sultan Orkhan in the mid-fourteenth century initiated a long succession of such arrangements. During the century and a half which followed, all the major Italian powers at one time or another cultivated Ottoman friendship for commercial and political purposes.[5] Even the participation of the papacy in the Djem affair was explained as in the best interests of Christendom. The possession of Djem by a Christian power was believed to have served as an effective curb on the aggressive intentions of the Turks and a guarantee that Bayezid would remain cooperative. Moreover, it was expected, naïvely it is true, that when the time was ripe for an attack on Turkey, Djem would prove an invaluable instrument for dividing the Turks and winning Ottoman support for the crusaders.[6] The fact is, apologists had traditionally defended cooperation with a Moslem power by identifying the special interest of their government with the common good of Christendom. In a commentary on a bull of Pope Paul II, the Spanish diplomat and papal apologist Rodrigo Sánchez de Arévalo wrote that alliances between Christians and infidels were forbidden except that a Christian prince might join with one infidel power to fight another in defense of the faith. With the case of Spain in mind, however, he made the further exception that if a great Christian state were threatened with destruction by another Christian power the former was justified in seeking the aid of the Moslems on the grounds that the extinction of such a Christian state would be a severe loss to the faith.[7]

While today we may interpret the diplomatic relations of the West with the Ottomans as *de facto* recognition of the Turks and an acknowledgment of a policy of coexistence such was not the case in the eyes of contemporaries. The negotiations and alliances were not accompanied by any official redefinition of the status of the Turks or their acceptance as legitimate members of the community of nations. An unofficial effort in this direction appears to have been the intention of the anonymous author of a spurious letter circulated in the West shortly after the fall of Constantinople. The writer, speaking as, or for, the Grand Turk, censured the pope for stirring up Christians to make war on his people. He questioned the pope's right to grant indulgences and commented that if God had given such power to the pontiff he was obligated then to exercise it reasonably. Moreover, he continued, it was his understanding that the law of Christ forbade its followers to obtain their aims by use of force, and he entreated the pope to cease his warmongering. The Turks, he asserted, did not attack Christians because of their faith or belief. "For even if we do not worship Jesus Christ", he explained, "we do acknowledge him to be your prophet." Clearly the author appealed for the recognition of the Turks as a duly constituted power. He employed the myth of the Turks' antique lineage and historic right to justify their possession of Asia Minor, as did somewhat later the chaplain of Sir Richard Guylforde. But he went further and, like Giovanni Mario Filelfo in his *Amyris*, he legitimized the Ottoman subjugation of Greece as the just revenge of the descendants of Troy. As for the Turks' treatment of the Venetians, the offense of the latter was more than the fact that they held portions of the Trojan heritage. They had gained their empire without authority and by force; therefore, the Turks made war on them *a juste tiltre*. Again, the author stressed, the Turks attacked the Venetians not in the name of religion but to recover their temporal rights.[8] Obviously the work of an anti-Venetian propagandist, as well as a critic of the papacy, its author nonetheless removed the question from the realm of religion and with the aid of the Trojan mythology explained the Turkish conquests in terms of a temporal just war. At the end of the century the Florentine diarist, Luca Landucci, hinted at a similar conception, when, commenting on a report that the king of Naples was planning to summon the Turks to Italy, he observed that it was not at all unlikely since "the Turk had now a way of conquering without interfering with the faith"; but Landucci added that "God did not will that such an evil should befall unfortunate Italy".[9] But we find no elaboration of these sentiments by the spokesmen of those rulers who dealt with the Turks; rather, they were careful to justify their actions along traditional lines and usually went out of their way to proclaim their orthodoxy.[10]

But if the growth of diplomatic relations was not accompanied by any official declaration of an amoral political doctrine, certainly the opportunities to gain a better knowledge of the Turks were enhanced and in some instances resulted in a more critical assessment of the Ottomans, their customs, and their institutions. Western powers and private individuals participated in what may be appropriately described as cultural missions. An important case occured early in the century during the reigns of Murad II and Mehmed II. Although representing no government, but motivated by commercial interests and intellectual curiosity, Ciriaco de' Pizzicolli of Ancona several times visited the Turkish court. In 1430 he appeared before Murad II who entertained him royally. Fourteen years later he returned to Turkey and was present in Adrianople during the fateful negotiations between Murad and Ladislas of Hungary which led to the charge of deceit and broken faith when Hungary joined the crusade of Varna. In the years which followed Ciriaco traveled widely in the Levant in search of antiquities returning to Murad's court at Lydia in 1446. In 1448-1449 he was back in Italy but in 1452 we find him in the company of Mehmed II. He remained with the sultan during the siege of Constantinople and presumably entered the fallen capital with the victors. His relations with the Turks provoked a modern scholar to observe that for men like Ciriaco "there was neither Christian nor Turk. . .". This estimate is strengthened by the knowledge that while the Turks besieged Constantinople, Ciriaco nourished the sultan's ambitions to emulate Alexander the Great by reading to him from Diogenes Laertius, Herodotus, Livy, Quintus Curtius, the chronicles of the popes, emperors, kings of France, and the Lombards.[11]

Yet this same Ciriaco of Ancona was an ardent advocate of the crusade. In 1432 he urged the new pope Eugenius IV to take up the holy war. In the same year he pleaded the cause of the crusade before Sigismund, the king of the Romans, at Siena; and in 1433, and again in 1441, he addressed the duke of Milan to the same end. Distressed by the sufferings of eastern Christians religion and with the aid of the Trojan mythology explained the Turkish he was present at the Council of Florence following which he wrote the pope arguing that the favorable time for an expedition had arrived. In the months preceding the crusade of Varna he was busily occupied with writing stirring appeals to various princes in behalf of the war against the Turks. And in 1448 he wrote a letter celebrating the victory of the Hungarian Hunyadi over the Turks at Kossovo. While curiosity and opportunity attracted him to the Turkish court, in light of the evidence, we can hardly agree that for Ciriaco of Ancona Turks and Christians were all the same.[12]

It was the Venetian Senate which sent the Turks the best-known cultural mission of the fifteenth century. At the request of Mehmed II the government dispatched the painter Gentile Bellini. The story of his stay in the palace of the sultan has been too well told elsewhere to bear repeating here. His famous portrait of the conqueror, owned since 1917 by the National Gallery in London, has made Mehmed II the most familiar of all Turkish sultans to the twentieth century.[13] Other princes who were believed to have sent artists to the Turks are King Ferrante of Naples and Sigismondo Pandolfo Malatesta, tyrant of Rimini. There is no proof that either of these missions ever materialized. We do know that the court painter of Rimini, Matteo de' Pasti, was apprehended enroute to Constantinople by the Venetians, who charged him with espionage. He was alleged to have been taking the sultan a map of Italy containing strategic information. Also he carried a presentation copy of Roberto Valturio's *De re militari* which included scaled drawings of military machines and devices. At the same time a rumor spread through the peninsula that Malatesta had invited the Grand Turk to come to Italy, promising him a splendid reception and offering his services as a condottiere. Less than three years later the same terrible Malatesta commanded the Venetian land forces in their unsuccessful campaign against the Turks in the Morea. Coexistence was not meant to be always peaceful. A major source for the de' Pasti mission is the letter which was written to introduce the artist to Mehmed II. Composed by Valturio in the name of his patron, it is another example of that pragmatic eulogizing which has so exercised modern historians. But even if we disregard the author's flattery of the sultan, the letter is proof that the court of Rimini desired friendly relations with the Moslem power.[14]

The experiences of Ciriaco and of Gentile Bellini were the source of tales about the Turks, and particularly of Sultan Mehmed II, which were frequently repeated by western writers. The text which mentions Ciriaco's reading to the sultan was the work of a member of a Venetian embassy, Giacomo de'Langusto and was inserted in the chronicle of Zorzi Dolfin. Langusto described Mehmed II as having a good complexion, of medium build, expert in arms, and with a bearing which inspired fear. Although lacking in humor he thirsted for knowledge, was generous, determined, and possessed the virtues of a warrior such as courage, vigilance, and the ability to endure fatigue, cold, heat, thirst, and hunger. Langusto asserted that he ceaselessly sought knowledge of the West and had a map with details of the Latin states. Nothing, he declared, gave the sultan more pleasure than the study of world affairs and military science. He concluded by warning that the sultan was determined to unite the world under one empire and in one faith.[15]

The tales told about the sultan in connection with Bellini's visit were not so flattering, and reflect the tendency toward sensationalism when writing about the Turks. The sultan, it was reported, was greatly impressed by the Venetian's ability to reproduce the human likeness on canvas. But when Bellini attempted a painting showing the beheading of St. John the Baptist, Mehmed allegedly criticized the work as failing to show faithfully a beheaded person. To correct this shortcoming he was supposed to have ordered for the artist's enlightenment that one of his slaves be beheaded in Bellini's presence. Similar tales of cruelty, whether true or false, were repeated with relish. One concerns a particularly lovely and enchanting woman among the sultan's wives who so captivated him that he was unable to attend to any other business. Though wholly taken by the woman, he was reported to have recognized that his love for her was interfering with his duty to the empire and thus he personally slew her to be free of her enchantments.[16]

Representing a very different level of thinking and a purely pragmatic reaction, we may include the observation of the French political commentator Philippe de Commines. In Venice at the time of the formation of the league against the victorious Charles VIII (March 31, 1495), Commines spent an evening entertaining a Turkish ambassador in his own apartment. He recorded that the Turk was most anxious to cultivate the friendship of their two nations. For his own part, the Frenchman regarded Mehmed II as one of the two wisest and most valiant rulers of his day. The other was Mathias Corvinus, king of Hungary. Commines, however, attributed Mehmed's great accomplishments more to his use of cunning than of courage, indicating that he personally transacted most of his important business. He went on to emphasize that Mehmed, Mathias Corvinus, and his own master, Charles VIII, were the wisest princes to have reigned for a hundred years. He acknowledged that the sultan did possess certain fatal weaknesses, namely his addiction to worldly pleasures especially to all manner of sensuality and to gluttony. The latter, he alleged, brought Mehmed great distress in that it caused his legs to swell to the size of a man's waist every spring. Although the swelling disappeared of itself, it was attributed by the sultan's physicians to his gluttony; although, Commines added, it may have been a judgment from heaven. At any rate, had it not been for his vices the Turk, Commines concluded, would have effected greater damage to Christendom. It is clear from his summary of the sultan's conquests that the French diplomat judged the Grand Turk in terms of power politics and military success.[17]

Increased relations, whether peaceful or otherwise, between the western powers and the Turks resulted in a small but growing body of descriptive-historical literature dealing with the Turks. In contrast with the great bulk of the crusading tracts and anti-Moslem polemics, these accounts are uncommonly sober, critical treatments by authors with a first-hand acquaintance of their subject. Though in some cases based on experiences dating from an earlier period, their printing history, beginning in 1480 or thereafter, is a further indication of a more tempered attitude toward the Turks during the reign of Bayezid II. Perhaps the most remarkable work in this category is the *Tractatus de moribus condicionibus et nequicia Turcorum*. Written in 1479 or 1480 it was first printed in Rome in the latter year. Altogether in our period it was published seven times; and, counting both Latin and German editions, it appeared a dozen times more between the years 1530-1596.[18] The author, George of Hungary, was a native of Transylvania and was captured while still a schoolboy during a Turkish raid on Sebes in 1438. He remained in captivity until 1458. He wrote not for the usual reason of exhorting Christians to the crusade, but rather to prepare them, and himself, should they fall subject to the Turks. The book, then, was intended as a guide for survival in captivity and in particular was dedicated to alerting future captives to the subtle dangers by which they might be won from their faith to the religion of the prophet. Admitting that he himself had perched precariously on the brink of apostasy, George dealt in detail with the hardships and indignities endured by enslaved Christians, the plight and sufferings of the Balkan peoples, and the various pressures and inducements which led many to renounce Christ. The author had both an extensive and an unusually accurate knowledge of Islam. He was not above praising the Turks. He extolled their high standards of morality, the modesty of their women (which he contrasted to the behavior of Christian women), and the strength of the family institution. He was impressed by the strict discipline in the army and the manner in which the Turks conducted themselves in camp during the siege of Constantinople. During the reign of Murad II and the early days of his successor, the Turks, even those of rank, distinguished themselves by the simplicity of their habits. However, George criticized a growing taste for luxury which he recognized as creating a greater need for more slaves. His discussion of Mehmed II's personality, however, was in general favorable. He contributed to the western belief that the sultan was tolerant and even well-disposed toward Christianity by recounting a visit which the Grand Turk made to a Dominican church in Pera where he witnessed the celebration of the Mass. Apart from the material on Turkish life, religion, and the problems of Christians living under Ottoman dominion, George's work is of the utmost importance for the information he included on the origins of the Turks, on the janissaries, and the development of the *devshirme*.[19]

Judged on the bases of its reliability, objectivity, and comprehensiveness, *La Genealogie du grant Turc à present regnant* by Teodoro Spandugino ranks next after the *Tractatus* among the works in this category dating from our period.[20] Although it was not printed until 1519, it was written in 1503, and was to be widely used in the sixteenth century. Manuscript copies in Italian were presented by the author to Pope Leo X and to the French rulers Louis XII and Henry II. The French translation, which was printed in Paris in 1519, based on the earliest version of the work, was the first to be published, and is the text analyzed here. The Italian editions, printed in Lucca, 1550, and Florence, 1551, were augmented by the author to include material subsequent to the reign of Bayezid II (abdicated 1512), beyond which the first French edition does not go. Spandugino had visited Gallipoli in the company of his father in the year 1465. He journeyed to Constantinople in 1503, at the close of the Turco-Venetian war (1499-1503) for the purpose of assisting his brother Alexander, a merchant in the Turkish capital, to recover goods seized during the hostilities. Finding his brother dead and unable to reclaim his wealth, Spandugino occupied himself by writing a book on the Turks. In addition to his own observations he drew upon the knowledge of two highly placed officials of the Grand Porte who were probably related to the author, who was himself of Greek-Italian extraction. Moreover he made repeated references to the testimony of Turkish historians which he obviously consulted in doing his research.[21]

Spandugino's expressed purposes for writing the work are both legitimate and conventional: "pour alleger ma griefve douleur et soubstrayre les ennuyeuses pensées de mon inoppinée et maulvaise fortune...", he wrote, "je me mys à investiguer et vouloir congnoistre les gestes et meurs de la maison de Othoman et, par quelz moyens et personnaiges, elle avoit esté si fort exaulcée". At the same time he was concerned to show the miserable and unhappy state of the Greeks and arouse support in the West for their cause. He had a clear conception of the structure of his book. Following a short resumé of the history of the Ottoman dynasty, he explained that he would deal with the order of the sultan's court, its officers and ministers, and their manners and customs. And by way of justifying his efforts he warned his readers that in all these matters the Turks differed from any other nation or principality. In light of the favorable treatment he accorded most Turkish institutions it is significant that Spandugino specifically emphasized the contrast between those of the Turks and the Christians.[22] Judging from an explanatory note appended to the Italian edition of 1550, it would appear that Spandugino had been criticized, or at least anticipated criticism, of his description of the Turks. At any rate he felt obliged to elaborate on the circumstances and motives which led to his writing the book. He declared categorically that he did not regard himself as a historian! He had included, he claimed, only that material which he was able to remember and that which he judged worthy of being known.[23]

The contrast between the practices of Turks and Christians was reiterated in the body of the work, usually to the disadvantage of the latter.[24] But even where he pronounced no judgment Spandugino's objective and detailed description of Ottoman institutions bespoke the author's approval. Like other writers in this genre he was explicit in his praise of the personal virtues of the Turks—their hospitality to strangers, their mutual respect, their scrupulous observance of religious laws, etc.[25] Mehmed II he described as "hardy, rude, belliqueux, liberal, vaillant, et magnanime". He recorded the tales which asserted the unusual cruelty of the conqueror but was careful to introduce them with the phrases, "on dit", or "on escript de luy que. . .".[26] As a warrior Bayezid II was no less ruthless. In commenting on the taking of Modon he wrote: "A la fin, il la print par force et usa de tresgrande cruaulté et occision contre celluy loyal peuple". But after concluding peace with Venice in 1503, Spandugino asserted that the sultan occupied himself only with praiseworthy pursuits, and that it was common opinion that since the beginning of the dynasty there was no sultan more devoted to ruling justly.[27]

Spandugino dealt with the problem of religion in that part of the work where he discussed "l'usaige de leur vivre, leurs coustumes et façon et leur gouvernment". He noted that Christians and Jews were forbidden by law to discuss their religion with the Turks. The latter on the other hand went to great length to convert Christians to their faith. His discussion of the means and pressures exerted to this end, such as the use of false accusations, seem most familiar.[28] In describing the taxes levied on the Christian subjects of the sultan, Spandugino expressed great sympathy for those unfortunate creatures caught between the levy of tribute children and the tax collectors. He explained that it was the custom of Christians to marry their children early since the sultan's agents took only single youths to be raised as janissaries. The result, however, was that they produced large families which increased their tax assessment. But, he observed, "ung pauvre crestien aymera mieulx despendre tout son bien pour saulver son filz et evacq luy son ame". Spandugino expressed his amazement that the poor Christians were able to survive considering the weight of their burdens.[29]

But sympathy for the plight of fellow Christians did not result in a distorted description of the Turkish regime as a whole. Spandugino gave credence to the stories about the rude origins of the house of Osman, and admitted the cruelties of the Turks in combat. But *La Genealogie du grant Turc* is not an account of a barbarous horde but a description of a highly organized and well-governed state. The strength of the work is to be found in the detailed and informed description of the Ottoman government, its various functions, officers, and military institutions. No doubt the character of the work must be credited in large part to the critical facility of its author whose objective attitude was shared by a few observers, such as Pero Tafur and La Broquière earlier in the century. But the composition and publication of the book was further made possible by the easing of tensions between the Latins and the Turks in the generation after the death of Mehmed II and is itself a reflection of these new, if temporary, conditions.[30]

Some modern scholars have tried to show that admiration for the Turkish administration was not restricted to a few knowledgeable and objective observers but was shared by many common folk particularly in southeastern Europe who desired to enjoy the benefits of the Grand Turk's regime. In this vein the system of the *devshirme*, the levying of tribute children from among Christian youths between ages eight and fifteen, has been defended as offering such brilliant prospects for those enslaved that it aroused no resistance. On the relations of the Moslem conquerors and their Christian subjects we have been offered this idyllic conjecture: "It is hard to believe that the women of mixed villages, gathering at the well, did not come by degrees to exchange ideas on costume and embroidery patterns, charms or the evil eye, and methods of infant hygiene".[31] It is difficult to substantiate or refute such generalizations. Certainly the available evidence is conflicting. In Bosnia, for example, where the Orthodox and Latin authorities had competed for converts from the Bogomile heresy, many people were easily won over to Islam following the Turkish conquest. Similarly for Serbia it has been reported that "the Serbs in general feared Catholic domination. Thus the Ottomans were able to establish their rule without serious resistance by the Serbs".[32] Yet in 1483 Mathias Corvinus claimed in a letter to the pope that more than 200,000 Serbs had fled Turkish domination and in a period of only four years had settled in the south of his kingdom.[33] Much work remains but it is obvious that for the Balkans the results are going to vary considerably from one locality to the next.

I think we can question more seriously the assertion that pro-Turkish sentiments were also prevalent among the inhabitants of the Holy Roman Empire. The chief text which has been cited in support of this opinion is the carnival play, *Des Türken Vasnachtspil*, written by Hans Rosenblüt in 1456. The author has the "türkische Kaiser", accompanied by his councillors, travel to the city of Nuremberg and there attempt to persuade the citizens of the advantages of Turkish rule. In the opening arguments by the Ottoman spokesman and in the various statements of other Turks including the sultan himself, a rosy picture of life in Turkey is set forth. The peace and order maintained by the sultan's strong government, his justice and light taxation, his toleration of Christians are all emphasized in contrast to the social and political evils of the empire and the corruption of the church and its hierarchy. Indeed the Turkish regime is made to appear by far the superior. But Rosenblüt's purpose is not to praise the Turk; and it is made quite clear that what is said about them is purely in the way of propaganda.[34]

Admittedly, Turkish rule was not everywhere and at all times harsh and intolerable. When it fitted their purposes the sultans were capable of clemency and tolerance. Moreover, we cannot deny that a large number of Christian adventurers and renegades voluntarily placed their talents at the disposal of the Turks. The great peasant population of South Germany and Hungary, however, cannot be compared with those opportunists, present in every society and in every age, who seek their fortunes and sell their wares in the most lucrative markets. In contrast to the imaginary warm reception the Turks received at Nuremberg, in Rosenblüt's *Fashnachtspiel*, we have the actual experience recorded by a Burgundian traveler, Bertrandon de la Broquière, who visited Vienna in 1433, after traveling through Palestine, Syria, Turkey, and the Balkans. When he appeared in Vienna he was dressed like a Turk and carried weapons which were distinctly Turkish. He reported that the innkeepers of Vienna, thinking him an infidel, refused him lodging until he convinced them that he was a Christian. And in the same year in which Rosenblüt wrote his *Türkenspiel*, thousands of peasants and other common folk flocked to the standard of the cross and marched to the rescue of Belgrade. Only three years later in a ballad entitled *Von den Türken*, though he continued his criticism of the Germans, Rosenblüt characterized the Turkish menace in familiar terms and emphasized the need for a crusade.[35]

In *Des Türken Vasnachtspil* the author's concern is with the problem of Germany. The abuses and injustices perpetrated by the ruling class are brilliantly satirized in the condemnatory speeches of the Turks and the absurd defenses offered by the official spokesmen of the empire and the church. The criticism of Christian behavior and institutions by contrasting them unfavorably with those of the "infidels" was not an invention of Rosenblüt's or his generation. The technique was long employed by travelers to the Levant who were surprised to find that all the Moslems they met were not wild savages thirsting for the blood of Christians but that sometimes they showed more courtesy and charity than Christians did one another.[36] Such experiences may well have resulted in a more tolerant attitude on the part of the travelers in question. And the cumulative effect of such observations may in the long run have contributed to altering the generally shared Latin Christian view of Islam. But for the most part the comparisons are made not to extol the Turks or the Saracens but to chastise wayward Christians. The latter, it was assumed, were and ought to have been morally superior. Thus when a prince was unjust or particularly cruel he was compared to or even called a Turk. To cite one among hundreds of examples, the Florentine Landucci wrote (1501) concerning the troops of Cesare Borgia, that they "behaved like the Turks, putting all the villages to fire and flame, and carrying off girls and women" etc.[37] But to make the denunciation of one's enemy a shade stronger he was declared to be worse than the Turk; thus in a Venetian dispatch (1509), we read: "The Emperor is still in Paduan territory, accompanied by the French, Papal, and Ferrarese forces, perpetrating against the Christians such cruelties that greater could not be committed by the infidels."[38] To be fair we will quote from an address of the German ambassador at the court of Henry VII in which he declared that "they [the other Latin powers] ought all to join against these rascally Venetians, who are worse than the Turk".[39] Such backhanded compliments, we can be sure, did little to improve the image of the Turks.

It is in a similar context, I believe, that we must understand much of the political and popular criticism of papal plans for a holy war. Criticism of the crusade was nearly as old as the institution itself.[40] Some of the opposition was unquestionably based on the sincere belief that killing ran contrary to the Gospel and that warfare was no proper means for winning souls to Christ.[41] Moreover, incipient notions of the principle of coexistence and the idea of the just war may be found even in various statements of popes, canonists, and theologians. In the thirteenth century Innocent IV had officially established that it was forbidden to war upon Moslems either for the purpose of conversion or to conquer their lands when they had done no harm to Christians. Aquinas concurred with this but stressed the qualification that it was just to attack them when they interfered with the practice of the Christian faith. Similarly Augustinus Triumphis held that since infidel rulers did not derive their power from the pope they therefore were not to be attacked without cause.[42] But while the conditions for a crusade were thereby more carefully circumscribed the principle of the holy war was left intact. The authoritative position represented by these pronouncements was, moreover, fully explained, for the benefit of the laity, in the famous second chapter "By What Law Or On What Ground Can War Be Made Against the Saracens?" in the fourth part of Honoré Bonet's *The Tree of Battles*.[43] Written in 1387, the work was widely read and much copied, in part or in its entirety, in the fifteenth century. Thus Gilbert of the Haye in a Scottish version done in 1456, and entitled *The Buke of the Law of Armys or Buke of Bataillis* states that wars fought indiscriminately against the infidels or for the purpose of converting them are forbidden. But wars to recover the Holy Land, which Christ had conquered with his own blood, are allowed, as are wars against infidels who "mak ony molestacioun to cristyn that is in thair jurisdiction. . .".[44]

Political polemicists and popular critics alike took little account of such reasoning which they regarded as the legalisms of subtle canonists and obscure theologians. To both the former the crusade was largely a device by which the pope and clergy extracted money and privileges. Such antagonisms, while not wholly without some basis in fact, were only one current in the rapidly rising tide of anti-clericalism which was the result of complex forces and deep-rooted sentiments at work in Renaissance society.[45] The important point is that criticism of the crusade did not necessarily imply a constructive view of the Turks any more than anti-clericalism represented a repudiation of Christianity. While the negative tendencies in each case ultimately contributed to breaking down established attitudes and beliefs, we must not rush to hasty conclusions and imbue Renaissance minds with modern concepts. In the sixteenth century violent anti-papalists among the protestants were still denouncing the Turks as the enemy of the faith and praying for the protection of Christendom![46]

Although we must be cautious in estimating the contribution of the Turks to the revolt which came in the sixteenth century, we cannot deny their significance for the fortunes of the church and the papal program during the critical period 1453-1517. As the reactions of the *Curia Romana* to the Ottoman peril greatly colored the public image of the Turks in the West, the Turkish advance and the papal responses to it no less affected the pope's image. The succession of crises which opened with the fall of Constantinople and culminated with the siege of Rhodes and the capture of Otranto, provided papal apologists with a unique occasion for demonstrating the need for common Christian action under the leadership of the pope. Thus the Turkish advance breathed new life into the old forms which comprised the program of the post-conciliar popes. In effect the hopes for a *Republica Christiana* and a universal papal monarchy were given a new lease on life. But the opportunity, if it ever existed in fact, proved elusive, and the best efforts of the conservative reformers abortive. Neither the Turkish attack on Italy in 1480 nor the favorable circumstances for dealing a decisive blow subsequent to the death of Mehmed II were sufficient to unite the West.

In the altered conditions of the last two decades of the *Quattrocento* even the papacy, as we have seen, turned to negotiating with the Turks. Ideologically there was no radical change. The idea of the crusade and discussions for its prosecution continued as before. The Turk was still, officially, the enemy of the faith. But the favorable conditions of the mid-fifteenth century had passed; and when the Turk once again loomed as the fierce aggressor, the church was no longer one and the disunity of Christendom was an established fact.[47] The failure of the papal crusade in the fifteenth century, for which the popes alone were hardly responsible, yet resulted in a further diminution of confidence in the authority, effectiveness, and integrity of the See of St. Peter.[48] For those for whom the Turk remained a matter of serious concern, it meant relying even more heavily upon that authority which in most areas offered the best hope for peace, order, and security, the Renaissance prince or king.

A foreshadowing of future developments along these lines, and the novel ideas which were to accompany the laity's assumption of responsibility for the war against the Turks, occurred in the very heart of our period. The special case was that of George Podiebrad, the Bohemian king of heretics. Not that George bore any love for the Turks; indeed it was alleged that he coveted among other prizes the former capital of Byzantium and the crown of Constantine. But once pronounced a heretic and cut off from communion with Rome he was not likely to champion papal leadership of the crusade. He therefore proposed a grand and unique scheme by which he hoped to achieve both the internal pacification of Europe and the expulsion of the Turks. What George called for was nothing less than a league of European powers, a permanent union of Christian princes with a standing general assembly, a supranational military force supported by taxes levied on all members, a common currency, and an international court. The incongruous position in which Podiebrad found himself as the enemy at once of Rome and the sultan, as well as the requirements of his policies *vis-à-vis* his Christian neighbors, gave birth to a radical conception of a united states of Europe which ignored the traditional claims of both emperor and pope. The latter, it is true, was called upon to assist in the collection of taxes to finance the war against the Turks and to put pressure on the Italian states to provide the necessary naval forces; otherwise, the pope was excluded.[49]

Unquestionably Podiebrad saw the league as a means of solving his outstanding problems as well as fulfilling his ambition to be a dominant force in European affairs. Yet the concern for the Turkish peril, graphically described in the preamble and reiterated throughout the plan, was not simply a matter of form. The continued advance of the Turks was a threat to George's position in Bohemia as well as his future plans. Podiebrad knew that he could not count on the pope, and his own alienation from Rome, which came shortly after the failure of Pius II's congress at Mantua, led to the realization that the papal crusade was no longer possible. In proposing a league of temporal princes to deal with the Turk, Podiebrad not only removed the crusade from the jurisdiction of the pope but moved one step closer to the concept of a secular just war. The king of Bohemia knew that he was breaking with tradition and therefore appealed to a new principle for the regulation of state relations and the maintenance of peace. The latter, the ultimate objective of the whole scheme, was only possible through the administration of justice, hence the need for a *jus gentium naturalis* or as the draft put it: *de naturae gremio nova jura producere*.[50]

The dilemma of George Podiebrad, caught between the Turk and the pope, anticipated that of German protestants in the next century. But already reform-minded patriots were calling for a war against the Turks in which they emphasized the role of the emperor at the expense of the pope. Peace and unity, the rehabilitation of the empire, the renewal of religion and morality, together with the defense of Germany against France and the Turks were the main constituents of the proposals associated with the plans and policies of the emperor-elect Maximilian. The king himself, as well as his political publicists, seized every opportunity to gain adherents to this program. The spread of *die bösen Blattern* was cited as an example of God's punishment for the corrupt and dissolute life of the Germans and their failure to take the cross.[51] The Augsburg poet Hans Schneider praised Maximilian's plans to proceed against the French in 1492 and urged that the campaign against the Turks be pressed with equal ardor.[52] The German victory over the French at Salins in 1493 was celebrated by Sebastian Brant who proclaimed that the moment had at last arrived for dealing with the Turkish peril. The alleged appearance of crosses on the clothing of the citizens of Alsace was interpreted by Brant among others as a summons to the emperor to organize the war against the Ottomans.[53] In general Brant, like the conservative scholar-reformer, Jakob Wimpfeling, called for a combined effort on the part of pope and emperor to cleanse Christendom and exterminate the Turk. Such was the burden of

Brant's *De origine et conversatione bonorum regum et laude civitatis Hierosolymae* and the bulk of his *Varia carmina* published three times in 1498.[54] But in chapter 99, "Von Abgang des Glouben" in his best known work, *Das Narrenschiff*, the Germans are summoned to support their king:

> By God, you princes, please behold
> What injury there'll be untold
> If once the empire should decay,
> Not even you will live for ay.

Lamenting the decline of Christendom, the rise and spread of Islam, the conquests of the Ottomans:

> So strong the Turks have grown to be
> They hold the ocean not alone,
> The Danube too is now their own.
> They make their inroads when they will,
> Bishoprics, churches suffer ill,
> Now they attack Apulia,
> Tomorrow e'en Sicilia
> And next to it is Italy,
> Wherefore a victim Rome may be
> And Lombardy and Romance land,
> We have the arch foe close at hand,

Brant does not fail to chide the pope:

> We perish sleeping one and all,
> The wolf has come into the stall
> And steals the Holy Church's sheep
> The while the shepherd lies asleep.

Nor does he spare the conscience of all Christians:

> Our sins I blame and not the others',
> We have no patience now with brothers
> Nor pity we their misery.
> Each state would grow and greater be;
> . . . .
> We find each man to his wall turning
> To ascertain if it is burning,
> Not thinking e'er to quench with vim
> The fire before it reaches him.

And yet it is clear that the Turk is determined to crush Christendom:

> For Europe's gates are open wide,
> The foe encircles every side,
> With sleep or rest he's not content,
> On Christian blood alone he's bent.

He therefore calls upon the princes:

> Do not permit such shameful things!
> If you'll support the ship of state
> It will not sink but bear its freight.
> Your king is all benignity,
> He'll don for you knight's panoply,
> Rebellious lands he will subdue,
> But you must help, he needs you to.
> The noble Maximilian,
> He merits well the Roman crown.
> They'll surely come into his hand,
> The Holy Earth, the Promised Land,
> He'll undertake it any day
> If he can trust in you and may.[55]

The rambling and repetitive but nonetheless ardent exhortation addressed to the princes of Germany by Ulrich von Hutten marks the new trend in reform thought at the end of our period. Although he acknowledged the responsibility of the empire for the defense of Christendom and the true religion, he regarded the Turkish war as fundamentally a German problem. He appealed not to all Christian rulers but to the lords of Germany, and it was within the context of imperial concerns that he treated the Ottoman menace. Arch-defender of the privileges of his class, he blamed all the misfortunes of the Germans, including the Turkish threat, upon the princes. Divided, self-seeking, disloyal, and disobedient, they wallowed day and night in their drinking cups boasting of past achievements and proclaiming the weakness of Asiatic soldiers. But while the Germans amused themselves, the Turks were winning battles; while the princes pursued the pleasures of the hunt, the Turkish rulers snared Asia, Africa, and a large part of Europe. More in the manner of the traditional crusade exhortation, Hutten drew a sensational account of the origin and rise of the Turks, dwelling especially on the conquests of Mehmed II, whom he called "the Great", and the recent victories of Selim in Syria and Egypt. It was folly, he warned, to think that Germany was immune, and he spared no superlatives in describing the strength and forces of the Turks. Moreover, he explained that owing to their savage nature their desire for conquest was insatiable. They conquered not to rule but to destroy. Bloodthirsty, sprung from the filthiest barbaric rabble, they were, he declared, the enemies of humanity, of religion, and of God. Hutten contended that they planned to extinguish the entire German race; already the provinces of southeastern Germany had been devastated and depopulated. There was little time, he urged. Unless the princes came to their senses there would be no Germany. The Turks, he insisted, were not invincible, but it was necessary to raise an army at once. He appealed to the princes' honor, valor, and patriotism, and he pleaded with them to consult quickly and to take immediate action. What was most required, for the war against the Turks and the reform of Germany, was that the princes cooperate with one another and follow obediently the commands of their emperor.[56]

Criticisms of the crusade, pope, and clergy were sometimes coupled with a more benevolent attitude toward the adherents of Islam. In the fourteenth century John Wyclif had not merely anticipated Luther but had advanced the radical proposition that some among the Moslems might be saved just as many so-called Christians were surely to be condemned. In the main, however, he, like Luther, regarding Islam as a corruption of true religion and a rationalization of innumerable vices, employed it as a base standard of iniquity against which he gauged the shortcomings of Christians and especially the church. False Christians were at one with the Moslems; in fact the former had been the condition for the rise of the latter. The obvious means of combatting Islam was to purge those practices among Christians which had called it into being. Although he stipulated that at the moment of death they must accept Christ, Wyclif asserted that there were those of other sects, even Saracens, who might be saved providing they had not thwarted the will of God. Thus at the end of the fourteenth century Wyclif posited a dualistic universalism in which Christians were those who truely followed Christ, wherever they were to be found; and Moslems were those, including many within Christendom, who failed to do so.[57]

We cannot follow here the universalist tendencies among the various radicals of the fifteenth century. But pacifism was regarded, however, as a fundamental tenet of the "plain Law of Christ" as professed by certain radical sects whose revolutionary teachings found favor among the war-weary and depressed lower orders of southeastern Europe. The behavior of pacifist sects located in the path of the Ottoman advance is not sufficiently documented. Contemporary testimony affirmed, however, that in the case of the *Unitas Fratrum* their pacifist outlook extended to the Turks, at least in theory:

> Et hoc dicunt, quod si Turci prosequerentur eos aut quicunque inimici, nollent se defendere, sed pocius mori in simplicitate sua, et ex hoc concludunt, quod neque pro iusticia aut pro fide liceat bellari, sed simpliciter mala pati, allegentes apostolum: 'Non vosmet ipsos defendentes'. Et Christum: 'Diligite inimicos'.[58]

Radicals of various persuasions espoused a universalism which accorded the Turks and all Moslems a place in God's plan for salvation. The apocalyptic spiritual Johannes Baptista Italus claimed that while visiting Turkey he had had a vision in which it was revealed to him that both Moslems and Jews were to be won to Christianity. He shared with others the conviction that the great movement was to commence with the year 1517. In the sixteenth century spiritual and Anabaptist preachers not only predicted the conversion of the Turks and called for nonresistance, but praised the Ottomans as being true to their own nature (in contrast to most Christians) and claimed that the Turk as a Turk was also a creature of God.[59]

The peaceful approach to Islam, though generally related to reform impulses within Christianity, did not for the most part stray so far from the bounds of orthodoxy. Plans for the conversion of Moslems were not, of course, an innovation in the Renaissance. In the mid-twelfth century, as is well known, Peter the Venerable, reflecting the rational outlook of the new philosophy, believed that Moslems might be converted if shown the error of their ways. He had the Koran translated by the Englishman Robert of Ketton and wrote at length on the subject. Peter's program found little sympathy among Christians and none with the adherents of Islam. But the policy of conversion, in one form or another, was frequently revived in the following centuries. The efforts and failures of Jacques de Vitry, St. Francis, St. Louis, Roger Bacon, Raymond Lull, and others have been given fair attention by students of Christian missions.[60]

The miserable results of these endeavors, however, did not discredit the peaceful approach to Islam. The failure of the West to organize a crusade in face of the continued advance of the Turks and the growing doubts about the validity of a religious war or a military solution to the problem led to a renewed interest in preaching missions among the Moslems. Despite all, Latins remained convinced of the superiority of Christian doctrine, and, of course, the ultimate victory of Christ, and equally certain of the vulnerability of Islam. The author of the crusade plan appended to Tedaldi's account of the fall of Constantinople believed that the West could count on the aid of the

Turkish prince of Karamania, who "with some inducements may probably become a Christian". The English pilgrim and mystic, Margery Kempe, prayed for the conversion of Saracens and Jews. And as astute an observer as Arnold von Harff observed that "if preachers were sent among them, they would all be converted to Christianity because they were so credulous". Such credulity on the part of Latins was nourished by the convincing arguments (that is, convincing to Christians), such as those put forward in the letter of Pius II to Mehmed II. The fact that such works were quickly reproduced in print, documents not only a contemporary interest in the possibility of converting the Turks but the naïvete of a reading public eager to be persuaded by easy solutions to the Turkish peril.[61]

Such optimism, born of anxiety, was no doubt further strengthened by the few known cases of the actual baptism of Turkish prisoners and political refugees. On the basis of one incident the Franciscan preacher Bernardino de'Bustis projected the possibility of mass conversions. His example, related in the third sermon, for Quinquagesima Sunday, of his *Rosarium Sermonum*, is connected with the mission of Alberto da Sarteano to the East as envoy of Eugenius IV for the cause of church union. Taking his text from Isaiah (9:2: "The people who walked in darkness have seen a great light; those who dwelt in a land of deep darkness, on them has light shined."), he went on to illustrate how da Sarteano had brought back from Cairo a Christian renegade. The man, believed to have been the famed traveler, Nicolo de'Conti, having been a Moslem for forty years was converted by the pope's emissary. Moreover, according to de'Bustis, the convert upon hearing da Sarteano preach before the pope, wept "because of the tragedy of there being Saracens and because of the ingratitude of Christians, for, if that sermon had been preached in the center of Cairo or Damascus, and if those infidels had understood the language, out of a hundred thousand, eighty-six thousand would have been converted".[62]

Unbounded optimism, as that displayed by preachers like de'Bustis, whether real, or expressed for homiletic effect (and we have already been warned by Erasmus about the methods of the contemporary *ars predicandi*), drew the criticism it justly deserved. Thus Andreas de Escobar, titular bishop of Megara and a supporter of the council of Basel, wrote that he doubted that the Turks, Saracens, Jews, or pagans would ever be converted before the day of judgment; but he agreed that the effort should be made along with a crusade to recover the Holy Land.[63] A letter purporting to be from a certain Sultan John of Babylon to Pope Pius II, obviously mocking the letter of the latter to Mehmed II, condemned not only the pope's appeal to the Grand Turk but all plans to convert the Moslems by use of reason.[64] However valid, the criticism of the skeptics must not blind us to the fact that there were some strong and sincere proposals in support of the benevolent approach. The desire for reform and peace at home, denunciation of the crusade, and an eloquent appeal for the peaceful conversion of Moslems are significantly combined in one of the best known pieces of English literature of the late fourteenth century. In *The Vision of Piers Plowman*, the author is able to conceive of a reformed church, a just government, and a universal peace when

> Batailles shal non be ne no man bere wepne,
> And what smyth þat ony smytheth be smyte þerwith to dethe.[65]

The author's portrait of the prophet Mohammed is consistent with the unsympathetic representations common throughout the Middle Ages. And he repeats the favorite tale about Mohammed's having been a cardinal, who frustrated in his design to become pope, purposefully distorted the teachings of Scripture and deceived the Saracens by trickery.[66] But echoing Wyclif, it was not just Mohammed but all evil clergy, "manered after Makometh", that had led Christians astray so "þat no man vseth treuth". Let the clergy reform and all people who are contrary to Christ's law would be converted. He bemoans the fact that men "so longe on Makometh shulde byleue", especially since the Moslems "Han a lippe of owre byleue". Indeed the poet goes on to express his own belief in a universal faith based on the common tenets shared by Christianity, Judaism, and Islam; but reaffirming the superiority of Christianity he calls for a renewed effort to bring all men to Christ:

> And sitthen þat þe sarasenes and also þe iewes
> Konne þe firste clause of owre bileue *credo in deum patrem omnipotentem*,
> Prelates of crystene prouynces shulde preue, if þei myzte,
> Lere hem litlum & litlum & *in ihesum christum filium*,
> Tyl þei couthe speke and spelle *et in spiritum sanctam*,
> And rendren it & recorden it with *remissionem peccatorum*,
> *Carnis resurreccionem, et vitam eternam; amen.*[67]

In his lectures at Harvard in 1961, R. W. Southern associated the revival of conversion schemes among the scholars of the fifteenth century with their authors' experience in conciliar diplomacy. Negotiations and compromise had, after all, restored papal unity, ended the Hussite problem, and temporarily brought together the Greeks and Latins.[68] But the peaceful approach to the Turks was also the result of expanding intellectual horizons, especially the encounter with Byzantine Platonism and its early Christian commentators. The Greek Platonist Gemistos Plethon was accused of preaching a universal religion, a blend of existing faiths including Christianity and Islam.[69] In the years immediately following the fall of Constantinople the program for the peaceful conversion of the Turks occupied the attention of a handful of orthodox Catholic theologians and statesmen. Certainly the most dedicated and unswerving advocate of the new policy was the Spaniard Juan de Segovia. He had backed the wrong side at Basel, had been made cardinal by the council's anti-pope, Felix V, and when it was all over retired from active affairs to the priory of Aiton in Savoy. Juan remained, however, an apostle of conciliation. Moreover, he approached the doctrine of Islam in the Renaissance spirit of critical scholarship. Eschewing the work of Robert of Ketton, he produced with the help of a Moslem jurist from Salamanca a new translation of the Koran.[70] Juan opposed the crusade on both moral and practical grounds. He believed it was contrary to the true nature of Christianity, and he cited the long, inglorious history of the Holy War as proof that it was not the will of God. On the contrary it was Islam that was born of war and was sustained by it. He made it very clear that he was not opposed to Christians fighting a just war. "I want to emphasize", he wrote, "that I do not condemn the lawful wars against the Moslems owing to their invasion of Christian lands or other similar causes, but only those undertaken with religious motives in mind or for the purpose of conversion." Indeed, he conceded that before making any constructive peaceful move it was necessary to build up a strong defense to halt the advance of the Turks.[71]

If Segovia's observations on war strike a familiar chord, his analysis of the problems and pitfalls of evangelical preaching might seem to have been taken from a modern textbook on the psychology of homiletics. Dispatching preachers into Moslem lands, he believed, was as useless and harmful as the crusade, and past efforts had been every bit as fruitless. To begin with, unless they were supported by military force they did not have a chance. But worse, Christian preachers knew nothing about Islam and little enough about their own faith. Their method consisted of condemning Moslem beliefs and practices which ran counter to Christian doctrine, and their sermons were sweeping denunciations of Mohammed and his followers. The correct approach, he asserted, was to begin with those beliefs Christians and Moslems held in common. Preachers were to be trained in the teachings of the Koran, the religious traditions of Islam, and the ways of the Moslem people. Preaching had its role but only after a long period of preparation during which the contacts of missionaries with the Moslems were to be restricted to charitable and intellectual activities. In place of the crusade or the usual preaching mission Juan de Segovia recommended the method of conciliation. Christians were urged first to maintain peace with the Moslems as much as possible. Then in an atmosphere of concord they were to work for closer ties, especially in the cultural areas. From increased peaceful relations Segovia expected a mutual understanding to develop between the two peoples and a diminution of fanaticism and prejudice. Once these aims were accomplished, Christians were to institute discussions on doctrine beginning of course with those teachings both professed. The discussions were to be held with Moslem jurists but in the presence of their lords, who in the end had to be convinced. After citing in support of his method arguments drawn from natural law, theology, and the record of history, Segovia examined at length the benefits he expected to accrue from such conferences even if the final end of conversion were not realized. Such a program was not the work of an impractical visionary. In addition to the experience of Basel, Segovia had actually held doctrinal discussions with Moslems in Spain and had a personal acquaintance with Moslem believers as well as an extensive knowledge of Islam based upon his studies. He did not minimize the dangers and difficulties. Patience and understanding were his watchwords. But he was optimistic. He claimed that even well-educated Moslems were ill-informed about the teachings of both Christ and Mohammed and he expected conversion to follow enlightenment. Since he occupied no position of prominence himself, Juan de Segovia advocated the adoption of his method in letters to leading churchmen.[72]

Among his correspondents Segovia got the strongest encouragement from Nicholas of Cusa, with whom the Spaniard had first discussed at the Council of Basel the possibility of converting the Moslems. Cusa's interest in the eastern question has been outlined by his biographer, Edmond Vansteenberghe, and his writings bearing on the subject have been carefully studied in recent years.[73] At Basel he had obtained a copy of the Latin Koran and a history of Islam. Also he was probably present when a Turkish embassy came to the council to negotiate with the Emperor Sigismund. His knowledge and interest in the subject were enhanced by the journey he made to Constantinople in 1437 to complete the arrangements for the council of Ferrara-Florence. In the Byzantine capital he found another copy of Ketton's translation, an Arabic text of the Koran which was explained to him by its owners at the Franciscan convent of Holy Cross, and the writings of St. John of Damascus refuting Islam. Cusa reported that during his stay in Constantinople a certain Balthazar told him of a prominent Turk, an ardent student of the Scriptures, who together with twelve companions wished to go to Rome and learn more from the pope. He claimed that among the Moslems the most learned praised the Gospel and preferred it to the Koran.[74]

Although in the decade and a half preceding the fall of Constantinople Cusa was preoccupied with restoring relations between Germany and Rome and directing ecclesiastical reform in the empire, he found time to discuss the eastern question with learned churchmen along the way. It was at his suggestion that Denis of Rickel examined the teachings of Islam and composed his *Contra perfidiam Mahometi* which the author dedicated to Cusa.[75] When in response to the Turkish victory over Byzantium Segovia set to work on the program outlined above, Nicholas of Cusa independently employed the conference method to achieve unity among the various faiths in his *De pace fidei*. The work was represented as the gist of a vision which came to the author while meditating upon the recent reports of the terrible atrocities committed by the king of the Turks at Constantinople. But in place of the customary invective Cusa, in a spirit of charity and compassion, allowed that even non-Christian religions worshipped, however imperfectly, the true God and possessed some knowledge of Him. *De pace fidei* together with his one surviving letter to Segovia and his major study of Islam, *Cribratio Alchoran*, show that in his thinking on Islam, as in his purely speculative works, Nicholas of Cusa was, as Copleston put it, "governed by the idea of unity as the harmonious synthesis of differences".[76]

If the pleas of the peace-minded (a minority in every age) had no immediate effect upon the policies of contemporary rulers, they formed, however, the essential background for the work of the heroic apostles of peace in the next generation when Sebastian Franck was able to write, "To me, anyone who wishes my good, and can bear with me, is a good brother, whether papist, Lutheran, Zwinglian, Anabaptist or even Turk", and when Erasmus, while admitting the legitimacy of fighting the Turks, advised that it was better to attract them to the Christian religion by doctrine, good deeds, and a pure life.[77] Obviously this charitable outlook involved a conception of the Ottomans which conflicted with the so-called humanist view of the Turk as the barbarian enemy of culture and the orthodox religious estimate of Mohammed's people as the children of Lucifer. The proponents of peaceful conversion granted the Turks and all Moslems a rightful place in God's creation and in His plan for history. They attributed to them a capacity for salvation, and claimed that in the Koran they already possessed a portion of the truth.

It is understandable, in light of recent history and our present concern for world peace, that scholars should emphasize the pragmatic and charitable approaches to the Turkish problem in the Renaissance. Certainly the ideas of Juan de Segovia or Nicholas of Cusa are more congenial to our generation than those of the crusade proponents. It would be misleading, however, to imply that the benevolent or even the realistic viewpoints were widespread in the half-century after the fall of Constantinople. At odds with the orthodox tradition they were hardly encouraged by what was known about the victorious advance of the Ottomans and what was believed to be the latter's intentions regarding the West. It is therefore, I think, equally understandable that most Latin Christians in the Renaissance failed to realize a more sympathetic or objective view of the Turks. Apart from the unhappy but apparently universal tendency to represent one's enemy as the personification of evil, the western characterization of the Ottomans as the sworn foe of Christendom had some basis in fact. On this we may cite the authority of the distinguished orientalist Bernard Lewis, who wrote that "among the Christian peoples of Europe it was common practice, at one time, to use the word Turk as a synonym of Muslim, and to speak of a convert to Islam, of whatever nationality, as having 'turned Turk'. This usage was not without good reasons. The Ottoman Empire from its foundation to its end was an Islamic state, dedicated first to the advancement, then to the defense of Islam against the infidels."[78]

Yet the conflict of East and West in the Renaissance was not without consequences of significance for a better understanding between peoples of diverse cultures. In this connection we should now place alongside the apostles of peace the authors of the descriptive-historical works the significance of which we can now see more clearly. For the most part the latter gained their knowledge of the Turks by first-hand experience, whether as agents of a western power (e.g. La Broquière), or as captives of the Turks (e.g. George of Hungary), or involved in the pursuit of wealth (Spandugino). Such men demonstrated that the Turk was an acceptable subject for the writing of history and that a foreign culture could be studied successfully by an outsider. And if their own compositions were framed by conventional explanations and justifications, the body of their texts reveal an objective approach and critical facility. In short, the authors of the descriptive literature contributed to one of the most important intellectual developments of the Renaissance—the rehabilitation of historical studies based on travel, first-hand observation, and the study of oral tradition—a development which has been described as "the first contribution of modern historiography to an independent study of the past."[79]

NOTES TO CHAPTER VIII

1. On reactions to the death of Mehmed II see e.g. Infessura, *Diario*, cols. 1147, 1148; Volterranus, *Diarium*, cols. 133-135; Iorga, *Notes et extraits*, V, 86, 87. On the new appeals for the crusade see G. Müller, *Documenti sulle relazioni della città toscane*, p. 233; and cf. Pastor, *HP*, II, 342ff.; D. Bouhours, *Histoire de Pierre d'Aubusson*,

2nd ed. (Paris, 1677), pp. 236-238. For the civil war in Turkey, Grasso, "Documenti riguardanti la constituzione di una lega contro il Turco nel 1481", *Giornale ligustico di archeologia, storia e bell arti*, VI (1879), 321-494. S. N. Fisher, *The Foreign Relations of Turkey* 1481-1512 (Urbana, 1948), pp.21-27.

2. On Charles VIII and the crusade see P. Durrieu, "La Déliverance de la Grèce projetée en France à la fin du quinzième siècle", *Revue d'histoire diplomatique*, XXVI (1912), 333-351; H-F. Delaborde, *L'Expedition de Charles VIII en Italie* (Paris, 1888); Djuvara, *Cent Projets*, pp. 46-66. On the negotiations at Cambray see B. Knös, *Un Ambassadeur de l'hellénisme, Janus Lascaris*, pp. 112ff.; and Bonardi, "Venezia e la lega di Cambrai", *Nuovo archivio veneto*, ser. III, VII (1904), 209-244. And for the period 1517-1518, J. Martin, "Le Saint-Siège et la question d'Orient au seizième siècle. Projets de croisade sous le règne de Léon X", *Revue d'histoire diplomatique*, XXX (1916), 35-56; and F. le Van Baumer, "England, the Turk and the Common Corps of Christendom", *AHR*, L (1944-45), 26-48.

3. See the chapters by J. R. Hale, C. M. Ady, D. Hay, and R. Doucet in *NCMH*, I: *The Renaissance*; and G. Mattingly, *Renaissance Dilpomacy*.

4. The negotiations turning on Djem were carefully studied by L. Thuasne, *Djem-sultan fils de Mohammed II, frère de Bayezid II (1459-1495)* (Paris, 1892); see also F. Cognasso, "Il Sultano Djem all Corte di Alessandro VI", *Popoli*, II (1942), 96-103; and Armenag Sakisian, "Djem Sultan et les fresques de Pinturicchio", *La Revue de l'art*, XLVII (1925), 81-91. See also S. N. Fisher, *The Foreign Relations of Turkey*, pp. 28-50.

5. For the negotiations of the Italian powers with the Ottomans see F. Babinger, "Lorenzo de'Medici e la Corte ottomana", *Archivio storico italiano*, CXX (1963), 305-361, with copious references; and for the larger picture D. Vaughan, *Europe and the Turk*, pp. 1-103.

6. See e.g. the speech of Innocent VIII before the congress in Rome March 25, 1490, cited in Thuasne, *Djem-Sultan*, pp. 266, 267.

7. *Commentum et apparatus super bulla privationis et depositionis Georgii regis Bohemiae*, cited in R. H. Trame, *Rodrigo Sánchez de Arévalo, 1404-1470* (Washington, 1958), pp. 165, 166.

8. This letter was patterned after a false epistle addressed to Pope Clement VI by one Morbassan. It was often copied by anonymous publicists who accommodated its substance to their own purposes. The text I quote was copied into the *Mémoires* of Jacques du Clercq, V, 86; it is also found appended to Jacopo Tedaldi's account of the fall of Constantinople (see M. L. Concasty, "Les 'Informations' de Jacques Tedaldi sur le siège et la prise de Constantinople", *Byzantion* XXIV, 1954, 95-110), and in the *Chronique de Mathieu d'Escouchy*, II, 58-61; cf. Iorga, *ROL* VIII (1900-1901), 298-299. The letter was probably composed at one of the courts hostile to Venice and its chief purpose seems to have been that of anti-Venetian propaganda.

9. Landucci, *A Florentine Diary*, p. 161.

10. See references cited in note 2 above.

11. See especially E. Jacobs, "Cyriacus von Ancona und Mehmed II", *Byzantinische Zeitschrift*, XXX (1929-30), 197-202; but compare W. Bodnar, *Cyriacus of Ancona and Athens* (Brussels, 1960), pp. 19, 28, 29, 64-69. F. Babinger, "Notes on Ciriaco of

Ancona and Some of His Friends", *Journal of the Warburg and Courtauld Institute*, XXV (1962), 321-323.

12. F. Pall, "Ciriaco d'Ancona e la crociata contro i Turchi", *Bulletin de la section historique, Académie Roumaine*, XX (1938), 9-68. Bodnar, *op. cit.*, p. 49, noting Ciriaco's presence at the Council of Florence which was called to reunite the Latins and Greeks admitted that "This, together with the idea of a crusade against the Turks, was one of his pet projects".

13. L. Thuasne, *Gentile Bellini et Sultan Mohammed II* (Paris, 1888); cf. F. Babinger, "Ein vorgeblicher Gnadenbrief Mehmeds II. für Gentile Bellini", *Italia medioevale e umanistica*, V (1962), 85-101.

14. Valturio's letter is in S. Baluze, *Miscellanea* (Lucca, 1762), III, cols. 113, 114. Cf. F. Babinger, *Mahomet II*, pp. 242, 243, 613-615; and his "Mehmed II und Italien", *Byzantion*, XXI (1951), 127-170; and E. Jacobs, "Mehmed II Beziehungen zur Renaissance", *Oriens*, II (1949), 7-30. For Malatesta's campaign, G. Soranzo, "Una Missione de Sigismondo Pandolfo Malatesta a Maometto II nel 1461", *Romagna*, III (1902).

15. Zorzi Dolfin, "Cronaca delle famiglie nobili di Venezia e della stessa città dalla sua origine sino l'anno 1478", ed. G. Thomas in *Sitzungsberichte der königlich bayerischen Akademie der Wissenschaften*, II (1868), 5, 6.

16. Cf. the tales in the works by two former slaves of the Turks, Giovanni Mario Angiolello, *Historia Turchesca*, ed. I. Ursu (Bucharest, 1909), pp. 6-8, 121, 122; and Teodoro Spandugino, *La Genéalogie du grant Turc à present regnant*, ed. C. Schefer (with the title *Petit traicté de l'origine des Turcqz*, Paris, 1896), pp. 40, 41. Thuasne, *Gentile Bellini*, pp. 52-56. See also the ninth tale in Matteo Bandello's *Le Novelle*, ed. G. Brognoligo (Bari, 1928), I, 135ff.

17. Commines, *Mémoires*, ed. Mlle Dupont (Paris, 1847), II, 282-288; 322, 399; 424.

18. For the various editions see J. A. B. Palmer, "Fr. Georgius De Hungaria, O.P. and the *Tractatus de moribus Condicionibus et Nequicia Turcorum*", *Bulletin of the John Ryland Library*, XXXIV (1951-52), 44-68. Translated into German by Sebastian Franck, the work was printed in 1530 with an introduction by Luther. The *Historia Turchesca* (see note 16 above), was the work of another captive of the Turks, Giovanni Mario Angiolello who was seized at the fall of Negropont in 1470. Put in the service of the sultan he participated in the campaigns against Usan Hasan in 1473, 1474 and in the Balkans in 1476 and 1477. He escaped during the civil war after Mehmed's death and returned to Italy. An important source for the reign of Mehmed II, the work, however, was not printed in our period. The *Reisebuch* of Johann Schiltberger is another work by a former Turkish captive. Seized at the battle of Nicopolis, Schiltberger entered the service of Bayezid I and was in turn captured and forced to serve Timur. He returned to Germany in 1427. The bulk of the book deals with the campains of Timur and his son and is much less informative about the Turks than the others in this category; it does, however, include material on the reign of Bayezid I which is important; moreover, the *Reisebuch* was printed for the first time in our period. Somewhat more informative though hardly an objective or careful account is the *Anzeygung kurtzlichen und volfurung den ursprung dess Thurckyschen unnd hundtyschen volcks...* of Joerg von Nuremberg. Entering the service of Stephen of Bosnia as gunmaster in 1456, Joerg fell into the Turks' hands and served the sultan

in the same capacity until 1480 when he escaped by way of Egypt. The work was first printed at Memmingen in 1482-83 and consisted of only eight quarto leaves. A new edition, with much added material, was printed at Memmingen in 1496 and appeared again at Nuremberg in 1500. For other works in this category, but which were little known in their own time in the West, see the introduction of Franz Babinger to his *Die Aufzeichnungen des Genuesen Jacopo de Promontorio de Campis über den Osmanenstaat um 1475* in *Sitzungsberichte der Bayerishe Akademie der Wissenschaften. Philosophisch-Historische Klasse*, Heft 8 (1956), 5-28.

19. George of Hungary, *Tractatus*. The edition of the *Tractatus* used here is that published together with Ricoldus, *Contra sectam Mahumeticam*, printed in Paris in 1511. For George's motives in writing see fols. 29^r-29^v; the description of his being taken captive, fols. 29^v-30^v; on the origin and rise of the house of Osman, chapters I and II, fols. 30^v-32^r; on the Janissaries, chapters VII, fols. 35^v-36^v; XI, fols 40^r-41^r; XXII, fol. 58^r; on Turkish women, chapter XII, 41^r-42^r; on the treatment of Christian subjects, chapters VI and VII, 34^v-36^v; and on Islam and especially the problem of Christians converting to the "law of the Turks", chapters XIII-XVII, 42^v-51^r, and XX, XXI, 54^r-57^r.

20. The edition used here was edited by C. Schefer under the title *Petit traicté de l'origine des Turcqz* (Paris, 1896). For the Italian text based on the MS presented to Henry II see C. N. Sathas, *Documents inédits relatifs à l'histoire de la Grèce au moyen âge* (Paris, 1890), IX, 139-261.

21. *Petit traicté*, pp. 2, 12, 32. Cf. Sathas, *Documents*, IX, iii-xxxi for the various editions and Spandugino's biography.

22. *Petit traicté*, pp. 2-4.

23. Cited by Schefer in his introduction, *ibid.*, pp. lxii-lxiii.

24. *Ibid.*, pp. 54, 55, 161, 162, 191-193.

25. *Ibid.*, pp. 151, 159, 161, 162, 182, 191-193, 207, 208, 255, 256.

26. *Ibid.*, pp. 40-43.

27. *Ibid.*, pp. 46-53.

28. *Ibid.*, pp. 198, 199; cf. 208, 209, 244ff.

29. *Ibid.*, pp. 142-145.

30. *Ibid.*, pp. 5-11.

31. E.g. D. Vaughan, *Europe and the Turk*, pp. 25-29.

32. See John V. A. Fine, Jr., review of Sima Ćirković, *Istorija srednjovekovne bosanske drzave* (Belgrade, 1964), in *Speculum*, XLI (1966), 527, 528; Halil Inalcik, "Mehmed the Conqueror (1432-1481), and His Time", *Speculum*, XXXV (1960), 419. Cf. L. von Thallóczy, *Studien zur Geschichte Bosniens und Serbiens im Mittelalter* (Munich, 1914), p. 107.

33. *NCMH*, I, 37. See also A. Apponyi, *Lectures on the Peace Program and the Constitutional Growth of Hungary* (Budapest, 1911), p. 51. Cf. A. Buzmov, "Les Problèmes de la conquête de la péninsule des Balkans par les Turcs", *Etudes historiques à l'occasion des XIe congrès international des sciences historiques* (Sofia, 1960), pp. 135-142; E. Albrecht, *Das Türkenbild in der ragusanisch-dalmatinischen Litteratur des XVI Jahrhunderts* (*Slavistische Beiträge*, 15, Munich, 1965).

34. In *Fashnachtspiele aus dem fünfzehnten Jahrhundert (Bibliothek des litterarischen Vereins in Stuttgart,* 1853), pp. 288-304. Cf. Vaughan, *op. cit.,* p. 28.

35. La Broquière, *op. cit.,* p. 248; and Chapter II above on the Christian defense of Belgrade. R. Liliencron, *Die historischen Volkslieder der Deutschen vom dreizehnten bis zum sechzehnten Jahrhundert* (Leipzig, 1869), I, 503-511; see in the same work, "Türkenschrei" (1453), 460-465.

36. On this point see Francis Rogers, *The Quest for Eastern Christians. Travels and Rumor in the Age of Discovery* (Minneapolis, 1962), pp. 15, 16, 29.

37. Landucci, *op. cit.,* pp. 182, 183.

38. *CSPVen,* II, 348, 349.

39. *Ibid.,* II, 5.

40. See e.g. P. A. Throop, *Criticism of the Crusade: A Study of Public Opinion and Crusade Propaganda* (Amsterdam, 1940).

41. See above pp. 219ff.

42. W. S. Holdworth, *A History of the English Law* (London, 1924), V, 31. On Augustinus Triumphis cf. J. N. Figgis, *Political Thought from Gerson to Grotius,* 1414-1625, Harper Torchbook ed. (New York, 1960), pp. 8, 21; and M. Wilks, *The Problem of Sovereignty in the Later Middle Ages* (Cambridge, 1963), pp. 413ff. Joan D. Tooke, *The Just War in Aquinas and Grotius* (London, 1965).

43. Honoré Bonet, *The Tree of Battles,* tr. G. W. Coopland (Cambridge, Mass., 1949), pp. 126-128.

44. Gilbert of the Haye, *The Buke of the Law of Armys,* ed. J. H. Stevenson (London, 1901), pp. 102-106.

45. D. Hay, *The Italian Renaissance in its Historical Background,* pp. 50-53.

46. Le Van Baumer "England, the Turk and the Common Corps of Christendom", pp. 31-33.

47. See Kenneth M. Setton, "Lutheranism and the Turkish Peril", *Balkan Studies,* III (1962), 133-168.

48. Cf. e.g. the remarks of Pius II, *Commentaries,* VII, 516; but the conclusions of R. Aubenas are unduly severe in *NCMH,* I, 92, 93.

49. H. Markgraf, "Über Georgs von Podiebrad Project eines christlichen Fürstenbundes", *Historische Zeitschrift,* XXI (1869), 245-304; N. Iorga, "Un Auteur des projets de croisades, Antoine Marini", *Études d'histoire du moyen âge dédiées à Gabriel Monod* (Paris, 1896), pp. 445-457. F. G. Heymann, *George of Bohemia. King of Heretics* (Princeton, 1965), pp. 293-315.

50. *Ibid.,* p. 308.

51. G. E. Maas, *The Legendary Character of Kaiser Maximilian* (New York, 1941), p. 101.

52. Liliencron, *op. cit.,* II, 305, 306.

53. *Ibid.,* II, 308, 312.

54. *De origine et conversatione bonorum regum et laude civitatis Hierosolymae* (Basel, 1494); *Varia Carmina,* ed. F. Zarncke in *Narrenschiff* (Leipzig, 1854), no. 46, p. 185; cf. "In laudem divi Maximiliani", *ibid.,* no. 13, p. 197.

55. *Ibid.,* pp. 93-96; but cited here in the translation of E. H. Zeydel, *The Ship of Fools* (New York, 1944), pp. 315-322.

56. Ulrich von Hutten, "Ad principes germanos ut bellum in Turcas concorditer susci-
piant exhortatoria", *Opera*, ed. E. Böcking (Leipzig, 1861), V, 101-103, 106-114,
121, 123, 124, 130, 131. For the German reaction in the sixteenth century see K. M.
Setton, "Lutheranism and the Turkish Peril", *op. cit.*; A. Scholtze, *Die orientalische
Frage in der öffentlichen Meinung des sechzenten Jahrhunderts* (Frankenberg, 1880);
R. Ebermann, *Die Türkenfurcht. Ein Beitrag zur Geschichte der öffentlichen Meinung
in Deutschland während der Reformationszeit* (Halle, 1904); S. H. Moore, "The Turkish
Menace in the Sixteenth Century", *Modern Language Review*, XL (1945), 30-36;
H. J. Kissling, "Die Türkenfrage als europäisches Problem", *Südostdeutsches Archiv*.
VII (1947), 39-57; H. J. Kissling, "Türkenfurcht und Türkenhoffnung im 15. 16.
Jahrhundert: Zur Geschichte eines 'Komplexes' ", *Südost-Forschungen* XXIII (1964),
1-18.

57. See R. W. Southern, *Western Views of Islam*, pp. 77-83.

58. Cited in P. Brock, *The Political and Social Doctrines of the Unity of Czech Brethren in
the Fifteenth and Early Sixteenth Centuries* (The Hague, 1957), p. 93, n. 44. See also
the observations of E. Troeltsch, *The Social Teachings of the Christian Chruches*, tr.
Olive Wyon (New York, 1960), I, 336-348.

59. On Italus see G. H. Williams, *The Radical Reformation* (Philadelphia, 1962), pp. 18,
19, 255. The tale of his stay in Turkey and the vision is found in *Elsass, I: Stadt
Strassburg*, 1522-1532, ed. M. Krebs and J. Rott (Gütersloh, 1959, *Quellen zur Geschichte der Täufer VII*), nos. 205, 206a. The same experience is identified with the
prophetic preacher Francesco da Meleto. Williams suggests that Italus and Meleto
may have been the same person. Cf. D. Cantimori, *Eretici italiani dei cinquecento*
(Florence, 1939), pp. 14-16, and D. Bongi, "Francesco da Meleto, un profeta fiorentino a' tempi del Machiavelli", *Archivio storico italiano*, ser. 5, III (1889), 62ff. Cf.
the views of Michael Sattler and Sebastian Franck in *Spiritual and anabaptist Writers*,
ed. G. H. Williams (Philadelphia, 1957, *Library of Christian Classics XXV*), pp. 141,
150, 156.

60. E.g. M. T. d'Alverny, "Deux traductions latines du Coran au moyen âge", *Archives
d'histoire doctrinale et litteraire du moyen âge* XVI (1948), 63-131; J. Kritzeck, *Peter
the Venerable and Islam* (Princeton, 1964); N. Daniel, *Islam and the West*, with an extensive bibliography on the subject.

61. Martène, *Thesaurus*, col. 1824; Margery Kempe; *op. cit.*, pp. 362, 372; von Harff,
op. cit., pp. 116, 119.

62. *Rosarium Sermonum* (Venice, 1498), pars prima, sermo, III, fols. 15ᵛ-16ʳ. On Sarteano's missions and the identification of Nicolo de'Conti see Rogers, *Quest for
Eastern Christians*, pp. 40-49.

63. Cited in Rogers, *Quest for Eastern Christians*, p. 57.

64. *Ibid.*, p. 83; the letter, together with an alleged reply of Pius II, was first published
in Joannes de Hese, *Itinerarius per diversas mundi partes* (Cologne, 1490).

65. *The Vision of William Concerning Piers Plowman*, ed. W. W. Skeat (London, 1869),
Passus III, p. 45.

66. *Ibid.*, Passus XV, pp. 276, 277; for another version of this medieval legend in a
fifteenth century text see E. Douté, *Mahomet Cardinal* (Chalons-sur-Marne, 1889).

67. *The Vision of William*, Passus XV, pp. 277, 281, 286; 287; and cf. John Lawlor,
Piers Plowman. An Essay in Criticism (New York, 1962), pp. 148-150.

68. R. W. Southern, *Western Views of Islam*, pp. 85, 86.

69. George of Trebizond wrote in his *Comparationes phylosophorum Aristotelis et Platonis* (Venice, 1523), sig. V6ᵛ: "Audiui ego ipsum Florentiae, uenit enim ad concilium cum graecis, asserentem unam eandemque religionem, uno animo, una mente, una praedicatione, uniuersum orbem, paucis post annis esse suscepturum. Cumque rogassem, christine an machumeti? neutram inquit, sed non à gentilitate, differentem". Cited by M. Creighton, *A History of the Papacy* (London, 1897), IV, 42. On Pletho see H. F. Tozer, "A Byzantine Reformer (Gemistus Plethon)", *Journal of Hellenic Studies*, VII (1886), 353-380; and F. Masai, *Pléthon et le platonisme de Mistra* (Paris, 1856).

70. The prologue to the now missing translation is printed in D. Cabanelas Rodríguez, *Juan de Segovia y el problema islámico*, appendix III, pp. 279-302. In it Segovia explained his philological method and described his unsuccessful search for a Christian Arabic scholar to help him. On the latter see N. Daniel, *op. cit.*, and K. H. Dannenfeldt, "The Renaissance Humanists and the Knowledge of Arabic", *Studies in the Renaissance*, II (1955), 96-117, neither of whom mentions Segovia.

71. Quoted in Cabanelas, *op. cit.*, p. 111. Segovia's program was worked out in detail in his unpublished *De mittendo gladio Divini Spiritus in corda saracenorum* (summary in Cabanelas, appendix I, pp. 265-272), and in Segovia's letters to Nicholas of Cusa, Jean Germain, Aeneas Sylvius (Pius II), and an anonymous friend, *ibid.*, appendices IV, VI, VII, IX, X, XI.

72. Letter of Segovia to Nicholas of Cusa, 2 December 1454, *ibid.*, pp. 303-310, where Juan stressed his actual experience in doctrinal discussions, as well as historical and scriptural examples, as proof of the validity of his approach; cf. Cabanelas, pp. 93-125, for detailed analysis of all the relevant texts.

73. E. Vansteenberghe, *Le Cardinal Nicolas de Cues*, 1401-1464 (Paris, 1920), pp. 227-234. See the preface of R. Klibansky and H. Bascour to their edition of *De pace fidei* (London, 1956, *Mediaeval and Renaissance Studies*, Supplement III), pp. ix-liii. Cusa's reply to Segovia, 29 December 1454 *(ibid.*, pp. 93-102, and Cabanelas, *op. cit.* appendix V, pp. 311-318), includes information on the cardinal's longstanding interest in the problem as well as a discussion of Segovia's program and some specific suggestions for implementing it.

74. Nicholas of Cusa, *Cribratio Alchorani in Oeuvres choisie de Nicolas de Cues*, ed. M. de Gandillac (Mesnil, 1942), pp. 503-505.

75. Letter of Cusa to Segovia, 29 December 1454, in Cabanelas, *op. cit.*, pp. 317, 318.

76. *De pace fidei*, eds. Klibansky and Bascour, pp. 3, 4. Cf. P. E. Sigmund, *Nicholas of Cusa and Medieval Political Thought* (Cambridge, Mass., 1963), pp. 293-295; E. F. Jacob, "Nicholas of Cusa", in *The Social and Political Ideas of Some Great Thinkers of the Renaissance and Reformation*, ed. F. J. C. Hearnshaw (New York, 1949), pp. 32-60; and B. Decker, "Die Toleranzidee bei Nikolaus von Kues und in der Neuzeit", in *Nicolo Cusano, Relazioni presentate al Convegno Interuniversitario di Bressanone* (Florence, 1962), pp. 5-24; and cf. F. Copelston, *A History of Philosophy, III: Late Mediaeval and Renaissance Philosophy* (Image Books edition, New York, 1963), pt. II, 39.

77. Sebastian Franck, *Das verbüthschierte mit sieben Sigeln verschlossene Buch* (1539), quoted in J. Lecler, *Toleration and the Reformation* tr. T. L. Westow (London, 1960), I, 175;

cf. Franck's letter to John Campanus in *Spiritual and Anabaptist Writers*, ed. G. H. Williams; Erasmus, *Querela pacis*, in *Opera omnia* (Leyden, 1703), IV, 638; see also his introduction to the *Novum instrumentum, ibid.*,VI, fol. ★ 3ʳ, where Erasmus hopes that his rendition will make the Scriptures attractive to the Turks.

78. B. Lewis, *Istanbul and the Civilization of the Ottoman Empire* (Norman Okla., 1963) p. 145.

79. Momigliano, *Studies in Historiography*, p. 137, where the whole problem is clarified.

Tandenaerde gheprendt

XII: Printer's device with oriental design.
(From the *Historie van Saladine*. Audenarde [Arend de Keysere, before 1483]. With the kind permission of the owner Lessing J. Rosenwald. One of only two copies known).

INDEX

Flanders, 11, 95, 98

Flemming, Robert, 178

Florence, 3, 4, 5, 6, 17, 32, 34, 37, 43, 51n21, 61, 78n16, 129, 132, 133, 134, 141n28, 143n63, 144n66, 153, 161, 162, 165, 205, 209, 213, 227n5

Florence, Council of, 7, 30, 99, 107, 153, 157, 206, 224, 228n12

Folco da Forli, Benedetto, 102

Foscari, Francesco, 8

Foscarini, Ludovico, 75, 76

France, 6, 21, 29n69, 33, 53n43, 59, 62, 78n18, 82, 83, 84, 88, 92, 93, 96, 98, 103, 105, 107, 113n63, 116, 117, 118, 131, 133, 134, 137, 160, 161, 164, 168, 179, 183, 189, 191, 192, 202, 203, 205, 207, 208, 213, 216

Franche Comté, estates of, 113n66

Francis I, King of France, 160, 164, 165

Franciscans, 2, 7, 19, 26n30, 39-56, 66, 84, 107, 110n21, 133, 157, 167, 179, 194, 221, 223-225

Franck, Sebastian, 225, 228n18, 231n59, 232n77

Franco, 189

Franconia, 189

Frankfort, Diet of, 33, 41, 42

Frederick II, Margrave of Brandenburg, 1

Frederick III, Holy Roman Emperor, 3, 4, 21, 32, 33, 51n22, 84, 85, 98, 119, 140n17, 141n27, 142n31, 143n51, 155, 156

Fullar, Erasmus, 48; Oswald, 48

Gaguin, Robert, 172n10

Gallipoli, 24n11, 63, 100, 106, 149, 164, 209

Garnet, Robert, 136

Garnet, Thomas, 136

Gascoigne, Thomas, 4, 48

Gattilusio, Niccolò, 64

Gauls, 158

Gaza, Theodore, 148

Geiler von Kaysersberg, Johann, 144n73

Geneva, 118, 119

Gennadios (George Scholarius), Patriarch of Constantinople, 36

Genoa, 2, 3, 5, 6, 14, 15, 20, 30, 31, 38, 78n22, 102, 133, 203

Georgia, 4

Germain, Jean, 84, 107, 108, 109n7

German tribes, 158

Germany, 3, 6, 9, 12, 18, 29n79, 32, 33, 39, 41-45, 53n43, 59, 60, 73, 82, 84, 88, 92, 93, 96, 105, 118, 121, 133, 134, 137, 158, 166, 167, 179, 180, 183,